INDUSTRIAL AND ORGANIZATIONAL PSYCHOLOGY

Research and Practice

INDUSTRIAL AND ORGANIZATIONAL PSYCHOLOGY

Research and Practice

SECOND EDITION

PAUL E. SPECTOR

Department of Psychology
University of South Florida

JOHN WILEY & SONS, INC.

New York • Chichester • Weinheim • Brisbane • Toronto • Singapore

ACQUISITIONS EDITOR	Ellen Schatz
MARKETING MANAGER	Bonnie Cabot
SENIOR PRODUCTION EDITOR	Deborah Herbert
DESIGNER	David Levy
ILLUSTRATION EDITOR	Edward Starr
PHOTO EDITOR	Nicole Horlacher

This book was set in 10.5 × 12.5 ITC/Berkeley Old Style Book by UG and printed and bound by Quebecor-Fairfield Printing. The cover was printed by Lehigh Press Lithographers.

This book is printed on acid-free paper.

Library of Congress Cataloging-in-Publication Data
Spector, Paul E.
      Industrial and organizational psychology : research and practice / Paul E. Spector. — 2nd ed.
          p.   cm.
      Includes bibliographical references and index.
      ISBN 0-471-24373-6 (cloth : alk. paper)
      1. Psychology, Industrial.   2. Personnel management.   I. Title
   HF5548.8.S625   2000
   158.7—dc21
                                                                                            98–50852
                                                                                            CIP

Printed in the United States of America

10 9 8 7 6 5 4 3 2 1

To Gail and Steven Spector

PREFACE

Industrial/organizational or I/O psychology is an exciting field that has been enjoying tremendous growth in the United States and throughout the industrialized world. What began in the United States as a tiny subspecialty of psychology, known only to a few practitioners and professors, has grown to be one of the major applied specialties in psychology worldwide. This attention is due to two factors. First, I/O is concerned with the workplace, so its findings and principles are relevant to everyone who has held a job. Second, I/O has developed proven methods that organizations find of value. I/O psychologists are often called upon to help organizations have a more efficient and healthier workforce.

The field of I/O psychology has a dual nature. First, it is the science of people at work. This aspect ties it to other areas of psychology, such as experimental and social. Second, I/O psychology is the application of psychological principles of organizational and work settings. In no other area of psychology does a closer correspondence between application and science exist, making I/O a good example of how society can benefit from the study of psychology.

The field of I/O is a large and diverse one. Many topics are covered, ranging from methods of hiring employees to theories of how organizations work. It is concerned with helping organizations get the most from their employees or human resources, as well as helping organizations take care of employee health and well-being. For this reason, a single textbook can provide only an overview of the major findings and methods that I/O psychologists use. The goal of this book is to provide such an overview, as well as a comprehensive understanding of the field. Each of the major areas that comprise I/O is covered.

Part One of this book provides an overview of the I/O field. Chapter 1 covers the nature of the field and its history and discusses I/O as both a practice and a science. The chapter describes what a career in I/O involves, as well as what it takes to become an I/O psychologist. Chapter 2 provides an overview of the basic principles of I/O research methods.

The remainder of the book is divided into four major sections. In Part Two, Chapter 3 discusses job analysis or the assessment of jobs. Chapter 4 focuses on the assessment of employee job performance. Chapter 5 explores the way in which employee characteristics are measured. Part Three contains two chapters. Chapter 6 deals with the methods that organizations use to hire new employees. Chapter 7 follows those new as well as experienced employees through their training programs.

The four chapters in Part Four discuss the relationship between the individual and the organization. Chapter 8 covers theories of motivation. Chapter 9 focuses on how people feel about their jobs—their level of job satisfaction and commitment to the organization. The topic of Chapter 10 is productive and counterproductive work behavior. Chapter 11 deals with worker health and safety.

The final part of the book, Part Five, is concerned with the social context of work. Chapter 12 explores small work groups or work teams and their effect on the individual. Chapter 13 discusses leadership and supervision in the workplace. Chapter 14, the last chapter, takes an organizational perspective. It covers organizational development and theory.

SPECIAL FEATURES

Each chapter except the first two contains two special features. The first is a detailed summary of a research study from one of the major I/O journals. Each "Research in Detail" was chosen to give added insight through a study relevant to topics covered in the chapter. The implications of each study for the practice of I/O are also discussed. The second feature is a case study that describes how a practicing I/O psychologist was able to help an organization with a problem. These "I/O Psychology in Practice" cases have been chosen to represent the wide variety of settings and applied work that involve I/O psychologists.

At the end of each "I/O Psychology in Practice" case are discussion questions. These questions seek to encourage students to think about the principles discussed in the book. They require the student to apply the chapter principles to a real situation. The questions can be used in a variety of ways. They can be assigned to groups of students or to individuals. They can be used for in-class debates, discussions, oral presentations, or written assignments. The cases themselves help show students the connections between practice and research in the I/O field. Students often have a difficult time seeing the relevance to their lives of what they study in college; I/O psychology is a field that is relevant to almost everyone.

CHANGES IN THE SECOND EDITION

The second edition of this book refines and updates the first. The organization is much the same, as reflected in very minor change to the table of contents. However, the content of the book has changed considerably, with over 100 new references, almost all from 1995 and later. A few new topics have been added, but most of the revision involves clarifying and updating material from the first edition. The present edition carries the same special features: cases, chapter objectives, glossary, and research in detail. Five of the cases are new, including new international cases, one from Australia and one from Canada.

Two trends in the I/O field are evident with this second edition. In the final decade of the present century, our field became international in scope. In Chapter 1, Table 1-2 contains a list of I/O graduate programs outside of the United States. This list is more than twice as long as the one in the first edition, reflecting the tremendous growth of the field. Quite a few of the programs listed in the table had just started or were about to start when I compiled the list. The large American I/O consulting firms, once limited to North America, are opening offices throughout the world. Two of the largest, Development Dimensions, Inc. or DDI, and Personnel Decisions, Inc. or PDI, changed the meaning of the I in their names to International, as they expanded their scope beyond the United States. The second edition of this book has included more international information than the first in response to this trend.

The other trend is the internet. This emerging technology has already changed the I/O field by facilitating communication among us throughout the world. Chapter 1 now contains a subsection about internet resources of interest to researchers and students. Several relevant discussion groups or listservs are mentioned. A short list of websites is also provided, which students can access to find out more information about I/O. A more extensive list of links can be found on my own website. A portion of this website has been set up as a resource to instructors and students. In addition to links, it contains class notes and internet exercises that are tied to topics in this textbook.

Textbook Internet Support Site.   Much of the information in a textbook is quickly outdated or time sensitive. It is not feasible for publishers to update more often than the four- to five-year revision cycle of most upper level texts. The internet, however, provides a means of doing just that. With this second edition, part of my website will be devoted to this purpose. The Industrial and Organizational Psychology: Research and Practice section will contain updated information, as well as other supplemental features.

I teach an introductory I/O course myself, and I will keep a copy of my own notes and overheads on the site. Some of the overheads are outlines of my lectures, whereas others provide additional information, such as lists or tables. Although my course tends to follow the text (or more correctly the text follows my course), there is supplemental information here. I often bring in additional material not covered in the book or present it in a somewhat different way. All of these notes and overheads can be downloaded and modified or printed for the instructor's own use. The text files are in HTML format, and the graphics files are in jpg format. As updated information becomes available (e.g., a new I/O salary survey), it will be put here. A date at the bottom of every document will show the last time it was updated.

I have also included some internet exercises that are tied to particular topics. At present there is at least one exercise per chapter. All require the student to find information on one or more internet sites and either answer questions or write a report. These exercises can be used in a variety of ways, including as the basis for in-class discussions. Most exercises are tied to particular portions of the text and make use of the links on my site. Finally, for each of the case people there is a link to their employer or the organization in which the case was conducted. Students can use these links to find more background information that can help put the case in context.

Outside of the textbook section are additional website features. Perhaps of most interest is the extensive links part. Although a few are shown in Chapter 1, web addresses change rapidly, so that by the time you read this book some might no longer be correct. A more extensive list with site descriptions can be found on the website, which I will keep updated. This includes links to professional associations, not all of which are in the United States, including the American Psychological Association, American Psychological Society, British Psychological Society, International Association of Applied Psychology, and Society of Industrial and Organizational Psychology (SIOP). Links to I/O journals are also provided, many of which contain abstracts and tables of contents to recent issues. A section includes sites that have I/O related information, such as the Gallup Organization, or the U.S. Bureau of Labor Statistics. Another section has links to I/O consulting firms, whose sites explain the services that these companies provide. As I learn of new, relevant sites, they will be added. Students can be referred to the links for additional information; for example, I regularly suggest students try the SIOP link for information about graduate schools in the United States and Canada. A student curious about what the large consulting firms do can check out their extensive and interesting websites (http://chuma.cas.usf.edu/~spector).

Content Changes in the Second Edition. Although all of the topics covered in the first edition are still here, some have been modified and some are new. Changes of particular note are the following:

Expansion of history section, including a discussion of the role of women in I/O.

I/O as a career, including salary information.

A comparison of I/O research topics in different countries.

Acceptance to and preparation for graduate school.

Frame of reference training to reduce performance appraisal rating errors.

Updated information about the validity of personality tests for selection.

Expanded discussion of affirmative action and procedures to reduce discrimination.

Discussion of German Action Theory.

Discussion of the Galatea effect.

Update on the relation between age and job satisfaction.

Inclusion of Hofstede's cultural values (e.g., individualism—collectivism).

Discussion of how excessive work hours relate to health and
   the European Council initiative to restrict working hours.

Update on accident prevention techniques.

Techniques for training managers to be charismatic.

Expanded material on women and leadership.

Discussion of negative effects of technology.

ACKNOWLEDGMENTS

In writing both the first and second editions of this book, I was lucky to have had advice and assistance from many people. I express my sincere thanks to the colleagues and students who provided this help as well as to the Wiley staff, who did a superb job.

First are the members of the USF I/O group:

Tammy Allen	Edward Levine
Walter Borman	Carnot Nelson
Michael Brannick	Louis Penner
Michael Coovert	Karen Oberne (I/O staff assistant).

There are colleagues and friends from around the world who provided feedback and information:

Seymour Adler, *Assessment Solutions, Inc.*

Julian Barling, *Queens University, Canada*

John Bernardin, *Florida Atlantic University*

Stephen Bluen, *South Africa*

Peter Chen, *Ohio University* and his undergraduate I/O class who provided critiques of the first edition

Steven Cronshaw, *University of Guelph, Canada*

Donald David, *Old Dominion University*

Laura Desmaris, *IBM*

Dov Eden, *Tel Aviv University, Israel*

Barbara Ellis, *University of Houston*

Michael Frese, *University of Giessen, Germany*

Yitzhak Fried, *Wayne State University*

Barbara Fritzsche, *University of Central Florida*

Joan Hall, *Naval Air Warfare Center Training Systems Division*

Paul Jackson, *University of Sheffield, England*

Richard Jeanneret, *PAQ Services, Inc.*

Steve Jex, *University of Wisconsin, Oshkosh*

Boris Kabanoff, *University of New South Wales, Australia*

Filip Lievens, *University of Ghent, Belgium*

Lakshmi Narayanan, *Florida Gulf Coast University*

Brian O'Connell, *American Institutes for Research*

Richard Perlow, *Clemson University*

Mark Peterson, *Florida Atlantic University*

Ivan Robertson, *University of Manchester Institute of Science and Technology, England*

Juan Sanchez, *Florida International University*

Arie Shirom, *Tel Aviv University, Israel*

Dirk Steiner, *Universite de Nice-Sophia, France*

Paul Taylor, *University of Waiko, New Zealand*

Richard Vosburgh, *Campbell Soup Company*

In addition, 12 I/O psychologists provided the "Psychology in Practice" cases:

Kerry Bunker, *Center for Creative Leadership*

Janis Cannon-Bowers, *Naval Air Warfare Center Training Systems Division*

Jeanne Carsten, *Chase Manhattan Bank*

Anna Erickson, *SBC Communications*

Chuck Evans, *RHR International*

Jeff McHenry, *Microsoft*

Kathleen McNellis, *Florida Progress Corporation*

Charles Michaels, *University of South Florida*

Karen Midkiff, *IBM*

Lynn Summers, *Mediappraise Corporation*

Paul Van Katwyk, *Personnel Decisions International*

Tom White, *Digital Equipment Corporation, Australia*

The reviewers of the various drafts of the book did a superb job, and the comments of each one of them were a tremendous help. Those who reviewed the first edition are:

Robert B. Bechtel, *University of Arizona*

David V. Day, *Pennsylvania State University*

Janet Barnes Farrell, *University of Connecticut*

M. Jocelyne Gessner, *University of Houston*

Sigrid Gustafson, *American Institutes for Research*

Jane Halpert, *De Paul University*

Leslie Hammer, *Portland State University*

David Kravitz,
    American Institutes of Research

Karl Kuhnert, *University of Georgia*

Dan Landis, *University of Mississippi*

Therese Macan,
    University of Missouri-St. Louis

John Meyer, *University of Western Ontario*

George Neuman, *Northern Illinois University*

Gerald L. Quatman, *Xavier University*

Mary Roznowski, *Ohio State University*

Ann Marie Ryan, *Michigan State University*

Ladd Wheeler, *University of Rochester*

Those who reviewed the second edition are:

Joseph Horn, *University of Texas at Austin*

Marjorie Krebs, *Gannon University*

Therese Macan,
    University of Missouri at St. Louis

Karen Maher, *California State University
    at Long Beach*

Patrick McCarthy,
    Indiana University Southeast

Steven Scher, *Eastern Illinois University*

Susan Shapiro, *Indiana University East*

Kenneth Shultz, *California State University
    at San Bernardino*

Steven Stern, *University of Pittsburgh at
    Johnstown*

I had the good fortune to be able to work with two wonderful acquisitions editors on this edition, Ellen Schatz and Chris Rogers. Caroline Ryan and Eman Hudson, Ellen's assistants, were helpful in handling many details, including the external reviews of the book.

The production staff at Wiley did an outstanding job of turning my manuscript into the final book form. They were production editor, Deborah Herbert, illustration editor, Edward Starr, photo editor, Nicole Horlacher, designers, Dawn Stanley and David Levey, and copyeditor, Betty Pessagno.

Finally, I thank my wife, Gail Spector, for assisting in so many ways, including helping me make the hundreds of little decisions involved in writing a book.

Paul E. Spector

BRIEF CONTENTS

CONTENTS

PART FOUR
THE INDIVIDUAL AND THE ORGANIZATION   173

PART FIVE
THE SOCIAL CONTEXT OF WORK   271

INTRODUCTION

Chapter 1

INTRODUCTION

Most people in the industrialized world come into direct or indirect contact with organizations every day. Organizations include the government agencies and private companies that provide most of the goods and services we use. They produce our automobiles, clothing, electronics, food, and furniture. Such organizations can employ tens or even hundreds of thousands of people, and running them can be extremely difficult. Many specialists are employed solely to help organizations run smoothly. Organizations often turn to industrial/organizational (I/O) psychologists for help with many of their employee-related problems. For example, I/O psychologists have helped

AT&T develop assessment centers to choose the best people to be managers

Digital Equipment Corporation employees cope with layoffs and reorganization

General Electric (GE) develop systems to provide job performance feedback to employees

The U.S. Army use psychological tests to place recruits in the appropriate jobs

The U.S. Postal Service develop procedures to reduce assaults by employees

If you go to work for a large organization, there is a good chance that your work life will be affected by industrial/organizational (I/O) psychology. An I/O psychologist may have designed the application form that you will fill out to get the job, the salary and benefit package that you will be offered, the training that you will receive, and the structure of the tasks that will comprise your job. I/O psychologists get involved in issues related to employee health, job performance, motivation, safety, selection (hiring), and training. They can also deal with the design of equipment and job tasks. This book discusses all of these areas, and more.

There are two equally important aspects of the I/O psychology field. First, I/O involves the study of the human side of organizations. Many I/O psychologists, particularly those who are professors at universities, conduct research about people at work. Second, I/O includes the application of the principles and findings of the research. Most I/O psychologists are involved in practice, either as consultants or as employees of organizations. This book reviews the major findings in I/O research and explores how practicing I/O psychologists apply those findings in organizational settings.

Industrial/organizational psychology is an eclectic field that has borrowed concepts, ideas, techniques, and theories from many other disciplines. Experimental psychology provided the historical basis of the I/O field. Its principles and techniques, such as psychological testing, were applied by several early experimental psychologists to problems of organizations. As we will discuss later in this chapter, psychologist Robert Yerkes convinced the army to use psychological tests during World War I. Other influences on the I/O field have come from industrial engineering, management, social psychology, and sociology. Although I/O psychology had its beginnings in the United States, it has become an international activity, especially in industrialized countries.

This chapter contains an overview of the I/O field. It covers the major activities and employment settings for I/O psychologists and presents a brief history of the field. The chapter discusses the training needed to become an I/O psychologist and where that training is offered, not only in the United States but throughout the world. The research process will be discussed, and the major publication outlets for I/O research will be listed. I/O psychologists are very concerned with the ethical treatment of people. The ethical principles of I/O psychology will be summarized.

Chapter 2 contains a discussion of the research methods used in I/O psychology. Chapters 3 to 14 cover the major topics of the field and begin with a focus on the assessment of jobs and people. Next they cover two major areas that are relevant to developing productive employees—selecting good people and training them to do their jobs well. Chapters 8 to 11 are concerned with the individual in the context of the organization and cover motivation, how people feel about their jobs, employee behavior, and employee health and safety. Chapters 12 to 14 deal with the individual employee in the social context of the organization. Major topics discussed include groups, leadership, techniques to change organizations, and theories of organizations.

Objectives   **The student who studies this chapter should be able to:**
1. Define I/O psychology.
2. Describe the major activities of I/O psychologists.
3. Summarize the history of the I/O field.
4. Explain the importance of research and how it relates to practice.

WHAT IS I/O PSYCHOLOGY?

Psychology is the science of human (and nonhuman) behavior, cognition, emotion, and motivation. It can be subdivided into many different specializations, some of which are concerned primarily with the science of psychology (experimental) and others with the application of scientific principles. The applied area with the largest number of psychologists is clinical psychology. Clinical psychologists deal with the treatment of psychological disorders and problems. **I/O psychology** is a smaller applied field that is concerned with the development and application of scientific principles to the workplace. I/O psychologists do not deal directly with employees' emotional or personal problems. This activity falls in the domain of clinical psychology. An I/O psychologist, however, might recommend hiring a clinical psychologist to help with such problems as employee alcoholism.

As its two-part name implies, the field of I/O psychology contains two major divisions: the industrial (or personnel) and the organizational. Although the content of the two major divisions overlaps and cannot be easily separated, each grew out of different traditions in the history of the field. Industrial psychology, which was the original name for the field, is the older branch and tended to take a management perspective of organizational efficiency through the appropriate use of human resources or people. It is concerned with issues of efficient job design, employee selection, employee training, and performance appraisal. Organizational psychology developed from the human relations movement in organizations. It focuses more than industrial psychology on the individual employee. It is concerned with understanding behavior and enhancing the well-being of employees in the workplace. Organizational topics include employee attitudes, employee behavior, job stress, and supervisory practices. The major topics of the field, however, cannot easily be characterized as strictly industrial (I) or organizational (O). Motivation, for example, is relevant to the I concerns of employee efficiency and performance, but it is also relevant to the O concern with the happiness and well-being of employees. Even though the I and O areas cannot always be clearly distinguished, together they suggest the broad nature of the field.

ACTIVITIES AND SETTINGS OF I/O PSYCHOLOGISTS

I/O psychologists do many different jobs in a wide variety of settings. We often divide I/O settings into those that are concerned with practice and those that are concerned with research. The practice activities involve the use of psychological principles to solve real-world problems, such as excessive job stress or poor job performance. Research provides principles that can be applied in practice. Both practice and research are equally important within the I/O field. One major objective of I/O is to help organizations function more effectively. In order to do so, the field must have research findings on which to base practice. Not all research is done with practice in mind, however. Some psychologists study work behavior just to learn why people do the things they do at work.

Although settings can be classified as either practice or research, there is considerable overlap in activities across the two. Many I/O psychologists in research settings get involved in practice, and psychologists in practice settings sometimes do research. Furthermore, some practice activities require research to determine the best approach to solve the problem at hand. Existing principles might not exist in all cases. In fact, I/O psychologists often don't have answers, but they have the means of finding solutions.

Most research settings are the colleges and universities in which I/O psychologists are professors. Practice settings include consulting firms, government, the military, and private corporations. Consulting firms provide I/O services to organizations that hire them. Large consulting firms might have dozens of employees providing services to organizations throughout the world. I/O psychologists often work for governments (city, county, state, or national), the military (usually as civilian specialists), and private corporations. I/O psychologists in each of these practice settings might be doing the same sorts of activities. Figure 1-1 shows the percentage of I/O psychologists found in each of the major settings.

Many I/O psychologists are college or university professors. Most are in psychology departments, but frequently they can be found in colleges of business administration as well. Although they spend much of their time doing research and teaching students, they

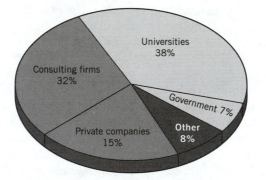

FIGURE 1-1

Percentage of I/O Psychologists Who Work in Various Settings. *Source:* SIOP Survey of Membership Report, 1996, Arlington Heights, IL: Society for Industrial and Organizational Psychology.

do far more than that. Many are involved in practice as consultants to organizations, and some have started their own consulting firms to pursue this interest. The following list describes the major activities of professors:

Teach courses

Do research

Write research papers and present them at meetings

Provide consulting services to organizations

Write textbooks

Supervise students

Provide information to the public

Develop courses

Keep up with their field

Help administer the teaching function of their university

The basic functions of a professor are to create and disseminate knowledge. Each activity on this list is concerned with one or both of these functions.

Practicing I/O psychologists do many of the same things as their academic colleagues, including conducting research and teaching college courses. The major focus of a practice job, however, is the application of the findings and principles of the field. The following list of activities shows what practicing I/O psychologists do:

Analyze the nature of a job (job analysis)

Conduct an analysis to determine the solution to an organizational problem

Conduct a survey of employee feelings and opinions

Design an employee performance appraisal system

Design an employee selection system

Design a training program

Develop psychological tests

Evaluate the effectiveness of an activity or practice, such as a training program

Implement an organizational change, such as a new reward system for employees who perform well

Much of the effort of I/O psychologists is directed toward enhancing the effectiveness and functioning of organizations. They do so by focusing on several aspects, including the selection of people who can do the job better, training people to do the job better, designing jobs that can be done better, or designing organizations to function better. I/O psychologists also attempt to change organizations so that they are better places for people to work, even if the effectiveness of the organization is not improved.

HISTORY OF THE FIELD OF I/O PSYCHOLOGY

(Unless otherwise noted, most of this section is based on Katzell and Austin's (1992) history of the I/O field.) I/O psychology is a twentieth-century invention, with roots in the late 1800s and early 1900s. It has existed almost from the beginning of the psychology field. The first psychologists to do I/O work were experimental psychologists who were interested in applying the new principles of psychology to problems in organizations. Early work focused on issues of job performance and organizational efficiency. As the field matured during the first half of the century, it expanded into the areas that it covers today. Figure 1-2 shows the major events in the development of I/O psychology.

Two psychologists are credited with being the main founders of the field. Hugo Münsterberg and Walter Dill Scott were both experimental psychologists and university professors who became involved in applying psychology to problems of organizations. Münsterberg was particularly interested in the selection of employees and the use of the new psychological tests. Landy (1997) posits that Münsterberg's inability to gain the respect of colleagues at Harvard was the motivation for his shift to the new emerging field of industrial psychology. Scott was interested in many of the same things as Münsterberg, as well as the psychology of advertising. Each wrote pioneering textbooks on these topics, including Scott's *The Theory of Advertising* (1903), and Münsterberg wrote the first I/O textbook, *Psychology and Industrial Efficiency* (1913).

A major influence on the I/O field was the work of Frederick Winslow Taylor, an engineer who studied employee productivity throughout his career during the late nineteenth and early twentieth centuries. Taylor developed what he called **Scientific Management** as an approach to handling production workers in factories. Scientific Management includes several principles to guide organizational practices. In his writings Taylor (1911) suggested the following:

1. Each job should be carefully analyzed so that the optimal way of doing tasks can be specified.
2. Employees should be selected (hired) according to characteristics that are related to job performance. Managers should study existing employees to find out what personal characteristics are important.
3. Employees should be carefully trained to do their job tasks.
4. Employees should be rewarded for their productivity to encourage high levels of performance.

Though refined over the years, these same ideas are still considered valuable today.

Hugo Münsterberg   Walter Dill Scott   Frederick Winslow Taylor   Robert Yerkes

Frank and Lillian Gilbreth

1991	Americans with Disabilities Act passes
1970	APA adopts the name Division of Industrial and Organizational Psychology
1964	Civil Rights Act passes
1941	World War II war effort begins
1924	Hawthorne studies begin
1921	First I/O Ph.D. is awarded; Psychological Corporation is founded
1917	Mental tests for job placement are developed
1913	First I/O textbook is published

FIGURE 1-2
A time line of major events in the history of I/O psychology.

Another influence from the field of engineering can be seen in the work of Frank and Lillian Gilbreth, a husband and wife team who studied efficient ways of performing tasks. They combined the fields of engineering and psychology (Frank was an engineer and Lillian a psychologist) in studying how people perform tasks. Their best known contribution was the **time and motion study**, which involved measuring and timing people's motions in doing tasks with the goal of developing more efficient ways of working. Although the basic ideas were Taylor's, the Gilbreths refined and used their new technique to help many organizations (Van De Water, 1997). Some historians claim that Lillian was the first to receive an I/O Ph.D. (Koppes, 1997), in 1915, although most historians give this distinction to Bruce V. Moore in 1921. The Gilbreths' work served as the foundation of what would later become the field of human factors, which is the study of how best to design technology for people. In later years, Lillian turned her attention to designing consumer products and invented the foot-pedal trash can and refrigerator door shelves, among other things (Koppes, 1997). However, the Gilbreths themselves are best known as the subjects of the popular movie *Cheaper by the Dozen*, which chronicled their lives as working parents of 12 children.

World War I saw the beginning of the use of I/O psychology by the U.S. military, which gave a boost to the development of the field. When the United States entered the war in 1917, a number of psychologists, led by Robert Yerkes, offered their services to the army. The best-known accomplishment of the group was the development of the Army Alpha and Army Beta group tests for mental ability. One of the biggest problems for the army was placing new recruits in the jobs for which they were best suited. The newly invented psychological tests seemed to the psychologists to be an efficient way to solve that problem. This was the first large-scale application of psychological testing to place individuals in jobs. It provided a foundation for mass testing that has been used ever since in educational (e.g., the Scholastic Aptitude Test or SAT) and employment settings.

During the decades between the two world wars, I/O psychology expanded into most of the areas in which it is used today. As organizations grew in size, they began hiring I/O psychologists to address many of their increasing employee problems, particularly those that were relevant to productivity. As suggested earlier, in 1921 Penn State University awarded what many consider the first Ph.D. in what was then called industrial psychology to Bruce V. Moore. I/O psychologists began organizing into consulting firms that would provide services to organizations for a fee. The most well-known of these was the Psychological Corporation, founded in 1921 by James McKeen Cattell, which is still in existence today. One of the most important events of this period was the Hawthorne studies, which continued for more than 10 years at the Western Electric Company.

Before the Hawthorne studies, I/O psychologists focused almost exclusively on issues of employee productivity and organizational efficiency, including the assessment of employee abilities and the efficient design of jobs. Although the Hawthorne researchers set out to study these topics, they quickly discovered that many social aspects of organizational life affected employee behavior and performance. Their study of supervision and work groups helped launch the O or organizational side of the field.

The best known of the Hawthorne studies was the investigation of lighting-level effects (Roethlisberger & Dickson, 1939). The objective of this study was to determine the lighting level that would produce optimal performance on a factory task. The researchers conducted an experiment in which a group of employees was taken to a special room where lighting levels were changed. Lights were made brighter and dimmer from day to day to see the effects on productivity. The researchers were surprised to find that over the course of the experiment, productivity increased and seemed to have little to do with lighting levels. Many explanations of these results have been advanced and debated. The most frequently discussed is that knowledge of being in an experiment, or what has come to be called the **Hawthorne Effect**, caused increases in performance. Whatever the reason, it seems clear that social factors can be more important than physical factors in people's job performance.

World War II had a tremendous stimulating effect on the development of the I/O field. Hundreds of psychologists from all specializations contributed to the war effort. Psychologists dealt with problems that spanned the entire scope of both I and O work, including the selection of recruits, placement of recruits in different jobs, training, morale, performance appraisal, team development, and equipment design. Prior to World War II, the American Psychological Association (APA) limited its interests to experimental psychology and rejected attempts by I/O psychologists to make practice part of its mission, which was considered nonscientific. As a result of the war, however, the APA opened its doors to applied psychology, and Division 14 of Industrial and Business Psychology was formed in 1944 (Benjamin, 1997). After the war, the two areas of industrial and organizational psychology continued to expand. Furthermore, by demonstrating its value to society on a large scale, private companies took increasing interest in the field, implementing many I/O procedures, such as psychological tests. In 1970 the Industrial Psychology Division 14 of the American Psychological Association changed its name to the Division of Industrial and Organizational Psychology and is today called the Society for Industrial and Organizational Psychology (SIOP).

Another event in the United States that helped shape the field of I/O psychology was the passage of the Civil Rights Act of 1964. This act set into motion forces that have had a tremendous impact on how organizations hire and treat employees. When discrimination against minorities became illegal, organizations had to change many of their employment practices. I/O psychologists were called upon to help develop procedures that would eliminate discrimination in the workplace. The passage of the Americans With Disabilities Act (ADA) in 1991 extended protection against discrimination to the disabled. Here again I/O psychologists have been called upon to find ways to eliminate unfair discrimination.

The history of the field is full of examples of how I/O psychologists have helped improve organizations and work conditions for employees. The field has grown from its initial concern with productivity to the many diverse areas we find today. I/O psychology has much to contribute to the operation of organizations and the well-being of employees. Its future looks bright as organizations continue to need help with employee issues, as discussed throughout this book.

I/O PSYCHOLOGY AROUND THE WORLD

So far our discussion of I/O psychology has focused on the United States, where the field had its beginnings and most of its early development. However, I/O psychology exists throughout the world, and many of its findings and principles have come from other countries. In addition, the practice of I/O psychology differs somewhat in different countries. For example, the techniques used to select employees varies among countries (Clark, 1993; Shackleton & Newell, 1991). I/O psychology in the United States has had a long tradition of paying somewhat greater attention to the I side than the O side of the field. In recent years, this tendency has been reinforced by increasing legal requirements that organizations avoid discriminatory hiring practices, as we will discuss in Chapter 6. Employers, feeling government pressure, turn to I/O psychologists to help design legally defensible hiring procedures. I/O psychology in other countries, for example, in Canada and Europe, focuses somewhat more on the organizational direction. In part this is because of the stronger labor union movements in these countries, which puts greater emphasis on employee rights than is true in the United States. Thus, much of the research on topics of employee attitudes, health, safety, and well-being comes from Canada and Europe.

These differences in research interests among scholars of I/O psychology in various countries are illustrated by a study of topic popularity in the major research journals conducted by Miriam Erez of the Israel Institute of Technology (1994). She tabulated the number of articles published in psychological research journals for each of 25 topics by country of author. Table 1-1 lists the most frequently studied topics for each country. The differences are quite striking. For example, in Scandinavian countries (Finland, Norway, and Sweden), 53 percent of studies were concerned with employee health and stress, with additional studies covering related issues. In the United States these topics were found in only 5 percent of studies. Conversely, in the United States employee selection was the most popular topic, but it was unstudied in Scandinavia. This difference in focus on employee health versus selection mirrors societal differences in emphasis on employee productivity versus well-being.

TABLE 1-1
Most frequently studied I/O research topics in eight countries listed in order of popularity within country

COUNTRY	TOPICS	COUNTRY	TOPICS
Canada	Employee selection	Israel	Career issues
	Job stress		Values
	Leadership		Cross-cultural issues
	Career development		Motivation
England	Employee selection		Performance appraisal
	Turnover		Job satisfaction
	Leadership	Japan	Job stress
	Gender differences		Leadership
	Job stress		Career issues
Germany	Job stress		Motivation
	Motivation	Scandinavia	Job stress
	Training		Shift work
	Work environment		Gender differences
India	Job satisfaction		Unemployment
	Motivation	United States	Employee selection
	Job level in the organization		Career issues
	Job stress		Performance appraisal
			Leadership

Source: From Erez, M. (1994). "Toward a Model of Cross-cultural Industrial and Organizational Psychology." In H. C. Triandis, M. D. Dunnette, and L. Hough (eds.), *Handbook of Industrial and Organizational Psychology*. Volume IV. *Theory in Industrial and Organizational Psychology*. Palo Alto, CA: Consulting Psychologists Press.

As Erez's results show, job stress is a research area that is international in scope. Many of the major developments have come from outside of the United States. For example, there has been an important program of job stress research at the University of Stockholm in Sweden, and the journal *Work & Stress*, which is devoted to work in this area, is published in England. Much of the research that we will discuss in Chapter 11 concerning job stress was not conducted in the United States but comes from a variety of countries. On the other hand, most of the research we will discuss on employee selection is from the United States.

During the twenty-first century, I/O psychology will almost certainly continue to develop and prosper throughout the world. The practice is spreading rapidly throughout the world as our techniques gain acceptance in more and more places. The international interest in I/O is well indicated by the rapid spread of I/O Master's and Ph.D. programs outside of the United States (see Table 1-3), which has doubled from the first to the second edition of this book! Although an I/O psychologist's focus can differ across countries, just as we saw with research topics, the field has available a wide variety of methods and techniques that can be helpful in dealing with employee issues in organizations. Although most of the research once came almost exclusively from the United States, more and more research is originating from other countries, including Australia, Canada, England, Germany, Israel, and New Zealand. Cross-cultural research comparing different countries, or replicating results from Western cultures in other contexts is becoming increasingly popular. This work is important because not all principles used in the United States will necessarily work in other countries or cultures. We will discuss some of these studies throughout the book.

WHAT IT TAKES TO BE AN I/O PSYCHOLOGIST

The most common route to becoming an I/O psychologist is to earn a graduate degree (master's or Ph.D.) in I/O psychology from one of the many I/O psychology graduate programs in the United States and other countries. Many people who do I/O work have other backgrounds, such as in other areas of psychology or in business administration. Some of these people consider themselves to be I/O psychologists and may hold jobs with that title. In the United States, most I/O psychologists hold a Ph.D. degree. Although it is possible to be an I/O psychologist with a master's degree in the I/O field, such people are often referred to as master's level I/O psychologists to reflect their lower degree status. One can have a successful career as an I/O psychologist with a master's degree, but opportunities and salaries are usually better with the Ph.D.

In some countries, such as Canada, the situation is similar to that in the United States. However, in other places, as in much of Europe, the Ph.D. is not as common as the master's degree. Rather, the master's degree is considered a practice degree, whereas the Ph.D. is a research credential. An individual who wishes to be a practitioner will likely have only the master's degree. If one continues on to earn a Ph.D., he or she is most likely to be interested in research and will be found in a research institute or a university. It is possible for a practitioner to have a Ph.D., but it is not considered as important as in the United States.

Table 1-2 lists master's and Ph.D. programs throughout the United States, and Table 1-3 lists a sample of graduate programs (mostly Ph.D.) from other countries. As the size of

<u>TABLE 1-2</u>
Universities in the U.S. with graduate programs in I/O psychology

STATE	MA PROGRAM	PH.D. PROGRAM
Alabama		Auburn University
		University of Alabama
California	California State Univ.	California School of Professional Psychology
	Long Beach	The Claremont Graduate University
	Sacramento	University of California at Berkeley
	San Bernardino	US International University (PsyD)
	San Diego State Univ.	
	San Francisco State Univ.	
	San Jose State Univ.	
Colorado	Univ. of Colorado at Denver	Colorado State University
Connecticut	Univ. of Hartford	Univ. of Connecticut
	Univ. of New Haven	
Washington, DC		The George Washington Univ.
Florida	Florida Institute of Technology	Florida International Univ.
	Univ. of Central Florida	University of South Florida
	Univ. of West Florida	
Georgia	Georgia State Univ.	Georgia Institute of Technology
	Valdosta State College	University of Georgia
Illinois	Illinois State Univ.	DePaul Univ.
	Roosevelt Univ.	Illinois Institute of Technology
	Southern Illinois Univ. at Edwardsville	Northern Illinois Univ.
		Univ. of Illinois Urbana-Champaign
Indiana	Indiana Univ.-Purdue Univ. at Indianapolis	Purdue Univ.
Iowa		Iowa State Univ.
Kansas	Emporia State Univ.	Kansas State Univ.
Kentucky	Western Kentucky Univ.	
Louisiana		Louisiana State Univ.
		Tulane Univ.
Maryland	Univ. of Baltimore	Univ. of Maryland
Massachusetts	Springfield College	
Michigan		Central Michigan Univ.
		Michigan State Univ.
		Univ. of Michigan
		Wayne State Univ.
Minnesota	Mankato State Univ.	Univ. of Minnesota
Mississippi		Univ. of Southern Mississippi
Missouri	Southwest Missouri State Univ.	Univ. of Missouri-St. Louis
Montana	Montana State Univ.	
Nebraska		Univ. of Nebraska at Omaha
New Jersey	Fairleigh Dickinson Univ.	Stevens Institute of Technology
	Montclair State College	
New York	City University	Baruch College, CUNY
	Hofstra Univ.	Columbia Univ., Teachers College
	Polytechnic Univ.	Fordham Univ.
	Rensselaer Polytechnic Institute	New York Univ.
		SUNY at Albany

TABLE 1-2 (continued)

STATE	MA PROGRAM	PH.D. PROGRAM
North Carolina	Appalachian State Univ. East Carolina Univ. Univ. of North Carolina-Charlotte	North Carolina State Univ.
Ohio	Xavier Univ.	Bowling Green State Univ. The Ohio State Univ. Ohio Univ. Univ. of Akron Wright State Univ.
Oklahoma		Univ. of Tulsa
Oregon		Portland State Univ.
Pennsylvania	West Chester Univ.	Carnegie Mellon Univ. Penn State Univ. Temple Univ.
South Carolina		Clemson Univ.
Tennessee	Austin Peay State Univ. Middle Tennessee State Univ. Univ. of Tennessee-Chattanooga	Univ. of Tennessee-Knoxville
Texas	Lamar Univ.-Beaumont	Rice Univ. Texas A & M Univ. Univ. of Houston Univ. of North Texas
Virginia	Radford Univ.	George Mason Univ. Old Dominion Univ. Virginia Tech
Wisconsin	Univ. of Wisconsin-Oshkosh	

Source: TIP Web Page, http://cmit.unomaha.edu/TIP, March 17, 1997.

the lists may suggest, the United States is the world leader in terms of number of programs, but there are many fine I/O programs throughout the rest of the world. I/O may have begun in the United States, but it has spread throughout the world, especially wherever there are large profit-making organizations.

Admission to American graduate programs is quite competitive, especially for the well-established Ph.D. programs. Most base admission mostly on undergraduate grade point average (usually just the junior and senior year) and Graduate Record Exam (GRE) scores. Prior applied and research experience can be helpful. Letters of recommendation from faculty members are usually required. I/O graduate programs are challenging and require both language and mathematical skills. Thus to do well, a student should properly prepare as an undergraduate. A solid background in basic mathematics (i.e., algebra) and statistics is a good start. Good basic language skills, especially writing, is also valuable. It is always wise to take a course in I/O before making the choice to pursue this career. Interestingly, many students enter graduate school without having taken this course. Finally, a good background in basic psychology will make things easier. Students who have

TABLE 1-3
A sample of universities outside of the United States that offer graduate degrees
in industrial/organizational psychology

COUNTRY	UNIVERSITY	COUNTRY	UNIVERSITY
Australia	Flinders University of South Australia	Germany	Technical University of Berlin
	Griffith University		Technical University of Dresden
	Macquarie University		University of Frankfurt
	Monash University		University of Giessen
	Murdoch University		University of Manheim
	University of New South		University of Munich
	Wales		University of Osnaerück
	University of Queensland	Hong Kong	Chinese University of Hong Kong
	University of Western	Ireland	University College Dublin
	Australia	Israel	Bar-Ilan University
Belgium	Free University of Brussels		Hebrew University of Jerusalem
	University of Ghent		Technion–Israel Institute of
	University of Levven		Technology
	University of Liege		Tel Aviv University[b]
	University of Louvain	Netherlands	Free University of Amsterdam
Canada	Queen's University		University of Amsterdam
	St. Mary's University		University of Groningen
	University of Calgary		University of Leiden
	University of Moncton		University of Nijmegan
	University of Montreal		University of Tilburg
	University of Waterloo/	New Zealand	University of Canterbury
	University of Guelph		University of Massey
	University of Western Ontario		University of Massey at Auckland
China	Beijing University		University of Waikato
	Beijing Normal University	Portugal	ISCTE Institute of Management
	China Eastern Normal		and Social Sciences – Lisbon
	University	Russia	Moscow State University
	Institute of Psychology, Chinese	Scotland	Heriot-Watt University/
	Academy of Science		Strathclyde University
	Zhejiang University[a]	Singapore	National University of Singapore
Costa Rica	Latin University of Costa Rica	South Africa	University of Capetown
England	University of Hull		University of South Africa
	University of London		University of Stellenbosch
	University of Manchester	Spain	Complutense University
	University of Sheffield		University of Barcelona
France	University of Provence		University of Santiago
	Aix-Marseille		University of Valencia
	University of Bordeaux	Sweden	Stockholm University
	University of Metz		University of Lund
	University of Paul Valéry	Switzerland	University of Bern
	Montpellier	Turkey	Istanbul University

[a]Formerly named Hangzhou University.
[b]Offers a similar Organizational Behavior degree.

other undergraduate majors and didn't have this background find they have a lot of catching up to do, especially in the first year.

The training of I/O psychologists includes both the practice and research sides of the field. An I/O psychologist is trained to be a scientist-practitioner, or someone who is able to conduct scientific research and apply principles to problems of organizations. Students are exposed to procedures for applying principles of the field, as well as to research methodology. The specific content and emphasis can differ among graduate programs, especially when comparing these programs across countries. The emphasis of most master's programs is on the practice side of the field, whereas a Ph.D. covers both more equally.

In the United States one must have a Ph.D. to be considered a full-fledged I/O psychologist, although it is possible to get an I/O job with a master's degree. There are many excellent programs offering terminal master's degrees to people who do not wish to spend the extra years it would take to earn the Ph.D. These programs offer training oriented more toward practice than science, in part because they do not have sufficient time to cover each side of the field in depth and in part because they are intended to train practitioners. The Ph.D. programs tend to offer a better balance between practice and science in part because they take over twice as long to complete. These programs train people to be both practitioners and researchers. In the United States most practitioners have a Ph.D.

A master's degree can be completed in about two years, while a Ph.D. can be completed in about four to five years by a person who has a bachelor's degree. Programs vary, but a master's program will include coursework on research methodology and the various areas of the I/O field, which will be discussed in this book. A Ph.D. program covers the same areas, as well as general psychology and more extensive research methodologies. For this degree, the Society for Industrial and Organizational Psychology (1985) includes the following areas:

Work Motivation Theory	Work Attitude
Work Groups	Employee Selection
Organization Theory	Work Performance
Performance Appraisal	Job Analysis
Organizational Development	Assessment of Individual Differences
Criterion Development	Training

In addition, there is practicum experience working in an organizational setting with a practicing I/O psychologist and research experience (e.g., a master's thesis or doctoral dissertation) done under the supervision of a committee of I/O faculty members.

The job market for I/O psychologists in the United States has been excellent, although it does fluctuate with general economic conditions. Surveys of I/O psychologists done by the American Psychological Association over the years have generally found less than 1% unemployment among those who wish to work. Zickar and Taylor (1995) reported the results of a salary survey of American I/O psychologists in 1994. The median salary was $59,500 per year for individuals with a master's degree and $71,000 per year for those with a Ph.D. The top 5% of I/O psychologists made from $200,000 to over $1 million per year. College professors made less (median $52,000) than individuals working for consulting firms and private companies (median $100,000). The median starting salary for a new Ph.D. was $45,000 per year. Women made considerably less than men ($58,000 versus $75,000 median salary per year), with some of the difference accounted for by women being less likely to have a Ph.D. and having less job experience. Finally, it should be kept in mind that these are median salaries, meaning that half the people make more and half less than these numbers. Salaries can range considerably among I/O psychologists who live in different places, and even among psychologists in the same organization.

The field of I/O psychology was at one time a predominantly male profession. In the 1960s, only about 8% of Ph.D.s in I/O were awarded to women. Interestingly, prior to 1930 women comprised a much higher proportion of practicing I/O psychologists than they did in 1960. Although accurate estimates of numbers are impossible to make (Koppes, 1997), women may have comprised as many as 25% of I/O psychologists. In the past few decades women have entered the field in increasing numbers, and today they earn about half of the Ph.D.s awarded in the United States. This trend can also be found elsewhere in the world.

I/O PSYCHOLOGY AS A PROFESSION

I/O psychology is a profession in many ways like the professions of accounting or law. Some states in the United States require that I/O psychologists be licensed; but in most states, only clinical psychologists must be licensed. Many I/O psychologists work for consulting firms that provide services for a fee to client organizations. These services are provided in much the same way that an accounting firm or law firm provides them.

I/O psychologists belong to several professional/scientific societies. The Society for Industrial and Organizational Psychology (SIOP), which is a division of the American Psychological Association (APA), is the largest organization in the United States that is comprised entirely of I/O psychologists. It currently has about 4,200 members, 1,600 of whom are student affiliates. All members of SIOP are also members of APA or the American Psychological Society (APS), which split from APA several years ago. The Academy of Management is a larger organization than SIOP, but the majority of its members are not psychologists. It is comprised of people who have interests in the broad field of management, mostly professors from colleges of business administration. Many I/O psychologists, primarily those who are college professors, are active members of this organization.

In addition to the national associations, there are many regional and state associations of I/O psychologists. Smaller local associations can be found in several areas, including central Florida, Michigan, New York City, and Washington, DC. Professional associations of I/O psychologists can be found in many countries throughout the world. Canada has its own Society for Industrial and Organizational Psychology; the British Psychological Society has its Division of Occupational Psychology; and many similar associations exist throughout Europe. Over a dozen of them have formed the European Association of Work and Organizational Psychology (EAWOP). Also very relevant to I/O psychologists is the International Association of Applied Psychology, Division of Organizational Psychology. I/O psychologists from around the world are members, especially those with interests in cross-cultural and international issues.

I/O PSYCHOLOGY AS A SCIENCE

Research is one of the major activities of I/O psychologists. Research can develop new methods and procedures for such activities as selecting or training employees. Other research focuses on understanding some organizational phenomenon, such as the causes of employee theft or the effects of job attitudes. Research conducted for organizations might find immediate application to a particular problem. Results of research studies are presented at professional meetings and published in scientific journals.

The associations noted earlier all have conferences, usually annually, where results of research are presented. The annual meeting of the Academy of Management, for example, attracts several thousand practitioners and researchers who can share and discuss their research findings and ideas. Practitioners often find such meetings to be a good place to learn about new solutions to their organizational problems. Researchers can find out about the latest findings before they are published in the scientific journals.

Scientific journals of the field represent the major outlet for research results. Some major journals are produced by professional associations, whereas others are published privately. For example, the *Journal of Applied Psychology* is published by APA, and the *Journal of Organizational Behavior* is published by John Wiley, the publisher of this textbook. Table 1-4 lists the major journals that publish research on I/O topics. Most are like magazines that are published in four to six issues per year. One, the *International Review of Industrial and Organizational Psychology*, is published once a year and summarizes the state of knowledge on various topics.

I/O researchers, most of whom are college professors, submit articles for possible publication to these journals. Their work is then sent to experts in the field for a critique. Articles are revised based on the critiques, and often several rounds of revision and resubmission will be necessary before an article is accepted for publication. Only the 10 to 20% of submitted articles that survive a rigorous peer review process will be published in the best journals. Peer review helps maintain high standards for published work so that the best research makes it into print.

Publication of research papers is a competitive and difficult endeavor. College professors, particularly those without tenure, are under tremendous pressure to be successful at publication. I/O programs at most universities have a "publish or perish" philosophy that requires professors to be active researchers who contribute to the knowledge base of the field. This is true of scientific disciplines in most universities. A publication record in the best journals is a major determiner of career success for a professor, as reflected in the ability to find a job, earn tenure, get promoted, and receive raises.

TABLE 1-4
Journals that publish I/O research and theory

Academy of Management Journal	*Journal of Business and Psychology*
Academy of Management Review	*Journal of Management*
Administrative Science Quarterly	*Journal of Occupational and Organizational Psychology*
Applied Psychology: An International Review	*Journal of Occupational Health Psychology*
Group and Organization Studies	*Journal of Organizational Behavior*
Human Factors	*Journal of Vocational Behavior*
Human Relations	*Organizational Behavior and Human Decision Processes*
Human Resources Management Review	*Organizational Research Methods*
International Journal of Selection and Assessment	*Personnel Psychology*
International Review of Industrial and Organizational Psychology	*Work & Stress*
Journal of Applied Psychology	

INTERNET RESOURCES FOR I/O PSYCHOLOGISTS AND STUDENTS

Over the past few years, the internet has become an increasingly important medium for sharing ideas and information. E-mail facilitates communication especially among people spread around the world. SIOP has its own world wide web site containing its publication *The Industrial/Organizational Psychologist* or *TIP*, as well as other useful information. Of perhaps most interest to students is detailed information on most of the I/O graduate programs in Canada and the United States. All I/O-related societies have their own websites. One of the most useful is the American Psychological Association website, which contains not only information about itself, but also abstracts of articles from all its journals and links to many psychology related sites. Addresses to these and other useful sites are in Table 1-5, and can be found on my own website, which is also listed. This website contains updated information about I/O psychology, including a section that supplements the textbook.

TABLE 1-5
I/O psychology internet resources

WEBSITES

WEB ADDRESS	DESCRIPTION
http://chuma.cas.usf.edu/~spector	Paul Spector's website: Contains updated information to supplement the textbook as well as links to many I/O sites. The author's own class notes are included.
http://www.aom.pace.edu	Academy of Management: Contains information about this I/O-related association and the field itself.
http://www.apa.com	American Psychological Association: Contains information about the association, lots of psychology links, and abstracts of articles in APA journals.
http://psych.hanover.edu/APS/exponnet.html	American Psychological Society's Research on the Net Page: You can participate in actual research studies on this site.
http://www.acd.ccac.edu/hr/EmploymentStatistics	Mostly selection-oriented information and links.
http://www.hfes.org	Human Factors and Ergonomics Society: Contains information about the association and its publications.
http://allserv.rug.ac.be/~pcoets/div/home.htm	International Association of Applied Psychology Organizational Psychology Division: Contains information and links about the field in Europe.
http://www.doleta.gov/programs/onet	Occupational Information Network, O*NET. The U.S. Department of Labor job information site.
http://www.siop.org	Society for Industrial and Organizational Psychology: Contents of *TIP* and lots of information about the field and about graduate programs.

LISTSERVS

LIST NAME	ADDRESS TO SUBSCRIBE TO LIST	DESCRIPTION
EAWOP-L	listserv@nic.surfnet.nl	European Association of Work and Organizational Psychologists' list
HRNET	listserv@cornell.edu	Human Resources Division of the Academy of Management list
IAAP-L	listserv@ucmail.ucm.es	International Association of Applied Psychology list
IOOBF-L	listserv@uga.cc.usg.edu	List devoted to I/O psychology

Another useful resource, discussion groups or listservs, exist on someone's computer and contain the e-mail addresses of people who subscribe. When a message is sent to the listserv, it is relayed to every subscriber. Individuals sharing a common interest, such as I/O psychology, can converse through this medium. A person can ask a question and receive answers and opinions from several people in the field. For example, the I/O listservs frequently get questions from students about graduate school. Most people, however, choose just to "listen," or what is called "lurk." Table 1-5 also contains the addresses of I/O related listservs.

To subscribe to one of the lists, you must send an e-mail message to the appropriate e-mail address. The message you would send to subscribe to a list is:

SUB [name of list] [your name]

For example, for Joan Smith to subscribe to EAWOP-L, she would send the following e-mail message:

SUB EAWOP-L Joan Smith

to the following address:

listserv@nic.surfnet.nl

In a short time, she would receive an e-mail message from the list welcoming her as a new subscriber and providing detailed instructions, including how to send messages. Joan would then begin receiving all messages sent to the list.

ETHICS OF THE I/O FIELD

Psychology has had a long tradition of concern with ethical behavior and the welfare of people. I/O psychologists in the United States follow an ethical code that has been developed over the years by the American Psychological Association. The code includes both ethical principles and statements of appropriate professional conduct. Although the association has little enforcement power other than to terminate a psychologist's membership, most I/O psychologists are guided by the principles in their professional work.

The basic philosophy of the ethical code is that psychologists should do their best to avoid harming other people through their professional work. This means that a psychologist should avoid committing any illegal or immoral act that might harm someone either physically or psychologically. On the other hand, psychologists have a social responsibility to use their talents to help other people. In other words, the goal of the profession is to improve the human condition through the application of psychology. For the I/O psychologist, this means helping to improve organizations so that they function better and helping to improve the well-being of employees.

The APA ethical code contains six principles, each of which is listed in Table 1-6 with a brief definition. As you can see from the table, these principles are concerned with basic ethical standards of honesty, integrity, respect for others, and responsibility. The code also contains a detailed list of appropriate and inappropriate behaviors; too long to reprint here, they can be found in the December 1992 issue of the *American Psychologist* (pp. 1597–1611).

Many psychologists follow the code of ethics of the Academy of Management. Although somewhat different from the APA code, the two codes are compatible. The Acad-

TABLE 1-6
Six ethical principles from the American Psychological Association code

Competence: A psychologist only does work that he or she is competent to perform.
Integrity: Psychologists are fair and honest in their professional dealings with others.
Professional and Scientific Responsibility: Psychologists maintain high standards of professional behavior.
Respect for People's Rights and Dignity: Psychologists respect the rights of confidentiality and privacy of others.
Concern for Other's Welfare: Psychologists attempt to help others through their professional work.
Social Responsibility: Psychologists have a responsibility to use their skills to benefit society.

Source: From "Ethical Principles of Psychologists and Code of Conduct," by the American Psychological Association, 1992, *American Psychologist,* 47, pp. 1597–1611.

emy of Management code deals with standards of behavior in three domains of organizational work by its members—practice, research, and teaching. It too is based on the principles that one does not harm others and that one has the responsibility to use his or her talents to benefit society.

CHAPTER SUMMARY

The field of industrial/organizational (I/O) psychology is one of the major applied areas of psychology. It is a diverse field concerned with the human side of organizations. The I/O field can be divided into two major areas. The industrial side is concerned with organizational efficiency through the appraisal, selection, and training of people and the design of jobs. The organizational side is concerned with understanding the behavior of people on the job.

I/O psychology is both a practice and a science. Most I/O psychologists can be found working for organizations to address issues and problems involving people. They are practitioners who work either as consultants to many organizations or as employees of a single organization. Thirty-eight percent of I/O psychologists are college professors (Howard, 1990), most of whom conduct research to develop better methods and procedures to deal with employee problems at work or to understand behavior.

An I/O psychologist needs to earn a graduate degree from an I/O psychology program in a university. Many such programs may be found throughout the United States and the rest of the industrialized world, especially Australia, Canada, Europe, Israel, New Zealand, and South Africa, with new programs being added in other places. Although the field began in the United States, it has rapidly expanded throughout most of the world. Many of the findings discussed in this book have come from studies done with organizations and people throughout the world.

There are many associations of I/O psychologists (and others with similar interests) that allow for the dissemination of ideas and research findings of the field. This is done by holding conventions and by publishing scientific journals. These associations also have developed codes of ethical conduct for their members. The basic philosophy in these ethical codes is that I/O psychologists should take care not to harm anyone and that I/O psychologists have a social responsibility to use their skills to benefit others. Both the Academy of Management and the American Psychological Association have published ethical standards.

Chapter 2

RESEARCH METHODS IN I/O PSYCHOLOGY

I magine that you are a practicing I/O psychologist working for a company. Suppose you are assigned the task of determining if a new training program is effective in producing better performance in employees. Perhaps employees are being trained in use of a new computer system that is supposed to increase employee productivity. How would you go about finding out if the training works? Would you review the program and see if it looks as if it should be effective, or would you conduct a research study to determine its effects?

The problem with the first approach is that a training program that looks as if it should be effective is not always effective. The only way to be certain that training accomplishes its purpose is to conduct a research study. To conduct a study to determine training effectiveness requires knowledge of research methodology, a topic in which I/O psychologists today are extensively trained. Whether an I/O psychologist is in a job that involves primarily practice or research, he or she needs to know the methods that are used for conducting studies.

Research is the foundation of both the practice and science of I/O. In many practice jobs, I/O psychologists are hired to provide research skills so that questions concerning whether or not programs work can be determined scientifically. This is important for evaluating the success of organizational practices (such as training programs). Research is also important for the development of new practices, such as procedures for hiring people.

I/O psychology is a science because the methods used to expand knowledge of organizational phenomena are scientific methods. This means that the I/O psychologist gathers data or information in a systematic way to address research questions of interest, such as:

"Does the training program work?"

Each scientific study begins with a research question, which defines the purpose of the study. An investigation is planned using a particular design or structure in which data are collected. For example, in a simple experiment to test a training program, you might divide a sample of employees into two groups, only one of which receives the training. After the training has been completed, the two groups would be compared on their job performance. The basic experiment defines one of the simplest designs for an investigation. Data would be collected on performance and analyzed using a statistical test, which in this case would probably be a *t* test. (See the discussion of inferential statistics later in this chapter.) Conclusions would be drawn concerning the effects of the training by considering statistical results in the context of the investigation design. With the training program, it is hoped that the trained group will perform better than the nontrained group after the training has been completed. If this were the finding, one feasible conclusion would be that the training worked. In any given study, however, there can be many competing explanations for results that must be addressed with further research. In the training study, perhaps the trained people performed better just because they knew they were in an experiment and not because the training worked, an example of the Hawthorne Effect. With organizational studies (as well as those in any science), one cannot always be certain why results occurred, but with proper research design competing explanations can be eliminated.

In this chapter, we cover the four major components of a research study. First, we discuss the nature of research questions and how they are refined into testable research hypotheses. Second, we review several types of research designs and how they are used as the basis of organizational research studies. Third, we cover the basic principles of measurement, which define how observations of the phenomena of interest are collected. Fourth, we show how statistics are used to draw conclusions from the data of an investigation. In addition, we review the major principles of research ethics.

Objectives   **The student who studies this chapter should be able to:**
1. Explain the major concepts of design.
2. Describe the major types of designs and list their advantages and limitations.
3. Discuss the types of reliability and validity.
4. Explain how inferential statistics can be used to make conclusions about data.
5. State the major principles of research ethics.

RESEARCH QUESTIONS

Every study begins with a research question. This is true for studies done by practicing I/O psychologists, whose questions address an immediate issue for an organization, such as the effectiveness of a procedure or program. It is just as true for the scientist whose research is addressing a question that he or she believes is important, even if it is not of immediate concern to any particular organization.

Research questions can be general or specific. A general question would be

"What causes people to like or dislike their jobs?"

The problem with this sort of question is that it is not sufficiently specific to provide the basis of a study. Too many different factors could be studied as possible influences on liking the job. To be useful, the question should specify exactly what is being studied. A better question that is more specific is

"Does level of pay affect how much people like their jobs?"

This question specifies the particular influence on liking the job. It tells the researcher exactly what to study as a possible cause of liking the job. To address this question, one needs to assess people's pay level and their feelings about their jobs.

As we will see in Chapter 9, pay itself is not as important as the fairness of pay policies. People tend to be satisfied when they believe that they have been treated fairly when it comes to pay. They will be dissatisfied if they believe they have been unfairly treated, even if their pay is very high. Thus, the amount of pay is not necessarily the most important factor.

Many investigations go beyond raising questions by stating specific theoretical hunches or hypotheses about the outcomes of a study. A hypothesis is the researcher's best guess about what the results of a study will be. Rather than merely raising the question, the hypothesis is a theoretical answer. Thus, one might hypothesize that

"People who are well-paid will like their jobs better than people who are not."

or

"People who are fairly paid will like their jobs more than people who are not."

The hypothesis is a statement of the results that the researcher expects to find. Research studies are conducted to confirm hypotheses. In other words, do the results come out the way they were predicted?

Most hypotheses and research questions come from prior research and theory. Although occasionally a researcher will have a sudden inspirational research idea, most studies and theories come from hard work in studying the research literature of an area. This is the way that all sciences advance and evolve as individual studies become the foundations for later work. The best advice one can give a new researcher is to look to other people's research for new hypotheses and research questions.

The hypothesis and research question are the basis of the study and in some ways its most critical aspect. Without a specific and well-formulated question, it is difficult to design a study that will adequately address it. The question defines the goal or objective of the study, as well as the phenomena of interest. When both are known, the design of the study and the choice of measurement techniques can be relatively easy and straightforward.

IMPORTANT RESEARCH DESIGN CONCEPTS

The design of an investigation specifies the structure of the study. A large number of common designs are used in organizational research. Each has its own particular strengths and weaknesses, so that no design is necessarily superior to the others. Before discussing the various types of designs, we will define several concepts that must be understood first.

Variables

Variables are the basic building blocks of a design. A **variable** is an attribute or characteristic of people or things that can vary (take on different values). People's abilities (e.g., intelligence), attitudes (e.g., job satisfaction), behavior (e.g., absence from work), and job performance (e.g., weekly sales) are all common variables in organizational research. Each subject's standing on each variable is quantified (converted to numbers) so that statistical methods can be applied.

Variables can be classified into one of two types. In experiments **independent variables** are those that are manipulated by the researcher, while **dependent variables** are those that are assessed in response to the independent variables. In other words, the independent variables are assumed to be the cause of the dependent variables. In the training program example, employees were assigned to either a group that was trained or a group that was not trained. Group assignment (trained or not trained) is the independent variable. It is manipulated because the researcher created the training and decided who does and does not get trained. Subsequent job performance would be the dependent variable, because it is not manipulated by the researcher but is merely assessed after training.

Research Setting

The research setting can be classified as either field or laboratory. A **field setting** is one in which the phenomenon of interest naturally occurs. Organizations are field settings in which to study employee behavior. **Laboratory settings** are artificial environments in which phenomena of interest do not normally occur. They occur only because the researcher created them in that setting. The same physical location can be the setting for either a field or a laboratory study, depending on what is studied. A university classroom is a field setting in which to study student learning but a laboratory setting in which to study reactions to job conditions.

Most I/O research occurs in organizational field settings, but much of it takes place in the laboratory as well. Dipboye (1990) reported that 29% of I/O studies published in major journals of the field are laboratory studies. Laboratory studies can involve any aspect of work. For example, many researchers have created simulated job conditions to test people's reactions. Taken together the results of both field and laboratory studies help enhance our understanding of organizational phenomena (Dipboye, 1990).

Generalizability

Generalizability of results means that the conclusions of a study can be extended to other groups of people, organizations, settings, or situations. Generalizability is often a concern with laboratory studies because one cannot be certain that results will hold for organizational settings. The more dissimilar the study is to the organizational setting in terms of both conditions and subjects, the less confidence there can be in the generalizability of the results. The only sure way to be certain about generalizability is to replicate the study in the field setting. If the results in the laboratory are also found in the field, you can have confidence in the generalizability of the laboratory findings.

Generalizability can also be a concern in field studies, for studies done in one organization or with one group of subjects might not have the same results in other places or with other groups of subjects. For example, a study done with nurses in a hospital might have different results from the same study done with physicians. Furthermore, results found in a hospital might be different from results found in a university. Of even greater concern is generalizability across countries and cultures. We cannot be certain that the findings from all of our American and Western research will generalize to countries with different cultures, such as China or India. Finally, even if we only wish to generalize within a single occupation in a single organization, conditions of the study might hold only for the setting in which the study is conducted. A training program that is conducted as part of a study might differ somewhat from the program that is implemented in the entire organization. Trainees and trainers can be affected by knowing they are participants in a research study, just as in the Hawthorne studies we discussed in Chapter 1. This knowledge can motivate the trainers to perform their training tasks in a more effective way than they would if the training was for other purposes. Thus, a training program might work well in the research phase but not in the implementation phase of a training development project.

Control

Every study offers are several possible explanations for why the results occurred. **Control** refers to procedures that allow researchers to rule out certain explanations for results other than the hypotheses they wish to test. For example, suppose we wish to find out if salary affects how much people like their jobs. We could conduct a survey of employees in various organizations, asking them how much they are paid and how much they like their jobs. We might find that the higher the salary, the greater the liking. However, with this sort of design, there are many uncontrolled variables that might be the real cause of liking. For example, perhaps the higher paid people are in different types of jobs than the lower paid people. If the higher paid people are all professional athletes and the lower paid people are sales clerks, it will be difficult to conclude that the pay caused the liking. This is because the type of job was uncontrolled, and it is a possible alternative explanation for results.

Control can be achieved by a number of procedures. For the most part, they involve either holding constant or systematically varying the levels of one or more variables. With the pay survey example, one might hold constant the type of job by limiting the survey to people of only one type of job. If the subjects of the study all had the same job, job type could not have accounted for the results because it was controlled. One could also control for job type by systematically varying it. Subjects could be chosen so that there would be equal numbers of higher and lower paid people in each job type. For example, the study might be limited to groups of actors and athletes that had about the same mix of higher and lower paid people.

Control can be achieved in experiments by the use of the **control group**. A control group is a collection of people who receive a condition or manipulation different from the one of interest. In determining the effectiveness of a training program, the group that does not get trained and is compared to the group that did get trained is called the *control group*. A control group can sometimes be exposed to some manipulation that is used to control specific variables of concern. For example, with a training study it is possible that training has a nonspecific or Hawthorne Effect. A person who knows he or she has been trained might perform better because of increased effort rather than increased skills. This is important to know because there is no need to send someone through expensive and time-consuming training if it does not have the intended effect. The control group can be given bogus or placebo training to control for the Hawthorne Effect. If individuals who are told they are being trained but receive little actual training perform as well as the trained group, the researcher will know that the training did not achieve its intended results.

Laboratory experiments are often conducted in I/O psychology because they provide the strongest control over many variables that might affect results. Even though they may lack the generalizability of a field study, a researcher might choose this more controlled approach. It is common for research on new topics to begin in the laboratory, so that a researcher can see if, under highly controlled conditions, a hypothesis might hold. If it does, field studies can follow to be sure the results generalize to the settings of real interest—organizations.

Random Assignment and Random Selection

Random refers to a process that eliminates systematic influences on how subjects are treated in a study. The term *random* is used in two ways—random assignment and random selection.

Random assignment occurs when people are assigned to various treatment conditions or levels of an independent variable in a nonsystematic way. This means that every subject of a study has an equal chance of being assigned to every condition. In a training study, each employee who participates would have an equal chance of being assigned to the trained group and an equal chance of being assigned to the control group. The random assignment process is a means of controlling for subject variables that are not of interest in the study. We expect that on average subjects in both groups will be more or less equivalent in their characteristics. For example, they should be of approximately the same ability, age, motivation, and tenure.

Random selection means that we choose the subjects of our investigation by a nonsystematic method: Every possible subject of our study has an equal chance of being chosen to participate. Random selection is important if we wish to draw accurate conclusions about the entire group of interest. If we wish to find out how the employees of a given organization feel about their jobs, unless we are going to study all of them, we want to be sure that the group we choose is a random sample. Otherwise we run the risk of choosing employees who do not feel the same way about their jobs as the majority of employees. It would not be a good idea to conduct a survey of a large organization and only get the views of top management. Their feelings are not likely to reflect those of employees at the lower levels of the organization.

Random assignment is used as a means of control by which groups of subjects can be made more or less equivalent to one another on variables not being studied. This is a powerful means of control used in experimental studies such as our training study example. Random selection enhances generalizability by choosing subjects who represent the people of interest. This might mean choosing from all employees of a given organization or from all working people in an entire country.

Confounding

Confounding occurs when two or more variables are intertwined in such a way that conclusions cannot be drawn about either one. For example, age is confounded with job tenure (how long people have been on their jobs). This is because one cannot be on the job a long time unless one is relatively old. A 25-year-old cannot have been on the job for 20 years. If you were to find that age was associated with job performance, you could not be certain that it was not job tenure that was the important variable. Age might relate to performance only because the older employees had longer job tenure.

With commission sales jobs, pay is determined by job performance. Employees who sell the most product have the highest pay. This confounds pay and performance. If you wished to relate either variable to another variable of interest, you could not easily know which was the more important factor. For example, if job satisfaction related to performance, you could not be certain if pay or performance were the reason for satisfaction.

Often control procedures can be used to unconfound variables. For example, one might study the age-performance connection in only a sample of newly hired employees. Control would have been achieved over tenure by limiting the study to those people with approximately the same low level of job tenure. You might study the performance–satisfaction connection by limiting the study to employees who were not on commission or other pay-for-performance systems.

Statistical procedures can also be used to control for confounding. Although it is beyond our scope here, there are many complex statistics that allow for statistical control of unwanted confounding variables. Much of the research in the literature of I/O psychology is concerned with testing for the confounding effects of variables. Often this helps us understand why two variables, such as performance and satisfaction, are related.

RESEARCH DESIGNS

A **research design** is the basic structure of a scientific study. Research designs can be classified along a continuum from those that involve active manipulation of conditions (experimental) to those that involve relatively passive observation of people. The various designs have their strengths and weaknesses, and rarely will a particular design allow us to draw definitive conclusions about a research question. To do so requires the use of a variety of designs that produce similar results.

The Experiment

An **experiment** is a design in which there are one or more independent variables and one or more dependent variables, as well as random assignment of subjects. An independent variable contains two or more levels or conditions of interest. The following have been independent variables in organizational experiments:

Length of daily work shift (in hours)

Pay categories (in dollars)

Availability or nonavailability of training

Setting or nonsetting of job goals

The dependent variable is measured but not manipulated by the researcher and is presumed to be caused by the independent variable. Frequently studied dependent variables in organizational research include the following:

Frequency of absences from work   Satisfaction with the job

Job performance   Turnover (quitting the job)

The experiment can be distinguished from other designs by two particular features. First, in an experiment subjects are assigned at random to two or more conditions that represent the levels of the independent variable or variables. Even though other research designs may have levels of independent variables, to be a true experiment there must be random assignment. Second, the experiment usually involves the creation of the independent variable levels by the researcher. For example, a researcher might design experimental training programs. Sometimes, however, the independent variable levels may occur naturally, and the researcher merely assigns subjects to those levels. In an organization, for example, there might be ongoing training programs that the researcher assigns people to at random.

Most experiments in the I/O literature have taken place in the laboratory (Schaubroeck & Kuehn, 1992). However, experiments can be conducted in more naturalistic settings. The **field experiment** is conducted within an organization rather than the laboratory. The many field experiments that have been conducted are often only approximations to true experiments and are called *quasi-experiments* (Cook & Campbell, 1979). In a **quasi-experiment design**, one or more of the features of a true experiment have been compromised. Very often there is not random assignment to the levels of the independent variable. In a training study, members of one work group might be given the training, while members of another serve as the control group. Observed differences between the trained and untrained employees might result from the work group itself rather than the training, because of the lack of random assignments.

The major advantage of the experiment is the ability to draw causal conclusions. If the experiment is done properly, one can be reasonably certain that the independent variable is the cause of the dependent variable. If the experiment is conducted in the laboratory, however, one cannot be certain that the results will generalize to the field. With field experiments, generalizability is more likely.

Even with the experiment, however, there can be alternative explanations for results. Often the independent variable will be confounded with another variable. For example, suppose you are interested in determining whether the number of training sessions employees receive affects their job performance. One group might get 5 sessions and the other 10 sessions. However, the total training time is confounded because the second group gets twice the amount of training as the first. You could control total time by making the sessions for the 5-session group twice as long as those for the 10-session group. Unfortunately, now the length of session is confounded with the number of sessions. Disentangling the effects of session length, session number, and total training time can be difficult. It can require several experiments to reach a definitive conclusion.

Survey Designs

The survey design is one of the simplest and easiest to conduct of all the major designs. A **survey design** uses a series of questions compiled to study one or more variables of interest. These questions are then asked of a sample of respondents at a single point in time. Most surveys are presented as paper-and-pencil **questionnaires** that respondents complete and return to the researcher. Other means of conducting surveys can involve computers, face-to-face interviews, telephone interviews, and even the internet via e-mail or the world wide web.

The most common version of the survey involves collecting all data directly from the respondent, but some studies use other data sources as well. For example, one can survey employees about their jobs and get additional information from co-workers or supervisors. Studies of job performance often get performance data from supervisors rather than the employees who are being studied. It is also common to ask customers or peers to provide assessments of job performance. For example, some restaurants ask customers to fill out a card indicating how good the service was. This can be used as a measure of performance if the waiter or waitress is identified.

Most surveys are **cross-sectional**, meaning that all data were collected at a single point in time. A **longitudinal design** is one in which data are collected at more than one point in time. For example, one might collect data on people's feelings about the job when they are first hired and on their performance a year later. This design allows one to see if initial feelings predict later job performance. Many studies of employee turnover are longitudinal, with turnover assessed a year or more after the initial survey. This sort of study involves both a survey and one other type of data, turnover assessed from organizational records.

Using a survey design to study organizational phenomena has two advantages. First, the survey is a quick and relatively inexpensive way to find out how people feel about the job. Second, surveys are usually conducted on employees who are asked about their own jobs. This means that generalizability is not as big a problem as it is with laboratory experiments.

Surveys have two major disadvantages. First, employees are not always good sources of information about the variables of interest. For example, self-appraisals of job performance are usually biased in favor of the employee (Harris & Schaubroeck, 1988). In other words people overrate their own performance. Second, the cross-sectional nature of most surveys makes it difficult to draw conclusions about which variables were likely to be the cause of which other variables. For example, a survey of teachers might find that their reports of their salaries relate to their reports of their job performance. From this alone it could not be determined that salary caused performance, performance caused salary, or a third variable (e.g., job tenure) caused both. The use of longitudinal designs can be more helpful in drawing causal conclusions. Studies in which employee feelings about their jobs predict their later turnover have provided convincing evidence that job attitudes are a causal factor in turnover (Gerhart, 1990).

Perhaps the biggest problem in conducting a survey is assuring a sufficiently high response rate. **Response rate** is the percentage of those surveyed who agree to participate. If the response rate is low because only a small percentage of people are willing to provide data, the generalizability of results is questionable. The responses of these few people might not be the same as those of the people who did not participate. Procedures have been developed to increase response rates, such as avoiding threatening questions and sending reminder letters (Fowler, 1988; Kalton, 1983).

Observational Designs

In an **observational design**, the researcher observes employees in their organizational settings. Observations can be done either with (obtrusive) or without (unobtrusive) the employees' knowledge. With obtrusive methods, the researcher might watch individual employees conducting their jobs for a period of time. Employees would know that the observer was conducting research about a particular aspect of their jobs. With **unobtrusive**

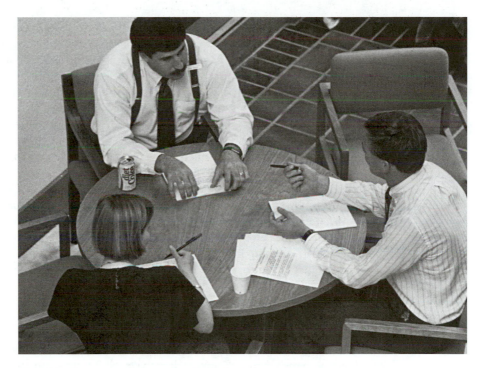

Most I/O research is conducted in the workplace.

methods, the subjects of study might be aware that the researcher is present, but they would not know that they are being studied.

In some obtrusive studies, observers assess specific behaviors or events of interest. For example, observers might record the number of times workers take breaks. In other obtrusive studies, the observer might be asked to rate the person's job conditions or reactions to their jobs. For example, Glick, Jenkins, and Gupta (1986) asked observers to estimate how much employees liked their jobs after watching them for about two hours.

The unobtrusive observational study can be conducted in many ways. A well-designed study can be quite simple but requires creativity and ingenuity to think of a reasonable way to assess the variables of interest. Often such studies are done by having a person pretend to be doing something other than recording people's behavior. The guard at the entrance of an office building can keep track of the arrival times of employees in a study of tardiness. Such data might also be gathered from a videotape of the entrance that has the time recorded on the picture.

One disadvantage of the obtrusive study is that the researcher can affect the phenomenon being studied. Remember how in the Hawthorne study job performance kept going up no matter what lighting levels were chosen (see Chapter 1)? Employee motivation was affected by the research process, making it seem that lighting had no effect on performance. This is why unobtrusive methods can be valuable, although it is not often possible to use them because we can't ethically and perhaps even legally record or watch people's behavior at work.

MEASUREMENT

Measurement is the process of assigning numbers to characteristics of people or things. Variables in every study must be measured or quantified so that data analysis can be conducted to draw conclusions. One of the most critical steps in planning a research study is deciding how each variable will be measured. The nature of measurement determines in part the type of data analysis that can be done.

Measurement can be classified as either categorical or continuous. With **categorical measurement**, the values of the variable represent discrete categories and not the amount of the characteristic of interest. Numbers are assigned arbitrarily to people or things so that low values do not represent less of the characteristic than high values. Player numbers on a sports team or job titles are categorical because (in most cases) they are arbitrary substitutes for the name of the person in the former case or the name of the job in the latter.

Continuous measurement is used when the numbers represent the amount of the characteristic in question. Higher numbers represent more of the characteristic than lower numbers, so that inferences can be made based on the value of a variable. Dependent variables are usually continuous in large part because continuous measurement allows for a variety of sophisticated data analytic methods. Much of the work of both the I/O practitioner and researcher involves the assessment or measurement of jobs and people. Number of training sessions or total time spent in training would be continuous measures.

In experiments, the levels of the independent variables are often categorically measured by numbering them arbitrarily when the levels do not represent an underlying characteristic that can be measured continuously. For example, the independent variable of the method of information presentation in a training program would not represent a continuously quantified dimension. There might be four levels of presentation, for example,

1 = Book

2 = Computer

3 = Lecture

4 = Videotape

These are four discrete items that are numbered arbitrarily.

Over the past decade there has been increasing interest in the use of nonquantitative methods to study organizational phenomena. These **qualitative methods** (Strauss & Corbin, 1990) offer an alternative to the highly quantitatively oriented approaches of most I/O psychologists. In pure form, the qualitative approach involves observing behavior in an organization and then recording those observations in a narrative form. Conclusions and generalizations can be drawn from repeated observations of the same phenomenon without quantifying the results. The qualitative approach can be a good means of generating hypotheses and theories from observations of what happens in organizational settings.

Classical Measurement Theory

According to **classical measurement theory**, every observation of a variable can be divided into two components: true score and error. The true score is assumed to represent the variable of interest. The error is comprised of random influences on the observed score that are independent of the true score. Because errors are random, they are as likely to deflate as inflate the observed values of the variable. Thus, if multiple observations of a variable are taken on the same person or thing, the errors will average out to approximately zero and disappear. Suppose you wish to weigh yourself on a bathroom scale with a needle that tends to stick, randomly indicating a too high or too low weight on successive attempts. If you weigh yourself several times and average the observations, the resulting mean is likely to be close to your true weight. For example, suppose you weigh 120 pounds and the observed scores are

$$116, 118, 122, 124.$$

Each of these observed weights is inaccurate because of an error component. The magnitudes of the error components are

$$-4, -2, 2, 4, \text{ respectively.}$$

The average of the four error components is zero. This means that if you average the four observations of weight, the errors will disappear and the resulting mean will be the correct weight of 120 pounds.

Psychological tests use multiple items to increase accuracy of measurement by averaging out error. Each item of the test contains both a true score and an error component. By combining the items with random errors, those errors should cancel each other out. This leaves a more accurate measurement of the true score.

Even the elimination of error with multiple measures, however, does not guarantee that what was assessed reflects what was intended to be assessed. Depending on the measurement process, many factors may affect the observed score beyond the intended variable and error. For example, rating scales that ask people to indicate the characteristics of their jobs can be affected by the responder's cognitive processes, feelings about the job, mood, and personality (Spector, 1992). The multitude of influences on an observed score is one factor that makes it difficult to interpret the meaning of results from a single study.

Reliability

Reliability is the consistency of measurement across repeated observations of a variable on the same subject. In classical measurement theory terms, it reflects the relative size of the error to true score components. When the error component is small, there will be little variation from observed score to observed score on the same subject. As the error component increases, observations will differ each time the subject is assessed.

There are several types of reliability that can be classified as either internal consistency or test-retest. We often take multiple measurements of each subject on the variable of interest to increase the accuracy of measurement by averaging out the error components, as we discussed in the previous section. **Internal consistency reliability** refers to how well the multiple measures on the same subject agree. If each measure is presumed to assess the same true score, then differences in scores on each measure reflect error or unreliability.

The instrument that uses multiple measures most often is a psychological test that combines multiple items into a total score for the variable of interest. The items must be interrelated for the test to have internal consistency reliability. Usually the more items there are in a test, the better will be its internal consistency. Multiple-item measures are used to assess many of the variables discussed throughout this book, including abilities, job attitudes, perceptions of the job environment, and personality.

Multiple measures are also used when we ask people to rate variables of interest. For example, employee job performance can be assessed by asking supervisors to rate the performance of subordinates. Supervisors are asked to indicate how well subordinates perform by using a rating scale, such as the following:

How would you rate the performance of the following person?

————Excellent

————Good

————Fair

————Poor

Performance ratings are very much like grades given to students by teachers. For research purposes, two or more people might be asked to rate each employee's performance. The ratings can be combined in the same way that multiple items on a test are combined. **Inter-rater reliability** is the extent to which two or more raters agree with one another.

Test–retest reliability refers to the consistency of measurement when it is repeated over time. If you were to assess a person's job satisfaction several times in a row, a reliable scale would give you the same score each time. This assumes, of course, that the satisfaction remained constant. Similarly, a psychological test or other measuring device should give you the same value for a subject each time, unless the true score changes. The time span over which test–retest reliability is assessed is dependent on how stable the variable is assumed to be. With tests of some human attributes such as intelligence, high levels of reliability have been found over time spans of decades.

Both internal consistency and test–retest reliability are necessary properties for a useful measuring device. If a measure contains too much error, it will not give sufficiently accurate measurement to be useful. The first required property of a measure is reliability. Reliability is not enough, however. Just because a measuring device is consistent does not mean that it actually assesses the variable of interest. The interpretation of scores from any measuring device represents its validity, which we discuss next.

Validity

Validity has to do with the inferences that are made about what an observed score measures or represents. In classical measurement theory, it refers to our interpretation of what the true score component represents. Thus, validity refers to the inferences made about a measuring device rather than the device itself. For example, an intelligence test is considered valid if people who score high do better than people who score low on tasks that in theory require intelligence. **Construct validity** means that we are able to give an interpretation to scores on a measure. To say that a measure has construct validity is to say that we have confidence in our interpretation of what that measure represents.

There are several different ways to assess validity, all of which involve inferences that can be made about measures. **Face validity** means that a measure appears to assess what it was designed to assess. An item from a scale to assess how people feel about their jobs, such as,

"Do you like your job?"

might be considered to have face validity because it appears to assess what was intended. An issue of concern with face validity is the perspective of those judging it. Sometimes experts in a domain are asked to judge the face validity of a measure. I/O psychologists can be used as experts for measures of organizational variables.

Face validity does not provide particularly strong evidence to support construct validity. Often a measuring device might appear to be face valid, but it does not assess what was intended. The question, "Have you stolen from your employer?" might appear to be a face valid measure of honesty, but if dishonest employees lie in their answers, the question will not be a valid measure of honesty. Although we sometimes rely on face validity to interpret our measures, it is far from sufficient for establishing construct validity.

Content validity means that a multiple-item measure of a variable does an adequate job of covering the entire domain of the variable. This is best seen in determining whether or not the questions on a course examination do a good or poor job of adequately covering the semester's material. A single question would generally be inadequate to cover all the material in an entire chapter of a textbook. The question

"What is content validity?"

would not represent an adequate and content valid examination on this chapter. A content-valid exam would ask many questions and cover all of the topics in the chapter. As with face validity, experts are used to judge the content validity of a measure.

Criterion-related validity means that scores on a measure of interest relate to other measures that they should relate to in theory. As noted earlier, scores on an intelligence test that is considered valid should relate to performance on tasks that in theory should require intelligence, such as taking examinations in college courses. Intelligence tests have been shown to relate to many variables, including job and school performance, lending confidence to the interpretation of what they represent. The ability of intelligence tests to predict performance makes them valuable tools for the practitioner who wishes to select employees for jobs (see Chapter 5). Although criterion-related validity is important for building a case for construct validity, it is not sufficient. Sometimes we can find support for our predictions for reasons other than what we expect.

The four types of validity are summarized in Table 2-1. The first three—face, content, and criterion-related—represent ways to assess validity. Combined they provide evidence

TABLE 2-1
Four types of validity for a measure and what each one means

TYPE	MEANING
Face	Measure looks like what it assesses
Content	Measure assesses entire variable
Criterion-related	Measure relates to what is expected
Construct	Interpretation of a measure's meaning

for the construct validity of a measure. Construct validity is inferred based on research evidence. It is our best guess about what a measure represents.

STATISTICS

Most studies carried out by I/O psychologists require statistical methods for the data analysis. Two types of statistics are used. Descriptive statistics summarize the results of a study, and inferential statistics help interpret the results using a variety of statistical tests. In this section, we review descriptive statistics and the purpose of several inferential statistics tests.

Descriptive Statistics

The designs discussed in this chapter result in the collection of data on samples of several individuals or jobs. When such data are collected in a study, it is all but impossible to make sense of it without some sort of summary analysis. **Descriptive statistics** provide ways of reducing large amounts of data to summary statistics, such as means or variances. These statistics can be interpreted much more easily than the original data.

Measures of Central Tendency and Dispersion. Several different statistics measure the center of a group of scores. The **arithmetic mean** is the sum of the observations di-

I/O researchers analyze their data by computer.

vided by the number of observations. For example, suppose we have the following numbers of absences in a year for five employees:

$$2, 3, 4, 5, 6.$$

The mean of these five numbers is four absences per year. It is computed by taking the sum of the five numbers (20) and dividing it by the number of employees (5). The **median** is the middle number when the observations are rank ordered from lowest to highest. In this case, 4 is also the median because there are two observations below and two above this value.

The measure of central tendency might indicate the middle score, but it does not give any indication about how much the observations differ from one another in value. For example, the following five observations:

$$48, 49, 50, 51, 52$$

have the same mean of 50 as

$$0, 1, 50, 99, 100$$

even though there is a larger difference among observations in the second case. Measures of dispersion indicate the degree to which the observations differ from one another.

The **variance** is a dispersion measure that is the arithmetic mean of the squared differences between each observation and the arithmetic mean of the same observations. For example, the arithmetic mean of the following absence frequencies:

$$2, 3, 4, 5, 6$$

is 4. The differences between each observation and the mean of 4 are

$$-2, -1, 0, 1, 2$$

Each of these differences squared results in

$$4, 1, 0, 1, 4.$$

The arithmetic mean of these numbers is 2 (10 divided by 5), which is the variance. The **standard deviation** is the square root of the variance, which is 1.4 in this example. It is frequently reported in research papers as the measure of dispersion.

Correlation. Measures of central tendency and dispersion are useful for summarizing groups of observations from a single variable. **Correlation** is a statistic used to indicate the degree to which two continuous variables are related (magnitude) and the direction of the relation. This is important because many research questions concern the relations among variables. For example, a question such as,

"Does level of pay relate to job performance?"

is likely to be answered by computing a correlation statistic between a measure of pay and a measure of job performance.

The most commonly used descriptive statistic to assess correlation is the **Pearson product -moment correlation coefficient**. This statistic can be computed when there are

TABLE 2-2
Hypothetical data showing three possible associations between pay and job performance

POSITIVE ASSOCIATION		NEGATIVE ASSOCIATION		NO ASSOCIATION	
JOB PERFORMANCE	PAY	JOB PERFORMANCE	PAY	JOB PERFORMANCE	PAY
1	1	1	12	1	1
2	2	2	11	2	12
3	3	3	10	3	3
4	4	4	9	4	10
5	5	5	8	5	5
6	6	6	7	6	8
7	7	7	6	7	7
8	8	8	5	8	6
9	9	9	4	9	9
10	10	10	3	10	4
11	11	11	2	11	11
12	12	12	1	12	2

two observations, each representing a different variable, on every subject in a given sample. Table 2-2 contains hypothetical observations of pay and job performance for 12 employees of an organization. Each employee has an observation for each variable. The table contains three possible associations reflected in how the observations of the two variables are paired. Each of the three cases is plotted in Figure 2-1.

In the first case, a positive association or correlation exists between pay and job performance. Employees who have low pay also have low job performance, and employees who have high pay have high job performance. In Figure 2-1a the two variables are plotted with performance on the vertical axis and pay on the horizontal axis. The observations form a straight line from the lower left to upper right portions of the graph. This means that pay and performance are positively correlated, with a value of 1.0.

Figure 2-1b illustrates negative association or correlation. Employees who have low pay have high job performance, and employees who have high pay have low job performance. The observations form a straight line from the upper left to the lower right on the graph. This indicates negative correlation between pay and job performance. This time the value for the correlation coefficient is −1.0.

Figure 2-1c illustrates little association between pay and performance. Some employees with low pay have low job performance, and some have high job performance. Some employees with high pay have low performance, and some have high performance. The observations do not form a straight line but are scattered widely throughout the graph, meaning that the value for the correlation coefficient is approximately zero (0).

Figures 2-1a and 2-1b illustrate perfect correlation because the observations formed a straight line. In almost all studies, there is likely to be a much smaller association between variables, reflected in correlation coefficients that are closer to 0 than the upper limit of 1 in absolute value. In I/O research, correlation coefficients rarely exceed .50. In many do-

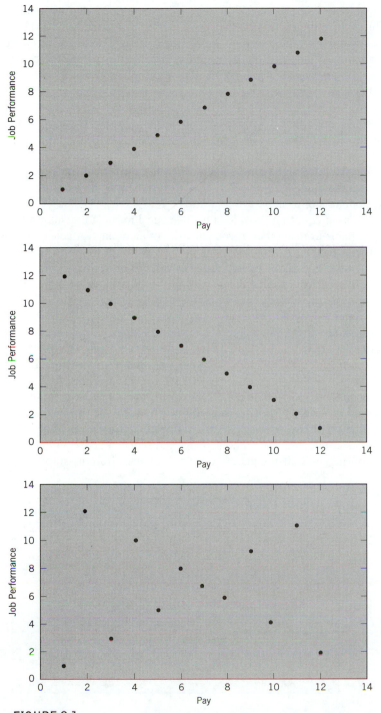

FIGURE 2-1

Three possible associations between income and job performance: (a) positive association; (b) negative association; (c) no association.

mains correlations can be considerably smaller. Figure 2-2 is a plot of 50 observations on two variables where the correlation between them is approximately .50. The points form an elliptical shape from the lower left to the upper right. The direction of the plot indicates a positive association. If the observations had lined up from the upper left to the lower right, the magnitude of the correlation would have been the same, but it would have been negative in sign ($-.50$).

Regression. An important byproduct of correlated variables is that you can use one to predict the other. With the case illustrated in Figure 2-1*a*, you can predict that employees with low pay will have low performance, and employees with high pay will have high performance. Precise predictions can be made when the numerical value for performance is predicted from the numerical value for pay. This is done with a regression equation that is computed from a set of data.

The **regression equation** provides a mathematical formula that allows for the prediction of one variable from another. If you enter the value of one variable (called the **predictor**) into the equation, it will give you the value for the other variable (called the **criterion**). In almost all cases, the two variables will not be perfectly correlated, so prediction of the criterion from the predictor will not be completely accurate. However, even relatively imprecise predictions can be helpful in many situations in which predictions are made. For example, psychological tests (e.g., the Scholastic Aptitude Test or SAT) are used to select students for admission to colleges and universities because they have been shown to predict grade point average. Even though predictions are imperfect, use of the test can result in better average performance by the students, who are admitted based on test scores.

It is also possible to combine data from two or more predictor variables in order to predict a criterion variable. **Multiple regression** is a technique that enables the researcher to combine the predictive power of several variables to improve prediction of a criterion variable. For example, both high school grades and scores on the SAT could be combined to predict college grades. An equation can be developed from a sample of subjects that

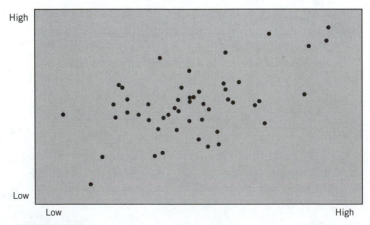

FIGURE 2-2

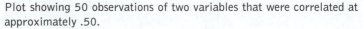
Plot showing 50 observations of two variables that were correlated at approximately .50.

can plug in values of the predictor variables (e.g., high school grades and SAT) to predict a criterion variable (e.g., college grades).

Inferential Statistics

The hypotheses and research questions of most studies cannot be adequately addressed by descriptive statistics alone because data from a limited sample of people must be generalized to a much larger group. In other words, the data from a small sample of employees who are studied are generalized to all employees of the organization or to all employees of all organizations. We are not satisfied in just noting the results with the subjects studied. We wish to draw conclusions about larger groups of people so that we can make general statements about the variables of interest.

Inferential statistics allow us to draw conclusions that generalize from the subjects we have studied to all the people of interest by allowing us to make inferences based on probabilities. The descriptive statistics from a small group of subjects from a research study are extended to the findings to other subjects by using statistical tests that are based on probability.

For example, suppose we conduct a training experiment and wish to extend the results to a larger population of employees. Twenty employees of an organization are randomly assigned to one of two groups of 10 each. One group receives the training, and the other is a control group that does not. The dependent variable is performance on the job. Table 2-3 contains hypothetical data from the study. The performance scores of subjects within each group varied from one another, even though every subject in each of the two groups had the same treatment assigned to that group. This variability among subjects who receive the same treatment in an experiment is called **error variance**, which makes it difficult to draw conclusions just by looking at descriptive statistics. This is because the variability among subjects treated the same will produce differences in means between groups. If we were to place subjects into groups randomly, it is unlikely that those groups would have the same mean on the variable of interest. If many different groups of subjects

TABLE 2-3

Hypothetical data for an experiment comparing a trained group to a control group

CONTROL GROUP PERFORMANCE	TRAINED GROUP PERFORMANCE
1	2
1	4
2	5
2	5
3	6
3	6
4	7
4	8
5	8
10	9
Mean 3.6	6.0

are taken at random from the same organization, it is unlikely that the mean performance of many of them will be the same. There will be variability from sample to sample. Interpreting the results of a study means deciding if observed differences between means is due to error variance or the treatment in question.

If the performance scores in each group are equivalent and produce the same mean, it would be obvious that the training was ineffective. On the other hand, if the performance scores of the trained subjects were all higher than the performance scores of the control group subjects, it would be obvious that the training worked as expected. Neither case is likely to occur in an actual study, making the interpretation of results difficult based on inspection of means alone. The data illustrated in Table 2-3 are typical of the results usually found. Even though the trained group mean is higher than the control group mean, there is overlap in the scores of subjects across the two groups. Some control group subjects performed better than some trained group subjects, and the best performer was in the control group. To interpret these results, you must decide if there is enough difference between the groups to conclude that the training worked or that the differences were due to error variance.

Inferential statistics or **statistical tests** are procedures that help you decide if the results can be attributed to error variance or the experimental treatment. The tests allow you to calculate the probability that the observed results, the differences between means in this case, were not due to error variance. If the probability of finding the mean difference by chance is less than 1 in 20 (.05), the conclusion is reached that the difference was likely due to the training rather than error variance. This is called **statistical significance**, meaning that the probability of finding the observed value of the statistical test by chance alone is less than .05.

There are dozens of different statistical tests, each used for a different situation. Some are used for various experimental designs, whereas others are used for nonexperimental designs. Some are limited to two variables, such as the one independent variable and one dependent variable in the present example. Others can be used with an unlimited number of variables. Table 2-4 lists several of the most commonly used statistical tests in I/O research. Although they may have different purposes, all are based on the same underlying principle of determining if the probability of the test statistic is statistically significant.

TABLE 2-4
Five commonly used inferential statistics tests and their usage

Independent Group *t* test: Used to determine if two groups of subjects differ significantly on a dependent variable.

Analysis of Variance (ANOVA): Used to determine if two or more groups of subjects differ significantly on a dependent variable.

Factorial ANOVA: Used to determine the significance of effects of two or more independent variables on a dependent variable.

t test for Correlation: Used to determine if the correlation between two variables is significantly greater than zero.

Multiple Regression: Used to determine if two or more predictor variables can significantly predict a criterion variable.

An independent group t test is used in the present example to see if the two groups differ significantly on a dependent variable. If there are two or more groups, the analysis of variance (ANOVA) would be used. This would allow you to compare two different training methods to a control group. In most experiments, however, there are two or more independent variables. For example, suppose you wish to compare the trained group to the control group separately for men and women. You could randomly assign 10 men to the control group and 10 men to the trained group. Similarly, you could randomly assign 10 women to the control group and 10 women to the trained group. This would produce a factorial design consisting of the training variable and the gender variable, each of which had two levels. A **factorial design** has two or more independent variables. **Factorial ANOVA** is a statistical test that is used to analyze the data from a factorial design. It tells us if the subjects in the various groups differed significantly on the dependent variable.

The correlation coefficient can be tested to see if it is significantly different from zero. This is done with a variation of the t test. A significant correlation means that significant association exists between two variables and that you can predict one variable from another better than by chance. When more than two variables are related to a third, multiple regression is used. There are significance tests to show that two or more predictor variables in the regression analysis are related significantly to the criterion variable. Again, significance means that the criterion can be predicted by the predictors better than by chance.

Meta-Analysis

A single study is never considered to offer a definitive answer to a research question. To achieve confidence in a conclusion about a phenomenon of interest, we need to conduct several studies. It is not unusual, however, for different studies to yield somewhat different results. The same sampling error that produces differences among means taken from the same population will produce differences in the results of inferential statistical tests. To make sense of conflicting results across studies requires the use of a special type of analysis called meta-analysis.

A **meta-analysis** is a quantitative way of combining results of studies, much like our statistics summarize the results across individual subjects (Hunter & Schmidt, 1990; Rosenthal, 1991). A meta-analysis can summarize statistically the results of different studies in the domains of interest to I/O psychologists. Such analyses can be simple descriptive summaries of results or very complex mathematical and statistical procedures.

Perhaps the simplest form of meta-analysis summarizes the results of multiple studies with means of statistics. A meta-analysis might report that the mean correlation between two variables has been found to be a particular value, such as .40. For example, suppose you found five studies that reported the following correlations between job satisfaction and pay level:

.20, .22, .24, .26, .28.

A simple meta-analysis of these five studies would conclude that the mean correlation between these two variables was .24. More complex analyses could also be conducted to explore other aspects of these studies. If some studies were conducted on managers and others on nonmanagers, one could test to see if the correlations were different for the two types of employees.

In this book, the results of studies are often summarized by referring to meta-analysis. These analyses have become popular in the I/O research literature. It can be difficult to read several studies and make sense of the findings without the use of some sort of method such as meta-analysis. In most areas that have been frequently studied, meta-analyses can be found to help interpret what those individual studies have found.

ETHICS OF RESEARCH

The ethical principles of I/O psychologists hold for research as well as for practice. The overriding ethical consideration is that the researcher must protect the well-being of subjects. This means that manipulations, such as an experimental training procedure, should not be used if they are known to cause harm. Even with nonexperimental studies, such as surveys, the researcher must take care to protect identities when appropriate. If respondents to a survey provide negative feedback about their supervisors, supervisors should not be able to find out who provided the feedback. This way there can be no retaliation against a subordinate for saying something that the supervisor did not like.

At times, however, conflicting demands can make it difficult to decide what is correct ethically. It would be considered unethical to violate confidentiality and disclose the identities of surveyed employees. On the other hand, a psychologist who works for an organization has an ethical responsibility to that organization much as he or she would have to an individual. That responsibility might extend to identifying disgruntled employees who might cause trouble or need help. A psychologist might have to weigh the well-being of individuals against the well-being of the organization. This responsibility to two parties creates an ethical dilemma because two conflicting demands are placed on the psychologist. It is difficult to know what is the right thing to do in all such situations. An I/O psychologist must carefully weigh the costs to all people involved in taking different actions. An ethical psychologist will discuss the issue with other psychologists and with superiors in the hope of reaching an ethical and satisfactory decision. In some cases the psychologist might be forced to take the organization's side or risk being fired.

It is a good idea to try to foresee these situations and avoid them. If you suspect that supervisors might demand to know employee identities, conduct surveys anonymously. If you do not know the identities, you cannot disclose them. Even so, ethical dilemmas can arise in both practice and research. They can be difficult to resolve because someone might be harmed no matter what action is taken. For example, a psychologist might become aware of company policy violations committed by an employee. If nothing is said, the company might suffer damage, but if the person is turned in, he or she might get fired.

Another ethical principle is that subjects of studies should be informed about the nature and purpose of a study before they participate. If there is even a slight possibility that participation has some drawbacks, the person should be asked to sign an **informed consent form**. These forms explain the nature of a study and what is expected of the subject, and alerts them that withdrawal from the experiment can be done at any time. Although using these forms can be awkward in field settings, informed consent means that the subjects understand possible risks. This protects the researcher from legal action resulting in harm, either real or imagined, that someone claims occurred from participation.

CHAPTER SUMMARY

I/O psychology is a science because the methods used in research are scientific methods. This means that I/O psychologists collect and analyze data to address organizational issues and questions. An I/O research study begins with a research question, which defines the purpose of the study. The question leads to a research hypothesis, which is the researcher's best guess about how a study will turn out. A specific hypothesis will serve as the basis for the design of a study.

An I/O study can take place in either a field or laboratory setting. In a field setting, the phenomenon in question occurs naturally; in a laboratory, it is created. Generalizability means that the results of a given study can be extended to other settings and situations. Control is an important component of research studies in that it allows one to rule out alternative explanations for results. There are many different approaches to achieving control in studies. Random assignment refers to choosing subjects in a nonsystematic way so that every individual has an equal chance of being assigned to different treatment conditions. Random selection means that every possible subject has an equal chance of being chosen to participate in the study. Confounding occurs when two or more variables are intertwined and related in a way that makes it difficult to draw conclusions about either one.

Research designs can be divided into experimental and nonexperimental forms. In experimental designs, the researcher randomly assigns subjects to conditions that are constructed for the study. Nonexperimental designs involve observation without assignment of subjects or construction of conditions.

Measurement is the process by which characteristics of people or things are quantified. Reliability refers to the consistency of measurement, whereas validity means that inferences can be drawn about the meaning of a measure. The data generated by a study are analyzed with statistical methods. Descriptive statistics summarize the data from a study, and inferential statistics allow for the interpretation of findings.

Ethical principles of I/O psychologists apply to research studies. In general, researchers should ensure that their studies do not harm anyone. This is accomplished by taking care that procedures are not dangerous or harmful. Subjects should be informed about the nature of a study by having them read and sign an informed consent form. They should be allowed the opportunity to decline participation. Care should be taken to protect the identities of subjects when information they provide could be used against them in a detrimental way.

Part TWO

ASSESSMENT OF JOBS, PERFORMANCE, AND PEOPLE

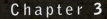

JOB ANALYSIS

How would you describe the job of a police officer? What are the different tasks that police officers do, and how much time do they spend doing each one? How difficult is it to learn the various tasks, and how long does it take? What personal characteristics does it take to do each task, as well as the entire job? These questions are addressed by a variety of techniques that I/O psychologists refer to as job analysis.

Even for the most familiar jobs, a job analysis is necessary to provide an accurate picture of all the details of the job and all the characteristics required of the people who will do it. For example, everyone is somewhat familiar with the job of a police officer. However, the public perception of the job is based to a large extent on depictions in popular movies and television programs. Even the most realistic shows, such as "Homicide: Life on the Streets" and "N.Y.P.D. Blue," undoubtedly give a distorted view. Television programs focus on the more dramatic aspects of the job, which may be rarely performed. Most police officers spend more time on routine patrol duties and paperwork than on apprehending criminals (Bernardin, 1988). The firing of a weapon is a common occurrence on television, but it is rarely done by most police officers on the job. A thorough job analysis would provide an accurate picture of what police officers do all day on the job. The police officer's job has been thoroughly studied with many different job analysis methods and procedures. We look at some of them throughout this chapter.

There are two different types of job analyses—the job oriented and the person (or employee) oriented. The job-oriented job analysis focuses on the tasks that are done on the job, whereas the person-oriented analysis is concerned with the personal characteristics needed for a job. In other words, the job-oriented procedures describe jobs, and the person-oriented procedures describe the characteristics people need to perform jobs. Both are important tools for describing jobs and their requirements.

In this chapter we discuss the job-oriented and person-oriented approaches, and the particular methods that are used for each. In addition, we discuss the uses and purposes of job analysis information, the sources of information that go into a job analysis, and the reliability and validity of job analysis methods. Finally, we discuss job evaluation, which is a job analysis technique used to set salary levels.

<u>Objectives</u>   **The student who studies this chapter should be able to:**
1. List the uses of job analysis information.
2. Describe the sources and ways of collecting job analysis information.
3. Discuss the different job analysis methods.
4. Describe the evidence for reliability and validity of job analysis methods.
5. Explain how job evaluation is used to set salary levels for jobs.

WHAT IS JOB ANALYSIS?

Job analysis is a method for describing jobs and the human attributes necessary to perform them. There is no one way to do a job analysis. Many methods provide different types of information about jobs and job requirements. As noted earlier, job analysis techniques can be used to collect information that is job oriented or person oriented, depending on the purpose of the job analyst.

The Job-Oriented Approach

The **job-oriented job analysis** provides information about the nature of tasks done on the job. Some methods describe the tasks themselves. Other methods provide information about characteristics of tasks. For example, a task for a police officer would be:

Completes report after arresting a suspect

This describes something a police officer does. A characteristic of an officer's job would be:

Uses pencils and pens

The characteristic isn't a specific task but describes common features that cut across tasks. A police officer performs many tasks involving writing, such as completing reports of many types and giving citations to motorists. The purposes of the job analysis determine which type of approach would be most useful. The task descriptions provide a picture of what people do on a job. Characteristics of tasks can be used to compare the nature of tasks across different kinds of jobs. Police officers and teachers share the characteristic of using pencils and pens to do tasks, so there can be some similarities in types of tasks, even though the specific tasks themselves may vary.

Tasks can be divided into a hierarchy in which higher level descriptions are broken down into smaller and smaller pieces of the job. For example, one of the major tasks performed by police officers is apprehending suspects. This police function can be further broken down into the specific actions that are involved, such as

Go to suspect's house to make arrest

Knock on door and identify self

Handcuff suspect

Inform suspect of legal rights

Put suspect in car

Drive suspect to police station

A job analysis is needed to describe what a police officer does at work.

Levine (1983) has developed a system that can be used to produce a hierarchy. He divides the major functions of a job into four levels of specificity:

1. Duty
2. Task
3. Activity
4. Element

A *duty* is a major component of a job. For a police officer a duty would be

Arrest suspects

Each duty is accomplished by performing one or more associated tasks. A *task* is a complete piece of work that accomplishes some particular objective. One of the tasks involved in arresting someone might be

Drive to suspect's house in police car to take person into custody

Each task can be divided into *activities*, which are the individual parts that make up the task. In this case activities would include

Put handcuffs on suspect

To accomplish this activity, a number of very specific *actions* or elements are involved, such as

Release clip holding handcuffs on belt

Take handcuffs in right hand

Open handcuffs with left hand

Place handcuff on suspect's wrist

Close handcuff

For most jobs there are several duties; each duty is associated with several tasks; each task is associated with several activities; and each activity can be broken down into several actions. This means that a job analysis can contain a great deal of very specific information about what happens on a particular job. A job analysis that goes to the level of job actions produces a long and detailed report.

The Person-Oriented Approach

A **person-oriented job analysis** provides a description of the attributes, characteristics, or KSAOs necessary for a person to successfully perform a particular job. **KSAOs** are the knowledge, skills, abilities, and other personal characteristics necessary for a job. The first three characteristics focus mainly on job performance itself; the "other" characteristics relate to job adjustment and satisfaction, as well as performance.

Knowledge is what a person needs to know to do a particular job. For example, a carpenter should have knowledge of local building codes and power tool safety.

Skill is what a person is able to do on the job. A carpenter should have skill in reading blueprints and in using power tools.

Ability is a person's aptitude or capability to do job tasks or learn to do job tasks. It is a person's potential to develop skills. Most skills require one or more abilities. The skill of using power tools requires several abilities, including hand–eye coordination. In order to build the roof on a house, a carpenter should have good balance and ability to work quickly.

Finally, **other personal characteristics** include anything relevant to the job that is not covered by the other three. A carpenter should have a willingness to do manual tasks and to work outdoors.

Although they might seem to overlap, KSAOs and tasks are very distinct. A task is something a person does. A KSAO is an attribute or characteristic of the person required to do a particular task or tasks. Tasks define what is done on a job, whereas KSAOs describe the sort of person needed. Table 3-1 provides some examples of tasks and associated KSAOs.

Many job analysis methods have been developed to do both job- and person-oriented analyses. Some are specific to one of the two major types of analyses, whereas others can be used for either one or both. The appropriateness of a particular method is determined by its purpose, the next topic we discuss.

TABLE 3-1
Examples of KSAOs and associated tasks

KSAO	TASK
Knowledge of legal arrest procedures	Arrest suspects
Skill in using a firearm	Practice shooting firearm on firing range
Ability to communicate with others	Mediate a dispute between two people to prevent violent incident
Courage (as other personal characteristic)	Enter dark alley to apprehend suspect

PURPOSES OF JOB ANALYSIS

Job analysis information has many purposes. It can serve as the foundation on which many other activities and functions are built. Ash and Levine (1980) outlined 11 common uses of job analysis information, five of which we discuss in this section of the chapter. The use of job analysis information for setting salary levels will be discussed later under the heading "Job Evaluation." The 11 uses are listed in Table 3-2.

Career Development

Many organizations have systems that allow employees to move up through the ranks to higher and higher positions. This is referred to as a **career ladder**: A progression of positions is established for individuals who acquire the necessary skills and maintain good job performance. Perhaps the best known career ladder system is in the military. Personnel move up through the ranks from lieutenant to captain to major to colonel to general. Not everyone can climb to the top of the ladder because of limited opportunities for promotion and inability to achieve the necessary KSAOs.

Job analysis contributes to career development by providing a picture of the KSAO requirements for jobs at each level of the career ladder. Knowledge of KSAO requirements can be incorporated into employee development and training programs that can focus on skills necessary for career advancement. This benefits employees because they are told exactly what they need to be eligible for promotion. It benefits organizations because they develop a readily available supply of candidates for upper level positions.

Legal Issues

Most industrialized countries have laws prohibiting discriminatory employment practices, especially in the hiring of employees. In Canada and the United States, for example, it is

TABLE 3-2
Eleven uses of job analysis information

USE	DESCRIPTION
Career development	Define KSAOs necessary for advancement
Legal issues	Show job relevance of KSAOs
Performance appraisal	Set criteria to evaluate performance
Recruitment and selection of employees	Delineate applicant characteristics to be used as the basis for hiring
Training	Suggest areas for training
Setting salaries	Determine salary levels for jobs
Efficiency/safety	Design jobs for efficiency and safety
Job classification	Place similar jobs into groupings
Job description	Write brief descriptions of jobs
Job design	Design content of jobs
Planning	Forecast future need for employees with specific KSAOs

Source: Based on "A Framework for Evaluating Job Analysis Methods," by R. A. Ash and E. L. Levine, 1980, *Personnel, 57,* 53–59.

illegal to discriminate on the basis of age, color, disability, gender, race, or religion. Although the specific groups that are protected against discrimination vary from country to country, the basic idea that decisions affecting people should be fair is almost universal. Fairness in employment means that decisions should be based on job performance or job potential rather than irrelevant personal characteristics. Job analysis provides a list of relevant KSAOs as the basis for hiring rather than irrelevant personal characteristics.

An important legal concept in U.S. employment is **essential functions**, which are actions that must be done on a job. A receptionist must answer the telephone, for example. A nonessential function might be done occasionally but is not important for a person in that position to do. A custodian might receive an occasional phone call, but answering the phone is not an important part of the job.

The concept of essential function is important in deciding whether or not to hire a disabled person. In the United States an organization might be able to legally deny employment to a disabled person who cannot perform essential functions under certain conditions (see Chapter 6). It is illegal to refuse to hire disabled individuals because they cannot perform nonessential functions because these functions can easily be done by someone else, or they do not need to be done at all. With nonessential functions, and at times with essential functions, an organization is required to make accommodations so that the person is able to do the job (Cleveland, Barnes-Farrell, & Ratz, 1997), as we will discuss at greater length in Chapter 5.

Job analysis is used to identify essential functions and KSAOs (Mitchell, Alliger, & Morfopoulos, 1997). This can help ensure that decisions about actions that affect people are based on personal factors that are job relevant. For example, a legally defensible system to hire people should be based on KSAOs that have been shown to be relevant to the job in question. Promotion decisions should be based at least in part on the KSAOs of the possible candidates for the position. Only those individuals who possess the established characteristics that are necessary for the job should be considered. When KSAOs are derived from a properly conducted job analysis, employee actions based on those KSAOs are likely to be legal. Furthermore, employees and job applicants will probably believe that they were fairly treated.

Performance Appraisal

A well-designed performance appraisal system will be based on a job analysis. Criterion development, determining the major components of job performance to be evaluated, is one of the major uses of job analysis information. A job-oriented analysis provides a list of the major components of a job, which can be used as dimensions for performance evaluation.

The behavior-focused performance appraisal methods to be discussed in Chapter 4 are based on a job analysis. The specific behaviors contained in such instruments are collected with **critical incidents** from a job analysis (Flanagan, 1954). These incidents are instances of behavior that represent different levels of job performance from outstanding to poor, and they become an important part of the assessment of performance. A poor incident would describe how a person actually did something that was ineffective, such as a police officer getting into an argument with a citizen that resulted in violence. A good incident would describe how a person did something that worked well, such as a police officer defusing a potentially violent encounter by allowing a person to explain his or her side of the story.

Selection

The first step in deciding who to hire for a job is determining the human attributes or KSAOs necessary for success on that job. This means that a person-oriented job analysis should be the first step in the design of an employee selection system. Once the KSAOs for a job are identified, procedures can be chosen to determine how well job applicants fit the requirements for the job. This is done by using methods to assess individual characteristics, such as interviews and psychological tests (see Chapter 5).

A person-oriented job analysis produces a list of the KSAOs for a particular job. These KSAOs include both the characteristics that a job applicant is usually expected to have at the time of hiring and characteristics that will be developed on the job through experience and training. Most accountant positions in large organizations, for example, require a college degree in accounting. This ensures that most applicants will have a reasonable level of knowledge about accounting principles and procedures. Specific knowledge about the organization's own policies and practices are learned on the job. This leads us to the next use of job analysis information—training.

Training

The KSAOs for a job suggest the areas in which training efforts should be directed. The KSAOs that applicants do not have when they apply for a position are areas for training after they are hired. An effective training program in an organization should be based on a thorough analysis of the KSAO requirements for a job. The KSAO requirements can be compared to the KSAOs of applicants or employees. Deficiencies on the part of applicants or employees are the areas in which training efforts might be directed if the characteristics can be acquired. For example, one cannot train a person to be taller if there is a height requirement for a job.

SOURCES OF JOB ANALYSIS INFORMATION

Job analysis information is collected in several ways. All of them use people who are trained in quantifying job characteristics and the KSAOs necessary to accomplish the different aspects of jobs. These people either survey the employees who do the jobs in question or experience the job firsthand by doing it themselves or observing it being done.

Who Provides the Information?

Most job analysis information comes from one of four different sources:

Job analysts	Supervisors
Job incumbents	Trained observers

Job analysts and trained observers actually do the job or spend time observing employees doing the job and translate those experiences into a job analysis. Incumbents and supervisors are considered to be **subject matter experts**, people with detailed knowledge about the content and requirements of their own jobs or the jobs they supervise. They are asked to provide information about jobs either in interviews or by completing job analysis questionnaires.

How Do People Provide Job Analysis Information?

People can provide job analysis information in many ways. The four most commonly used are

Perform the job

Observe employees on the job

Interview subject matter expert

Administer questionnaires to subject matter experts

Perform Job. One way to collect job analysis information is for the job analyst to actually do some of the job tasks or the whole job. The job can be performed as an employee would, or the tasks can be performed under simulated conditions. By doing the job, the analyst gains insight into the nature of the job tasks and how the job tasks interrelate. It also provides an appreciation for the context in which employees do their jobs. Both an insurance salesperson and a police officer, for example, operate an automobile, but the conditions under which they do so can be very different.

Although this method can provide good information, it is not often used. Experiencing the job by doing it can be costly and time consuming. It can require extensive training before the analyst can do the job. Some jobs are dangerous, particularly for an inexperienced person. Finally, this approach does not clearly indicate that tasks can differ among employees with the same job title.

Observe. Another way to experience the job is by observing others performing it. Observers can be job analysts or people trained to observe others. Observers are often given forms to complete. The form might contain a list of activities, and the observer indicates how often the subject does each one. As with the prior technique, observing employees can give insights into the context in which job tasks are performed. It can also be expensive and time-consuming.

Interview. One of the most popular ways to collect information about jobs is by interviewing subject matter experts who are familiar with them. The experts are usually job incumbents and their supervisors. Interviews are carried out by job analysts or trained interviewers. Interviews are often used to generate lists of all tasks and activities done by everyone who has the same job title. Many of the tasks might be performed by few employees. Other tasks might be performed by every employee but only on rare occasions.

Questionnaire. The questionnaire is the most efficient means of collecting job analysis information. It can contain hundreds of questions about the job and can be administered easily to thousands of employees. No other technique can provide as much information about jobs with as little effort on the part of the job analyst. The same questionnaire can be given to every employee with the same job title. Comparisons can be made among groups that have the same job title but may differ on some characteristics, such as location.

Multiple Methods. Each of the four ways of collecting job analysis information has its own set of advantages and limitations in providing a picture of what a job is like. (Table 3-3 lists the advantages and limitations of each method.) In practice, multiple ways are

TABLE 3-3
Advantages and limitations of four techniques for collecting job analysis information

Job Analyst Performs the Job

Advantages:	Provides the context in which job is done
	Provides extensive detail about the job
Limitations:	Fails to show differences among jobs with same title
	Expensive and time-consuming
	Can take extensive training of analyst
	Can be dangerous to analyst

Interview

Advantages:	Provides multiple perspectives on a job
	Can show differences among incumbents with the same job
Limitations:	Time-consuming, compared to questionnaires
	Fails to show context in which tasks are done

Observe Employees Doing the Job

Advantages:	Provides relatively objective view of the job
	Provides the context in which the job is done
Limitations:	Time-consuming
	Employees might change their behavior because they know they are being observed

Questionnaires

Advantages:	Efficient and inexpensive
	Shows differences among incumbents in the same job
	Easy to quantify and analyze statistically
	Easy to compare different jobs on common job dimensions
Limitations:	Ignores context in which job is done
	Limits respondent to questions asked
	Requires knowledge of job to design questionnaire
	Easy for job incumbents to distort to make their jobs seem more important than they are

often used so that the limitations of one are offset by the strengths of another. For example, a job analyst might do the job to get a feel for the context of the job and then administer questionnaires to get detailed information from a wide cross section of employees with the same job title.

METHODS OF JOB ANALYSIS

Many methods have been developed to conduct job analysis. These methods use the different sources of information and the different ways of collecting information. Some of the methods focus on either the job or the person, whereas others focus on both. The methods vary in their use of the four sources of job analysis information and the four ways of collecting information. Many of these methods use more than one source and more than one way of collecting information. One reason that so many methods exist is that they are not all suited to the same purposes. Levine, Ash, Hall, and Sistrunk (1983) found that job analysts rated different methods as being best suited to different purposes.

In this section we discuss four frequently used job analysis methods: The Job Components Inventory, Functional Job Analysis, and the Position Analysis Questionnaire are general methods that can be used to compare different jobs; task inventories are used to provide a description of the specific components and tasks of individual jobs. Each method has its own particular strengths and was developed to address a particular purpose.

Job Components Inventory

The **Job Components Inventory (JCI)** was developed in Great Britain to address the need to match job requirements to worker characteristics (Banks, Jackson, Stafford, & Warr, 1983). This method allows for the simultaneous assessment of the job requirements and a person's KSAOs. In other words, the KSAOs for a job and for an individual are listed. The degree of correspondence of the lists is used to determine if an individual is suited to a particular job or if the person needs additional training in order to perform a job adequately. The JCI has been used in school settings for both curriculum development and vocational guidance.

The JCI covers over 400 features of jobs that can be translated into skill requirements. Five components of job features are represented in the JCI:

1. Use of tools and equipment
2. Perceptual and physical requirements
3. Mathematics
4. Communication
5. Decision making and responsibility

Examples of the skill requirements for each of the five components for clerical jobs in Great Britain can be found in Table 3-4. Just about any job can be analyzed with the JCI,

TABLE 3-4

Examples of frequently needed skills for British clerical occupations grouped by the five components of the Job Components Inventory

COMPONENT	SKILL
Use of tools and equipment	Use of pens
	Use of telephone
Perceptual and physical requirements	Selective attention
	Wrist/finger/hand speed
Mathematics	Use decimals
	Use whole numbers
Communication	Advise or help people
	Receive written information
Decision making and responsibility	Decide on sequencing of work
	Decide on standards of work

Source: From "Skills Training for Clerical Work: Action Research Within the Youth Opportunities Programme," by M. H. Banks and E. M. Stafford, 1982, *BACIE Journal,* 37, 57–66.

TABLE 3-5
The first and last entries in the *Dictionary of
Occupational Titles*, fourth edition, 1977 index

ABALONE DIVER: Gathers or harvests marine life, such as sponges, abalone, pearl
oysters, and geoducks from sea bottom wearing wet suit and scuba gear, or diving
suit with air line extending to surface.

ZYGLO INSPECTOR: Applies iron oxide and zyglo solutions to ferrous metal parts
and examines parts under fluorescent and black lighting to detect defects, such as
fissures, weld breaks, or fractures.

Condensed.

so that its skill requirements can be matched to those of potential employees. An existing
database of job requirements for many jobs can be used with people who wish to know
how well their own skills match those of a chosen career.

Functional Job Analysis

Functional Job Analysis (FJA) (Fine & Wiley, 1971) provides both a description of a
job and scores on several dimensions concerning the job and potential workers. The dimensions are applicable to all jobs, so that the procedure can be used to make comparisons among jobs. FJA was the job analysis method used by the U.S. Department of Labor
to produce the *Dictionary of Occupational Titles* (U.S. Department of Labor, 1977, 1991).
This rather large document contains job analysis information on over 20,000 different
jobs. The index from the 1977 edition lists jobs from abalone diver to zyglo inspector,
both of which are described in Table 3-5.

The **Dictionary of Occupational Titles** (DOT) contains a description of each job's
content and scores representing the complexity with which incumbents work with: data,
people, and things. Data is any sort of information (e.g., financial); people can be co-
workers, subordinates, clients, or customers; and things are animate (e.g., animals) or
inanimate (e.g., tools) objects. The description provides an overview of the nature of the
job and the major tasks involved. The description for a police officer job is shown in
Table 3-6.

TABLE 3-6
Description of a police officer job from the *Dictionary
of Occupational Titles,* fourth edition, 1977

Patrols assigned beat to control traffic, prevent crime and arrest violators. Notes
suspicious persons and establishments and reports to superior officer. Disperses
unruly crowds at public gatherings. Issues tickets to traffic violators. May notify
public works department of location of abandoned vehicles to tow away. May
accompany parking meter personnel to protect money collected.

Condensed.

Data, people, and things are scored for the complexity with which they are handled in a job. Data ranges in complexity from comparing (e.g., verifying numbers entered in a computer) to synthesizing (e.g., writing a research report), people ranges from taking instructions (e.g., doing what one is told to do) or helping to mentor (e.g., training an apprentice), and things ranges from handling (e.g., unloading a truck) to setting up (e.g., making objects in a machine shop). Table 3-7 contains examples of jobs that represent each of these levels of data, people, and things. As shown in the table, data is handled at the lowest level of complexity (comparing) by a spear fisher and at the highest level of complexity (synthesizing) by a mechanical engineer.

Occupational Information Network, O*NET. The DOT last underwent a complete revision in 1977, and so much of it is obsolete and out of date. Many of today's jobs didn't exist in the 1970s (e.g., computer network administrator and website designer), and others have changed. For example, many jobs today require the use of personal computers (newspaper reporter and secretary). Rather than just updating the DOT, the U.S. Department of Labor decided to take a new approach. Enlisting the help of many I/O psychologists, the **Occupational Information Network** or **O*NET** was launched. This information system, which should be operational by the time you read this chapter, is a computer-based resource for job-related information. It is available in a number of forms, including a CD-ROM and via the world wide web. The idea is to make this database widely available to individuals and organizations.

The contents of the O*NET is far more extensive than anything yet attempted. It encompasses a tremendous amount of information about the content of jobs and the KSAOs needed by individuals in those jobs. Hundreds of pieces of data are provided on each job, which cover many of the concepts discussed throughout this book. On the job side are types of activities (e.g., operating vehicles), how employees for the job are recruited (e.g., through college recruiters), the nature of training required, types of compensation (pay and fringe benefits), and workplace hazards (e.g., exposure to infectious disease). On the person side are extensive KSAO requirements listed, with 33 under the knowledge cate-

TABLE 3-7

Examples of jobs that are high and low on data, people, and things from the *Dictionary of Occupational Titles,* fourth edition, 1977

Data

Synthesizing (high)	Mechanical engineer
Comparing (low)	Spear fisher

People

Mentoring (high)	Counselor]
Taking instructions/Helping (low)	Factory worker

Things

Setting up (high)	Machinist
Handling (low)	Laborer

gory, 46 under skills, 52 under abilities, and 43 under other (U.S. Department of Labor, 1998). This is quite an advance over just data, people, and things! The best way to see this amazing resource on jobs is by visiting the O*NET website, which as of this writing is at:

http://www.doleta.gov/programs/onet.

Position Analysis Questionnaire

The **Position Analysis Questionnaire (PAQ)** (McCormick, Jeanneret, & Mecham, 1972) is an instrument that can be used to analyze any job. The questionnaire itself contains 189 items dealing with the task requirements or elements of jobs. A KSAO profile for a job can be developed from the elements. The elements of the PAQ are general and allow comparisons of different jobs on a common set of dimensions or KSAOs.

The elements of the PAQ are organized into six major categories, each of which is further divided into several minor categories (Table 3-8). The elements cover a wide variety of task requirements, including the inputting and processing of information, the use of equipment and tools, general body movements, interpersonal interaction, and work context. The elements can be translated into KSAOs for any job. A job that involves using mathematics, for example, requires skill in this area. Because the PAQ generates a standard list of KSAOs, jobs can be compared on their KSAO requirements.

The PAQ produces a profile of the task elements and KSAOs for a job. The profile compares a given job to the hundreds of jobs in the PAQ database. It indicates the percentile score for each element and KSAO in comparison to all jobs. A low score means that the element or KSAO is a less important part of the target job than it is for jobs in general. A high score means that the element or KSAO is a more important part of the target job than jobs in general. A percentile of 50 means that the job is average on the element or dimension in question.

Table 3-9 contains a sample of the most important elements and KSAOs for a police officer job. As the table shows, a police officer job involves engaging in general personal contact and wearing specified versus optional apparel. Table 3-9 also contains several sample KSAOs for a police officer job. The two most important are far visual acuity and simple reaction time.

TABLE 3-8
Major categories of the PAQ

CATEGORY	EXAMPLE
Information input	Collecting or observing information
Mediation processes	Decision making and information processing
Work output	Manipulating objects
Interpersonal activities	Communicating with other people
Work situation and job context	Physical and psychological working conditions
Miscellaneous aspects	Work schedule

Source: From "A Study of Job Characteristics and Job Dimensions as Based on the Position Analysis Questionnaire (PAQ)," by E. J. McCormick, P. R. Jeanneret, and R. C. Mecham, 1972, *Journal of Applied Psychology, 56,* 347–368.

TABLE 3-9
PAQ KSAOs and task elements for a police officer

KSAOs
Far visual acuity
Simple reaction time
Movement detection
Rate control
Auditory acuity

Task Elements
Interpreting what is sensed
Being aware of environmental conditions
Controlling machines and/or processes
Engaging in general personal contact
Wearing specified versus optional apparel

Source: Job Profile, PAQ Number 003127, used by permission of PAQ Services.

Task Inventories

A **task inventory** is a questionnaire that contains a list of specific tasks that might be done on a job that is being analyzed. The inventory also contains one or more rating scales for each task. Ratings might be made on dimensions such as

Amount of time spent doing the task

Criticality of the task for doing a good job

Difficulty of learning the task

Importance of the task

Job incumbents usually are asked to complete the inventory for their own job. Results are compiled across incumbents to give a picture of the average importance or time spent for each task in a particular job.

When several people complete a task inventory, they are certain to give somewhat different ratings on the same dimensions for each task. This can reflect differences in how individuals make judgments about their jobs. In other words, if two people spend the same amount of time on a task, one might give it a higher time-spent rating than the other. An alternative possibility is that differences in ratings across people reflect real differences in tasks. There can be large differences in the content of jobs with the same title in the same organization. For example, some secretaries take dictation, but many do not. Some use computers for word processing, but there are still secretaries who use typewriters.

Most task inventories are used for purposes in which differences among people with the same job are of no particular interest. In a study of stockbrokers, however, ratings of time spent in several tasks predicted the individual's sales performance (Borman, Dorsey, & Ackerman, 1992). For example, stockbrokers who spent more time with clients away from the office sold more than their counterparts who spent less time (see the Research in Detail box in this chapter). Whether the time spent is the cause or the result of good per-

RESEARCH IN DETAIL

LACK OF AGREEMENT among raters of a task inventory is usually interpreted as lack of reliability. In this study the authors viewed disagreement from a different perspective. They believed that people in the same job would differ in the amount of time they spent in various tasks. Furthermore, the researchers believed that the time-spent differences might relate to sales performance of stockbrokers. In other words, people who are high performers might spend their time differently on the job than people who are low performers.

To test this idea, the authors conducted a job analysis with 580 stockbrokers as subject matter experts. Each one completed a task inventory with 160 tasks. Ratings of amount of time spent were made for each task. In addition, data were collected for each stockbroker's sales performance (dollars sold) for the prior year.

The amount of time spent in some of the tasks correlated significantly with sales performance. For example, the following tasks were associated with high sales:

Dealing with corporate clients and clients in nonbusiness settings

Advising and helping other stockbrokers

The authors noted that it might be tempting to conclude that their results suggest effective strategies for stockbrokers to adopt for good sales performance. They believed, however, that the strategies might be the effect rather than the cause of good performance. A stockbroker with many clients is likely to have many opportunities to spend time with them away from the office setting. He or she is also likely to have high sales volume because of the number of clients. A stockbroker with few clients has fewer opportunities for client contact outside the office setting or for sales. Thus, the activity of spending time with clients away from the office may not be the cause of high sales volume, but just the by-product of having many clients. The major contribution of this study is that it shows that there can be important differences among people in the same job. It might prove useful if job analysts provided information to organizations about employee differences in time spent doing tasks.

Source: W. C. Borman, D. Dorsey, and L. Ackerman. (1992). "Time-spent responses as time allocation strategies: Relations with sales performance in a stockbroker sample." *Personnel Psychology,* 45, 763–777.

formance is not totally clear in this study. Further study is needed to determine why task inventory ratings related to job performance.

A task inventory for even a fairly simple job can contain hundreds of tasks. To make interpretation easier, tasks are often placed into dimensions that represent the major components of a job. The dimensions for a police officer job that came from a task inventory are shown in Table 3-10. Each of these dimensions was associated with several specific tasks, and each task was rated by subject matter experts on a variety of different scales. A better understanding of this job can be gained by considering the individual tasks in the context of the major dimensions.

A task inventory often is a major component of an extensive job analysis project that collects several different types of information about jobs and people. The **Combination**

TABLE 3-10

Major dimensions of a police officer job from a task analysis

Driving a car or other police vehicle
Making arrests
Interviewing witnesses and other people
Maintaining vigilance during routine patrol
Writing reports
Investigating accidents and related problems
Issuing tickets and citations, such as those for traffic violations
Responding to disturbances, such as family quarrels
Providing service to citizens

Source: From *Selection of Police Officers,* Report Supplement No. 1: Job Analysis, by R. M. Guion and K. M. Alvares, 1980. Bowling Green, OH: Bowling Green State University.

Job Analysis Method (C-JAM) (Levine, 1983) is one such approach. C-JAM uses both interviews and questionnaires to collect information about KSAOs and tasks. It produces a detailed picture of the KSAOs for a job and the tasks performed. Table 3-11 contains an example of several KSAOs for a police officer job analyzed with C-JAM.

Choosing a Job Analysis Method

We have discussed only a few of the many available job analysis methods. With such a wide variety of methods, how can one choose? Each method has its own advantages and limitations, and not every method is appropriate for every application. Levine et al. (1983) asked job analysis experts to rate the effectiveness of seven job analysis methods for eleven purposes. Each method was better suited for some purposes than others. Functional job analysis was seen as being relatively effective for almost all purposes; however, it was also seen as one of the most time-consuming to complete. Choice of method requires consideration of several factors, including cost and purpose.

TABLE 3-11

Examples of KSAOs for a police officer job analyzed with C-JAM

Knowledge of laws, statutes, ordinances (including types of crimes)
Knowledge of where/when to conduct interview/interrogation
Skill in operating special equipment (helicopter, boat, MDT, voice radio, etc.)
Skill in handling/maintaining handgun/shotgun
Ability to enforce laws, statutes, ordinances
Ability to take charge of a situation
Integrity (moral/ethical/honesty)
Courage

Source: From Job Analysis of Deputy Sheriff in the Pinellas County Sheriff's Office, by E. L. Levine and D. P. Baker, 1987, unpublished paper, University of South Florida, Tampa.

RELIABILITY AND VALIDITY OF JOB ANALYSIS INFORMATION

Job analysis information depends on the judgment of people who either do or observe others do a job. People's judgments are imperfect, so it is important to determine how reliable and valid each job analysis method is. Many studies have addressed this issue for some methods. In general, results suggest that different people's ratings of jobs are often reasonably reliable. In other words, there will be a relatively high correlation among different people's ratings of the same job for at least some job analysis methods. Validity is a more difficult question, and some researchers have begun to study the question of whether job analysis ratings are good indicators of what they are intended to assess.

Reliability

Spector, Brannick, and Coovert (1989) summarized the results of a dozen studies that reported reliabilities for various job analysis methods. They found that test–retest reliabilities ranged from .68 to .90. In other words, people showed that they could be reasonably consistent in their job analysis ratings when they repeated them over time. Inter-rater agreement (whether or not different job analysts agree in their ratings) was somewhat lower. Correlations among ratings of different people ranged from .46 to .79.

Several studies have examined the reliability of task inventory ratings. Wilson, Harvey, and Macy (1990) found that test–retest reliabilities varied considerably for different rating scales, such as amount of time spent doing the task or importance of the task. Although some reliabilities were very high, others were unacceptably low. Sanchez and Fraser (1992) also found that inter-rater reliabilities among job incumbents varied across different rating scales and across different jobs as well.

Taken together, the studies suggest that job analysis ratings can be reasonably reliable. As noted here, there are exceptions with task inventory ratings. Care should be taken in deciding which scales to use for rating tasks when job incumbents are the subject matter experts. The next question is whether or not job analysis ratings are valid.

Validity

The best evidence for the validity of job analysis ratings comes from studies that compared different methods or sources of information, such as incumbents versus supervisors. Spector et al. (1989) summarized the results of nine studies that reported correlations among methods or sources that ranged from .47 to .94. These results are suggestive of validity for job analysis ratings, but an intriguing study raises some doubts about the interpretation of source agreement. J. E. Smith and Hakel (1979) compared the PAQ ratings of trained job analysts with college students who were given only job titles. The students' ratings correlated very well with the ratings of the analysts. This seemed strange because the analysts conducted in-depth interviews with incumbents, whereas the students were given limited information about the job. Smith and Hakel wondered if the analyst ratings reflected preconceived notions about the job rather than the information gathered with the job analysis procedures. If this is the case, then job analysis ratings might be less valid than I/O psychologists usually assume.

Other researchers who have studied the correspondence in ratings of students and trained job analysts have reached different conclusions. Cornelius, DeNisi, and Blencoe (1984) believe that students have accurate knowledge about many jobs; therefore, both job analysts and students can provide valid indicators of job information. Although students have accurate knowledge, more extensive information can be gathered in a thorough job analysis conducted by trained analysts (Cornelius et al., 1984).

Green and Stutzman (1986) conducted a job analysis in which they had job incumbents complete a task inventory. The task inventory included tasks that no one did on the job the researchers were analyzing. Over half of the incumbents indicated that they did at least one fake task. This finding suggests that many people are either careless or not completely honest when they complete task inventories. Whether or not this reduces the accuracy of the task inventory was not determined by this study. Hacker (1996) followed up on this research by conducting a similar study and comparing incumbents who endorsed fake tasks with those who did not. He found that both groups of people did not differ in their ratings of all other tasks, or in the reliability of their ratings of all other tasks. His results suggest that this phenomenon does not affect job analysis results.

The research on the validity of job analysis ratings suggests that they can provide useful information, but they are not perfect and are potentially subject to some biases because they are based on human judgment (Morgeson & Campion, 1997). Green and Stutzman's results emphasize that incumbents are not necessarily accurate in making their ratings. Sanchez and Levine (1994) attempted to improve job analysis results by training incumbents in how to rate their jobs. Although their results were only partially successful, such training might prove useful in the future. Even though there is a need to improve job analysis procedures, the various methods are important tools used by I/O psychologists.

JOB EVALUATION

Job evaluation refers to a family of quantitative techniques that are used to determine the salary levels of jobs. These techniques are very much like the job analysis methods we have already discussed. In fact, the job analysis methods sometimes are used to conduct job evaluation. For example, Robinson, Wahlstrom, and Mecham (1974) used the PAQ to conduct a job evaluation. The major difference between job analysis and job evaluation is that job evaluation determines the relative salaries for different jobs by mathematically combining job information.

Perhaps the most popular job evaluation method is the point method (Treiman, 1979). There are four steps involved in conducting a point method job evaluation. First, a panel, often managers or other organization members, determines the compensable factors for the job. Compensable factors are characteristics that will serve as the basis for the evaluation. They include

Consequences of error on the job	Responsibility
Education required	Skill required

Second, a panel (comprised of new people or the same people) judges the degree to which each job has each compensable factor. This is done on a quantitative scale so that each job gets points for each factor. A particular job, for example, might get 2 points out of a possible 20 for consequences of errors made and 20 points out of a possible 20 for education. This would mean that the job would be low on consequences for error and high on education level required. Third, the points for the factors are summed for each job. In this example, the job would get a total of 22 points (2 + 20) for the two factors. Each job gets a total point score. These numbers are not in dollar units, and so they do not indicate the actual salary level. Rather, the numbers are relative, so that the higher the number the higher the salary the job should have.

The fourth and final step is to plot the actual salaries for each job against the point totals for each job. If the salary system is fair according to the compensable factors, the plot should be a straight line. This means that the higher the points, the higher the salary. If the point for a particular job is not on the straight line, the job is either overpaid (point is above the line) or underpaid (point is below the line). Steps can then be taken to bring the job into line with the other jobs with similar totals. Jobs that are paid too much according to the system can have salaries frozen. Jobs that are paid too little can be given salary increases.

Although the job evaluation can indicate the relative value of a job, other factors enter into salary levels. One of the biggest influences is the market wage for a job. A hospital is likely to find, for example, that physicians are overpaid in relation to nurses. However, it would not be feasible for a hospital to set salaries completely according to compensable factors. The cost of paying nurses much higher salaries would be prohibitive. Paying physicians much lower wages would result in not being able to hire or retain them. Thus, the wages paid throughout the area or country must be considered. A salary survey can be conducted to find out what other organizations pay each position. To conduct such a survey, all hospitals in the area could be contacted to determine their salary levels for nurses and physicians.

The point system is just one of many different job evaluation methods. There are also several varieties of point systems. They are all used to determine the pay levels of jobs by estimating their comparative worth. Research on the various methods suggests that they may be interchangeable. Studies have shown that the results of different methods are often quite similar (Gomez-Mejia, Page, & Tornow, 1982; Robinson et al., 1974).

Comparable Worth

Job evaluation has been used to demonstrate pay discrimination against women. It is well-known that in the United States women's salaries are lower on average than men's. Some of the differences are attributable to the fact that jobs held primarily by women (e.g., secretaries) are paid less than jobs held primarily by men (e.g., electricians). Although the Equal Pay Act of 1963 made it illegal to pay a woman less than a man for the same job, there is no law preventing an organization from paying a woman less than a man in a different job.

The concept of **comparable worth** means that different but comparable jobs should be paid the same. If jobs that are held predominantly by females contribute as much to the organization as jobs held primarily by men, the jobs should be paid the same. The difficulty is finding a common measure by which to gauge the comparable worth of jobs. Job evaluation provides a means of doing so.

To do a comparable worth study with job evaluation, one would first apply one of the methods to the jobs of an organization. Those jobs that are held primarily by men would be compared to those held primarily by women. In most instances, the women's jobs would likely be underpaid according to the compensable factors. Using mathematical procedures, it would be possible to calculate how much adjustment each of the underpaid jobs should receive. If made, those adjustments could accomplish comparable worth between the predominantly female and predominantly male jobs.

The use of job evaluation to establish comparable worth has not been without critics (e.g., Eyde, 1983; Rytina, 1981). Part of the difficulty is that the judgments used in a job evaluation can be biased in ways that perpetuate the lower salaries of women. For example, Schwab and Grams (1985) found that people who assign points to jobs in organizations are influenced by knowledge of current salaries. As a result, lower paid jobs are given fewer points than they deserve, and higher paid jobs are given more points than they deserve. Job evaluations might undervalue lower paid predominantly female jobs and overvalue the higher paid predominantly male jobs.

Perhaps the biggest impediment to achieving comparable worth is not bias in job evaluation, but the cost involved in substantially raising salaries in predominantly female occupations, such as clerks and elementary school teachers. The adjustments of these salaries would be extremely expensive, unless they were accompanied by reductions in the salaries of other jobs. In addition, there is the issue of market wages, which is a major influence on the salary levels set by organizations. Although some progress has been made in the United States, it seems unlikely that comparable worth will be achieved in the near future.

FUTURE ISSUES AND CHALLENGES

Job analysis is one of the most frequently used tools of practicing I/O psychologists. Therefore, we might expect that a lot of research has been conducted on its accuracy and validity. This is not the case, however; on the contrary, most research on job analysis has been concerned with developing new methods rather than studying the validity of old methods. There is a need for more research on the validity of methods, for the existing research has raised some alarming questions. The human judgments on which job analysis is based are imperfect. To understand job analysis better and to improve it, we need to understand the judgment process (Morgeson & Campion, 1997).

Several approaches could be taken to improve the accuracy of job analysis judgments. Morgeson and Campion (1997) provide a number of suggestions for reducing bias and inaccuracy. For example, they suggest that job incumbents will be more motivated to distort their ratings than job analysts. Incumbents might inflate their ratings of how often important tasks are performed (arrest suspects) and deflate ratings of seemingly less important tasks (take a coffee break). Although many of their propositions have never been tested, Morgeson and Campion provide a reasonable prescription for maximizing job analysis accuracy.

Rater training is another area of possible research. A better understanding of how people make their ratings would suggest useful ways of training raters. It may be that accuracy could be increased with training. Perhaps the inaccurate raters who endorse tasks they do not do on task inventories could benefit from training.

One final area that offers future challenges to the field is helping organizations keep their employee actions, such as promotions and selection, job relevant. The present worldwide trend toward fairness in actions that affect people will require the use of job analysis. A job analysis can help ensure that decisions about who to hire or promote will be based on the KSAOs for a job rather than arbitrary or discriminatory criteria. Job analysis is being used for this purpose extensively, especially in the United States. This use is likely to spread throughout the world over the next decade.

CHAPTER SUMMARY

Job analysis is a method for describing jobs and the personal attributes necessary to do a job. The job-oriented approach provides information about the nature of a job and the tasks involved in a job. The person-oriented approach describes the knowledge, skills, abilities, and other personal characteristics a person must have for a job. There are dozens of job analysis methods that provide information about either the job, the person, or both.

Job analysis information has many purposes. It can be used for

Career development of employees

Legal issues, such as ensuring fairness in employee actions

Performance appraisal

Selection

Training

Most job analysis information comes from one of four different sources:

Job analysts   Supervisors

Job incumbents   Trained observers

They provide their information with one of the following ways:

Performing the job themselves

Interviewing people who do the job

Observing people doing the job

Giving questionnaires to people who do the job

ARLO AND JANIS By Jimmy Johnson

© 1993 by NEA, Inc.

Many different methods can be used to conduct a job analysis; no one method stands out as being superior to the others. Each has its particular advantages and limitations. The job analyst's purpose should determine which method is chosen. Four popular methods are

Job Components Inventory

Functional Job Analysis

Position Analysis Questionnaire

Task Inventories

Most job analysis methods have been found to be reasonably reliable. Inadequate research attention has been given to exploring their validity. Existing research has shown promise, but there is evidence that people are not always accurate in their job analysis ratings. More attention should be directed to studying ways to increase the accuracy of job analysis information.

Job evaluation is one of a family of techniques that are used to set salary levels. Job evaluation procedures are much like job analysis, and often job analysis methods are used to conduct job evaluation. Research suggests that many of the different job evaluation techniques give similar results when applied to the same jobs. Job evaluation has been used in an attempt to reduce the salary inequities between men and women. The concept of comparable worth means that jobs that make equivalent contributions to organizations should be paid the same.

I/O PSYCHOLOGY IN PRACTICE

THIS CASE IS a job analysis conducted at IBM by Karen Midkiff. Dr. Midkiff received her Ph.D. in 1989 in I/O psychology from Bowling Green State University. She is presently senior market researcher for IBM's Worldwide Customer Satisfaction Research and Measurement Department in New York. In her present position, she is part of a team that studies customer satisfaction with company products and services worldwide. Whereas most corporate I/O psychologists work in the human resources or training areas, Dr. Midkiff is in the marketing division of her company. Before coming to this department, she was a member of a team that conducted an extensive job analysis project for the purpose of developing more effective procedures to hire manufacturing employees.

The major focus of the assessment project was to determine KSAOs for assemblers in factories that manufacture computers and computer components, such as hard drives and memory chips. Because it is involved in a rapidly changing industry, IBM must be constantly concerned about the KSAO requirements for jobs. At the time of this study, the manufacturing process was becoming more complex, requiring a more highly skilled workforce. New methods were needed to hire people who had these skills.

Dr. Midkiff and her team decided to use several different methods of job analysis to provide a complete picture of the jobs and the KSAOs. They toured five plants, observed employees doing their jobs, tried out some of the equipment, and reviewed technical manuals. They interviewed first-line managers and gave out questionnaires

(Continued next page)

to job incumbents. They collected hundreds of critical incidents of good and poor job performance. From all of this information, they developed a list of KSAOs for the manufacturing jobs.

Once they knew the KSAOs, Dr. Midkiff and her team could proceed to choose the assessment procedures. They decided to develop a multimedia computerized assessment battery containing a number of subsets. The computer is able to present a variety of tasks to an individual using computer graphics, full-motion video, and sound. This procedure can make the assessment interesting to assessees and expands the kind of problems that can be presented. For example, actual video clips of the equipment used on the job can be shown, providing a high level of perceived job relevance. Before the test could be used, however, the IBM team had to collect more data showing the relationship of test scores to actual job success. Data from over 2,000 employees showed that the assessment test could predict actual job performance. Since it was shown to predict how well people perform, the test was adopted for use in hiring all entry-level manufacturing employees.

Discussion Questions

1. Why is job analysis the first step in designing an employee assessment device?

2. Why did Dr. Midriff's team actually try out parts of the jobs they were analyzing?

3. What impact will the use of computers in manufacturing have on KSAO requirements for assembly-line jobs?

4. What are the advantages and limitations of Dr. Midkiff's new multimedia computer testing system?

PERFORMANCE APPRAISAL

Imagine that you are a manager for a large organization and you are given the task of determining how well your subordinates are doing their jobs. How would you go about appraising their job performance to see who is and who is not doing a good job? Would you watch each person perform his or her job? If you did watch people, how would you know what to look for? Some people might appear to work very hard but in fact accomplish little that contributes to the organization's objectives. For many jobs it might not be readily apparent how well a person is doing just by observing him or her, unless you had a good idea of what constitutes good job performance. Performance is best appraised by measuring a person's work against a criterion or standard of comparison.

In this chapter we are concerned with issues involved in the appraisal of employee job performance. First, there is the issue of the criterion or standard of comparison by which performance is judged and measured. Before we can appraise performance, we must have a clear idea of what good performance is. Once we know that, we can address the second issue of developing a procedure to assess it. Performance appraisal is a two-step process of first defining what is meant by good performance (criterion development) followed by the implementation of a procedure to appraise employees by determining how well they meet the criteria. Before we discuss criteria and procedures for appraising performance, we look at the major reasons for engaging in this potentially time-consuming activity.

Objectives   **The student who studies this chapter should be able to:**
1. List the uses of job performance information.
2. Discuss the importance of criteria for performance appraisal.
3. Describe the various methods of performance appraisal, as well as their advantages and limitations.
4. Discuss how to conduct a legally defensible performance appraisal.

WHY DO WE APPRAISE EMPLOYEES?

The first question that we address is the rationale for organizations to appraise the performance of their employees. Performance appraisal can be a time-consuming chore that most managers and their subordinates dislike. Why then do most large organizations appraise employee job performance at least once per year? The reason is that job performance data can benefit both employees and organizations. Performance data can be used for administrative decisions, employee development and feedback, and research to determine the effectiveness of organizational practices and procedures.

Administrative Decisions

Many administrative decisions that affect employees are based, at least in part, on their job performance. Many organizations use job performance as the basis for many punishments and rewards. Punishments can include both demotion and termination (firing), and some organizations have policies that require the firing of unsatisfactory employees. Rewards can include promotion and pay raises, and many organizations have merit pay systems that tie raises to the level of job performance.

The basis for using job performance data for administrative decisions can be found in both contract and law. A union contract will often specify that job performance is the basis for particular administrative decisions, such as pay raises. A contract can also state that performance appraisals will not be done. Civil service (government) employees in the United States can be fired only for unsatisfactory job performance or violation of work rules. Rule violations include assaulting a co-worker, being convicted of a felony, falling asleep on the job, or not showing up for work when scheduled. Even so, many fired U.S. government employees have been reinstated because of long records of satisfactory performance on the job. The United States is not the only country in which laws can be found that require administrative decisions to be based on job performance. In Canada, for example, the legal requirement that employee firing must be based on job performance has been extended to private companies as well as the government.

Employee Development and Feedback

In order for employees to improve and maintain their job performance and job skills, they need job performance feedback from their supervisors. One of the major roles of supervisors is to provide information to their subordinates about what is expected on the job, and how well they are meeting those expectations. Employees need to know when they are performing well so that they will continue to do so, and when they are not so that they can change what they are doing. Even employees who are performing well on the job can benefit from feedback about how to perform even better. Feedback can also be helpful in telling employees how to enhance their skills to move up to higher positions.

Criteria for Research

Many of the activities of practicing I/O psychologists concern the improvement of employee job performance. The efforts of I/O psychologists can be directed toward designing better equipment, hiring better people, motivating employees, and training employees. Job performance data can serve as the criterion against which such activities are evaluated. To do so, one can conduct a research study. A common design for such a study involves comparing employee performance before and after the implementation of a new program designed to enhance it. A better design would be an experiment in which one group of employees receives a new procedure while a control group of employees does not. The two groups could be compared to see if the group receiving the new procedure had better job performance than the control group that did not. Better job performance by the trained group would serve as good evidence for the effectiveness of the training program.

PERFORMANCE CRITERIA

A criterion is a standard against which you can judge the performance of anything, including a person. It allows you to distinguish good from bad performance. Trying to assess performance without a criterion is like helping a friend find a lost object when the friend will not tell you what it is. You cannot be of much help until you know what it is you are looking for. In a similar way, you cannot adequately evaluate someone's job performance until you know what the performance should be.

Characteristics of Criteria

Actual Versus Theoretical Criteria. Criteria can be classified as either actual or theoretical. The theoretical criterion is the definition of what good performance is rather than how it is measured. In research terminology, the **theoretical criterion** is a theoretical construct. It is the idea of what good performance is. The **actual criterion** is the way in which the theoretical criterion is assessed or operationalized. It is the performance appraisal technique that is used, such as counting a salesperson's sales.

Table 4-1 contains theoretical and corresponding actual criteria for five different jobs. As can be seen, both criteria can be quite different for some jobs. For others, the correspondence between the theoretical and actual criteria is quite close. For example, for an insurance salesperson, the theoretical criterion is to sell, and the actual criterion is a count of the sales the person made. For an artist the correspondence is not as close. The theoretical criterion of producing great works of art is matched to the actual criterion of asking art experts for an opinion about the person's work. In this case there is room for subjectivity about who is deemed an art expert and about the expert judgments of what is and is not good art. As these cases illustrate, the criteria for different jobs may require quite different assessment approaches.

TABLE 4-1
Examples of theoretical and actual criteria for five jobs

JOB	*THEORETICAL CRITERION*	*ACTUAL CRITERION*
Artist	Create great works of art	Judgments of art experts
Insurance salesperson	Sell insurance	Monthly sales
Store clerk	Provide good service to customers	Survey of customer satisfaction with service
Teacher	Impart knowledge to students	Student achievement test scores
Weather forecaster	Accurately predict the weather	Compare predictions to actual weather

Contamination, Deficiency, and Relevance. Our actual criteria are intended to assess the underlying theoretical criteria of interest. In practice, however, our actual criteria are imperfect indicators of their intended theoretical performance criteria. Even though an actual criterion might assess a piece of the intended theoretical criterion, there is likely some part of the theoretical criterion that is left out. On the other hand, the actual criterion can be biased and can assess something other than the theoretical criterion. Thus, the actual criterion often provides only a rough estimate of the theoretical criterion it is supposed to assess.

Three concepts help explain this situation: criterion contamination, criterion deficiency, and criterion relevance. **Criterion contamination** refers to that part of the actual criterion that reflects something other than what it was designed to measure. Contamination can arise from biases in the criterion and from unreliability. Biases are common when people's judgments and opinions are used as the actual criterion. For example, using the judgments of art experts as the actual criterion for the quality of someone's art works can reveal as much about the biases of the judges as it does about the work itself. Because there are no objective standards for the quality of art, experts will likely disagree with one another when their judgments are the actual criteria for performance.

Unreliability in the actual criterion refers to errors in measurement that occur any time we try to assess something. As discussed in Chapter 2, measurement error is part of the measurement process and is comprised of random errors that make our measurement inaccurate. It is reflected in the inconsistency in measurement over time. If we were to assess the job performance of someone repeatedly over time, the measure of performance would vary from testing to testing even if the performance (theoretical criterion) remained constant. This means that our actual performance criterion measures will have less than perfect reliabilities.

Criterion deficiency means that the actual criterion does not adequately cover the entire theoretical criterion. In other words, the actual criterion is an incomplete representation of what we are trying to assess. This concept was referred to in Chapter 2 as content validity. For example, student achievement test scores in mathematics could be used as an actual performance criterion for elementary school teachers. It would be a deficient criterion because elementary school teachers teach more than just mathematics. A less deficient criterion would be student scores on a comprehensive achievement test battery, including mathematics, reading, science, and writing.

Criterion relevance is the extent to which the actual criterion assesses the theoretical criterion it is designed to measure, or its construct validity (see Chapter 2). The closer the correspondence between the actual and theoretical criteria, the greater is the relevance of the actual criterion. All of the actual criteria in Table 4-1 would seem to have some degree of relevance for assessing their intended theoretical criterion. Theoretical criteria can be quite abstract, such as producing great works of art; therefore, it can be difficult to determine the relevance of a criterion. As with the validity of any assessment device, relevance concerns the inferences and interpretations made about the meaning of our measurements of performance.

Criterion contamination, deficiency, and relevance are illustrated in Figure 4-1. The actual criterion is represented in the figure by the lower circle, and the theoretical criterion is represented by the upper circle. The overlap between the two circles (shaded area) represents the extent to which the actual criterion is assessing the theoretical, which is criterion relevance. The part of the lower circle that does not overlap the theoretical criterion (unshaded area) is contamination because it is assessing something else or is measurement error. The part of the upper circle that does not overlap the lower (unshaded area) is criterion deficiency because part of the theoretical criterion is not assessed.

Level of Specificity. Most jobs are complex and involve many different functions and tasks. Job performance criteria can be developed for individual tasks or for entire jobs. For some purposes, it may be better to assess performance on an individual task, such as typing memos, whereas for other purposes the entire person's job performance is of interest. For developing an employee's skills, it is better to focus at the individual task level so that feedback can be specific. The person might be told that he or she types too slowly or makes too many errors. This sort of specific feedback can be helpful for an employee who wishes to improve performance. For administrative purposes, overall job performance might be of more concern. The person who gets promoted might be the one whose overall performance has been the best. The particular methods used to assess performance should be based on the purposes of the assessment information.

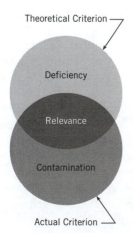

Theoretical Criterion

Deficiency

Relevance

Contamination

Actual Criterion

FIGURE 4-1

Criterion contamination, relevance, and deficiency. The lower circle represents the actual criterion, and the upper circle represents the theoretical criterion. Contamination is the part of the actual criterion (nonshaded area) that does not overlap the theoretical criterion. Deficiency is the part of the theoretical criterion that is not overlapped by the actual criterion (nonshaded area). Relevance is represented by the overlap between the actual and theoretical criteria (shaded area).

It takes close observation to see how well an employee is doing the job.

Criterion Complexity

Because most jobs involve multiple tasks, and most tasks can be evaluated from several perspectives, criteria can become quite complex. Job performance even on a single task can usually be assessed along a quality dimension (how well the person does the job) and a quantity dimension (how much or how quickly the person does the job). The complexity of job performance means that multiple criterion measures are necessary to assess performance adequately. These might involve only quality, only quantity, or both. It can be at the level of specificity of a single task or at the level of the entire person's job. The nature of the job and the purposes of the assessment information determine the nature of the criteria that are used as well as the level of specificity.

The nature of some jobs requires that quality is the major focus, whereas for others quantity may take priority. In athletics, sometimes one or the other serves as the criterion for winning a competition. In gymnastics, quality is the criterion used. Judges score each gymnast's performance along a quality dimension, and the person with the highest score wins. In track and field events, the criterion is concerned with quantity—jumping farthest, jumping highest, running fastest, or throwing farthest. With jobs there can be an emphasis on quality or quantity, often depending on the nature of the tasks involved. For a sales job, the emphasis is usually on the quantity of sales, whereas for a teacher it is on the quality of instruction.

There are many other possible criteria beyond work quality and quantity. Table 4-2 contains a performance appraisal form that has eight rather general criteria that might be relevant to a specific job. For example, maintaining a professional appearance on the job is relevant when public image is important. Many organizations expect employees who meet the public to display a certain image. This might involve a dress code that specifies the sort of clothing that is appropriate for work, such as a business suit. Factories generally do not have dress codes because they are not concerned with public image. Their dress rules are concerned with safety. Ties are often forbidden because they could get caught in machinery.

There are two ways to deal with the complex nature of criteria. The *composite criterion approach* involves combining individual criteria into a single score. If employees receive a number to represent performance on each of four dimensions, a composite would be the sum of the four dimension scores for each employee. If a person received the following performance scores on a one to five scale:

Attendance = 5

Professional appearance = 4

Work quality = 4

Work quantity = 5

his or her composite performance score would be the sum of the dimension scores or 18 (5 + 4 + 4 + 5). A grade point average would be a composite score for school performance. The *multidimensional approach* does not combine the individual criterion measures. In the previous example, there would be four scores per employee.

The composite approach is preferred for comparing individual employee performance. It is easier to compare employees when each has a single performance score. The

TABLE 4-2

Example of a performance appraisal form with eight criterion dimensions

DIMENSION	RATING CATEGORIES				
	POOR	FAIR	ADEQUATE	GOOD	OUTSTANDING
Attendance	_____	_____	_____	_____	_____
Communicating with others	_____	_____	_____	_____	_____
Following directions	_____	_____	_____	_____	_____
Instructing others	_____	_____	_____	_____	_____
Motivating others	_____	_____	_____	_____	_____
Professional appearance	_____	_____	_____	_____	_____
Work quality	_____	_____	_____	_____	_____
Work quantity	_____	_____	_____	_____	_____

multidimensional approach is preferred when feedback is given to employees. It gives specific information about the various dimensions of performance rather than general feedback about overall performance.

Dynamic Criteria

Criteria are usually considered as constant or static standards by which employee performance can be judged. Some I/O psychologists believe, however, that job performance itself is variable over time. This means that the best performer on the job at one point in time will not be best at another point in time. When job performance is assessed, the variability would produce a difficulty because the performance in question would not have been the same throughout the entire time period. If someone performs well for part of the year and not well for the other part, how should their performance be assessed?

Variability of performance over time is referred to as the **dynamic criterion**, although it is the performance and not the standard that changes. The dynamic criterion idea has generated some controversy among I/O psychologists. For example, Barrett, Caldwell, and Alexander (1985) take the position that job performance tends to be stable over time. They do not believe that criteria are dynamic. On the other hand, Deadrick and Madigan (1990) provide data that support the dynamic criterion idea. They collected weekly performance data of sewing machine operators in a clothing factory. Performance was very consistent over short periods of time (weeks) but was not very consistent over long periods of time (months). In a similar study, Vinchur, Schippmann, Smalley, and Rothe (1991) found that job performance of manufacturing employees was reasonably stable over a five-year time span. They suggested that the nature of the job and job setting determined the stability of job performance. Although it seems likely that there will be some variability in people's performance over time, there have not been enough studies done from which to draw confident conclusions about how dynamic or static job performance is for various jobs.

METHODS FOR ASSESSING JOB PERFORMANCE

The job performance of individuals can be assessed in many ways. The most common procedures can be divided into two categories—objective performance measures and subjective judgments. *Objective measures* are counts of various behaviors (e.g., number of days absent from work) or the results of job behaviors (e.g., total monthly sales). *Subjective measures* are ratings by people who should be knowledgeable about the person's job performance. Usually supervisors provide job performance ratings of their subordinates. Both objective and subjective measures of job performance will be presented in the following discussion.

Objective Measures of Job Performance

Organizations keep track of many employee behaviors and results of behavior. Human resource departments record the number of absences, accidents, incidents, and latenesses for each employee. Some organizations keep track of the productivity of each employee as well. Productivity data must be collected if an organization has an incentive system that pays employees for what they produce, such as a commission or piece-rate.

TABLE 4-3
Examples of objective measures of job performance

ABSENCES	DAYS ABSENT PER YEAR
Accidents	Number of accidents per year
Incidents at work (e.g., assaults)	Number of incidents per year
Latenesses	Days late per year
Productivity (e.g., sales)	Dollar amount of sales

Five common objective measures of job performance are listed in Table 4-3. Each is an objective count of the number of behaviors or amount of work produced. Such data are usually found in organizational records, but they can be collected specifically to assess performance. Two of the measures are concerned with attendance—number of times absent and number of times late for work. Accidents include both automotive and nonautomotive, such as being injured by a machine in a factory. Incidents are the number of times the individual is involved in a work incident that is considered important for the particular job. For example, in a psychiatric inpatient facility, the number of times a staff person is assaulted by a patient is recorded in an incident report. For police officers, shooting incidents become part of the employee's record. Productivity is the amount of work produced by an individual.

The attendance measures are applicable to the majority of jobs because they have scheduled work hours. For jobs that are unstructured in terms of work schedule (e.g., college professor), attendance is not a criterion for job performance. The other three objective measures are specific to a particular job. For example, the type of incidents recorded is a function of the nature of the job and job environment. Records of incidents of assaults by students might be kept for urban public school teachers, but they are not likely to be kept for college professors. Teachers are assaulted relatively frequently in large American cities, but college professors are rarely the target for violence. The productivity measure chosen must match the nature of the work done. Specific productivity measures for some common jobs are listed in Table 4-4. As you can see, the nature of productivity can be very different from job to job. This makes it difficult to compare the performance of people who hold different jobs.

Using objective measures to assess job performance has several advantages. First, it can be easy to interpret the meaning of objective measures in relation to job performance criteria. For example, it is obvious that no absences in the past year is a good indicator of satis-

TABLE 4-4
Examples of objective productivity measures for several jobs

JOB	MEASURE
Assembly-line worker	Number of units produced
College professor	Number of publications
Lawyer	Number of cases won
Salesperson	Amount of sales
Surgeon	Number of operations performed

factory attendance, but four work-related traffic accidents in the prior six months is an indicator of unsatisfactory driving performance. Second, the quantitative nature of objective measures makes it easy to compare the job performance of different individuals in the same job. For attendance measures, comparisons can be made of individuals across different jobs, as long as they all require that the person work on a particular schedule. Third, objective measures can be tied directly to organizational objectives, such as making a product or providing a service. Finally, objective measures can often be found in organizational records, so that special performance appraisal systems do not have to be initiated. These data often are collected and stored, frequently in computers, for reasons other than employee performance appraisal, making performance appraisal a relatively easy task to accomplish.

Unfortunately, objective performance measures also have several limitations. Many of the objective measures are not appropriate for all jobs. When jobs do not involve countable output, productivity is not a feasible measure of performance. Also, it is not always obvious what number is considered satisfactory performance. For example, how many absences per year should be considered good performance? Data taken from records can be contaminated and inaccurate. Sometimes behaviors and productivity are attributed to the wrong person or are never recorded. People can also distort records by omitting bad or good incidents for individuals who are intentionally being helped or hurt.

Objective measures are often deficient as indicators of job performance criteria. They tend to focus on specific behaviors, which may be only part of the criterion, and they may ignore equally important parts. Measures of productivity focus on work quantity rather than quality. Although quantity might be more important in some jobs, it is difficult to imagine a job in which quality is not also important. Finally, what is reflected in an objective measure is not necessarily under the control of the individual being assessed. Differences in the productivity of factory workers can be caused by differences in the machinery they use, and differences in the sales performance of salespeople can be caused by differences in sales territories. A person who is assaulted at work may have done nothing wrong and may have been unable to avoid the incident. A police officer who uses his or her weapon might have been forced into it by circumstances rather than poor job performance. In using objective measures to assess individuals, these other factors should be taken into account.

Subjective Measures of Job Performance

Subjective measures are the most frequently used means of assessing the job performance of employees. Most organizations require that supervisors complete performance appraisal rating forms on each of their subordinates annually. There are a wide variety of types of rating forms that different organizations use to assess the performance of their employees. In this section, we discuss several different types.

Graphic Rating Form. The most popular type of subjective measure is the **graphic rating form**, which is used to assess individuals on several dimensions of performance. The graphic rating form focuses on characteristics or traits of the person or the person's performance. For example, most forms ask for ratings of work quality and quantity. Many include personal traits such as appearance, attitude, dependability, and motivation.

A graphic rating form, illustrated in Table 4-2, consists of a multipoint scale and several dimensions. The scale represents a continuum of performance from low to high and usually contains from four to seven values. The scale in the table contains five scale points, ranging from "poor" to "outstanding" with "adequate" in the middle. The form also contains several dimensions of job performance along which the employee is to be rated. This form includes attendance and work quality. To use the form, a supervisor checks off his or her rating for each of the dimensions.

Behavior-Focused Rating Forms. The graphic rating forms just discussed focus on dimensions that are trait oriented, such as dependability, or general aspects of performance, such as attendance. The behavior-focused forms concentrate on specific instances of behavior that the person has done or could be expected to do. Behaviors are chosen to represent different levels of performance. For attendance, an example of a good behavior would be, "can be counted on to be at work every day on time," while a poor behavior would be, "comes to work late several times per week." The rater's job is to indicate which behaviors are characteristic of the person being rated. The way in which the form is scored is dependent on the particular type of form.

There are several different types of behavior-focused rating forms. We will discuss three of them:

Behaviorally Anchored Rating Scale (BARS) (Smith & Kendall, 1963)

Mixed Standard Scale (MSS) (Blanz & Ghiselli, 1972)

Behavior Observation Scale (BOS) (Latham & Wexley, 1977).

All three of these scales provide descriptions of behavior or performance rather than traits, but they differ in the way they present the descriptions and/or the responses.

The **Behaviorally Anchored Rating Scale (BARS)** is a rating scale in which the response choices are defined in behavioral terms. An example for the job of college professor is shown in Figure 4-2. This scale is designed to assess performance on the dimension of Organizational Skills in the Classroom. The rater chooses the behavior that comes closest to describing the performance of the person in question. The behaviors are ordered from bottom to top on the scale along the continuum of performance effectiveness.

A BARS performance evaluation form contains several individual scales, each designed to assess an important dimension of job performance. A BARS can be used to assess the same dimensions as a graphic rating form. The major difference is that the BARS uses response choices that represent behaviors, and the graphic rating form asks for a rating of how well the person performs along the dimension in question. Thus, both types of rating forms can be used to assess the same dimensions of performance for the same jobs.

The **Mixed Standard Scale (MSS)** provides the rater with a list of behaviors that vary in their effectiveness. For each statement, the rater is asked to indicate if

1. the ratee is better than the statement
2. the statement fits the ratee
3. the ratee is worse than the statement

There are several dimensions of performance in a Mixed Standard Scale, and each dimension has several behaviors associated with it. An example of three statements that reflect performance for the dimension of Relations with Other People is shown in Table 4-5. The three statements represent good, satisfactory, and poor job performance along the dimension.

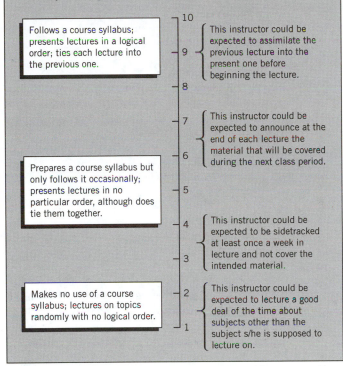

Organizational skills: A good constructional order of material slides smoothly from one topic to another; design of course optimizes interest; students can easily follow organizational strategy; course outline followed.

Follows a course syllabus; presents lectures in a logical order; ties each lecture into the previous one.

This instructor could be expected to assimilate the previous lecture into the present one before beginning the lecture.

This instructor could be expected to announce at the end of each lecture the material that will be covered during the next class period.

Prepares a course syllabus but only follows it occasionally; presents lectures in no particular order, although does tie them together.

This instructor could be expected to be sidetracked at least once a week in lecture and not cover the intended material.

Makes no use of a course syllabus; lectures on topics randomly with no logical order.

This instructor could be expected to lecture a good deal of the time about subjects other than the subject s/he is supposed to lecture on.

FIGURE 4-2

An example of a behaviorally anchored rating scale for a college professor. *Note.* From *Performance Appraisal: Assessing Human Behavior at Work* by H. J. Bernardin and R. W. Beatty, 1984, Boston, MA: Kent. Reprinted with permission.

In a mixed standard scale, the statements for the various dimensions are presented in a random order. The rater is not told the specific dimensions associated with each behavior, although the nature of the behaviors is certainly clear. The original idea of Blanz and Ghiselli (1972) was that the mixed order of presentation of the statements would make it more difficult for the raters to bias their ratings than is true of the other types of rating forms. When Dickinson and Glebocki (1990) compared responses to both the mixed and sorted (by dimension) orders, they found that subjects responded similarly in their ratings with both orders. Thus, it does not seem to matter if the dimensions are identified or if the statements are mixed up.

The **Behavior Observation Scale (BOS)** contains items that are based on critical incidents, making it somewhat like a Mixed Standard Scale. With the BOS, however, raters are asked to indicate for each item the amount of time the employee engaged in that be-

TABLE 4-5
Three items for a mixed standard scale to assess the dimension of relations with other people

Good Performance

Is on good terms with everyone. Can get along with people even when he or she doesn't agree with them.

Satisfactory Performance

Gets along with most people. Only very occasionally does he or she have conflicts with others on the job, and these are likely to be minor.

Poor Performance

Has the tendency to get into unnecessary conflicts with other people.

Note: Each item is rated on the following scale:
For each item on the scale, indicate if the employee is
  Better than the item
  As good as the item
  Worse than the item

Source: From "The Mixed Standard Scale: A New Rating System," by F. Blanz and E. E. Ghiselli, 1972, *Personnel Psychology,* 25, 185–199.

havior. The developers of the scale recommend having raters indicate the percentage of time the employee does each behavior by using the following percentage options:

  0% to 64%

  65% to 74%

  75% to 84%

  85% to 94%

  95% to 100%

This scale is different from the MSS in that the raters indicate frequency rather than comparisons of employee behavior with the item. In theory, it should indicate how often employees engage in performance-relevant behavior.

Use of the frequency ratings has been criticized by Kane and Bernardin (1982). They point out that frequency of a behavior is not a good indicator of performance in many instances because the specific behavior in question determines the criterion for good performance in terms of frequency. They give as examples two behaviors for police officers. An 85% to 94% frequency of occurrence would be outstanding for obtaining arrest warrants but abysmal for being vindicated in the use of lethal force. Thus, considerable judgment can be required in interpreting the meaning of frequency ratings with the BOS. Of course, judgment is required in interpreting many measures of job performance.

Development of Behavior-Focused Forms. Development of behavior-focused forms takes considerable effort from several people in an organization. Because it focuses on specific behaviors, a form must be developed for a specific job or family of jobs. The process involves four steps and can take a long time to complete. Each of the four steps is listed in Table 4-6.

TABLE 4-6
Four steps in developing a behavior-focused rating form to assess job performance

Step 1: Perform job analysis to define job dimensions
Step 2: Develop descriptions of effective and ineffective job performance from critical incidents
Step 3: Have knowledgeable judges place descriptions into job dimensions
Step 4: Have knowledgeable judges rate the effectiveness of the descriptions

Step 1 is a job analysis that identifies the specific dimensions of performance, such as making arrests or writing reports for a police officer. Step 2 involves writing the descriptions of behaviors that vary in their effectiveness or ineffectiveness on the job. This can be done by collecting critical incidents from people who are knowledgeable about the job in question, such as employees who do the job or their supervisors. A **critical incident** (Flanagan, 1954) is an event reflecting either effective or ineffective behavior by an employee. Descriptions of behavior that can be used in a rating form are derived from the critical incidents provided by employees or their supervisors.

Step 3 involves having judges (knowledgeable people) sort the descriptions of behavior into dimensions to verify that the descriptions reflect the intended dimensions. The final step is to have judges rate the descriptions of behavior along a continuum of effectiveness. With a BARS these ratings allow for the placement of the descriptions along the scale for each dimension, as in Figure 4-2. With the MSS, the ratings are used to place statements into the three categories of good, satisfactory, and poor.

Cognitive Processes Underlying Ratings. The development of sound performance appraisal methods requires that we understand the cognitive processes that affect rating behavior. I/O psychologists have studied these processes and have devised several models to explain ratings. Some of these models focus on how people utilize information to make judgments. Others are concerned with how people's views of job performance influence their evaluation of an employee.

Models of the Rating Process. There have been several competing models of the cognitive processes that influence ratings of performance (e.g., DeNisi, Caferty, & Meglino, 1984; Feldman, 1981). These models suggest that the rating process involves several steps (see Ilgen, Barnes-Farrell, & McKellin, 1993), including:

Observing performance

Storing information about performance

Retrieving information about performance from memory

Translating retrieved information into ratings

The process begins with observation of the employee by the supervisor. Next, observations of performance are stored in the supervisor's memory. When asked to rate performance, the supervisor must retrieve information about the employee from his or her memory. The information is then used in some manner to decide what performance rating to give for each dimension of job performance.

The various models describe how humans process information at each step. One idea is that people use **schemata** (categories or frames of reference) to help interpret and organize their experiences (Borman, 1987). Perhaps the best-known schema is the *stereotype*—a belief about characteristics of the members of a group. The characteristics can be favorable or unfavorable. For example, one might believe that private sector managers are hard working.

Another type of schema is a *prototype*, which is a model of some characteristic or type of person. One might think of a particular fictional or real person as the prototype of a good manager. Some people might consider Bill Gates, the founder and head of Microsoft, to be a prototype of a good corporate manager. A person who had the salient characteristics of the prototype might be thought of as a good manager. If the salient characteristics of the prototype are blond hair (or looking like Gates), managers who are blond (or look like Gates) might be seen as better in performance than their counterparts who have brown hair (or do not resemble Gates). The prototype is the standard used to assign people to the good manager category.

Schemata might influence all four steps in the evaluation process. They might affect the behaviors that a supervisor chooses to observe, how the behaviors are organized and stored in memory, how they are retrieved, and how they are used to decide on ratings. The use of schemata, however, does not necessarily imply that they lead to inaccurate ratings. In many ways, the use of schemata can simplify experience so that it can be more easily interpreted. It is possible that this leads to accurate judgments about employee performance (Lord & Maher, 1989).

Content of Subordinate Effectiveness. If schemata affect job performance ratings, it is important that we understand the schemata of people who appraise performance. In other words, appraisal techniques might be improved by designing them to effectively utilize the schemata of supervisors. If the dimensions on an appraisal form match the dimensions in supervisor schemata about performance, it will be easier for supervisors to do their ratings. There has been some research that is relevant to this issue.

Borman (1987) studied the content of army officers' schemata of subordinate job performance. U.S. Army officers were asked to describe the differences in characteristics between effective and ineffective soldiers. They generated 189 descriptive items, which were subject to complex statistical analysis. The analysis reduced the 189 items to six meaningful dimensions. Effective soldiers were seen as having the following characteristics:

Working hard

Being responsible

Being organized

Knowing the technical parts of the job

Being in control of subordinates

Displaying concern for subordinates

Borman concluded that these dimensions represent the characteristics that officers use to judge soldiers' performance. He also noted that in his sample of experienced officers, there was good agreement about what constituted good job performance. These results suggest that experienced supervisors might have schemata that accurately represent effective performance. These six dimensions could be used as the basis for any of the rating forms we discussed earlier.

Werner (1994) conducted a study in which he asked experienced supervisors to rate the performance of secretaries as described in a series of incidents. One of the variables of interest in this study was the sort of information that the supervisors used in making their ratings. Werner found that the following dimensions were seen as most important:

Attendance	Work accuracy
Job knowledge	Work quantity

Werner suggested that these four dimensions might represent the characteristics that define the schemata of his subjects. He also suggested that supervisors should let subordinates know the content of their schemata. Subordinates are likely to attempt to perform well in those areas that the supervisor believes are important for good performance.

Who Should Rate Performance? In most organizations, the direct supervisor of each employee is responsible for assessing job performance. However, it can be helpful to get multiple perspectives on job performance (Furnham & Stringfield, 1994). Ratings by peers, self, and subordinates (if appropriate) can be a useful complement to supervisor ratings. In particular, discrepancies between self (employee's own ratings of performance) and others can be used for employee development. It shows employees those areas in which other people see them differently from how they see themselves.

The use of multiple perspectives for manager feedback has been called **360 degree feedback** (Baldwin & Padgett, 1993) and has become a popular feedback tool for managers. A manager is evaluated by peers, subordinates, and supervisors on several dimensions of performance. In addition, the manager completes a rating of his or her own performance. All of this information is used for employee development as the multiple perspectives provide a complete picture of the person's performance. Another advantage of using multiple raters is that the biases of individuals can be reduced. Favoritism by the immediate supervisor is diminished when additional information from other raters is added to the appraisal.

Rater Bias and Error. It is the nature of human judgment to be imperfect. When supervisors or other people make performance ratings, they are likely to exhibit rating biases and rating errors. These biases and errors can be seen in the pattern of ratings, both within the rating forms for individuals and across rating forms for different people. These within-form and across-form patterns are called halo and distributional errors, respectively.

Halo Errors. Halo error occurs when a rater gives an individual the same rating across all rating dimensions, despite differences in performance across dimensions. In other words, if the person is rated as being outstanding in one area, he or she is rated outstanding in all areas, even though he or she may be only average or even poor in some areas. For example, a police officer might be outstanding in completing many arrests (high quantity) but do a poor job in paperwork. A supervisor might rate this officer high on all dimensions, even though it is not uniformly deserved. Similarly, if a person is rated as poor in one

TABLE 4-7
Job performance ratings for four employees on
five dimensions illustrating a halo error pattern

DIMENSION	EMPLOYEE 1	EMPLOYEE 2	EMPLOYEE 3	EMPLOYEE 4
Attendance	5	3	1	4
Communication	5	3	1	4
Following directions	5	3	1	4
Work quality	5	3	1	4
Work quantity	5	3	1	4

area, the ratings are poor for all areas, even though he or she may be satisfactory on some performance dimensions. This rating error occurs within the rating forms of individuals as opposed to occurring across forms of different individuals.

Table 4-7 shows a pattern of responses that reflects a halo error. The table shows the ratings of four individuals across five dimensions of performance. Ratings ranged from 1 (poorest performance) to 5 (best performance). This is a halo pattern because the ratings for each individual employee are the same across the different dimensions, even though each person received different ratings. Halo also exists if each individual receives almost the same rating across dimensions. Such a pattern suggests that raters are unable to distinguish among dimensions. The person is seen as uniform in performance across dimensions.

Although a pattern of similar ratings might indicate a rating error, it is possible that employee performance is consistent across dimensions. This means that halo patterns might accurately indicate that dimensions of actual performance are related. This possibility has led to considerable discussion in the I/O literature about the meaning of halo (e.g., Balzer & Sulsky, 1992; Murphy & Jako, 1989; Murphy, Jako, & Anhalt, 1993; Pulakos,

"He's not a perfect boss, but he *does* give you plenty of feedback."

© 1995; Reprinted courtesy of Bunny Hoest and Parade Magazine.

Schmitt, & Ostroff, 1986; Solomonson & Lance, 1997). Part of this discussion concerns how to separate the error from "true" halo. *True halo* means that an employee performs at the same level on all dimensions.

Another concern with halo has been explaining cognitive processes that would lead a rater to exhibit halo error. Several researchers have theorized that raters rely on a general impression of the employee when making dimension ratings (Lance, LaPoint, & Stewart, 1994; Nathan & Lord, 1983). According to this view, salient pieces of information are used to form a general impression of an employee. The impression forms the basis of performance ratings. This suggests that raters may be better able to provide information about global performance than dimensions of performance.

Distributional Errors. Distributional errors occur when a rater tends to rate everyone the same. **Leniency errors** occur when the rater rates everyone at the favorable end of the performance scale. **Severity errors** occur when the rater rates everyone at the unfavorable end of the performance scale. **Central tendency errors** occur when a rater rates everyone in the middle of the performance scale. The leniency pattern can be seen across ratings of different people. Table 4-8 shows a leniency pattern in that all four people are given ratings at the favorable end of the performance scale. Each person received ratings of 4 and 5 on a five-point scale. It is possible that a distributed error pattern does not reflect errors. All ratees might have performed the same, leading to similar ratings.

Control of Rater Bias and Error. Two approaches have been developed to control and eliminate rater bias and error. One approach is to design better performance appraisal forms that will be resistant to these problems. The other is to train raters to avoid rating errors. Although both approaches have shown promise, research studies have yielded conflicting results about their ability to reduce errors (Bernardin & Beatty, 1984).

Error-Resistant Forms to Assess Performance. The behavior-focused rating scales, such as the Behaviorally Anchored Rating Scale and the Mixed Standard Scale, were originally developed in part to eliminate rating errors. The idea is that raters will be able to make more accurate ratings if they focus on specific behavior rather than traits. These behaviors are more concrete and require less idiosyncratic judgment about what they represent. For example, it should be easier to rate accurately how often a person is absent from work than the somewhat abstract trait of dependability.

TABLE 4-8

Job performance ratings for four employees on five dimensions illustrating a leniency error pattern

DIMENSION	EMPLOYEE 1	EMPLOYEE 2	EMPLOYEE 3	EMPLOYEE 4
Attendance	4	5	5	5
Communication	4	5	5	5
Following directions	5	4	4	4
Work quality	4	5	4	5
Work quantity	5	4	5	5

Many studies have compared the various behavior-focused rating forms with graphic rating forms, as well as with one another. Results of these comparisons have found that the behavior-focused forms sometimes yield fewer errors (such as halo and leniency) than the graphic rating scales, and sometimes they do not (Bernardin & Beatty, 1984; Latham, Skarlicki, Irvine, & Siegel, 1993) As Bernardin and Beatty (1984) point out, many of the studies have compared scales that have not been carefully developed. They believe that carefully developed behavior-focused scales will have better rating error resistance than graphic rating scales. Future studies will be necessary to test their supposition.

Rater Training to Reduce Errors. Rater training has also been attempted in many studies with quite mixed results (Hedge & Kavanagh, 1988; Latham, 1986). At least some of the discrepancy in research findings may be the result of differences in the types of training that have been studied. Perhaps the most popular training is **rater error training** or **RET**. The objective of RET is to familiarize raters with rater errors and to teach them to avoid these ratings patterns. Although most studies have found that this sort of training reduces rating errors, it is often at the cost of rating accuracy (e.g., Bernardin & Pence, 1980; Hedge & Kavanagh, 1988). In other words, the raters might reduce the number of halo and leniency patterns in their ratings, but those ratings are less accurate in reflecting the true level of performance.

How could it be possible that the reduction of errors also results in the reduction in accuracy? One possible explanation lies in the nature of the rating errors. As noted earlier in this discussion, rater errors are inferred from the pattern of ratings. It is possible that the performance of individuals is similar across different performance dimensions or that all individuals in a supervisor's department perform their jobs equally well. Training raters to avoid the same ratings across either dimensions or people will result in their concentrating on avoiding certain patterns rather than on accurately assessing job performance. Bernardin and Pence (1980) suggested that RET might be substituting one series of rating errors for another.

Nathan and Tippins (1990) offer a different explanation of why halo errors are associated with greater accuracy in job performance ratings. They speculated that raters who exhibited less halo in their ratings might have given too much weight to inconsequential negative events. For example, a supervisor might have given an otherwise reliable employee a low rating in attendance because he or she was sick for one week in the prior year. Raters who exhibited a halo pattern in their ratings paid less attention to such rare instances and tended to consider the person's usual performance. This may have resulted in ratings that were more accurate because they were influenced more by general performance than by rare instances of good or poor performance in one or more dimensions.

Results have been more promising with types of training other than RET. Those training procedures teach raters how to observe performance-relevant behavior and how to make judgments based on those observations. Hedge and Kavanagh (1988), for example, found that this observation training increased rating accuracy but did not reduce rating errors (see Research in Detail box in this chapter). Day and Sulsky (1995) demonstrated promising results with **frame of reference training**, which attempts to provide a common understanding of the rating task. Raters are given specific examples of behavior that would represent various levels of performance for each dimension to be rated. Although these results are encouraging, more research is needed before we can confidently con-

| RESEARCH IN DETAIL |

SEVERAL STUDIES HAVE found that training raters to avoid rating errors can reduce their accuracy in evaluating job performance. Hedge and Kavanagh (1988) wanted to see if other types of training would be more effective in increasing the accuracy of performance ratings.

Fifty-two supervisors were randomly assigned to one of four treatment groups. The first group received rater error training designed to familiarize the rater with rating errors and ways to avoid them. The second group received training in ways to observe behavior relevant to job performance. The third group received training in ways to make proper judgments about performance based on observed behavior. The last group was a control group that received no training.

Both before and after training, all groups watched a videotape of a person performing a job. They then rated the person's performance on several performance dimensions. The videotaped performance was assessed by a panel of experts who provided a standard for comparison of the appraisals by members of each group in the study. Accuracy of performance rating was assessed as the discrepancy between the raters' appraisal of the videotape and the expert panel's judgment of the videotape.

The results showed that those who received rater error training had decreased rating errors and accuracy. This finding was consistent with prior research on this sort of training. The other two types of training were successful in increasing accuracy as well as rating errors. The authors concluded that these two types of training showed promise for increasing rating accuracy. They also concluded that the rating patterns often thought to reflect rating errors may not represent mistakes. Rather, these patterns may accurately indicate the level of performance of individuals on the job. For example, individuals might perform at the same level for different dimensions. The implications of this study are that different types of rater training might help organizations get more accurate performance appraisals.

Source: Hedge, J. W., and Kavanagh, M. J. (1988). "Improving the Accuracy of Performance Evaluations: Comparisons of Three Methods of Performance Appraiser Training." *Journal of Applied Psychology, 73,* 68–73.

clude that training can improve performance appraisal ratings because most of the studies have been conducted in the laboratory with college student subjects. It is not certain that actual managers will respond to training in the same way when ratings are not just for research purposes.

Factors That Influence Job Performance Ratings. So far we have discussed how the ratings of supervisors can be affected by their cognitive processes and by the design of the rating form (and training in how to use it). Now we turn to other factors that can affect the ratings made by supervisors. Banks and Murphy (1985) point out that much of the research on cognitive processes in performance appraisal actually addresses a supervisor's ability to provide accurate ratings. In organizational settings, many factors may influence the willingness of a supervisor to give accurate ratings, including characteristics of supervisors themselves and the rating situation. Fried and Tiegs (1995) developed a scale to assess intentional inflation of ratings. Leniency can be a strategy adopted by supervisors who have objectives other than providing the most accurate ratings possible. We will discuss two factors that can affect ratings:

How much the supervisor likes the subordinate

Supervisor's mood at the time of the rating

The idea that supervisors give better ratings to subordinates they like is supported by research (e.g., Ferris, Judge, Rowland, & Fitzgibbons, 1994). The higher ratings can be attributed to personal biases by supervisors; however, supervisors seem to like subordinates who perform well (Robbins & DeNisi, 1994). It is particularly important for a new employee to be seen as a good performer because that perception will likely lead to being liked by supervisors, which can result in good performance ratings in the future.

The continuation of good performance ratings can be influenced by supervisor expectations about performance independent of liking. Murphy, Gannett, Herr, and Chen (1986) found that judgments of performance were influenced by subject expectancies about the ratee's performance. People are likely to forget instances of behavior that do not fit their view of the person they are evaluating. Thus, a person who is liked and performs well will continue to be seen as a good performer, even if performance has recently slipped. This can produce biased ratings when performance changes over time.

The mood of the rater at the time of appraisal can affect ratings. In a laboratory study, Sinclair (1988) assigned subjects to a mood manipulation condition in which their mood was experimentally manipulated to be more depressed or elated. They were then asked to read a description of a professor's behavior and rate that professor's performance. Results showed that subjects in a depressed mood rated the professor's performance lower than subjects in the elated mood condition. The depressed subjects were also more accurate and exhibited less halo. Sinclair explained the results as reflecting the better information processing ability of people when they are in depressed moods.

LEGAL ISSUES IN PERFORMANCE APPRAISAL

Many countries have laws that prohibit discrimination against minorities and women (as well as other groups) in the workplace. These laws cover organizational actions that affect the employment status of people, such as promotions and terminations. Such employee actions are often based at least in part on the person's performance; therefore, the performance appraisal system of an organization can become the target for legal action. In the United States, it is illegal to discriminate in performance appraisal on the basis of certain nonperformance-related factors, such as age, gender, mental or physical disability, or minority status.

In the United States there have been an increasing number of court challenges to performance-based employee actions, such as promotions and terminations (Latham et al., 1993). Organizations that have lost such cases have been unable to demonstrate to the court's satisfaction that their performance appraisal systems did not discriminate against certain groups. Subjective methods are especially likely to evoke legal challenges because they allow room for supervisors to express prejudices against certain groups of people. It can be difficult for a supervisor to prove in court that his or her ratings were fair and unbiased.

Barrett and Kernan (1987) suggested six components that should be part of a legally defensible performance appraisal system. As shown in Table 4-9, the system should begin with a job analysis to derive the dimensions of performance for the particular job. The job

TABLE 4-9
Six points of a legally defensible performance appraisal system

1. Perform job analysis to define dimensions of performance
2. Develop rating form to assess dimensions from prior point
3. Train raters in how to assess performance
4. Have higher management review ratings and allow employees to appeal their evaluations
5. Document performance and maintain detailed records
6. Provide assistance and counseling to poor-performing employees prior to taking actions against them

Source: Adapted from "Performance Appraisal and Terminations: A Review of Court Decisions Since *Brito v. Zia* with Implications for Personnel Practices," by G. V. Barrett and M. G. Kernan, 1987, *Personnel Psychology,* 40, 489–503.

analysis will ensure that the dimensions are job relevant. Raters should receive training in how the rating form is to be used to assess performance. To help minimize personal bias, upper management should review performance appraisals. Performance and the reasons for the employee action should be documented and recorded. It is easier to take legal action against an employee when the performance, good or poor, has been documented for a long period of time. This eliminates the appearance that the latest appraisal was given to justify a particular action affecting an employee. Finally, it is a good idea to provide assistance and counseling to employees whose performance is unsatisfactory. This shows that the organization has done everything possible for an unsatisfactory employee before taking action against him or her.

Werner and Bolino (1997) analyzed the outcomes of 295 U.S. court cases in which performance appraisals were challenged as being discriminatory. Performance appraisal systems that were based on a job analysis, gave written instructions to raters, offered employees the opportunity to have input, and used multiple raters were far less likely to result in an organization losing the case. For example, while overall organizations lost 41% of cases, those that used multiple raters only lost 11% of cases. The use of these four practices combined should result in a relatively safe performance appraisal system from a legal perspective.

Allowing employees to have input into performance appraisals also has benefits beyond legal issues. Research has shown that giving employees the opportunity to sit down with supervisors and discuss appraisals openly can lead to better attitudes (Korsgaard & Roberson, 1995). In one study, this occurred even though employees allowed input actually had lower ratings than those who did not (Taylor, Tracy, Renard, Harrison, & Carroll, 1995). Perceptions of fairness in this study even reduced employee intentions of quitting the job. To be effective and perceived as fair, performance appraisal systems should include the Barrett and Kernan (1987) six steps, as well as input by employees.

FUTURE ISSUES AND CHALLENGES

Improving performance appraisal systems represents a major challenge to the I/O field. Objective measures are often deficient in not adequately representing the entire scope of people's job performance. Subjective measures suffer from contamination as a result of rating biases and errors of the supervisors who assess performance. There is considerable room for improvement with both types of performance measures.

The development of good performance measures must begin with the definition of performance criteria. For jobs with clear and countable output, such as sales, the development of criteria can be relatively easy and straightforward. For jobs without countable output, such as teaching, the development of criteria can be more difficult. It is not easy to define what good teaching is, so it is not easy to come up with sound performance appraisal methods to assess teachers.

Research with some forms of rater training shows promise in improving the accuracy of subjective ratings. Training that focuses on how to observe good job performance and how to transform those observations into accurate appraisals of people's performance seems likely to be effective.

A challenge for practicing I/O psychologists is to convince organizations that they should have the most complete and unbiased performance appraisal systems possible. This means investing resources and time in the development and maintenance of such systems. There are two practical reasons for such investment. First, a sound system is less likely to be challenged in court by an employee who believes that he or she has been unfairly evaluated. Second, a sound system is likely to be more effective in meeting its various objectives, such as providing feedback to employees so that they can improve their job performance.

CHAPTER SUMMARY

Job performance data have many organizational uses, including administrative decision making, employee development, employee feedback, and research. The first step in evaluating job performance is to develop performance criteria that define good and poor performance. Once criteria are set, specific methods to measure them can be chosen.

Job performance measures can be classified as either objective or subjective. Objective measures are counts of the output of a job, such as the number of sales for a salesperson or the number of units produced for a factory worker. Subjective measures are ratings by supervisors (or other individuals who are familiar with the person's job performance). Subjective measures are the more commonly used of the two methods, but they suffer from biases and errors attributable to human judgment. Two different approaches have been taken to reduce rating errors in subjective measures.

Several different types of rating forms have been devised to increase the accuracy of performance ratings. The Behaviorally Anchored Rating Scale (BARS) asks raters to indicate which of several behaviors comes closest to representing the job performance of the individual. The Mixed Standard Scale (MSS) asks raters to indicate if the individual's performance is worse than, as good as, or better than each of several items of performance behavior. The Behavior Observation Scale (BOS) asks raters to indicate how often ratees perform each of the listed behaviors. Research comparing the behavior-focused rating forms with other types of measures has failed to find consistent evidence for greater accuracy.

Rater training is another approach that has been attempted to reduce errors. Research has suggested that rater error training can reduce rating accuracy, even if it is successful in reducing rating errors. Observation training that focuses on observing performance-related behavior and making judgments of performance has shown promise in increasing accuracy. At the present time, however, it would be premature to conclude that either approach will prove useful in ensuring that supervisors will provide accurate performance ratings.

I/O PSYCHOLOGY IN PRACTICE

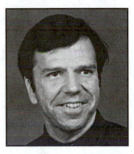

THIS CASE CONCERNS the enhancement of a performance appraisal system that involved Dr. Jeff McHenry. Dr. McHenry received his Ph.D. in differential psychology in 1981 from the University of Minnesota. Although his doctoral training was not in the I/O field, Dr. McHenry has become an I/O psychologist through his experiences and work. A graduate degree in the field is not required, although most I/O psychologists have I/O degrees. Dr. McHenry is presently a senior consultant for Microsoft Corporation, which develops and markets software for personal computers worldwide. Dr. McHenry is responsible for two major areas. He is in charge of employee surveys and he is responsible for supporting the management development program. Dr. McHenry is a member of the Performance Review Task Force, which has been assigned the job of improving the performance appraisal system for the company. Microsoft is an achievement-oriented company with a great deal of emphasis on employee performance. The performance appraisal system is an important element in the management of high productivity. Every employee at Microsoft receives a formal performance review twice each year. Merit raises are based on the performance appraisal system, and not everyone can get a merit raise. The task force in studying the performance appraisal system has come up with a number of specific recommendations for top management to consider. Four areas of concern have been targeted:

Focusing performance appraisal on employee goals linked to company goals

Incorporating company values into performance appraisal

Finding ways to avoid demotivating employees who do not get top performance ratings

Separating the administrative (e.g., determining who gets merit raises) from the employee development (helping employees improve their performance through feedback) uses of performance appraisal information

The task force will present its recommendations to top management, who will decide what steps to take next.

Discussion Questions

1. Why is performance appraisal important to a company such as Microsoft?

2. What is the advantage of linking performance appraisal to organizational goals?

3. Why does Dr. McHenry want to separate administrative from employee development uses of performance appraisal?

4. How could you minimize the demotivating impact of criticism in performance appraisals?

Chapter 5

ASSESSMENT METHODS FOR SELECTION AND PLACEMENT

Suppose you find yourself responsible for deciding whom to hire for a particular job. It might be hiring a nurse, or a plumber, or a police officer, or a teacher. There are several job applicants, and your task is to decide which one to hire. How would you go about making your choice? Would you interview each one and pick the person who seemed to be best suited for the job? How would you know what characteristics or qualities to look for in a potential employee? Furthermore, how would you go about finding out if applicants had the necessary characteristics? Procedures for the assessment of characteristics for selection (hiring) and placement (assigning current employees to jobs) are the topic of this chapter.

One of the earliest applications of psychology to the human problems of organizations had to do with the assessment of people for selection and placement. During World War I, the first use of large-scale testing of people to determine their job assignments (placement) in the U.S. Army took place. After the war, large organizations saw the potential value of assessing job applicants for selection and other employment decisions, and the use of testing and other techniques became commonplace. This is true today not only in the United States, but also in most of the industrialized world including Canada, Western Europe, and Israel (McCulloch, 1993).

This chapter discusses five techniques for the assessment of characteristics that are frequently used for selection and placement. A *psychological test* consists of a standard set of items or tasks that a person completes under controlled conditions. Most involve paper-and-pencil tasks, such as answering questions or solving problems, although some involve manipulation of physical objects to assess such characteristics as manual dexterity of eye–hand coordination. Psychological tests can be used to assess ability, interests, knowledge, personality, and skill. *Biographical information* asks about relevant prior experiences, such as level of education and work experience. Some forms can be quite detailed, asking not only about objective facts, but opinions and subjective reactions as well. The *interview* is a face-to-face meeting between the job applicant and someone at the employing organization who will have input into the hiring decision. A *work sample* is a test that asks a person to perform a simulated job. The person is given the necessary materials and tools and must perform a particular task, such as assembling a motor, under controlled conditions. An *assessment center* involves a series of exercises that measure how well a person can perform a sample of tasks from a job. It is commonly used to assess potential for a management or other white-collar job.

Each of the five assessment techniques can be used to determine a person's suitability for a particular job. Often more than one technique is used at the same time to try to get a complete picture of how well an individual's characteristics match those necessary for a job. These assessment techniques can have uses other than selection and placement, however. They can be useful for employee development by showing a person's strengths and weaknesses, which can then be addressed by training. In the next chapter on employee selection, we will see how the five techniques are used.

<u>Objectives</u>   **The student who studies this chapter should be able to:**
1. Define KSAOs.
2. Describe the five assessment methods.
3. Discuss the advantages and limitations of each assessment tool.
4. Explain how computers are changing assessment.

JOB-RELATED CHARACTERISTICS

Many different characteristics of people or KSAOs (knowledge, skill, ability, and other personal characteristics) are needed for a job. (See Chapter 3 for a more extensive discussion of KSAOs in the context of job analysis.) *Knowledge* refers to what the person knows about a job, such as legal knowledge for an attorney. A *skill* is something that a person is able to do, such as program a computer or type. *Ability* is the capability to learn something, such as the ability to learn to play a musical instrument or to speak a foreign language. *Other personal characteristics* are every other human attribute not covered by the first three. Included are interests, personality, physical characteristics (such as height or strength), and prior experience relevant for the job.

Table 5-1 contains examples of KSAOs for a sales associate in a computer store. Such a person should have knowledge of the product that he or she will sell, as well as the ability to understand complex computer systems. It is important that the person can work a cash register and handle monetary transactions. Finally, the person must have a neat appearance and a friendly, outgoing personality.

The KSAOs for each job can be determined by a detailed and thorough study, which is called a *job analysis.* (See Chapter 3 for a discussion of job analysis.) This involves a number of techniques that result in a list of the necessary KSAOs for the job in question. Once KSAOs are determined, procedures can be chosen or developed to assess them in job applicants or current employees. The idea is to select or place people into jobs who have the necessary KSAOs. Although this process does not guarantee that the people chosen will be successful on the job, it increases the chances of making good choices over using other selection and placement approaches.

TABLE 5-1
KSAOs for a computer sales associate

Knowledge	Knowledge of computer systems
	Knowledge of computer software
Skills	Skill in using a cash register
	Skill in completing monetary transactions
Abilities	Ability to understand complex technology
	Ability to communicate with other people
Other	Neat appearance
	Outgoing, friendly personality

All five of the assessment techniques that we discuss attempt to measure KSAOs that are relevant for job performance and other organizationally relevant variables. As with all assessment techniques, the properties of reliability and validity are critical. That is, all measures must be consistent (reliable) and must pass stringent tests for validity. In other words, evidence must exist that they can accomplish the tasks for which they are used in organizations. If a test is to be used to select police officers, for example, it must be shown to be able to predict how well a police officer will do on the job. Assessment techniques that cannot pass the test of validity should not be used.

PSYCHOLOGICAL TESTS

A **psychological test** is a standardized series of problems or questions that assess a particular individual characteristic. Tests are commonly used to assess many KSAOs, including knowledge, skill, ability, attitudes, interests, and personality. Tests are comprised of multiple items, which are indicators of the characteristic of interest. Each item can be completed relatively quickly, making it feasible to include many items to assess each characteristic and to assess several characteristics at one time.

Multiple items provide increased reliability and validity over a single indicator of the characteristic. Single-item measures tend to have low reliability because a person can easily make a mistake on any one item. For example, an item can be misinterpreted or misread. Consider the following item that might be encountered on a test:

I'm not usually the first one to volunteer for a new work assignment.

If a person misreads the item and does not notice that the second word is *not*, the meaning of the item will be reversed. His or her response to the item will be the opposite of what it should be to reflect the characteristic of interest, and the item will not be an accurate indicator of the characteristic of interest. If it is likely that only a few people will make this error, the item may retain some reliability and validity. The reliability and validity of a multiple-item test is better than that for the single-item test because the impact of occasional errors on each person's score is reduced. The contribution of each item to the total score when there are many items is quite small.

Characteristics of Tests

Many different types of tests are available that can assess hundreds of individual characteristics. The nature of the characteristic of interest helps determine which test is used.

© 1993, Ziggy and Friends, Inc./Distributed by
Universal Press Syndicate.

For example, a test to assess mathematical ability will most certainly be composed of math problems to be completed with paper and pencil. A test of physical strength, on the other hand, will likely involve the lifting of heavy objects. A discussion of the four distinguishing characteristics of tests follows.

Group Versus Individually Administered Tests. A **group test** can be administered to several people at once. The test itself is usually in a booklet form that can be given to hundreds or thousands of people at one time. The test administrator usually hands out the tests and instructs the test takers when they are to begin and stop. The test taker determines the pace of the completion of individual test items. An individual test is one that a test administrator gives to a single test taker at a time rather than to groups of individuals. This is necessary because either the administrator has to score the items as the test proceeds or an apparatus is involved that only one person can use at a time. The test administrator sets the pace of the individual items. Because of its greater efficiency, the group test is preferred when it is feasible.

Objective Versus Open-Ended Tests. With an **objective test**, the test taker must choose one from several possible responses. Such multiple-choice exams test ability and knowledge. An **open-ended test** is like an essay exam. The test taker must generate a response, rather than choose a correct response. Whereas the objective test is preferred because of its greater ease in scoring, the open-ended test is more appropriate for some characteristics. For example, writing ability is best assessed by asking a person to write an essay. Experts can read and score the essay for a number of characteristics, such as clarity of expression and grammatical accuracy. These characteristics would be more difficult to assess with an objective test.

Paper-and-Pencil Versus Performance Tests. With a **paper-and-pencil test**, the test itself is on a piece of paper or other printed medium, and the responses are made in written form, often with a pencil. A multiple-choice course examination is a paper-and-pencil test that presents the exam questions on paper, and the responses are made in pencil on the exam itself or on a separate answer sheet. Open-ended tests can also be paper-and-pencil if they ask people to write their responses in some form. A **performance test** involves the manipulation of apparatus, equipment, materials, or tools. Perhaps the most widely used performance test is a typing test. With this sort of performance test, the test taker demonstrates his or her typing ability by using an actual typewriter under standardized conditions. This tests the typing ability itself, rather than typing knowledge, which could be assessed with a paper-and-pencil test of knowledge about typing.

Power Versus Speed Tests. A **power test** gives the test taker almost unlimited time to complete the test. A **speed test** has a strict time limit. It is designed so that almost no one could finish all items in the allotted time. There are two ways in which the speed test is used. First, a speed test can contain challenging items, and the test indicates how quickly the test taker can answer them. Some instructors use speed tests for classroom examinations under the presumption that the better prepared students will be able to answer the questions more quickly than the less well-prepared students. The drawback to this use of speed tests is that the test taker is at a disadvantage if he or she is a slow reader. The second use is with a test that is designed to assess a person's speed in doing a particular task. A typing test is timed because its purpose is to assess a person's typing speed, as well as accuracy.

Ability Tests

An ability or aptitude is a person's capacity to do or learn to do a particular task. Cognitive abilities, such as intelligence, are relevant to tasks that involve information processing and learning. Psychomotor abilities, such as manual dexterity, involve body movements and manipulation of objects. The importance of each ability is dependent on the nature of the tasks of interest. Some job tasks require mostly cognitive abilities (e.g., programming a computer), whereas others rely mainly on psychomotor abilities (e.g., sweeping a floor). Many tasks require both types of abilities (e.g., repairing a computer or complex piece of equipment).

Cognitive Ability Tests. An intelligence or IQ test of general cognitive ability is the best known **cognitive ability test**. There are also tests of individual cognitive abilities, such as mathematical or verbal ability. Most cognitive ability tests are paper-and-pencil tests, in which the items represent individual problems to solve. Such tests can be administered to large groups of individuals and provide an inexpensive and efficient means of assessing job applicants.

Figure 5-1 contains two sample items from the Personnel Tests for Industry (PTI), a test designed to assess mathematical and verbal ability. The items are problems involving

Numerical

> For answers which should have a decimal point, the decimal point is printed on the answer line for you to use.
>
> **EXAMPLE**
>
> There are 8 gallons of water in a tank
> which can hold 16.5 gallons. How many
> gallons can be added to this tank? . . . . *8.5* . . gals.
>
> | 16.5
> | −8
> | 8.5

Verbal

> **EXAMPLE A:**
> Which does not belong?
> (A) red, (B) green, (C) purple, (D) sweet   A   B   C   Ⓓ
>
> *Red, green, and purple* are colors but sweet (choice D) is not a color and does not belong with the words. Therefore, the D has been marked as shown on the right of the question.

FIGURE 5-1

Two sample items from the Personnel Tests for Industry (PTI). Reproduced by permission. Copyright © 1969 by the Psychological Corporation. All rights reserved.

mathematical and verbal reasoning. The test was designed for group administration and can be completed in about 25 minutes. The PTI was produced by the Psychological Corporation, which is one of the oldest and best known publishers of employment tests.

All test takers are not proficient in the local language; therefore, tests have been developed that do not rely on reading ability. Figure 5-2 contains two items from Beta-II, which is a nonverbal intelligence test. The items involve problem solving without words. The first item asks the test taker to find his or her way through the maze. The second item asks the test taker to solve a coding problem using numbers and shapes. The test administrator reads instructions to test takers for each type of item. Instructions can be given in any language.

Cognitive ability tests have a long history of use by large organizations for employee selection because of their efficiency and validity. Group tests can be administered to many people simultaneously, and they are easy to score. The cost of a single copy of a test is low—no more than a dollar or two. Besides their low cost, cognitive ability tests have been shown to be valid predictors of job performance across a large number of different kinds of jobs (Murphy, 1988; Ree & Carretta, 1998). People who score well on cognitive ability tests tend to perform better on the job.

Psychomotor Ability Tests. **Psychomotor ability tests** assess such things as ability to manipulate objects and use tools. They involve both the coordination between senses and movement (e.g., eye–hand coordination) and the accuracy of movements. Many psychomotor tests are performance tests rather than paper-and-pencil tests because the abili-

Mazes ask examinees to mark the shortest distance
through a mase without crossing any lines (1.5 minutes)

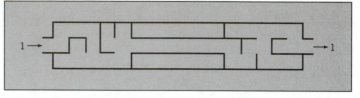

Coding requires labelling figures with their corresponding numbers (2 minutes)

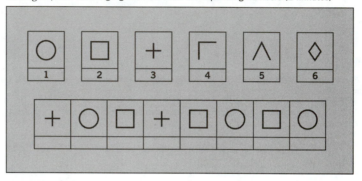

FIGURE 5-2

Two sample items from the Beta II Examination: 2nd edition nonverbal intelligence test. Reproduced by permission. Copyright © 1978 by the Psychological Corporation. All rights reserved.

ties of interest involve manipulation of objects rather than cognitive elements. People are scored on their ability to perform motor tasks, such as putting pegs in holes or using simple tools to manipulate objects.

Figures 5-3 and 5-4 are pictures of two psychomotor tests. Figure 5-3 is the Hand-Tool Dexterity Test, which assesses the ability to use simple tools to manipulate small objects. This test involves removing and reassembling several fasteners using wrenches and a screwdriver. The score is based on the time it takes to complete the task. Figure 5-4 shows the Stromberg Dexterity Test, which assesses arm and hand movement accuracy and speed. The person must place the colored disks into the correct color-coded holes. Again, scores are based on the speed with which the person can accomplish the task.

Knowledge and Skill Tests

An ability test is intended to assess a person's capability of learning or potential. A **knowledge and skill test**, often called an **achievement test**, is designed to assess a person's present level of proficiency. A knowledge test assesses what the person knows, and a skill test assesses what a person is able to do.

In practice, it is difficult to totally separate ability from knowledge and skill, for ability tests rely to some extent on knowledge and skill, and knowledge and skill tests rely to some extent on ability. The major difference between the two types of tests is the empha-

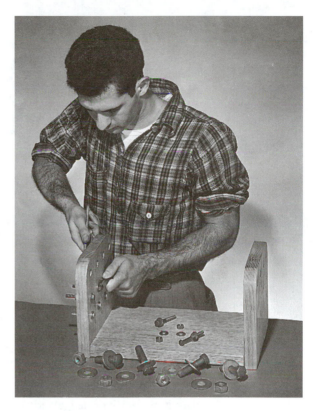

FIGURE 5-3
The Hand-Tool Dexterity Test.

FIGURE 5-4
The Stromberg Dexterity Test.

Which person carries more weight?
(if equal mark C.)

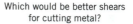

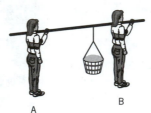

A   B

Which room has more of an echo?   Which would be better shears
for cutting metal?

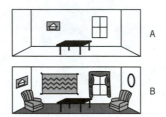

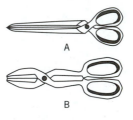

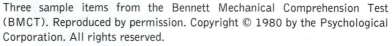

FIGURE 5-5

Three sample items from the Bennett Mechanical Comprehension Test
(BMCT). Reproduced by permission. Copyright © 1980 by the Psychological
Corporation. All rights reserved.

sis placed on prior knowledge and skill in performing specific tasks. For example, a psychomotor ability test might assess how quickly a person could put pegs in holes as an indicator of eye–hand coordination, whereas a psychomotor skill test might assess how well a person can type. Typing skill is the product of several different abilities.

Many different knowledge and skill areas can be assessed with a test. Some tests focus on general skills, such as math and reading. Others are useful for assessing skills at particular job tasks, such as typing. With a typing test the test taker is given the task of typing some materials under standardized conditions. The person is scored on the number of words per minute typed and the number of typing errors. As with ability tests, some knowledge and skill tests are paper and pencil, and some are performance tests.

Figure 5-5 contains three items from the Bennett Mechanical Comprehension Test. This test assesses a combination of mechanical ability and knowledge about tools. This sort of test is useful for determining if a person has a good understanding of how mechanical things work and how tools can be used. Note that this is a knowledge test and assesses a person's knowledge about tools rather than his or her skill in using tools. Actual tool use is a skill that involves both cognitive and psychomotor elements rather than just a cognitive knowledge element.

Personality Tests

A **personality trait** is the predisposition or tendency to behave in a particular way across different situations. A person who prefers to do things with other people is said to be high on the trait of sociability. A person who must always have his or her way with other people is said to be high on the trait of dominance. Personality traits can be important because certain classes of behavior can be relevant for job performance and other behaviors in organizations. Sociability can be an important trait for a salesperson who must interact with other people, whereas dominance can be an important trait for a supervisor who must direct the activities of others.

Paper-and-pencil **personality tests** can be useful tools for assessing personality traits. Some personality tests are designed to assess a single personality trait; personality inventories assess multiple dimensions and are sometimes used to provide profiles of individuals across several personality traits. They can also characterize people into types, which are combinations of different traits. For example, the extroverted type of person tends to be high on the traits of activity, optimism, sociability, and talkativeness, whereas the introverted type tends to be high on carefulness, quietness, passivity, and unsociability (Pervin, 1993).

Figure 5-6 contains two sample items from the NEO Personality Inventory-Revised (Costa & McCrae, 1992). This inventory assesses 30 traits and 5 domains. The traits include anxiety, warmth, compliance, and achievement striving. The domains fit the Big Five theory of personality structure, which we will discuss in Chapter 10.

Researchers frequently use personality tests to study many different aspects of people's behavior in organizations. The use of such tests in practice, however, has been widely criticized. There are two major concerns with the use of personality tests for employee selection. First, there is the possibility that job applicants will fake responses to the test by answering the items in the manner they believe will put them in the most favorable light. Therefore, scores for individuals who fake answers will not be valid, and the validity of the test itself will be compromised. Recent research has revealed, however, that attempts at distortion will not necessarily invalidate a personality test used for employee selection (Schmit, Ryan, Stierwalt, & Powell, 1995). Second, personality tests do not always appear to be as job relevant as other assessment devices. *Job relevance* means that what an assessment tool measures is obviously related to specific job tasks. A typing test, for example, is obviously relevant for a secretary who must type as part of the job requirements. It is harder to show that a personality trait such as dominance is related to particular job tasks.

Despite concerns over the use of personality tests for employee selection, such tests have been popular among practitioners in organizations. Smith and George (1992) recommend caution in using personality inventories and tests for employee selection when those tests were not developed for such purposes. This is good advice because meta-analyses have found modest validities for general-purpose personality tests as predictors of job performance (e.g., Ones & Viswesvaran, 1996; Salgado, 1997). Personality tests de-

> Once I start a project, I almost always finish it.
> I often do things on the spur of the moment.

FIGURE 5-6

Two sample items from the NEO Personality Inventory-Revised. Reproduced by special permission of the Publisher, Psychological Assessment Resources, Inc., 16204 North Florida Avenue, Lutz, Florida 33549, from the NEO Personality Inventory-Revised, by Paul Costa and Robert McCrae. Copyright © 1978, 1985, 1989, 1992 by PAR, Inc. Further reproduction is prohibited without permission of PAR, Inc.

veloped for organizational settings, however, have been found to predict job performance reasonably well. One example is the Employee Reliability Scale that J. Hogan and Hogan (1989) found to predict job performance and other behaviors at work.

Hesketh and Robertson (1993) point out that personality tests are often used with little thought as to what particular traits should be related to job performance. One difficulty with drawing conclusions about the validity of personality tests from the existing meta-analyses is that those analyses tended to group together tests that assessed many different traits for the prediction of performance on many different types of jobs. Some of those traits may have represented job-relevant characteristics; others may have been unimportant for success. Existing evidence suggests that specific personality traits chosen to be relevant to job performance on particular jobs will do a reasonably good job of predicting performance (Hogan & Roberts, 1996; Schneider, Hough, & Dunnette, 1996). Although caution is certainly called for, personality tests have considerable potential as selection tools.

Integrity Tests

An **integrity test** is designed to predict whether or not an employee will engage in counterproductive or dishonest behavior on the job. The behaviors the tests are designed to predict include cheating, poor performance, sabotage, and theft. They also are sometimes used to predict absence and turnover. Sackett, Burris, and Callahan (1989) noted that there are two different types of integrity tests—overt and personality.

The *overt integrity test* assesses a person's attitudes and prior behavior. It asks the person to indicate agreement or disagreement with statements concerning honesty and moral behavior. An example of such an item would be the following:

> It is all right to lie if you know you won't get caught.

The test taker is also asked how often he or she has done a number of counterproductive behaviors. A possible item might be the following:

> How often have you stolen something from your employer?

The *personality integrity test* assesses personality characteristics that have been found to predict counterproductive behavior. Whereas the overt integrity tests are obvious assessments of honesty and integrity, the personality tests are hidden in their purpose. In fact, standard personality inventories often are used as integrity tests. We discussed personality tests earlier in this chapter.

Research on integrity tests has shown that they can predict theft and other counterproductive behavior (Ashton, 1998; Ones & Viswesvaran, 1998; Ones, Viswesvaran, & Schmidt, 1993). Collins and Schmidt (1993) compared whiter-collar criminals to white-collar employees using several personality tests that have been used as integrity tests. They found that the tests were able to distinguish between the groups. The criminals scored differently than the employees on several measures of personality. Woolley and Hakstian (1993) found that both overt and personality integrity tests related to college students' admissions of having engaged in counterproductive and dishonest behaviors on the job and in school.

Hogan and Hogan (1989) developed a personality test specifically as an integrity test. Their Employee Reliability Scale was intended to assess several specific personality characteristics that related to theft and other counterproductive behaviors that they called *organizational delinquency*. They developed the scale by determining how incarcerated delinquents differed in personality from other groups of people. The delinquents were found to be more exhibitionistic and experienced less guilt for their actions than the nondelinquents, for example. The resulting scale has been shown to predict several different delinquent behaviors as well as job performance.

Vocational Interest Tests

A **vocational interest test** matches either the interests or personality of the test taker to those of people in a variety of different occupations and occupational categories. Interests are assessed by asking the test taker to indicate his or her preferences for engaging in various activities, such as attending a sporting event or visiting a museum. Personality is assessed with a personality-type test. Data are available about the answers of people in many different occupations. The test taker's answers are matched to those of people in different occupations to see how well he or she fits each occupation.

Interest and personality profiles vary considerably from occupation to occupation. Therefore, any individual test taker will match some occupations and not others. Because occupations tend to group together into categories, a person can be matched to a category of occupation, such as artistic, which involve artistic creation and pursuits, such as interior design or photography.

One of the most popular vocational interest tests is the Self-Directed Search (Holland, 1994). This test provides scores on six personality types (Figure 5-7). Each type is associ-

The Realistic type likes realistic jobs such as automobile mechanic, aircraft controller, surveyor, farmer, or electrician.

The Investigative type likes investigative jobs such as biologist, chemist, physicist, anthropologist, geologist, or medical technologist.

The Artistic type likes artistic jobs such as composer, musician, stage director, writer, interior decorator, or actor/actress.

The Social type likes social jobs such as teacher, religious worker, counselor, clinical psychologist, psychiatric case worker, or speech therapist.

The Enterprising type likes enterprising jobs such as salesperson, manager, business executive, television producer, sports promoter, or buyer.

The Conventional type likes conventional jobs such as bookkeeper, stenographer, financial analyst, banker, cost estimator, or tax expert.

FIGURE 5-7
The six personality types and associated occupations as assessed by the Self-Directed Search. Adapted and reproduced by special permission of the Publisher, Psychological Assessment Resources, Inc., 16204 North Florida Avenue, Lutz, FL 33549, from You and Your Career by John L. Holland, Ph.D. Copyright © 1985 by PAR, Inc. Further reproduction is prohibited without permission from PAR, Inc.

ated with a particular family of occupations. As shown in the figure, the investigative type likes investigative-type jobs that include scientific fields such as biology or geology. The profile of scores on the six types can guide a person in choosing a career.

The match between a person's vocational interests and those of people in occupations is presumed to predict a person's satisfaction with the occupation. A person who takes a job that is a poor match will likely be unhappy with it, whereas a person who takes a job that is a good match will probably like it. The idea behind the tests is to encourage people to select careers that match their interests. Vocational interest tests are frequently used for vocational guidance in helping people decide what careers to pursue.

BIOGRAPHICAL INFORMATION

One of the easiest ways to find out about people is to ask them what you wish to know. In an employment setting, basic information about people is obtained from an application form. Although they can differ from organization to organization, standard application forms contain questions about education, job skills, personal characteristics, and work history. Some forms can be quite detailed, asking about specific experiences, such as extracurricular school activities (e.g., participation in sports).

The **biographical inventory** asks much more detailed questions than an application form about a person's background. Where application forms ask about prior level of education and work experience, the biographical inventory asks about specific experiences at school and work, or even other areas of life. Some of the questions ask about objective, verifiable facts, such as

"What was your grade point average in college?"

Others ask about opinions or subjective experiences, such as

"Did you enjoy college?"

If a biographical inventory contains enough of the second type of question, it begins to approximate a psychological test that assesses interests and personality instead of prior life experiences. The items of a biographical inventory focus more on past experiences and reactions than do psychological test items (Stokes & Reddy, 1992). Most inventories use a multiple-choice response format that can be easily scored. Possible answers to the questions about enjoying college might be

"Enjoyed very much"

"Enjoyed somewhat"

"Enjoyed a little"

"Didn't enjoy at all"

Table 5-2 contains some examples of inventory items.

Biographical information is useful to organizations in the selection process. Application forms contain information about education and work experience that might be necessary for a particular job. Biographical inventories can be scored in a way that can predict job performance and job tenure (how long a person stays on the job before quitting). Systems have been developed to provide a score for each job applicant by combining responses to the various questions. Such scores have been shown to be predictive of job

TABLE 5-2
Sample items from a biographical inventory

When you were in grade school and people were being picked for teams, when were you usually
  picked?
During high school, what grades did you get in chemistry class?
Did you attend your high school prom?
In your first full-time job, how often did you initiate conversation with your immediate supervisor?

performance (Hunter & Hunter, 1984; Rothstein, Schmidt, Erwin, Owens, & Sparks,
1990).

The biggest criticism of biographical inventories has been that they too often take a
purely empirical approach. Items are chosen based entirely on their ability to predict performance. Sometimes an item can predict performance even though it cannot be linked to
a KSAO necessary for job performance. These items are combined into scores that predict
performance but do not reflect job-related KSAOs. Many questions in such inventories can
appear completely unrelated to the job or job performance. Applicants may consider some
questions as an invasion of privacy, such as questions about high school dating behavior.

Many examples can be found, however, of biographical inventories that assess meaningful, job-related characteristics (Stokes & Reddy, 1992). This latter conceptual approach will likely continue, for it is important to link selection and placement decisions to
job-relevant characteristics. One important reason has to do with requirements for legal
selection, which we address in the following chapter. A major principle of legal employee
selection in the United States and many countries is that the basis for hiring decisions
must be job relevant. Another issue is that applicants will find questions to be more acceptable if they can be linked to the job.

INTERVIEWS

An interview is a face-to-face meeting between one or more interviewers who are collecting information or making hiring decisions and an interviewee. Almost all organizations
use the interview in hiring for almost all positions. Perhaps one reason for the universal
use of this technique is that it is widely accepted. Steiner and Gilliland (1996) found that
it was rated most acceptable of all commonly used selection procedures by college students in both France and the United States.

There are two types of interviews conducted in organizational settings. During an *unstructured interview*, the interviewer asks whatever questions come to mind. It can be
much like a conversation between the interviewer and interviewee in which the nature of
the interaction between the two people determines in large part what is discussed. By
contrast, during a **structured interview**, the interviewer has a preplanned series of questions that are asked of every person who is interviewed. This makes the interview relatively standard, although the interaction between the two people can still affect what gets
discussed. Nevertheless, the use of a standard set of questions allows the interviewer to
collect the same information about each interviewee.

Campion, Palmer, and Campion (1997) discuss 15 ways in which structure can be introduced into an interview. There is no one way in which such interviews are conducted.

Some interviews are moderately structured in that questions to be asked or just the topics to be covered are specified and standardized. Others have strict requirements that questions be asked in a set order, that the same phrasing be used, that interviewees not be asked to elaborate on any answer even if it is unclear, and that interviewees not ask questions themselves until the end. In the extreme, the interview is much like an open-ended test with an oral response rather than written. Campion et al. (1997) suggest that the more highly structured approaches are probably the most valid, and therefore as much structure as possible should be introduced into the interview.

The interview can be used in two ways. One is as an alternative to an application form or a written questionnaire to collect information. Questions can ask about attitudes (Did you like your last job?); job experiences (Have you ever supervised anyone?); personal background (What was your major in college?); and preferences (Would you mind working weekends?). The other way the interview can be used is to make inferences about a person's suitability for a job based on both their answers to questions and their behavior in the interview situation. The interview can be considered as a sample of interpersonal behavior, showing how well a person communicates and relates to the interviewer.

Interviewers can be asked to make ratings on job-related dimensions, such as communication skills or relevant experience. They sometimes make overall ratings of applicant suitability for the job. These ratings can be subject to the same problems as performance appraisal ratings, which we discussed in Chapter 4. Interviewer biases and cognitive processes can reduce the accuracy of judgments and ratings (Dipboye & Gaugler, 1993).

The structured interview can be a good way to collect information that builds on that provided in the application form. Specific questions can ask for more detail about the provided information. For example, an application form will typically ask the person to list all prior jobs. In the interview, the interviewee might be asked to describe each job and to explain how his or her prior work experiences might be relevant to the job at hand.

An interview has two advantages over an application form. First, the interview allows for longer and more detailed answers to questions that do not have short or simple answers. Most people find it easier to talk than write. Second, the interview allows both the interviewer and the interviewee to ask one another for clarification. The interviewer can ask the interviewee to explain an unclear answer or to provide additional details. The interviewee can ask the interviewer to rephrase an unclear question or to indicate if the appropriate level of detail has been given.

The disadvantage of the interview is that the interviewer can affect the answers of the interviewee. Even with the most carefully constructed structured interview and thoroughly trained interviewer, the interaction between interviewer and interviewee will differ from interview to interview. Differences among interviewers in their ability to conduct an interview and in their personalities could affect the interview process and the interviewee's responses (Dipboye & Gaugler, 1993). This is not a concern with application forms because there is relatively little interaction between the person administering it and the person completing it.

The wisdom of using the interview to help decide who to hire has been the subject of controversy within the I/O field for many years. The most recent research evidence supports the use of structured but not necessarily unstructured interviews in making employment decisions. Ratings of interviewee employment suitability from a structured interview have been shown to predict future job performance across many different studies (Cam-

The interview is used for almost all hiring.

pion, Pursell, & Brown, 1988; Harris, 1989; Huffcutt & Arthur, 1994; Wiesner & Cronshaw, 1988; Wright, Lichtenfels, & Pursell, 1989). The unstructured interview has been found to be less valid as a predictor of job performance (Marchese & Muchinsky, 1993; Wiesner & Cronshaw, 1988). The problem with the unstructured interview is that it leaves too much room for biases. An interviewer might decide on the basis of appearance, for example, that an applicant is unsuited. Cable and Judge (1997) found that an interviewer's hiring decisions were related to how attractive they found the applicant and how much they liked him or her. Such interviewers might not be as thorough in questioning a disliked or unattractive applicant, and fail to discover important job-related qualifications that might lead to hiring.

Wiesner and Cronshaw (1988) conducted a meta-analysis of over 100 interview studies. This technique of data analysis allows for the combination of results across multiple studies of the same phenomenon. They classified each study as representing either a structured or unstructured interview and computed the average correlation across studies within each group. The average correlation between interview outcome and job performance was larger for the structured interview studies ($r = .34$) than for the unstructured interview studies ($r = .17$).

The Wiesner and Cronshaw study, as well as others that have followed, has provided convincing evidence for the validity of the structured interview for selecting employees. Before these studies were published, there was widespread belief in the field that the interview was invalid for employee selection. This conclusion is one that is accepted today only for the unstructured interview. The best advice that can be given to people who use interviews to select employees is to be sure to use structured rather than unstructured interviews.

TABLE 5-3
Factors that can enhance the reliability and validity of a structured interview

The interviewer should ask standardized questions.

The interviewer should have detailed information about the job in question.

The interviewer should not have prior information about the interviewee, such as psychological test scores.

Evaluations of the interviewee should not be made until the interview is completed.

The interviewer should make ratings of individual dimensions of the interviewee, such as educational background or relevance of prior work history, rather than a global rating of suitability for the job.

Interviewers should receive training in how to conduct a valid structured interview.

Source: Adapted from "Cognitive and Behavioral Processes in the Selection Interview," by R. L. Dipboye and B. B. Gaugler, 1993, in N. Schmitt and W. C. Borman (Eds.), *Personnel Selection in Organizations.* San Francisco: Jossey-Bass.

Several factors contribute to the validity of the structured interview. Huffcutt, Roth, and McDaniel (1996) conducted a meta-analysis showing that cognitive ability was related to interview outcomes and is a factor in their validity. Dipboye and Gaugler (1993) discussed six factors that are listed in Table 5-3. These factors involve the design of the questions asked, the information available and not available to the interviewer, the ratings made by the interviewer, and the training given to the interviewer. Roth and Campion (1992) found good validity for a structured interview that contained most of the factors noted as important by Dipboye and Gaugler (1993).

WORK SAMPLES

A **work sample** is an assessment device that requires a person to demonstrate how well he or she can perform the tasks involved in a job under standardized conditions. It is a type of simulation in which a person does a job or part of a job under testing conditions rather than actual job conditions.

A work sample is like a psychological test except that it is designed to measure a higher level skill. A test measures a basic skill, such as eye–hand coordination or manual dexterity. A work sample assesses the skill in doing a particular task, such as driving a bulldozer, which is composed of several basic skills performed in the context of a particular set of conditions. For some applications, the higher level skill may be more important to assess than the basic skills because a work sample indicates how well a person can actually do a particular task. The psychological test indicates if a person has the requisite basic skills that should in theory predict how well he or she could do the task.

The typical work sample gives the applicant the materials and tools necessary to accomplish the task. The person is instructed to complete the task quickly but accurately. A score is computed based on the accuracy with which the task is completed and the amount of time it took. For example, a person might be asked to disassemble and reassemble an electric motor or a small gasoline engine. A trained observer would score the person on accuracy and speed. Perhaps the most familiar work sample is the driving test that is required of applicants for a driver's license. The applicant is asked to complete a series of maneuvers with the automobile, while the test administrator records the scores for each one. To get the license, the applicant must achieve a total score that meets a pre-arranged criterion. A work sample in an organizational setting might be used the same way to determine if a person is suitable for a particular job.

Work samples have been found to be good predictors of future job performance (e.g., Hunter & Hunter, 1984; Robertson & Kandola, 1982). The close correspondence between the assessment situation and the job itself certainly has much to do with the success of the work sample in predicting performance. As with most simulation techniques, the work sample has a high degree of job relevance. This increases the likelihood that people will accept their use as predictors of important skills in employee selection.

ASSESSMENT CENTERS

An **assessment center** measures how well a person is able to perform the tasks of a specific job. It consists of several exercises that are designed to simulate various job tasks. Most assessment centers are designed to assess management skills, but they are used for nonmanagement jobs as well. The exercises can take several days to complete and are often administered to several individuals at a time. This technique is widely used by many types of employers. For example, in a survey of British employers, Keenan (1995) found that 44% used assessment centers to hire college graduates. In the United States the assessment center is used primarily for hiring and promotion decisions, although it can also be used to help employees enhance job skills (Spychalski, Quiñones, Gaugler, & Pohley, 1997).

Assessment center exercises have a high level of realism because they simulate many of the actual tasks conducted on the job. For example, the person being assessed, or *assessee*, may be asked to pretend or role play being a manager in a given situation. This might involve dealing with a subordinate or handling the paperwork for the job. The assessee's performance on each exercise is scored by a panel of trained *assessors*. The assessors are asked to evaluate the person's performance on each of several dimensions relevant to the job in question. For a manager's job, these can involve communication, dealing with other people, decision making, and planning. Table 5-4 contains the dimensions from a typical assessment center for managers described by Harris, Becker, and Smith (1993).

TABLE 5-4
Dimensions scored in an assessment center

Oral communication
Oral comprehension
Problem solving
Interpersonal relations
Coaching
Planning
Written communication

Source: "Does the Assessment Center Scoring Method Affect the Cross-Situational Consistency of Ratings?" by M. M. Harris, A. S. Becker, and D. E. Smith, 1993, *Journal of Applied Psychology, 78,* 675–678.

An assessment center can contain many different activities and exercises. The assessee might be interviewed and take a battery of psychological tests, in addition to completing several simulation exercises. The exercises might include an in-basket, a leaderless group exercise, a problem-solving simulation, and role plays. Each exercise yields scores on several dimensions, and usually each dimension is assessed by several exercises. In addition there is an overall assessment of the person's potential for the job in question.

An **in-basket exercise** asks the assessee to pretend that it is the first day of a new job and he or she has found a series of items in his or her in-basket. Items include letters, memos, notes from co-workers, and phone messages. The assessee's task is to deal with each item in an appropriate manner, deciding what action if any to take by making notes on each item. An example of a memo that could be part of an in-basket exercise is shown in Table 5-5. To score well, the person must handle the memo in an appropriate and constructive manner. Ignoring the memo or writing a nasty reply to the sender would not be constructive actions. Leaving a note for the secretary to complete the report or doing so him or herself would be better.

In a **leaderless group exercise** several assessees are given a problem to solve together. The problem might be a competitive one, such as dividing up a scarce resource. Each member of the group might be asked to role play a particular management position. They must decide which department gets a new piece of equipment. The problem can also be a cooperative one, for which all group members must generate a solution to an organizational problem, such as deciding whether or not to market a new product.

In a *problem-solving simulation*, the assessee is given a problem and is asked to come up with a solution, perhaps by producing a report. The problem would provide sufficient background information from which to write the report. For example, the assessee could be given information about the costs and projected income for opening a new assembly plant. His or her task would be to produce a feasibility report for opening the plant.

A *role-play exercise* requires that the assessees pretend to be a particular person in a specific organizational role, such as the manager of human resources. The task is to handle a problem or situation, such as counseling a troubled employee or dealing with an irate customer.

Assessors rate each assessee on each dimension by both observing behavior and reviewing materials produced during all the exercises. Each person will be scored on the various dimensions and may get an overall score. The dimension scores can be used to

TABLE 5-5
Example of a memorandum for an in-basket exercise

Memorandum
TO: Robert Jones, Manager of Marketing
FROM: Deborah Smith, Director of Human Resources
SUBJECT: New Position
On October 15 of this year you requested an additional secretarial position for your department. I have been instructed by the company president to provide you the position. Before I can do so, however, you need to provide me with a complete justification for why you need this position. Please complete a Position Justification Report and return it to me. I need it by the end of the week or the position will be delayed until the first of the year.

give the person feedback about his or her strengths and weaknesses. The overall score is useful if assessment center performance is to be used to make hiring decisions.

Research on the assessment center has found it to be a valid device for the selection of personnel (Gaugler, Rosenthal, Thornton, & Bentson, 1987; Smith & George, 1992). This means that scores on the assessment center are correlated with job performance. For example, Shechtman (1992) found that scores in an assessment center given to university students upon admission predicted their job performance as teachers from two to five years after graduation. McEvoy and Beatty (1989) found that assessment center ratings predicted job performance seven years later for state law enforcement managers.

Although the overall scores in an assessment center have been shown to be valid, questions have been raised about the construct validity of the individual dimension scores (e.g., Brannick, Michaels, & Baker, 1989; Bycio, Alvares, & Hahn, 1987; Chan, 1996; Joyce, Thayer, & Pond, 1994; Robertson, Gratton, & Sharpley, 1987). In other words, we are not certain that the intended dimensions of the assessment center are actually what is being measured. Different exercises are designed to assess a common set of dimensions. Because the same dimensions are assessed across exercises, scores on corresponding dimensions from different exercises should correlate well. For example, the score for leadership in an in-basket should relate to the score for leadership in the leaderless group exercise. On the other hand, the different dimension scores within the same exercise should not be highly correlated, because the dimensions are supposed to be measures of different distinct characteristics. High correlations among dimension ratings are similar to halo errors in performance appraisal (see Chapter 4).

The problem with assessment centers is that the various dimension scores given to assessees within an exercise, such as an in-basket, are too highly correlated. Furthermore, the scores given to assessees on the same dimensions across different exercises are not correlated enough. The high correlations across dimensions within exercises suggest that assessors are assessing only single dimension rather than multiple dimensions. One possibility is that assessors are able to judge only overall exercise performance rather than the individual dimensions. The low correlations between dimensions across exercises suggest that each exercise might assess a different characteristic.

Taken together, both findings raise the possibility that each exercise in an assessment center measures a single trait rather than multiple dimensions, and that the different exercises may assess different things. At the present time, we are not certain exactly what the different KSAOs assessed might be. Thus, use of the assessment center to give specific feedback about individual KSAOs (e.g., decision making or leadership) is questionable. Russell and Domm (1995) provided evidence that ratings reflect how well the individual performs the role for the job simulated rather than how well the person does each dimension. Regardless of why it works, the assessment center does a good job of predicting future job performance. For that reason it is a popular assessment device for selection and placement (see the Research in Detail box).

Research efforts have been made to improve the validity of dimension ratings in assessment centers. Reilly, Henry, and Smither (1990) reasoned that perhaps assessors are unable to adequately assess individual dimensions because they have too much information to process. Each exercise provides a great deal of information, and often that information must be organized in some way for judgments to be made. To help assessors organize information, the researchers provided a checklist of 273 behaviors to use to rate

RESEARCH IN DETAIL

ASSESSMENT CENTERS USE several different types of exercises to measure the various abilities thought to be essential for job success. The idea is to combine scores for each ability across several exercises, which should improve reliability and validity. Research has shown, however, that people's scores on individual ability dimensions from exercise to exercise are not highly correlated. In other words, a person might do well on a dimension (e.g., decision making) on one exercise and poorly on the same dimension on another exercise. This suggests that the assessment center may not measure the intended dimensions. If it did measure individual dimensions of ability, scores should be similar across different exercises.

Chan (1996) conducted a study that illustrates this problem of poor correlations among dimension scores across exercises in an assessment center that still has validity. The study was conducted at the Singapore Police Force, who asked the author to design an assessment center for them. Assessees were 46 officers who were possible candidates for promotion. Six exercises were written, including an in-basket and leaderless group. Fourteen dimensions were assessed, although not every dimension was measured in each exercise. The center was validated against two job performance criteria—current job performance rating and subsequent promotion two years after the assessment.

Correlations were computed among all ratings in the assessment center, both among all measures of the same dimension across exercises and among all ratings within exercises. If the dimension scores were valid, the former should have been larger than the latter. The results were the opposite in that the mean correlation among measures of the same dimension was larger than among measures of different dimensions within exercises (.07 vs. .71, respectively). The lack of significant relation among measures of the same dimensions suggests they measure different things, while the very high correlations among all ratings within exercises reflect a single thing for each exercise.

The assessment center resulted in two overall ratings—overall performance and promotability in the future. Overall performance correlated quite well with actual promotion assessed two years later, but not at all with the most recent performance appraisal by the supervisor. The assessment center rating of promotability also correlated with future promotion strongly and only modestly with supervisor rating of performance. These results demonstrate the validity of the center, even though the exercises did not do an adequate job of assessing what they were initially designed to measure.

Results of this study are quite consistent with many others in showing the doubtful validity of dimension scores. On the other hand, the strong prediction of future promotions was very encouraging. Whereas many assessment center studies are contaminated in that results are used to help determine future promotions, such was not the case here. The assessment center is an effective technique, even though we are not certain what it actually measures.

Source: Chan, D. (1996). Criterion and construct validation of an assessment centre. *Journal of Occupational and Organizational Psychology, 69,* 167–181.

performance in the exercises. The assessors used the checklist to note the specific behaviors performed by each assessee before making their ratings.

The results of the study showed that correlations between dimensions within exercises got smaller, and correlations between corresponding dimensions across exercises got larger than those typically found in assessment centers. Thus, the validities of the dimension scores improved. These results suggest that one problem with assessment centers as they are currently conducted is that they overload the assessor's ability to accurately assess dimensions. By providing checklists of behaviors, structure is put on the judgment task and improves validity of the exercise ratings. These results are promising, but more research needs to be conducted on the use of procedures to improve the accuracy of assessor ratings of assessment center dimensions.

USE OF COMPUTERS IN ASSESSMENT

Computers have had a large impact on many areas of organizations, and assessment is no exception. More and more assessment today involves computers for both the administration and scoring of tests and other devices. In addition, the computer has allowed the development of new types of assessment techniques that would be impossible without them. The future will undoubtedly see many new applications of computers to the assessment of people's characteristics.

Computer Administration of Psychological Tests

Paper-and-pencil psychological tests can be adapted for administration by computer. The test taker can read each item on the screen and respond with the keyboard or mouse. There are two major advantages to this approach. First, the test can be scored automatically as soon as the last item is answered, which can speed up the selection process. Second, a test can be put on an internet website, allowing access from almost anywhere in the world. An applicant doesn't have to come to a particular testing site to take the test. Of course, steps must be taken to monitor test taking so that cheating doesn't occur. There are two major disadvantages (McBride, 1998). First, developing a computer testing system can be expensive and time consuming. Both hardware and software costs can be considerable, especially compared to the small cost of printed test booklets and pencils. The use of computer-scannable answer sheets, however, allows for cheap computer scoring of large numbers of tests, thus eliminating one advantage of computer administration. Second, computerized tests are not necessarily equivalent to printed tests, especially for speeded tests, which time how many correct items a person can do in a given interval. One such test is a clerical speed and accuracy test in which the test taker must compare two strings of letters and indicate if they are the same or not, for example:

abdiel vs. abdifl

ghicbe vs. ghicbe

Response time can be different per item using computer versus paper and pencil for the same items, making scores nonequivalent.

It might seem that computer administration has the potential for increasing the accuracy of personality tests in which people often distort or fake their responses—people are sometimes better able to reveal themselves honestly to a machine, such as a computer, than to another person. A computer might seem more impersonal than a paper-and-pencil test to a test taker. Martin and Nagao (1989) compared the favorability of answers to personality questions administered with a computer or with paper and pencil. The computer administration resulted in less tendency by people to present themselves favorably. King and Miles (1995) found that this occurred only for a measure of impression management, but not other personality scales. Lautenschlager and Flaherty (1990) failed to find any difference between both types of administration. Potosky and Bobko (1997) compared computer administration with paper-and-pencil and found a very high degree of score similarity, suggesting little advantage of computer administration. Although it might seem that people will be more open to revealing themselves to a computer, so far research findings are inconsistent, suggesting that the effect is likely small and limited to certain scales.

Paper-and-pencil tests are not the only assessment technique that can be computerized, for even psychomotor skills can be assessed by computer. Computer versions of typing tests are in widespread use throughout the world. The computer version is no different from the noncomputer version, except that the test taker types on the computer with a word processing program rather than on a typewriter. The major advantage of the computer typing tests is that the scoring is done automatically when the person finishes the test.

An even more complex testing system for secretaries was developed by Schmitt, Gilliland, Landis, and Devine (1993). This system asks the test taker to complete eight "tests" on the computer and provides nine scores. Each of the eight tests is like a work sample in that it represents a simulated task done by a secretary. One test asks the test taker to compose and type a letter to a customer on a word processor. Although the validity of this system remains to be established, it seems likely that such computer assessment systems will be shown to be good predictors of future job performance.

Tailored Testing

Tailored testing selects the specific items given to a test taker according to the person's ability level. Although it is possible to administer tailored tests manually, a computer makes this approach more feasible (Murphy, 1988). A computerized tailored test begins by giving the test taker an item of moderate difficulty. If the person gets the item correct, a more difficult item is presented. If he or she gets is wrong, an easier item is chosen. As the test proceeds, the computer will choose items that are at the appropriate level of difficulty for the particular test taker. Tailored tests can be more efficient than standard tests because they can achieve the same level of reliability with fewer items. Each computer can be used by only one test taker at a time, however, making it difficult for mass testing. Unless tailored testing is shown to produce significantly better validities than paper-and-pencil tests, it is not likely to replace them in the near future.

FUTURE ISSUES AND CHALLENGES

The computer will undoubtedly produce the biggest changes in assessment in the future. So far the computer has been used primarily to administer and score tests. Most computerized tests are not much different from paper-and-pencil tests, and often a computerized test is just a paper-and-pencil test administered electronically (Bartram, 1994). The computer's tremendous potential to allow for new types of tests and new types of assessment methods is just beginning to be explored, although to date this potential has gone unrealized (McBride, 1998). A computer can be used to simulate many different job situations and tasks. The same technology that is used for computer games could be used to create an organizational simulation. Computer games that simulate piloting an airplane and performing surgery already exist. Extensions of such simulators might serve as assessment devices to assess critical KSAOs.

Computer software could be developed that would simulate many of the situations encountered on a real job. For example, a manager simulation could require that the person perform many of the tasks of a real manager, such as assigning people to tasks, deciding what to purchase, planning a budget, and scheduling people's work. Technological advances will allow the computer to create virtual reality simulations of organizational situations that will appear quite real to the person being assessed. The person will be able to hear and see subordinates and will be able to hold conversations with them as if they were really present. The high level of realism should provide good prediction of how a person would respond to the real situation.

CHAPTER SUMMARY

One of the major tasks I/O psychologists do for organizations is the assessment of people's characteristics for selection and placement. These characteristics can be classified as the knowledge, skill, ability, and other personal characteristics or KSAOs necessary for successful performance on the job.

The five major assessment methods used to assess KSAOs are:

Psychological test   Work sample

Biographical inventory   Assessment center

Interview

A psychological test is a standardized series of problems or questions given to a person to assess a particular individual characteristic. Tests are commonly used to assess many KSAOs, including knowledge, skill, ability, attitudes, interests, and personality.

The biographical inventory asks for detailed information about the person's past experience, both on and off the job. It asks for far more extensive information than the typical job application form.

An interview is a face-to-face meeting between one or more interviewers who are collecting information or making hiring decisions and an interviewee. During an unstructured interview, the interviewer asks whatever questions come to mind. By contrast, during a structured interview, the interviewer has a preplanned series of questions that are asked of every person who is interviewed. In both types, the interviewer often makes overall judgments about the interviewee's suitability for the job.

A work sample is an assessment device that requires a person to demonstrate how well he or she can perform job tasks under standardized conditions. It is a type of simulation in which a person does a job or part of a job under testing conditions rather than actual job conditions.

The assessment center consists of several different types of exercises that take place over one or more days. Although most assessment centers are used to identify future management potential, they can be used to assess the potential of people for many different types of jobs.

Computers are rapidly being introduced as tools to assist in assessment. Although so far most computer tests have been electronic versions of paper-and-pencil tests, researchers are beginning to develop new types of assessment devices that make full use of the computer's capabilities.

I/O PSYCHOLOGY IN PRACTICE

THIS CASE CONCERNS the development of an assessment center that is used by a consulting company to assess executives who come from a wide range of industries and countries. Dr. Paul Van Katwyk has been involved in the development and implementation of this new executive assessment center in his role as senior consultant at one of the world's largest I/O consulting firms, Personnel Decisions International, PDI. Dr. Van Katwyk received his master's degree in I/O psychology from the University of Guelph in Canada and his Ph.D. from the University of South Florida in 1996. He began working for PDI in 1995 as a consultant in the Assessment Solutions team which is responsible for developing assessment systems for organizations. In 1997 Dr. Van Katwyk accepted an assignment  to work in its Tokyo office where he delivers a wide range of I/O consulting services throughout Asia. The primary focus of these services is on assessment and coaching for managers and executives who are expatriates (working outside of their native countries) or who work within multinational organizations. He is also responsible for helping to develop new assessment tools for use in Asia.

PDI has been developing executive-level assessment centers throughout its 30-year history. Some centers are custom designed for a client organization, but PDI also offers some standard centers that have already been developed. The advantage of a standard center is that it is less expensive and quicker, for the client does not have to pay the cost of a time-consuming development effort, but the standard center is not always appropriate. When executives or potential executives are referred for assessment, the consultants must first determine if the standard center fits the requirements of the particular job in question. If this is the case, the assessees are sent to one of the 22 PDI offices worldwide for a one- to two-day assessment, including psychological testing, some simulations (e.g., in-basket or leaderless group discussion), and structured interviews. These assessment centers can be used for selection/placement of individuals into jobs or for development (helping people improve their job skills). The latter are more time consuming, for assessees are given extensive feedback throughout the process.

In recent years, it had become apparent that the standard assessment center was becoming dated. Globalization of PDI's business and rapid organizational change resulted in significant KSAO changes for the executive job. The challenge was to design a center that would be appropriate for people working in rapidly evolving, multinational companies. To accomplish this, several psychologists compiled results of studies done in many organizations to identify changing KSAOs needed for management jobs, and

(Continued next page)

I/O PSYCHOLOGY IN PRACTICE

interviewed senior consultants who were experts on executive assessment. They devised a list of KSAOs needed for a variety of executive positions, and designed exercises (e.g., in-basket or role play) for the center. To allow more flexibility, a menu system was devised. Rather than having a fixed number of exercises for each assessment, the consultant is able to match exercises to the job requirements for each situation. This allows much broader applicability, since not every job requires every KSAO.

Dr. Van Katwyk was a member of the new assessment center development team and helped design the exercises. He was also involved in introducing the assessment center concept to the Tokyo office of PDI. This included training the staff and also being one of the lead consultants in some of the first executive assessments done in Asia using this new assessment center. Currently, given the growing business with Japanese firms, the PDI office in Japan has completed a Japanese translation of the new executive assessment center. The assessment center is also being translated into several European languages as it is rolled out throughout PDI's offices in Europe.

Discussion Questions

1. Does it take the same KSAOs to be an executive in an American versus Japanese corporation?

2. How can we make sure that an assessment center yields comparable results when we use it in other countries or translate it into different languages?

3. Why would a company go to the expense of sending an executive to a developmental assessment center?

4. Why are the large US I/O consulting firms like PDI expanding overseas?

5. What sorts of challenges would an I/O consultant face moving from the United States to Japan or another Asian country?

Part Three

SELECTING AND TRAINING
EMPLOYEES

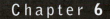

SELECTING EMPLOYEES

Imagine that you are a manager for a large organization and you have to hire a new employee. In many organizations it is the manager's responsibility to decide whom to hire. Often the manager determines the type of person needed for a job and decides which of several job applicants is best suited for a job. If you were in this situation, how would you go about making the decision? You would be fortunate if your organization employed an I/O psychologist to help with this important function. In fact, help with employee selection is one of the major contributions of the I/O field. As we have discussed in Chapters 3 and 5, I/O psychologists have many tools available to assist them in employee selection.

Two of the most important functions of any organization are the recruitment and selection of employees. The health and well-being of an organization depend in large part on a steady flow of new people. Employees must be hired to fill newly created positions and to replace people who have left. Acquiring new employees can be a costly and difficult undertaking. It involves the following four steps (Figure 6-1):

Planning the need for new employees

Getting appropriate people to apply for positions (recruitment)

Deciding whom to hire (selection)

Getting the selected people to take the jobs

Employee recruitment and selection involve legal issues in many countries, particularly Canada and the United States. As we have already discussed, there are strictly enforced laws in some countries prohibiting discrimination in actions that affect employees. The most frequent target of equal employment opportunity efforts has been the hiring process. An I/O psychologist who gets involved in employee selection must be an expert in the legal issues concerning selection.

In this chapter, we discuss how organizations recruit and select new employees, using the four steps listed earlier and shown in Figure 6-1. Most of the efforts of I/O psychologists involve selection, so we spend more time on that topic than the others. This is not to say, however, that the selection step is the most important. Rather, it is selection that has been the major focus of I/O practice and research

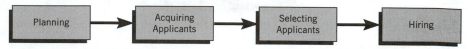

FIGURE 6-1

Four steps for acquiring new employees.

since the beginning of the field. In addition to the four steps, we discuss the value or utility of the scientific approach to selection. We also cover the legal issues involved in employee recruitment and selection from the perspective of civil rights legislation.

Objectives   **The student who studies this chapter should be able to:**
1. Explain how organizations conduct human resource planning.
2. Discuss methods of recruitment.
3. Explain the steps involved in conducting a validation study.
4. Describe how scientific approaches to selection can have utility for organizations.
5. Relate the principles of legal selection.

THE PLANNING OF HUMAN RESOURCE NEEDS

In order for an organization to stay healthy, it must have a steady supply of human resources or people. These human resources are necessary to fill vacancies created by people who leave the organization. They are also needed to fill new positions that are created by organizational changes or expansion. To do a good job in recruiting the people needed by an organization, careful planning is necessary. Human resource plans must include both a consideration of the organization's needs for people and the supply of possible people to hire (Cascio, 1987).

Forecasts of human resource demands usually list the number of people needed in each job category, such as number of clerks or teachers. Table 6-1 is an example of a projection that might be made by a manufacturing organization that is facing a gradual automation of its factories. The number of assembly-line workers needed declines steadily, while the number of technicians registers a corresponding increase. This is a common trend in industry, and it is important that organizations plan for reduction in one type of employee and increase in another. The organization can take a variety of actions to deal with the shifting nature of jobs and job requirements. The selection approach would re-

TABLE 6-1

Projections of employees needed for an organization undergoing automation of its manufacturing processes

JOB CLASSIFICATION	NOW	YEAR 1	YEAR 2	YEAR 3	YEAR 4
Assemblers	20,000	16,000	10,000	5,000	4,000
Technicians	20	200	400	600	1,000

TABLE 6-2

Sources of labor market information for the United States

Bureau of Labor Statistics of the U.S. Department of Labor
Engineering Manpower Commission
National Science Foundation
Office of Education
Public Health Service of the Department of Health and Human Services
U.S. Employment Service

Source: From *Applied Psychology in Personnel Management,* 3rd ed. (p. 224), by W. F. Cascio, 1987. Englewood Cliffs, NJ: Prentice Hall.

place assemblers with technicians. The training approach would turn assemblers into technicians. The first approach can be less expensive because it would cost more to provide training to employees who continue to get paid while they are learning a new job. The second approach has the advantage of doing the least harm to current employees. It provides considerable benefits to individuals who are given a new and more marketable skill. A training approach is necessary, however, when there is an inadequate supply of people with the necessary skills in the labor market.

The supply of people to hire in the labor market can be estimated in a variety of ways. Organizations can keep track of the number of people who apply for various positions. In addition, governmental agencies provide information about the number of available workers in different job categories. In the United States, several agencies provide this sort of information (Table 6-2). A comparison of the demand and supply of people for various jobs is an important component in choosing between a selection or training approach to meeting future human resource needs.

Both the globalization of the world economy and technological advances have produced tremendous shifts in the demand for people with various job-related skills. The demand for semiskilled and unskilled assemblers in factories has been declining in industrialized countries such as Canada and the United States. Highly skilled technical jobs have been increasing. Table 6-3 shows some trends for several categories of jobs in the United States through the year 2005. Demand is expected to decline for jobs in manufacturing and mining. Demand should increase for jobs in health-related fields and in re-

TABLE 6-3

Labor market trends in the United States, 1979, 1992, and 2005

OCCUPATIONAL CATEGORY	1979	1992	2005
Agriculture	3,398[a]	3,295	3,325
Construction	3,363	4,471	5,632
Government	15,947	18,653	22,021
Manufacturing	21,040	18,040	17,523
Mining	958	631	562
Service	47,083	66,093	87,222

[a]Thousands of people in the workforce.

Source: Projections for 2005 were from Franklin's moderate category. From "Industry Output and Employment," by J. C. Franklin, 1993, *Monthly Labor Review,* 116, 41–57.

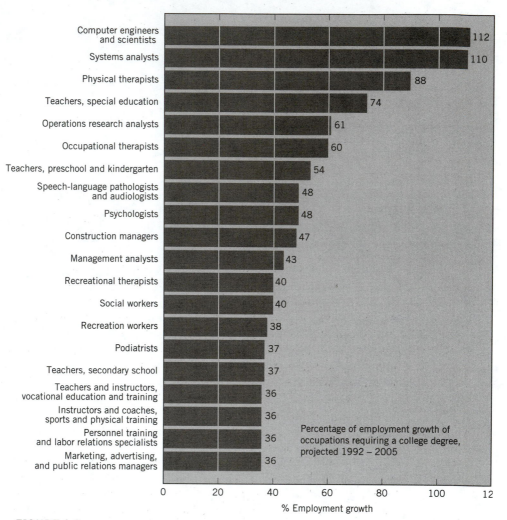

FIGURE 6-2

Fastest growing occupations requiring a college degree in the United States. Note that more than half are in the educational or medical-related occupations. Psychologists are listed ninth. Personnel training and labor relations specialists, which are relevant to the I/O field, are on the list. *Source:* From *Occupational Outlook Quarterly* (p. 42), by U.S. Department of Labor, 1993, Washington, DC: U.S. Government Printing Office.

tailing, such as in restaurants. Figure 6-2 shows the 20 fastest growing occupations in the United States requiring a college degree, projected from 1992 to 2005.

RECRUITING APPLICANTS

A challenge for many organizations is getting people to apply for available positions. To be able to hire good people, an organization must have a large number of possible employees from whom to choose. For some jobs it may be relatively easy to recruit applicants. For jobs in which there is an undersupply of people, an organization must expend considerable effort to attract the right people to fill their job vacancies. Several methods can be used to recruit applicants for a vacant position. Some require little effort, such as placing an advertisement in a local newspaper. Other actions may require the full-time efforts of one or more people, such as using college recruiters to interview potential employees across the country.

Five possible sources of applicants that are commonly used by organizations are

Advertising	School recruiters
Employee referral	Walk-ins
Employment agencies	

The choice of sources depends on the ease with which organizations can recruit applicants. Some organizations find that they get enough walk-in applicants to cover the jobs that they have, so more time-consuming methods are unnecessary. (A walk-in applicant is someone who applies for a job on his or her own without action on the part of the organization.) In competitive job markets, however, many organizations might be attempting to attract the same individuals. Here time-consuming methods might be necessary to attract the people who are needed.

The different sources of job applicants do not necessarily attract the same quality of applicant. Taylor and Schmidt (1983), for example, found that the attendance and performance of new hires depended on their source. In their study, applicants who were referred by employees had better attendance than applicants who were recruited from other sources. They noted that their results were somewhat different from those of prior studies. Thus, it seems that whereas there may be differences in the sorts of people acquired from different sources, no one source is superior in all situations.

The efforts made to recruit good applicants should be based on a detailed specification of the knowledge, skill, ability, and other person characteristics or KSAOs needed for a job (see Chapter 3). When the KSAOs are specified in advance, organizational efforts can be directed toward recruiting the right applicants, thereby increasing the efficiency of recruitment. For example, if an organization needs people who have computer skills, efforts can be centered in areas where such people are expected to be, such as large universities. On the other hand, if the organization needs a large supply of manual laborers, an area with a high unemployment rate because of factory closings might be a good place to look.

SELECTING EMPLOYEES

If an organization is lucky, it will have many more good applicants than the number of vacant jobs. As we will see in this section, the more selective an organization can be, the better the chances that the person hired will be a good employee. This is because many of the employee selection procedures developed by I/O psychologists work best when there are several applicants from whom to choose. These procedures are based on complex mathematical and statistical methodologies, which are beyond the scope of this book. We limit this discussion to the major concepts of selection and omit discussion of the statistical details. We first discuss the criterion-related validity approach to employee selection taken by I/O psychologists. This approach is based on scientific principles and statistics.

We then briefly discuss alternative procedures that are often used because of practical considerations. Next we cover the utility of our selection techniques. Utility is concerned with the benefits that organizations achieve from using scientific selection.

How Do We Select Employees?

The purpose of employee selection is to hire people who are likely to be successful on the job. To do so, several approaches can be taken. Perhaps the most often used approach is to have a manager interview the applicants and decide subjectively whom to hire. Purely subjective hiring procedures are likely to be biased and inaccurate. A better approach is to use scientific methods that have been shown to work in almost a century of research on employee selection.

Two important elements in employee selection must be considered. First is the *criterion*, which is the definition of a good employee. Although it may seem obvious that we hire the person who is expected to be the best performer, it is not easy to define what we mean by good performance. Job performance involves many different aspects. Some employees may work very accurately, whereas others work very fast. It is not always easy to decide if we should hire based on one aspect of the criterion (e.g., attendance) or another (e.g., work quantity). These issues were discussed at length in Chapter 4. To use scientific selection methods, we first must know what the criterion is for the job in question.

The second element is the *predictor*, which is anything that relates to the criterion. In Chapter 5 we discussed several methods for assessing characteristics that are relevant to job requirements. These techniques can be used to assess KSAOs that are necessary for job success. Measures of KSAOs can be used as predictors of a criterion of job performance. Knowledge of the subject matter, for example, should be a good predictor for the job performance of a classroom teacher. It is not the only predictor, for knowledge alone does not make someone a good teacher.

Determining if a given predictor relates to a criterion requires a *validation study*, which is a research study that attempts to show that the predictor relates to the criterion. To conduct this sort of study, both the criterion and predictor are quantified. Data are collected for a group of employees on both the criterion and the predictor variables. Because they are both quantified, a statistical test can be conducted to see if they are significantly related. The correlation coefficient indicates how well the two variables relate to each other. If the two variables are significantly related, you can conclude that the predictor is

FRANK & ERNEST ® by Bob Thaves

valid in terms of the criterion. The implication is that you could use information about the predictor to forecast the applicant's likely performance on the job.

Conducting a good validation study is a complex and difficult undertaking. First, you must carefully analyze the job and job requirements using job analysis. The results of the job analysis can be used to develop criteria for the job and to pick predictors. Data are collected to verify that the chosen predictors are valid. Valid predictors will become part of the organization's employee selection system. We discuss this process in greater detail in the next section of the chapter.

Conducting a Validation Study

Conducting a validation study involves five steps:

1. Conduct a job analysis
2. Specify job performance criteria
3. Choose predictors
4. Validate the predictors
5. Cross-validate

Conducting a job analysis provides the information needed to proceed with the next two steps of specifying criteria and choosing predictors. Once these steps are completed, data can be collected on a sample of employees to determine if the criteria are related to the predictors. If they are, the results must be replicated on a second sample to verify the results. The five steps are illustrated in Figure 6-3.

Step 1: Conduct a Job Analysis. As we discussed in Chapter 3, a job analysis provides information about the tasks involved in a job. It also provides information about the characteristics (KSAOs) an employee needs to be successful on a job. These two types of information are not independent, for the specification of KSAOs often is derived from an analysis of the tasks required for the job.

As we discuss later in the section on legal issues, an important concept in employee selection is job relevance—the correspondence between the KSAOs needed for job success and the KSAOs of the job applicant. For successful and legal selection, the two types of KSAO requirements should correspond. Hiring people with characteristics that are not related to the job requirements would be foolish at best and illegal at worst if it results in discrimination. Thus, it would make sense to hire on the basis of physical strength if the

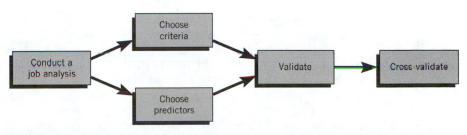

FIGURE 6-3
The five steps for conducting a validation study.

job requires heavy lifting, such as a dock worker. It makes little sense to have a strength requirement for schoolteachers.

A job analysis can be used in many ways as the basis for a validation study. The job analysis can identify the major components of the job. Next, an analysis can be done to specify the KSAOs necessary to accomplish each component. From this information a list of performance criteria and predictors can be made.

For example, for a manager's job one major component might be managing a budget. Managers often have to develop budgets and manage their resources so that they do not exceed them. One KSAO that would be important for managing a budget is knowledge of basic mathematics, such as addition and subtraction. People hired to be managers should have this basic knowledge.

Step 2: Specify Job Performance Criteria. Once you have a good idea about what a job entails, you can begin to develop criteria for good job performance. For example, if a manager is required to manage a budget, a reasonable criterion might be how well the manager stayed within the budget. There can be many reasons for not staying within the budget, so this criterion alone is not sufficient for evaluating how well a person performs the job. However, for a validation study we are interested in using criteria that might be predicted by one or more of our predictors. For example, if a test of mathematical ability is found to predict how well a manager can stay within a budget, then we can expect to hire managers who do better on the criterion if the test is used to help select them.

Step 3: Choose Predictors. As we develop our criteria for a job, we also choose potential predictors of job performance on those criteria. Potential predictors might be chosen to assess KSAOs directly, as with a psychological test of mathematical ability. Other predictors might be less direct as measures of a KSAO. We often assume that college graduates have certain knowledge and ability, such as being able to do basic mathematics and to write in their native language. Using education level as a predictor can eliminate the need to assess many KSAO requirements for a job. This is why many organizations prefer to hire college graduates. Care must be taken, however, that requiring a college degree is reasonable for the job in question. A degree would be overkill if the job required only basic arithmetic and a fourth-grade reading level.

In Chapter 5 we discussed five methods that can be used to assess KSAOs. All these methods are frequently used as predictors in validation studies and have been shown to be valid predictors of job performance:

Assessment centers	Psychological tests
Biographical inventories	Work samples
Interviews	

These tools might predict other nonperformance criteria, such as job satisfaction. Although few organizations select employees based on the likelihood that they will enjoy the job, it is possible to conduct a validation study to find appropriate and valid predictors. Criteria chosen for validity studies usually are concerned with an aspect of job performance or other behavior that is directly related to accomplishment of organizational objectives.

Step 4: Validate the Predictors. After the criteria and predictors are chosen, the data collection phase of the validation study can proceed. In this step, measures of the criterion and the predictors are taken on a sample of people to see if the predictor relates to the criterion. A good field test of the predictor is done in the organizational setting in which it is expected to be used in the future. Most validation studies are done in actual organizational settings as opposed to laboratory settings. In the laboratory you might determine that a human attribute relates to task performance, but you cannot be certain that it will generalize to the organization. By conducting field studies in the settings in which selection tools will ultimately be used, the likelihood of generalization is maximized.

There are two types of study designs for conducting a validation study. In a **concurrent validation study** both the criterion and predictor scores are collected from a sample of subjects at more or less the same point in time. Usually, the subjects are current employees who are assessed on both criteria and predictors. A sample of employees might be asked to provide predictor data by taking an assessment test. Test scores would then be correlated with subjects' most recent performance evaluation. If the two are related, we assume that scores on the predictor at the time of application for a job will predict later performance on the job.

In a **predictive validity study**, the predictor is measured before the criterion. A sample of job applicants might be given the predictor assessment. They would then be hired and some time later assessed on the criterion or criteria. The time span between predictor and criterion assessment could be months or years. The predictor scores would be correlated with the criterion scores to see if the predictor can forecast later criterion scores. If it can predict future performance, we can have reasonable confidence in the predictor as a valid selection device.

It might seem that the predictive design would be superior to the concurrent in validating predictors because the predictive design tests the predictor on applicants rather than employees who already have been selected and trained. Because the predictor is used on applicants, generalizability should be maximized. Research has shown, however, that the two designs are equally effective in validating predictors. Validity coefficients, the correlation between scores on the criterion and predictor, have been found to be about the same in studies using the two different types of designs (Schmitt, Gooding, Noe, & Kirsch, 1984). This is good news for organizations because predictive designs take too long to conduct. You might have to wait a year after collecting predictor scores to collect criterion scores. Furthermore, for some organizations it could take months or years before a sufficient number of people are hired to conduct the analysis. A concurrent study can be conducted in as little as a few days if the predictor can be administered quickly and the criterion scores are readily available.

Step 5: Cross-Validate. The final step in a validation study is to **cross-validate** or replicate the results of one sample with those of another sample. This is done to be certain that our results are not due to a statistical error as opposed to a real correlation between the criterion and predictor. In any study involving statistics, significance can occur by chance as opposed to real relations among the variables of interest. Such statistical errors are called Alpha or Type 1 errors. To protect ourselves from making an error in our conclusions about whether or not a predictor can forecast a criterion, we cross-validate or repeat our analyses on another sample of subjects. It is extremely unlikely that we will find the same results twice if there is no relation among the variables of interest. In other words, two successive Alpha errors are unlikely.

To conduct a cross-validation, we need two samples. The first sample is used to determine if the criterion and predictor are significantly correlated. A second sample is used to see if the significant relation found in the first sample can be repeated on the second. The predictor is validated on the first sample and then double checked or cross-validated on the second. Cross-validation adds to our confidence that the predictor can forecast the criterion or criteria of interest.

Validity Generalization

At times it is not necessary to collect data to validate a selection test or other device. Selection tests that are valid in one setting are often valid in many other settings. **Validity generalization** means that validities of selection devices are generalizable or transportable from job to job and organization to organization (Schmidt & Hunter, 1977). If a test predicts performance for a secretary in one organization, for example, it will predict for a secretary in another organization.

The idea of validity generalization has been widely accepted among I/O psychologists as long as the jobs and tests in question are comparable. If you validate a test for the selection of people in a particular job, the test should also be valid for the same job in a different organization. It should also be valid for a job that has the same KSAO requirements. If the second job is different from the job for which the test was valid, the test may or may not be valid. The only way to be certain would be to conduct a validation study on the second job to determine if the test predicts the criterion.

How Predictor Information Is Used for Selection

Once it is determined that a predictor or predictors are valid forecasters of future performance criteria, it must be decided how best to use the predictor information. Two popular uses of predictor information are as hurdles or as predictors in a regression equation. With either approach multiple predictors can be used in combination. Often prediction is better with several rather than single predictors because multiple KSAOs are necessary for job success.

Multiple Hurdles. The **multiple hurdle** approach sets a criterion for each predictor. If an applicant achieves that criterion, then the hurdle is passed. For example, a computer salesperson should have several KSAOs in order to be successful on the job. One obvious KSAO is knowledge of computer principles. Completion of a college degree in computers could serve as an indicator of the KSAO, and the applicant would pass this hurdle. Another important KSAO might be communication skills so that the person can relate well to customers. This might be assessed with a communication skills exercise. Applicants would have to have a passing score on the communication exercise to pass this hurdle.

It is efficient to use multiple hurdles in a specified order and eliminate applicants as the assessment process goes from hurdle to hurdle. For example, only those computer sales applicants with college degrees would be given the communication skills exercise. It would make financial sense to order the predictors in terms of cost from least to most expensive. Many organizations use relatively inexpensive preliminary screening methods as hurdles so that expensive assessments are not used with people who easily could have been screened out earlier in the process.

Regression Approach. The *regression approach* uses the score from each predictor in an equation to provide a numerical estimate of the criterion. With the computer sales job, an equation could predict the actual dollar amount of sales per month. Predictors for that job might be grade point average (GPA) in college and scores on the communication exercise. Both quantitative variables (GPA and exercise score) can be combined mathematically to provide predicted criterion scores (e.g., monthly sales). Individuals who are forecasted to have the best criterion scores would be those who are hired.

With a single-predictor variable, a linear regression equation is calculated from a sample of data. To compute an equation, you must have data on both the criterion and the predictor so that you can compare how well the predicted criterion scores match the real criterion scores. The general form of a linear regression equation is

$$Y = b \times X + a$$

where X is the predictor, Y is the criterion, b is the slope, and a is the intercept. When the equation is used, a and b are known quantities. A predicted value for the criterion (Y) can be computed by replacing X with values of the predictor.

The regression equation is developed from the data of a validation study. In addition to the correlation coefficient, a regression equation can be computed for a sample of data on a criterion and predictor. As noted earlier, this equation provides a means of predicting the criterion from the predictor. For example, monthly sales for a salesperson might be predicted from scores on the communication exercise. The most accurate prediction might be achieved from a regression equation such as the following:

Sales = $400 × Exercise Score + $2000

In this equation, a is $2000 and b is $400. If a person had an exercise score of 10, his or her sales would be predicted to be $6000:

Sales = $400 × 10 + $2000

Sales = $6000

If another person had a test score of 5, his or her sales would be predicted to be $4000:

Sales = $400 × 5 + $2000

Sales = $4000

Obviously, the first person would be preferred because his or her predicted performance is higher.

A similar procedure is applied when there are two or more predictors. This case involves the use of multiple correlation and multiple regression. Multiple correlation is the correlation between a criterion and two or more predictors. The multiple correlation coefficient is indicated by an R. Multiple regression is a statistical technique that provides an equation relating two or more predictors to a criterion. The equation can be used to forecast the criterion from scores on the predictors. In many cases, several predictors combined can provide a more accurate prediction of the criterion than any of them alone.

The general form of a multiple regression equation is

$$Y = (b_1 \times X_1) + (b_2 \times X_2) + a$$

for the two predictor case. In this equation the Xs are predictors, Y is the criterion, a is the intercept, and the bs are regression coefficients. The coefficients and intercept are computed from sample data. The equation is used by substituting values of the predictors for the Xs. A predicted value for the criterion is computed.

For example, we can combine the scores on the communication exercise with GPA in college. Assume that both of these predictors relate to sales performance. Combined they might provide more accurate forecasts than either one alone. If each predictor had a correlation of .40 with sales, both combined would likely have a multiple correlation that is greater than .40. The magnitude of the multiple correlation is a function of how strongly each predictor variable correlates with the criterion variable and how strongly the predictor variables correlate with one another. The multiple correlation will have the largest value when the predictor variables are uncorrelated. This would show that combined the predictors are more accurate than either one alone in forecasting the criterion.

A multiple regression analysis would provide an equation that would predict sales from both the exercise score and college grade point average. The equation could be used to forecast the sales from scores on the two predictors. Suppose that the predictor equation was the following:

$$\text{Sales} = (\$2000 \times \text{GPA}) + (\$1000 \times \text{Exercise}) + \$2000$$

In this equation, a is $2000, and the bs are $2000 and $1000. To use the equation, multiply GPA by $2000 and add it to the exercise score multiplied by $1000. To this total add $2000. The resulting number is an estimate of the person's future monthly sales. If a person had a college GPA of 2.0 and an exercise score of 4, his or her forecasted sales would be $10,000. A person with a 4.0 college GPA and an exercise score of 10 would be predicted to have sales of $20,000.

The magnitude of relation between the predictors and criterion determines how accurate the prediction is likely to be. If the predictors correlate strongly with the criterion, the predicted values for sales are likely to be fairly accurate. If the predictors do not correlate very well with the criterion, the predictions will not be very accurate. Even when predictors relate to criteria modestly, using the scientific approach we have discussed can still result in hiring better performing employees than using nonscientific approaches.

Every regression equation must be cross-validated to be sure that it continues to make reasonably accurate predictions. An equation that is generated on a sample of data will make the most accurate predictions possible for that sample. The same equation will not likely be as accurate when used on a second sample for statistical reasons that are beyond the scope of this book. To perform a cross-validation, the equation generated from one sample of data is applied to a second sample of data. Usually, the accuracy of prediction will be reduced when using the first sample equation on the second sample. If the regression equation yields nonsignificant results when used on a second sample, it should not be used.

An implication of using the regression approach is that a low score on one predictor can be compensated for by a high score on another. The multiple hurdle approach avoids this problem because an applicant must reach the criterion for each predictor. This can be important because a person often must have a reasonable level on every KSAO even if some KSAOs are very high. For example, in selecting a surgeon there are two equally important KSAOs. He or she must have the knowledge of how to operate and the manual skill to do so. A high level of one KSAO cannot overcome a deficiency in the other. Skill with a scalpel is insufficient if the surgeon does not know where to cut. The limitation of the regression approach can be overcome by combining it with the hurdles. First, applicants would be screened using the hurdles. A regression equation would then be applied only to those who made it past the hurdles.

Alternatives to Conducting Validation Studies. Most organizations select employees without going through costly and time-consuming validation studies. Organizations do not always hire enough people to conduct such studies, which can require more than 100 subjects to do properly. Other times organizations do not wish to invest the money or time to conduct these studies. For an organization with hundreds of different jobs, it could cost millions of dollars to conduct validation studies for every position.

An alternative approach is to rely on the established validity of selection tools that can be linked to KSAO requirements. With this approach one conducts a job analysis to determine KSAOs. Established methods to assess each KSAO are then chosen. If the job analysis results indicate that cognitive ability is needed, an existing cognitive ability test could be chosen. This approach relies heavily on existing research findings concerning the validities of existing methods. It does not involve data collection to test for validity of predictors. An organization can often rely on validity generalization results to help guide its choice of selection methods.

It is possible to purchase existing selection devices that have been developed elsewhere. Psychological testing companies have validated tests for sale to organizations. As we discussed in Chapter 5, many tests exist to assess hundreds of different characteristics. It is even possible to hire members of consulting firms to administer all sorts of assessments, including assessment centers, interviews, simulation exercises, and tests. Sometimes it is less expensive for an organization to buy assessment services than do their own. This is likely to be true with a small company that has few people to assess.

No matter how selection decisions are made, once it is decided whom to hire, procedures must be initiated to get that person to take the job. An organization has many ways to entice a person to join it, including offering fringe benefits or restructuring the job to suit the individual. One procedure that is often used is the realistic job preview, which we discuss next.

GETTING APPLICANTS TO ACCEPT AND KEEP JOB OFFERS

The recruitment job is not over when it is decided who will be offered a job. The next step is being sure that the applicants that an organization wishes to hire are interested in accepting the job offer. Installing the most accurate selection system possible is of little value if the applicants who are identified as potentially good employees will not take the job that is offered. Of equal importance is ensuring that individuals who take a job do not quit in a short period of time because they find that they do not like the job.

Convincing an applicant to accept a job involves several strategies. First, it is important that salary offers are comparable to those of other organizations for similar jobs in the same area. One way to make sure that offers are competitive is to conduct a salary survey to find out what other organizations are paying. This is done by contacting organizations and asking them what they pay for particular positions.

A second approach is to negotiate salary and other rewards with the potential employee. Many organizations are flexible in their benefits and salaries and may be able to tailor them to the demands of applicants. One such approach is the cafeteria benefits program, in which employees are allowed to choose their benefits from a long list of possibilities, such as different types of insurance policies. Organizations can also offer flexibility in the content of jobs so that a potential employee can modify the job to his or her liking.

In attempting to attract a potential employee, care must be taken so that the conditions are presented honestly. Providing a false positive view of an organization can result

RESEARCH IN DETAIL

FIELD EXPERIMENTS ARE difficult to conduct in organizational settings. This study by Meglino et al. (1993) is an example of a field experiment that was conducted over a relatively long period of time. Its purpose was to investigate the effects of a realistic job preview (RJP) on the turnover of employees who varied in experience on the job in question. Although many studies have shown the effects of realistic job previews on turnover, these researchers thought that the effects would differ between experienced and inexperienced employees.

Subjects were applicants for the job of correctional officer who were randomly assigned either to receive or not to receive the realistic job preview. The subjects were further divided into two groups depending on their prior experience in a similar job. Data were collected concerning whether or not the applicant took the job and how long each applicant stayed on the job. Thus, there were two dependent variables—job acceptance and job survival.

The results showed that the impact of the RJP was different for the experienced and inexperienced applicant groups. The experienced applicants were less likely to take the job if they were exposed to the RJP. They were more likely to quit the job during a three- to nine-month probationary period, and they were less likely to quit after the probationary period if they were given the realistic job preview. The inexperienced applicants were more likely to accept the job after seeing the RJP. The RJP had no significant effect on their turnover rate. These results show that the effects of the RJP might not be the same on everyone. Perhaps the RJP was more meaningful to experienced applicants who had a context in which to interpret the information. They knew that a particular feature of the job would be unpleasant, even though it might not initially seem to be so. Results also show that the effects can differ over time. Positive effects on turnover might not occur immediately.

Overall, it has been found that RJPs can be an effective and relatively inexpensive way of decreasing unwanted employee turnover. This study shows that organizations should consider carefully the characteristics of applicants when deciding to implement a preview because they might not reduce turnover for experienced employees.

Source: Meglino, B. M., DeNisi, A. S., & Ravlin, E. C. (1993). Effects of previous job exposure and subsequent job status on the functioning of a realistic job preview. *Personnel Psychology, 46,* 803–822.

in high turnover as new employees find that conditions are not as favorable as they were presented to be. A person may find that the job is intolerable because of some situation that he or she did not know about at the time the job was accepted. For example, a person may not have been told that the job involved extensive travel during the summer. A person who finds that job conditions are unacceptable will be likely to quit. Recruitment will have to begin again to find a replacement.

The **realistic job preview (RJP)** is used to give job applicants accurate information about the job and the organization. It is most typically accomplished with a brochure or videotaped presentation (Wanous, 1989). A good RJP provides an accurate view of both the favorable and unfavorable aspects of a job, so that a person who accepts a job will do so with accurate and realistic expectations. A person who knows what he or she is going to encounter will be more likely to remain on a job if unfavorable, but anticipated, conditions arise. If conditions exist that a person cannot tolerate, he or she will refuse the job offer. Another person who is willing to accept the situation will be hired and will be more likely to stay on the job.

Research with the RJP has shown that it is effective in achieving its objectives. Premack and Wanous (1985) conducted a meta-analysis of 21 RJP experiments conducted in organizations. This mathematical analysis of the results of these studies indicated that RJPs reduce initial expectations about the job and organization and lower subsequent employee turnover. They also reduce the number of employees who accept job offers by the organization. RJPs can increase job performance and job satisfaction, probably because people who would have been unhappy on a job are screened out before they accept the job. Those who accept the job are likely to have less favorable but probably more realistic perceptions of the organization because of the RJP.

A more recent study showed that the effects of an RJP can be complicated by the job experience of applicants. Meglino, DeNisi, and Ravlin (1993) conducted a field experiment in which applicants for a correctional officer position were assigned to either an RJP or a control condition without an RJP. Applicants in each group were classified according to prior experience as a correctional officer. The results showed that the impact of the RJP was different for the experienced and inexperienced applicant groups (see the Research in Detail box). These results show that the effects of the RJP might not be the same on everyone, although in general RJPs have been shown to be an effective and relatively inexpensive way of decreasing unwanted employee turnover.

THE UTILITY OF SCIENTIFIC SELECTION

Perhaps the most important question to ask about the scientific approach to employee selection concerns its utility or value. What is the payoff to an organization for using this difficult and time-consuming approach to selection? The answer is not easy to determine. Research has shown that scientific selection can result in the hiring of better employees, but its effects on overall organizational functioning are not as clear. The study of these effects is called **utility analysis**. I/O psychologists have developed mathematical procedures for conducting utility analyses of selection procedures. In this section, we first discuss in general how selection devices can result in the hiring of better employees. We then consider how utility analysis has been used to show how these selection procedures can have important effects on organizational functioning.

How Valid Selection Devices Work

An understanding of utility analysis must begin with an understanding of how selection devices work. Three basic concepts form the foundation of this discussion:

Baserate

Selection ratio

Validity

These three factors determine to what extent scientific selection will result in hiring better performing employees. If it does so, then we must consider the cost of using the selection device.

Baserate. The **baserate** is the percentage of applicants who would be successful on the job if all of them were hired. On some jobs most applicants would be capable of performing well, making the baserate close to 100%. On other jobs relatively few applicants would be successful, making the baserate close to 0%. A baserate of 50% results in the maximum utility because it offers the most room for improvement in accuracy of prediction. Suppose you know the baserate from prior experience with employees on a job. If 50% have been successful in the past, the best accuracy rate you could expect by guessing which applicants would be successful is 50%. If you guessed that every applicant would be successful or unsuccessful, you would expect to be correct half the time. Using a predictor, you could improve your accuracy up to 100%. This would represent a difference of 50% in accuracy between the baserate and your predictor.

If you know that the baserate is less or more than 50%, you can achieve better than 50% accuracy of prediction by guessing that every applicant will be successful (if the baserate is greater than 50%) or not successful (if the baserate is less than 50%). For example, a 60% baserate would give about 60% accuracy if you guess that everyone will be successful. A baserate of 40% would give about 60% accuracy if you guess that everyone will be unsuccessful (40% of people successful means that 60% are not successful). In both cases, the biggest possible gain in prediction accuracy is from 60% to 100%.

The more the baserate differs from 50% in either direction (the majority of employees are successful or not successful), the smaller is the room for improvement if we had perfect prediction. Thus, all baserates that are greater or less than 50% give less room for gain than 50%.

Selection Ratio. The **selection ratio** is the proportion of job applicants that an organization must hire. It is calculated as the number of positions to fill divided by the number of applicants. Some organizations find that they have many applicants for each vacant position. Their selection ratio will be low. Other organizations find that there are few applicants for each vacant position. Their selection ratio will be high. For example, if there are 100 job applicants for each job, the selection ratio will be 1/100. If there are two applicants for each position, the selection ratio will be 1/2. Low selection ratios produce the greatest utility because they allow an organization to be more selective in whom they hire for each position. In the long run, an organization can hire better people when there are many applicants from whom to choose.

Validity. The validity of a selection device is the magnitude of correlation between it and the criterion. The larger the correlation, the more accurately the criterion can be forecast by the selection device. The more accurate the forecast of the criterion, the greater is the utility because utility is based in part on increasing the success rate over the baserate.

How Valid Predictors Increase Success Rates

Figure 6-4 illustrates how baserate, selection ratio, and validity combine to increase the success rate of those hired. The figure graphs the criterion and predictor scores for a fictitious sample of 20 job applicants. The horizontal axis represents the predictor variable, and the vertical axis represents the criterion variable of job performance. The individual job applicants are represented by the points on the graph. Each point shows the criterion and predictor score for an applicant.

The baserate is represented by the horizontal line across the middle of the graph. Cases above the line are in the successful range on the criterion, and cases below the line are in the unsuccessful range. The cutoff score on the predictor is represented by the vertical line running down the center of the graph. Applicants who score higher than the cutoff (right side of vertical line) on the predictor are hired, and applicants who score lower than the cutoff (left side of vertical line) are not hired. In this case half of the applicants had predictor scores that were higher than the cutoff.

The graph is divided into four quadrants. The upper right quadrant contains applicants who would have been hired and who would have been successful on the job. They are referred to as *true positives*. The lower right quadrant contains people who would have been hired but would have been unsuccessful on the job. They are the *false positives*. The lower left quadrant contains people who would not have been hired and would not have been successful. They are the *true negatives*. Finally, the upper left quadrant contains applicants who would not have been hired and would have been successful on the job. They are the *false negatives*. There are eight true negatives and eight true positives, and there are two false negatives and two false positives.

If a predictor is valid, the points on the graph will be in the shape of an ellipse. This will produce a more accurate prediction over the baserate if a cutoff score on a predictor

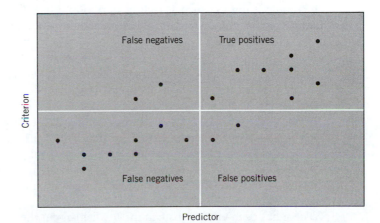

FIGURE 6-4
How a valid selection device increases the accuracy of selection.

is used to choose employees. The baserate in Figure 6-4 is 50%, meaning that half of the cases would be successful on the job if all were hired. If the predictor scores were used with the cutoff shown in the graph, eight people would have been successful and two would not have been. This improves the accuracy of prediction from the 50% baserate to 80%. This gain is a reflection of the potential utility of selection and can be substantial when conditions are favorable. As noted earlier in this discussion, the best situation occurs when the baserate is 50% and the selection ratio is low. The greater the validity, the greater is the potential utility of scientific selection.

So far we have seen how valid predictors can help identify those individuals who will be successful on the job. This is an important part of utility; however, the accuracy of a selection device or system is only part of utility. The other part concerns the relative cost of using the selection device versus the cost of poor selection. This more complete view of utility is discussed next.

Computing the Utility of Scientific Selection

Even though a predictor might result in the hiring of better employees, it is not necessarily the case that the result will be of benefit to the organization because the benefits of using a predictor might be less than the cost. For some types of factory work, for example, there is little in the way of skills or training necessary to do the job. It can be relatively inexpensive to replace an unsuccessful employee. In such a case, it would be difficult to justify using an expensive selection method, such as an assessment center. Jobs that result in a significant investment in individual employees warrant the use of expensive selection devices. For example, it takes millions of dollars for the U.S. Air Force to train a fighter pilot. It is certainly worth the cost to use expensive selection procedures in this case.

The utility concept we have discussed so far has concerned identifying successful versus unsuccessful employees. It is also possible to conduct utility analyses to see what sorts of performance improvements might occur from using a valid selection device to choose employees. If a selection device is valid, we would expect that on average individuals chosen with it will have better job performance. Several studies have shown that the highest performers can be up to 16 times more productive than the lowest performers on jobs with countable output, such as factory work (Campbell, Gasser, & Oswald, 1996). If we can compute the monetary value of that performance gain, we can compute the utility of using a selection device.

Several approaches have been suggested to conduct this sort of utility analysis (e.g., Raju, Burke, & Normand, 1990; Schmidt, Hunter, McKenzie, & Muldrow, 1979). Each is based on mathematical equations that provide estimates of monetary gain from using a selection device. The various approaches make their own assumptions and have their own variation on the equations. Each requires finding the relation between performance and monetary gain. For some jobs this can be straightforward. For example, the performance of a salesperson can be translated into the monetary value of sales made. For other jobs the translation is not so easy. How would you estimate the monetary value for a teacher's performance? It is possible to do so, usually by asking subject matter experts to make subjective judgments.

There has been much debate in the I/O field about the best approach to utility analysis. Some of the discussion has concerned how people make judgments about the monetary value of job performance (e.g., Becker & Huselid, 1992; Bobko, Shetzer, & Russell, 1991). These authors have expressed concern that people are not necessarily accurate in their judgments, making utility estimates inaccurate. Other authors have noted that utility analyses have failed to consider all the major factors involved in utility (Boudreau, 1983; Russell, Colella, & Bobko, 1993), resulting in somewhat inflated estimates of gains. As but one example, Boudreau (1983) discussed how increased profits from a more productive workforce should be adjusted for taxes to yield the real bottom line utility estimate.

Although utility analysis has limitations, results of such analyses have shown that scientific selection can offer considerable monetary benefits to organizations. Schmidt, Mack, and Hunter (1984) estimated that the U.S. Park Service might gain as much as $3.8 million in productivity if a cognitive ability test were used to select park rangers. This number was calculated for the case in which 130 rangers were hired per year. In organizations that hire larger numbers of people, expected gains might be considerably greater.

The idea of computing utility is not limited to employee selection. Landy, Farr, and Jacobs (1982) suggested that the approach could be used to estimate the monetary gain of other organizational practices, such as giving employees job performance feedback. If you can estimate the gain in performance from such a procedure, you can compute the utility in terms of monetary gain. Such analyses would share the same limitations as the utility analyses used for employee selection.

One further issue should be noted concerning the use of utility analysis. Such mathematical procedures provide a theoretical estimate of how much gain in performance would occur if more capable people were hired. Although in theory more capable people would perform better, in practice the expected gains may never occur. Organizations are complex social systems that affect people's behavior in a variety of ways. Job performance can be both enhanced and inhibited by organizations. As we will see throughout the remainder of this book, being able to perform does not mean that the organizational conditions and constraints will allow it. A capable person might not perform well because the equipment or support to do so are not available. Even a highly talented machinist will be unproductive if his or her machine is defective and keeps breaking. Nevertheless, utility analysis is valuable because it shows that selection procedures can be of benefit to organizations, even if we cannot be certain about the magnitude of the monetary benefits.

LEGAL ISSUES

Throughout the industrialized world, it is becoming an accepted value that organizations should not be discriminatory in their practices that affect employees, such as hiring and promotion. These countries have laws that protect the rights of people from discriminatory actions by organizations. The particular groups of people who are protected by these laws vary from country to country. Most offer protection to women, and many offer protection to blacks. A group is likely to be protected by law if it represents a reasonably large minority of a country. Thus, in countries with large black minorities, blacks are likely to be offered protection. In countries with few blacks, this protection might not be found in the law.

In this section, we discuss the legal issues involved in employee selection both inside and outside the United States. Although the United States was a leader in the development of legal protection from discrimination, many countries have not been far behind in this area. This discussion offers a contrast between the handling of the problem of discrimination in the United States and in other countries.

Legal Selection in the United States

Prior to 1964 in the United States, discrimination against ethnic minorities and women was widespread for many jobs, particularly the most desirable and highest paying ones. In 1964 the Civil Rights Act changed the way organizations had to select employees because it expanded legal protections from discrimination and provided a mechanism to enforce it. Legislation in the following years has broadened the legal protection to groups that were not covered by the Civil Rights Act of 1964. Although discrimination in hiring has not been eliminated completely in the United States, tremendous progress has been made over the past few decades.

The Civil Rights Act of 1964 made it illegal to discriminate against minorities and other groups in employment and other areas of life in U.S. society. Subsequent legislation and Supreme Court cases have produced a complex and confusing array of legal requirements for employee selection. The Civil Rights Act of 1991 was an attempt to rectify some of the confusion produced by years of sometimes conflicting Supreme Court decisions. Table 6-4 lists six of the most significant Supreme Court cases and the major outcome of each. Although the underlying principles of nondiscrimination are simple, implementing a selection system that meets legal requirements is complicated. This is due in part to

Civil rights legislation says that each of these people should have an equal opportunity to be hired for a job.

TABLE 6-4
Six significant U.S. Supreme Court discrimination cases and their outcomes

CASE	OUTCOME
Griggs vs. Duke Power (1971)	Selection methods that have adverse impact must be valid.
Rowe vs. General Motors (1972)	Legal protection against discrimination holds for performance appraisals.
Albermarle Paper Company vs. Moody (1975)	Organizations must use rigorous validation procedures.
Baake vs. Regents of the University of California (1978)	Discrimination laws protect everyone, and quotas for admission to graduate school are illegal.
Wards Cove Packing Company vs. Antonio (1987)	This case made it more difficult for individuals to win discrimination cases. It was an impetus for the Civil Rights Act of 1991.
Price Waterhouse vs. Hopkins (1988)	Promotions cannot be based on gender stereotyping (e.g., requiring a female employee to act or look more feminine).

changing requirements by the Congress and Supreme Court and in part to the technical complexities in employee selection systems.

The first issue that we address is the concept of *protected classes*. Although the law states that discrimination against anyone is illegal, certain groups of people have been the target of protection under the law. These groups are called **protected classes** and are comprised of people who have been the target of discrimination in the past. African Americans, Hispanics, Native Americans, and women all represent protected classes. Table 6-5 lists the major federal discrimination laws and the specific groups each covers. At the present time it is illegal to discriminate on the basis of

Age	Disability
Color	Gender
National Origin	Religion
Race	

It is conceivable that other groups will become protected classes in the future, and individual states are free to offer protection to additional groups not covered by U.S. law.

TABLE 6-5
Civil rights legislation in the United States protecting various groups

LEGISLATION	COVERS
Civil Rights Act of 1964	Color, gender, national origin, race, religion
Age Discrimination Act of 1967 (Amended 1968)	Age
Pregnancy Discrimination Act of 1978	Pregnancy
Americans With Disabilities Act of 1990	Mental and physical disabilities

Uniform Guidelines on Employee Selection. In 1978 the U.S. government produced a set of guidelines for legal selection called the **Uniform Guidelines on Employee Selection Procedures** (1978). Although originally intended to apply to government agencies, the guidelines were eventually adopted as acceptable legal practices for all organizations. The guidelines define several important concepts for selection and provide a procedure by which organizations can conduct legal selection. They provide more than just a statement of legal requirements. They outline the proper way to develop a valid employee selection system, which provides an additional advantage to an organization that follows them.

One of the most important concepts embodied in the Uniform Guidelines is **adverse impact**, which refers to the impact on a protected class of a given selection practice. It is usually defined in terms of selection ratios of the protected class and the majority group, which is usually white males. Adverse impact occurs when the selection ratio for the protected class is less than 80%, or four-fifths of the group with the highest ratio, which is usually white males but could be another protected class. For example, suppose that 60% of male applicants were offered a job. Female applicants would experience adverse impact if fewer than 48% of them (four-fifths of 60%) were offered a job (Table 6-6). This four-fifths rule recognizes that an equal number of applicants from every possible group is unlikely. Of importance here is the percentage of applicants who are hired, not the actual numbers.

Adverse impact is a threshold for possible discrimination in selection. It is not necessarily illegal to use a selection device that has adverse impact on a protected class. If a selection device or procedure has adverse impact, there are further tests to decide its legality. To be legal, a selection device must be job relevant. This means that it assesses a KSAO that is necessary for job success. One way to establish job relevance is by showing that a selection device is a valid predictor of job performance.

If selection practices produce adverse impact, an organization must be ready to defend itself from legal challenges. Tests of cognitive ability and physical strength are both likely

TABLE 6-6
Applying the four-fifths rule for adverse impact against women[a]

CASE 1: NO ADVERSE IMPACT AGAINST WOMEN

GENDER	NUMBER OF APPLICANTS	NUMBER HIRED	PERCENT HIRED	4/5THS THRESHOLD
Men	100	60	60%	
Women	80	40	50%	48%

No adverse impact because 50% is above the 48% threshold

CASE 2: ADVERSE IMPACT AGAINST WOMEN

GENDER	NUMBER OF APPLICANTS	NUMBER HIRED	PERCENT HIRED	4/5THS THRESHOLD
Men	100	60	60%	
Women	80	20	25%	48%

Adverse impact against women because 25% is below the 48% threshold

[a]In the first case, 60% of male applicants and 50% of female applicants were hired. Because 50% is more than four-fifths of 60%, there is no adverse impact against women. In the second case 60% of male applicants but only 25% of female applicants were hired. Because 25% is less than four-fifths of 60%, there is adverse impact against women.

to have adverse impact on some groups. Their use can be justified only if a job analysis shows that these attributes are necessary KSAOs for the job and if the tests are shown to be valid. Failure both to do a job analysis and to use valid selection methods risks using procedures that are unfair to the adversely affected groups. Although it is legal to require that those who are hired have the required KSAOs to do a job, it is illegal to require KSAOs that are not necessary for success on the job.

Essential Functions and Reasonable Accommodation. The 1990 Americans With Disabilities Act (ADA) extended legal protection from discrimination to people with disabilities. Two concepts came from this legislation. *Essential functions*, as we discussed in Chapter 3, refer to KSAOs that are an important part of the job. For example, typing is an essential function for a secretary, but lifting heavy objects is not. It can be illegal to deny a job to a person based on a KSAO that relates only to nonessential functions. The idea is that rarely done tasks, such as lifting a heavy object, that require a KSAO that an otherwise competent employee does not have can be done by someone else.

The second concept is **reasonable accommodation** for a disabled employee. An organization must make allowances that are feasible to enable a disabled person to perform the job. For example, an organization should provide someone to help an employee in a wheelchair get up a staircase to his or her workplace. This is a minor and reasonable accommodation that should be made. Providing help in doing nonessential functions for a job can be another reasonable accommodation. It is not yet clear what other actions are reasonable and what actions to help a disabled worker are too difficult or expensive for an organization. Undoubtedly, future court cases will determine how far organizations must go to make reasonable accommodations for disabled employees.

Affirmative Action. **Affirmative action** is a practice that many organizations have used to increase the number of protected class members in targeted jobs. Its purpose is to address the lingering effects of past discrimination in hiring by allowing certain groups to catch up in acquiring jobs that were at one time unavailable to them. An affirmative action program can involve many different steps, from extra efforts taken to attract applicants to preferential treatment in job offers or in promotions. Affirmative action is not a quota system; nor does it require the hiring of anyone without the necessary KSAOs. The U.S. Supreme Court has consistently ruled against such practices except in extraordinary circumstances (Kravitz, Harrison, Turner, Levine, Chaves, Brannick, Denning, Russell, & Conard, 1997). It also let stand the California law that prohibited most forms of preferential treatment. This does not mean, however, that other forms of affirmative action have been eliminated.

Organizations that have more than 50 employees or government contracts exceeding $50,000 are required by executive order to have an affirmative action program. This requirement affects most colleges and universities whose faculties have government research grants. For most other organizations this activity is voluntary, although some employers that have been caught using discriminatory practices may be ordered or strongly encouraged by a court to adopt an affirmative action program to end their illegal practices. Most large organizations in the United States practice some form of affirmative action, although some do so more rigorously than others. The widespread practice can be seen in the prominently displayed notice that an employer is an "Affirmative Action" employer, common on the stationery of many organizations and most universities.

The intent of an affirmative action program is to remedy the widespread problem of discrimination. Such programs should be introduced carefully because they can have unintended detrimental effects on the groups they are designed to help (e.g., Chacko, 1982; Kleiman & Faley, 1988). Madeline Heilman and her colleagues have found that women who are given preferential treatment in hiring can have a negative view of themselves and other women (Heilman & Herlihy, 1984; Heilman, Kaplow, Amato, & Stathatos, 1993). Furthermore, a person who is hired under affirmative action is likely to be seen as incompetent, and that stigma of affirmative action is difficult to overcome in the minds of co-workers (Heilman, Block, & Stathatos, 1997; Heilman, Battle, Keller, & Lee, 1998). Research has also shown adverse effects on nonbeneficiaries when preferential treatment has been perceived as unfair, e.g., reverse discrimination (Heilman, McCullough, & Gilbert, 1996; Leck, Saunders, & Charbonneau, 1996). To overcome these problems, an affirmative action program must be carefully designed so that it does not give the impression that people of protected classes are hired without the necessary qualifications. Otherwise, beneficiaries are likely to devalue themselves, and nonbeneficiaries are likely to undermine efforts to remedy past discrimination. When undertaken properly, an affirmative action program can be viewed by most employees as fair and nonthreatening (Parker, Baltes, & Christiansen, 1997).

An affirmative action program is one component of a selection system that will withstand a legal challenge. In the United States today, however, no system can be totally free of legal challenge on grounds of discrimination. The complexities of the law and inconsistencies in legal decisions mean that one cannot be certain what any particular judge will find to be legal (Cascio, Alexander, & Barrett, 1988). If an organization follows the steps in developing a job-relevant selection system, legal problems are likely to be minimized.

Legal Selection Outside the United States

Many countries throughout the industrialized world have discrimination laws similar to those in the United States. Some countries are as vigorous as the United States in enforcing discrimination laws (e.g., Canada and South Africa), whereas others are relatively lax (e.g., Australia and England). Although the United States may have taken the lead, other countries give employees even more protection and have extended protection to additional groups not specifically mentioned in U.S. law. For example, Canada disallows discrimination based on sexual preference, and Ireland disallows discrimination based on marital status.

How different countries approach their discrimination problems depends on the nature of those problems and their societies. Pearn (1989) compared the situation in England and the United States in terms of laws and practices. Although both countries have similar laws, England is far more lax in the enforcement of those laws. This is in part because blacks make up a smaller percentage of the English population (only 5%) and in part because of differences in the legal systems of the two countries (Pearn, 1989). South Africa began legal reforms in the 1970s motivated in large part by labor shortages among the minority white population (Barling, Fullagar, & Bluen, 1986). In recent years, political action by the black majority has resulted in rigorous affirmative action rules throughout the society.

Canada is much like the United States in terms of laws and vigor of enforcement. Although details may be different, organizations need to follow the same practices to avoid legal problems in Canada as they would in the United States. Ireland is a more homogeneous society than Canada or the United States, having fewer minority groups of sufficient size to push for legal protection. In Ireland discrimination is illegal on the basis of gender or marital status, but the law is silent about blacks or other minority groups (Federation of Irish Employers, 1991).

The countries discussed here, as well as the remainder of at least the industrialized world, have endorsed the idea that employee selection should be based on the job-relevant attributes of people. With this approach the person hired is the person who can best do the job. This will eliminate unfairness in selection from discriminatory practices. It should also help organizations enhance their effectiveness by hiring the best qualified people, regardless of age, color, disability, gender, race, religion, or other personal characteristics that are irrelevant for job success.

FUTURE ISSUES AND CHALLENGES

Perhaps the biggest challenge for the future of job selection has arisen from the changing nature of work and the workforce. KSAO requirements for jobs are changing in the United States and elsewhere. Dunnette (1998), for example, notes that the increasing use of work teams will require selecting people who are able to work well with others, as well as those who can perform job tasks. Basic arithmetic and reading skills are lacking among some applicant groups in the United States. Part of the problem is that the KSAO requirements for jobs have increased. Factory work that required few skills in the past is being replaced by jobs with substantial technical content. The problem for organizations will be to identify people who are trainable, as opposed to people who already have the necessary KSAOs. To do so will require the use of different selection approaches and a greater reliance on training. Both Reilly and Israelski (1988) and Robertson and Downs (1989) discussed how trainability tests for predicting future training success are different from tests that predict future job performance.

A second challenge is to end discrimination in employee selection. This will require a shift to making selection decisions based on job-relevant factors. The more widespread use of the scientific approach to selection will help eliminate unfair practices. One technique that has been used with some success is to have employment decisions made by groups or panels of managers rather than individuals (Powell, & Butterfield, 1997; Prewett-Livingston, Feild, Veres, & Lewis, 1996). It is apparently more difficult to engage in biased hiring when more than one person is responsible for decisions. When everyone has an equal opportunity for every job, organizations will benefit because they will have the widest range of talent from which to select employees. In the long run, everyone will benefit from the individual applicants who will be judged on their merits to the organizations, which will then have a more effective workforce.

CHAPTER SUMMARY

One of the most important functions of an organization is the recruitment and selection of new employees. To remain effective an organization must have a supply of skilled people with the necessary attributes or KSAOs to do the job. Acquiring such people involves a four-step procedure:

Planning the need for new employees

Getting appropriate people to apply for positions (recruitment)

Deciding who to hire (selection)

Getting the selected people to take the jobs

Planning the need for new employees requires the use of forecasting methods. This involves comparing the need for people with particular KSAOs with the number of such people who might be available in the area. Future planning for organizational changes and expansions must consider the availability of people to fill the necessary positions. Failure to consider these issues can result in the inability to find the people necessary to carry out an important organizational function.

Getting people to apply for jobs can be a difficult task if there is a shortage of qualified people. The problem is more often one of getting the right people to apply than of getting applicants because there can be a surplus of people with certain skills and a shortage of people with others. There are a number of ways that organizations acquire applicants, including advertising and using recruiters.

Scientific selection involves the use of selection devices that have been shown to predict job performance. To develop a system of effective or valid selection devices involves a five-step procedure: the KSAOs are identified with a job analysis; criteria are chosen; potential predictors are chosen; the predictors are validated with a research study; and finally, the predictors are cross-validated with a second sample or study.

Once an organization has decided whom to hire, it must convince the person to take the job. To do so an organization must be sure that it offers rewards that are equivalent to those offered by other organizations. One procedure that has been used to ensure a better match between a person and a job is the realistic job preview (RJP), which provides accurate information about the job that allows an applicant to make an informed decision about accepting a job offer.

Utility analysis is used to determine the benefits of using a predictor to hire people. These analyses are based on mathematical formulas that require an estimate of the monetary value of good job performance. There have been disagreements among researchers about the best way to conduct utility analysis. Nevertheless, the results of utility analyses have shown that scientific selection can have substantial benefits for organizations.

Employee selection is not only a scientific process; it is also a legal process. Most industrialized countries have laws against discriminatory selection practices. In the United States it is illegal to discriminate on the basis of age, color, disability, gender, national origin, race, or religion. To avoid legal problems, an organization must base selection decisions on job-relevant factors.

I/O PSYCHOLOGY IN PRACTICE

THIS CASE CONCERNS the development of an unusual assessment device to measure the artistic ability of employees. It was carried out by Dr. Anna Erickson, who is an I/O psychologist for SBC Communications Inc, which owns several telephone companies, including Pacific Bell and Southwestern Bell Inc. Dr. Erickson received her Ph.D. in I/O psychology in 1995 from Iowa State University. At the time of this project, her role in the company was to do selection research, although she also has done projects in the areas of job analysis, performance appraisal, planning for future employee needs, and surveys of employee opinions. At the present time, she is director of Marketing Research and is responsible for

(Continued next page)

conducting studies of customer preferences for and reactions to telephone company products and services, such as call waiting or caller id. This is not an unusual job for an I/O psychologist, for the methods and techniques are much the same as those for more traditional I/O work discussed in this book.

One type of employee hired by the telephone company is a yellow page artist who sketches ads for company customers. The company decided to expand the advertising services, which requires a higher level of artistic talent than is necessary for ad sketches. Supervisors of the ad artists were asked to recommend individuals for the more artistic jobs, but this procedure led to widespread controversy and a union grievance over favoritism. Clearly, a new procedure had to be found which would be seen as fair to the employees while providing a valid means of choosing good artists.

Dr. Erickson was asked to solve this problem, but unfortunately no existing assessments for artists could be found. She would have to invent a new assessment device, while at the same time gaining the support of the employees. To accomplish this objective, she put together a task force of employees and managers. At the same time, she studied the research literature on creativity and discovered that, despite the seeming subjective nature of art, experts show a high degree of interrater agreement when evaluating it. This gave her the idea of developing an assessment center in which raters would be faculty members from a well known university art department.

The first step in developing the center was to conduct a job analysis to identify KSAOs for the job. Results showed that there were two important components to assess. First, the artist had to deal with customers, and second, he or she had to do the creative work. The customer service part was assessed with a structured interview. The creative part was assessed by having experts rate the quality of a portfolio the person submitted and by expert ratings of performance in a simulation. All ratings were done blind, with the rater not knowing whose work was being assessed.

The task force was unanimous in approving this assessment procedure. It accomplished the goal of settling the union grievance. Dr. Erickson conducted a validation study of the assessment center and found it predicted very well professor ratings of their art students' employability. Those students who were rated most capable and employable did best in the assessment center. It is now being used for placement and selection in the company. This case illustrates how often employees perceive effective selection as fair selection.

Discussion Questions

1. Why was it important to have employee acceptance of the new assessment center?

2. Do you think supervisor nomination was an unfair way to decide who got the jobs?

3. How else could this assessment center be validated other than with the procedure used?

4. Can you think of other ways to measure artistic creativity?

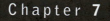

Chapter 7

TRAINING

If you accept a job with a large organization, it is almost certain that you will go through some sort of formal training program. Even people with college degrees need additional instruction in order to do most jobs. Even simple jobs require training. For example, every employee at a McDonald's restaurant gets trained. The person who makes french fries is taught the proper way to do the job. A restaurant manager receives hundreds of hours of training, much of it in a classroom setting. There is much to learn to be able to do most jobs well. Future trends suggest that the need for training will increase in most jobs as they become more and more technically oriented.

Training is one of the major activities of most large organizations, including private and public (government) sector organizations throughout the world. It is a necessary activity for both new and experienced employees. New employees must learn how to do their jobs, whereas experienced employees must learn to keep up with job changes. In many organizations a person will not be considered for a promotion until certain training has been completed and certain skills mastered. Learning in most jobs is a lifelong process that does not stop with a certain level of education.

Five steps are required for effective organizational training programs, as shown in Figure 7-1. The first step of a training program is to conduct a *needs assessment* study in order to determine who needs training and what kind of training is needed. The second step is to set objectives so that it will be clear what the training should accomplish. The third step is to design the training program. The fourth step is to delivering the training to those employees designated by the needs assessment. The final step is to evaluate the training to be certain that it reached its objectives. If the training was ineffective, the process should continue until an effective program is achieved. Each step should be based on the one that precedes it.

In this chapter we discuss all five steps in the training process. All but the delivery step fall within the domain of I/O psychology. Most training is conducted by professional trainers who specialize in its delivery. I/O psychologists are often behind the scenes helping to design the training that others will actually deliver. Most of the training conducted in organizations, however, does not involve I/O psychologists.

FIGURE 7-1
Five steps to developing an effective training program.

<u>Objectives</u>   **The student who studies this chapter should be able to:**
1. List the steps involved in developing and implementing a training program in an organization.
2. Describe how needs assessment is conducted.
3. Explain the various factors that affect learning and transfer of training.
4. Discuss how training is evaluated.

NEEDS ASSESSMENT

A needs assessment is conducted to determine which employees need training and what the content of their training should be. It is too often the case that training resources are wasted by training the wrong people or teaching the wrong content. A needs assessment can ensure that training resources are wisely spent on areas in which there is a demonstrated training need.

According to Goldstein (1993), needs assessment should focus on three levels: organization, job, and person.

The *organization level* is concerned with the objectives of the organization and how they are addressed by the performance of employees. An analysis of the organization's objectives can offer hints about the training that is needed. For example, if an organization has the goal of minimizing manufacturing defects, it would seem reasonable to train supervisors in principles of quality control. If the goal is to maximize productivity, training would involve principles of production efficiency.

The *job level* is concerned with the nature of tasks involved in each job. A job analysis can be used to identify the major tasks and then the necessary KSAOs for each task. From the list of KSAOs, a series of training needs can be specified. A police officer, for example, must have knowledge of legal arrest procedures. This would be a rather obvious area in which training would be provided.

The *person level* is concerned with how well job applicants or present employees are able to do job tasks. In other words, it assesses the KSAO levels of people rather than jobs. A comparison of the KSAOs of jobs and people suggests the areas of greatest potential training need. Part of an employee recruitment plan should consider if enough applicants have each KSAO. If they do, the KSAO can be used as a criterion for selection. If they do not, the KSAO will be the focus of training. Organizations do not expect to hire secretaries who need training in how to type. They might hire secretaries, however, who need training in how to use computers.

So far we have discussed needs assessment from the perspective of what should be trained. This approach, however, says nothing about the content of training programs that might already be in use. Ford and Wroten (1984) developed a procedure for determining the extent to which a training program meets training needs. It is somewhat like a job analysis, except that the training is analyzed rather than the job. To conduct such an analysis, subject matter experts review the content of a training program and compile a list of the KSAOs that are addressed. A separate group of subject matter experts reviews the KSAO list and makes ratings of how important each one is to the job in question. This procedure can identify how well the program components match training needs for the job. Programs can be adopted or modified on the basis of this procedure.

Despite the importance of needs assessment, organizations often do not use it. A recent survey of 1,000 large private companies in the United States found that only 27% used some sort of needs assessment before conducting training of their management-level people (Saari, Johnson, McLaughlin, & Zimmerle, 1988). Too often, training resources are wasted because the needs assessment that might have redirected that effort was never performed. More effort is often wasted in conducting the wrong training than might have been expended in first doing a proper needs assessment.

OBJECTIVES

One of the most important steps in developing a training program is setting objectives. Unless you are clear about the purpose of training, it is difficult to design a training program to achieve it. Part of this step is to define the criteria for good training success. The objectives of training are based on criteria and should include a statement of what a trainee should be able to do or know after training. The training criterion is a statement of how achievement of the training objective can be assessed. The training objective of acquiring knowledge can be assessed by seeing if trainees can meet a criterion of achieving a cutoff score on a knowledge test.

Criteria serve as the basis for the design of organizational training. Once we know what the training criterion is, we can design appropriate training to achieve it. Criteria also serve as the standards against which training programs can be evaluated, which we discuss in the section on training evaluation. Training objectives should be based on the results of the needs assessment.

TRAINING DESIGN

Most organizational training is conducted with the expectation that employees will apply what they have learned on the job. This is called **transfer of training**. Transfer is affected by a number of factors in both the job environment and the training itself. Individual differences in characteristics among trainees also are an important consideration in whether or not training will transfer. Figure 7-2 is a model of transfer developed by Baldwin and Ford (1988). Their model describes how features of the training design can affect how well trainees learn and in turn how well the training transfers to the job. They also note that individual differences among trainees and characteristics of the work environment are important influences.

In this section we discuss the training design factors that affect both learning and transfer. In addition, we cover eight popular training techniques that show how the train-

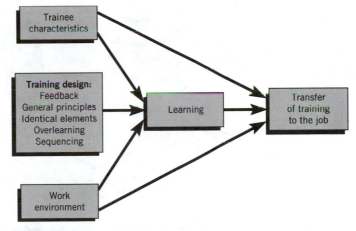

FIGURE 7-2

This model of transfer of training shows how characteristics of the trainee, training program, and work environment affect learning and transfer of training. *Source:* Adapted from "Transfer of Training: A Review and Directions for Future Research," by T. T. Baldwin and J. K. Ford, 1988, *Personnel Psychology, 41,* pp. 63–105.

ing is actually delivered. Training can be done in a variety of ways, from the relatively passive lecture to the very involving simulation. In the former case the trainee listens to a presentation, whereas in the latter case he or she gets to try out the new skill. Each of the eight methods is useful in some training situations.

Trainee Characteristics

People differ on many characteristics that are important in the training process. Perhaps most important, people differ in their capabilities to learn different tasks. Some people might be better able to learn cognitive tasks, whereas others might be more skilled at motor tasks. Thus, some people are skilled academicians and others are world-class athletes. These differences are important when it comes to the design of training. Not everyone has the same ability to learn a given task, and training needs to recognize these differences.

Bunker and Cohen (1977) studied the effectiveness of a training program designed to instruct telephone company employees in basic electronics theory. The mathematical ability of each trainee was assessed before training. A measure of electronics knowledge was taken before and after training. Results showed that those trainees with the highest level of mathematical ability gained the most from training. In order to get each trainee up to a given level of knowledge, more training would be necessary for the low-ability trainees. A good strategy for training is to give each individual trainee the amount of training necessary for him or her to reach the training criterion. This can mean that some people get a lot more training than others.

Ability is not the only individual trainee characteristic that affects training outcomes.

"I'm a hunter, but I've been cross-trained as a gatherer."

© 1995; Reprinted courtesy of Bunny Hoest and Parade Magazine.

Attitudes and motivation can affect outcomes both in training and on the job (Noe, 1986; Noe & Schmitt, 1986). People who do not wish to learn will not likely get much benefit from a training program. One of the most important factors that must be considered is how to motivate employees to do their best in a training situation. This can be done by giving external rewards for successful completion (e.g., promotion) or by making the training interesting to the trainees.

People also differ in the best way to learn new material. Some people are good at learning from a presentation, whereas others do well with written materials. People's capacities and preferences for different types of training are important considerations and should be taken into account if possible. People who do not read well should be trained with verbal approaches. Others who like to study and think about material might do better with a written manual.

Design Factors That Affect Transfer of Training

The transfer of training model in Figure 7-2 specifies five design factors that affect transfer. Each factor should be considered in the design of a training program. Appropriate use of the factors will maximize the likelihood of transfer. Ignoring them might result in a training program that is ineffective in affecting behavior on the job.

Feedback. **Feedback** is an important component of learning. Without some sort of feedback, it is doubtful that learning can occur at all. Feedback should be built into the training as appropriate so that the trainee can tell if he or she is learning the correct material.

Training that is intended to impart information or knowledge can build in feedback in two ways. First, trainees can be tested on the information with an examination. Second, trainees can ask questions of the trainer. Both of these procedures are a regular part of most college or university courses. Training that is intended to teach a skill should allow the trainees to practice and get feedback as they learn. For example, training in driving an automobile should allow the person to drive with an instructor who will give feedback. Feedback is also built into the task itself. Trainees can tell if they are staying on the road and if they are driving straight.

General Principles. General principles means that training should teach why something is done as well as how it should be done. Many training programs include a section on principles behind the material being taught. With computer training, there might be an introduction to the principles of computer and software design. This would be brief and rather general, but it would give the trainees a general idea of what the computer is and how it works. The purpose of teaching the general principles is that it provides a framework for learning. It has been found that including general principles where appropriate enhances learning (Baldwin & Ford, 1988).

Identical Elements. A training program that has good transfer of training capability should include **identical elements**, which means that the responses in the training situation are identical to those in the job situation. It also means that the stimuli the person perceives will be identical in both settings. The closer the match in both responses and stimuli, the easier it will be for trainees to apply what has been learned in training to the job setting.

A flight simulator is a training device that takes advantage of the identical elements idea. A flight simulator allows the trainee to fly an airplane without actually leaving the ground. There are two types—high fidelity and low fidelity. The high-fidelity simulator is extremely realistic and might be a cockpit from a real aircraft mounted on a moving platform that simulates the motion of the airplane. The motions of the simulator match the movements of the controls. If the trainee pulls back on the stick, for example, the front of the cockpit tilts upward. A low-fidelity simulator is best illustrated by a computer game that simulates flying. Even though these low-fidelity simulator games do not contain all the elements of a real airplane, many of the elements are authentic. For this reason the U.S. Navy uses such games to help train their pilots on some aspects of flying. To complete training, however, they must use the high-fidelity simulators. The simulator provides training that transfers well to actual flying because there are many identical elements (Figure 7-3).

Overlearning. Overlearning refers to giving the trainee practice beyond that necessary to reach a criterion for success in training. The idea is that a person first learns the material and then continues to overlearn it. Through overlearning, the person consolidates the new knowledge or skill so that he or she can use what has been learned with little thought. He or she has achieved **automaticity**, meaning that tasks can be done smoothly, without the person having to mentally monitor or pay attention to how he or she is performing. This results in much more effective performance and should be the goal for much organizational training (Ford & Kraiger, 1995).

Athletes practice their skills until they have become so overlearned that automaticity is achieved. In athletics the actions that are performed are often so complex and done in such short periods of time that it is not possible to think about all the elements. Overlearned elements are performed automatically and quickly. On the job the same principle

FIGURE 7-3
Pilots learn many of the skills of flying an airplane in a flight simulator, such as the one shown in this picture.

can apply as overlearned skills can be used when there is not enough time to think about how to perform a task. For example, in a hospital emergency room, there is little time to think about every task that needs to be done to save a person's life. Equipment must be used quickly and automatically when a person is in critical condition.

Overlearning can be built into training through practice and repetition. Information and knowledge training can include repetition of important concepts to ensure that the person rehearses the information. Examinations can also allow the person to rehearse, thus helping to consolidate what has been learned. With manual skills, sufficient practice should be allowed so that the skill becomes overlearned. It is not sufficient to allow the person to try the skill until he or she can do it correctly one time. Repeated practice is necessary to provide overlearning. The more the person gets to practice, the more likely it will be that he or she can apply what has been learned on the job.

Driskell, Willis, and Copper (1992) conducted a meta-analysis of overlearning studies. They analyzed the amount of performance gain as a function of the amount of overlearning. Overlearning was defined as practice in the training session that continued after the trainees first achieved the minimum criterion level for having learned the task. Overlearning in these studies ranged from 0% (no overlearning) to 200% (double the amount of training after the training criterion was reached as before it was reached). If it took two hours of training for the trainee to reach the criterion, 200% overlearning would be an

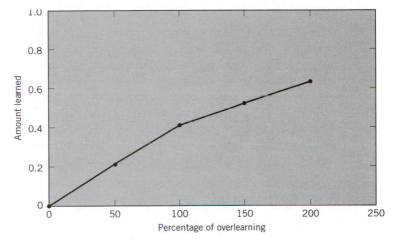

FIGURE 7-4

Learning is enhanced by the amount of overlearning training. Increasing the amount of training after the initial criterion is reached will increase the amount of learning (Driskell et al., 1992).

extra four hours of training. Figure 7-4 summarizes the results. The greater the overlearning (horizontal axis), the greater was the amount of learning (vertical axis). These results suggest that one should build in as much overlearning as possible in a training program.

Sequencing of Training Sessions. There are two aspects of sequencing training sessions: *part* versus *whole* and *massed* versus *spaced*. **Part training** refers to breaking a task into components, which are learned one at a time. After the components are learned, the entire task is taught as a whole. **Whole training** occurs when the entire task is taught at one time, rather than breaking it into individual components.

Part training is preferred over whole training when tasks are too complex to be learned all at once. It would be difficult to learn to play golf or tennis using the whole approach. It would be better in this case to learn one aspect of the game at a time, such as swinging the golf club or serving the tennis ball. To concentrate on all aspects of the game would be very difficult. Learning to ride a bicycle, on the other hand, is taught whole. One does not usually learn the components separately, such as pedaling or steering.

Massed training means that the training sessions are long in duration and take place over a relatively short period of time. **Spaced training** means that training sessions are relatively short and are spread out over time. Massed and spaced are relative terms that can be used to refer to some training programs as being more massed or spaced than other programs. A training program that holds sessions 1 hour per day for 10 days is more spaced than a program that meets for one 10-hour day.

Massed training can be very efficient. For that reason, it is often used for organizational training when it is easier to allow a person to leave work for training for a day than it is to allow one hour a day for eight days. With many jobs a replacement will have to be found while the person is in training, and it can be difficult to find a replacement for an hour at a time. The person might have to be paid for an entire day to fill in for one hour.

Furthermore, considerable travel time may be needed to get to the training site, which might be in another city. For these practical reasons, massed training is often used.

On the other hand, spaced training can be more effective than massed training in the long term. Massed training can produce fatigue, which interferes with learning and would not be possible with many motor tasks. Imagine learning to play tennis in 10-hour sessions. The fatigue would make it impossible to get the full benefit of the training. Even with mental tasks a person is not efficient when he or she is tired. Any student who has crammed for an exam has learned that massed training is not always the best procedure. Research on this approach has found that spaced training produces better retention of material over time (Baldwin & Ford, 1988).

Work Environment

Training in organizations takes place in the context of a complex work environment. Whether or not the skills learned in training are used on the job is dependent in large part on the environment on the job. Just because management provides training does not mean that employees or their direct supervisors will support its use on the job. It is not uncommon for direct supervisors of lower-level employees to tell their subordinates that the new skills learned in training are not to be used in their departments. Supportive environments where supervisors and other people encourage the application of learned principles produce employee motivation to learn and increased transfer of training (Facteau, Dobbins, Russell, Ladd, & Kudisch, 1995; Tracey, Tannenbaum, & Kavanagh, 1995). Unless there is support by employees and their supervisors, the best training will not have its intended effects. Getting that support is a complex problem that goes beyond the proper design of training.

Another issue concerns whether or not the opportunity arises to use the new training. For example, employees might be trained in using a new computer system. The system might not be available to them on the job, meaning that the training could have no effect. This issue goes back to the idea of needs assessment. People should not receive training in an area that they will not encounter on the job.

Training Methods

Many different methods for training are available. Because each has its advantages and limitations, there is no one best way to train. As noted earlier, different individuals may do well with different approaches. The best training programs are flexible so that employees can adapt to the demands of what and who are being trained.

In this section we discuss eight different training methods that are frequently used in organizational training. These methods can be used in combination, because a good training program may need to take advantage of the strengths of different methods for different aspects of training. For example, the training of pilots may involve many, if not all, of these methods. The learning of complex tasks can require the use of a variety of approaches. Table 7-1 lists all eight methods and summarizes the major advantages of each.

Audiovisual Instruction. **Audiovisual instruction** involves the presentation of materials using an audiotape or videotape. It can be a slide presentation or a computer presentation. Recently, interest has been shown in the use of multimedia presentations for

TABLE 7-1
Advantages of eight training methods

METHOD	ADVANTAGES
Audiovisual instruction	Material that could not otherwise be heard or seen
	Training of many people at once
Autoinstruction	Immediate feedback to trainees
	Individualized pacing
Conference	Feedback to trainees
	High level of trainee involvement
Lecture	Economical
	Good information-giving method
Modeling	High level of feedback
	Practice of new skills
On-the-job training	Exposure to actual job
	High level of transfer
Role playing	High level of feedback
	Practice of new skills
Simulation	High level of transfer
	Practice of new skills

Source: Adapted from "Selection, Training, and Development of Personnel," by W. C. Borman, N. G. Peterson, and T. L. Russell, 1992, in G. Salvendy (Ed.), *Handbook of Industrial Engineering,* 2nd ed. New York: John Wiley.

training. These presentations are computer based and use a variety of techniques to present the material. A multimedia encyclopedia combines pictures and text from a book format with animations and sound clips. We will undoubtedly see an expanded use of multimedia presentations for training in the future.

Autoinstruction. **Autoinstruction** refers to any method that is self-paced and does not use an instructor. The most well-known technique is **programmed instruction**, which divides the material to be covered into a series of individual chunks or frames. Each frame contains a piece of information, a question to be answered, and the answer to the question from the prior frame. The person works at his or her own pace. There is repetition built in as the same material is presented more than once. There is also feedback as the person must answer questions and is then given the correct answer almost immediately. Although the medium for programmed instruction was originally a book or manual, the computer is able to provide a much more flexible approach to autoinstruction training.

Conference. A **conference** is a meeting of trainees and a trainer to discuss the material in question. The distinguishing feature of the conference is that participants can discuss the material and ask questions. It also allows for a free flow of ideas so that the discussion can go beyond the prepackaged materials. Thus, the conference can be used to enhance learning more than the other methods. It is especially effective when used with trainees who have already acquired expertise with the material. It is the major teaching method used at the Ph.D. level in the training of I/O psychology students.

Lecture. A **lecture** is a presentation by a trainer to a group of trainees. Its major advantage is its efficiency: One trainer can present material to a large number of trainees. At some universities, lectures are given to thousands of students at one time. The greatest strength of the lecture is also its greatest weakness. The mass presentation to many people limits the amount of feedback that can be given. With even 40 people in a lecture, if each person asked one question the lecturer would have little time to present. For situations in which feedback is not needed, the lecture can be a very effective means of training.

Modeling. **Modeling** involves having trainees watch someone perform a task and then having them model what they have seen. The model can be on a film or videotape. Models can show both effective and ineffective examples of behavior. This approach is often used for the training of supervisory skills, such as giving negative feedback to an employee who is performing poorly. The examples of supervisory behavior are shown, and then the trainees attempt to imitate what they have seen. The trainer's role is to encourage the trainees to try the approaches and to give them feedback about how well they imitated what they saw.

Research on the modeling approach has provided support for its ability to train people in interpersonal skills, such as communicating with others. Latham and Saari (1979) evaluated the effects of a modeling program for supervisors. They found that trained supervisors were better able to deal with their subordinates on an interpersonal level as a result of the training experience. Modeling can be an effective training method not only for interpersonal skills, but also for technical skills such as using computers. Simon and Werner (1996) reported better learning with modeling than with autoinstruction or lecture in training U.S. naval personnel in using a new data processing system on a personal computer.

On-the-Job Training. **On-the-job training** is not a particular method but is any method used to show employees how to do the job while they are doing it. The greatest amount of job training often occurs while the person is doing the various job tasks. On-the-job training can be an informal system whereby a new employee watches an experienced employee to see how the job should be done. It can also involve a formal training program such as an **apprenticeship**, which is commonly used for jobs that may take years to be fully trained. For this sort of job, the other methods might not be feasible because the organization will not want to pay a person for years of training without productivity. If the person quits before training is completed, the training effort was wasted. An apprentice is an employee who can serve as an assistant to the trainer. The trainer is an employee who is doing the job and training the apprentice at the same time. This approach is often used to train people in trade occupations, such as electricians or plumbers.

Role Playing. A **role play** is a type of simulation in which the trainee pretends to be doing a task. It usually involves an interpersonal situation, such as giving a person advice or feedback. The role play is part of the modeling procedure we discussed earlier. The role play itself does not involve first observing another person perform the behavior. Role playing is frequently used for the training of interpersonal and supervisory skills. It can be an effective training technique, but it is costly in that only a few trainees can be trained at one time.

Simulations. As discussed earlier, a **simulation** is a technique in which specialized equipment or materials are used to portray a task situation. Trainees are to pretend that the situation is real and carry out their tasks as they would in the actual situation. Simulations can be used for training people in the use of equipment, such as automobiles or airplanes. They can also be used to simulate other situations, such as a business decision simulation that asks the trainees to pretend to be an organization member who has been given a problem to solve or task to accomplish. For example, a simulation might involve the planning of a new manufacturing plant. These simulations can be made very realistic, for they can be based on real examples from the same organization. The simulation shares the limitation of the role play in that only a few trainees can participate at one time.

DELIVERY OF A TRAINING PROGRAM

Even the most well-designed training program will be ineffective unless it is properly delivered. In most organizations specialists who are skilled in training deliver the program. They may or may not be experts in the content of the training or in training design. Content is the responsibility of subject matter experts who know the particular topics that the training will cover. I/O psychologists and people from several other fields are experts at program design. Because program delivery is not a frequent activity of an I/O psychologist, we continue with the next topic: training evaluation.

EVALUATION OF A TRAINING PROGRAM

As far as an I/O psychologist is concerned, a training program is not completed until it has been evaluated to determine its effectiveness. An evaluation is a piece of research to see whether or not the program had its intended effects. This is important because many training programs are ineffective. For example, Morrow, Jarrett, and Rupinski (1997) evaluated the utility of 18 training programs in an organization and found that 5 cost more than they returned in improved performance on the job. The principles of research design, as discussed in Chapter 2, are very much involved in the design of evaluation. There is little difference between conducting an evaluation study for a training program and conducting a research study to determine the effects of any intervention that is tried in an organization. Thus, the principles and techniques of research methodology that we discussed in Chapter 2 apply to the evaluation of a training program.

Carrying out a training evaluation requires five steps (Figure 7-5). The first step is to define the criteria for evaluation. As we have discussed several times in this book, you must have criteria before you can evaluate anything. Criteria are the standards for comparison so that you can determine if training has been effective. Once criteria have been selected, a design for the study and the measures used to assess the criteria can be selected (steps 2 and 3). Step 4 is collecting the data for the study. Step 5 is analyzing the data and reaching conclusions about the effectiveness of the training program. We discuss each of these steps in greater detail now.

Set Criteria

Training criteria serve as the standard by which training can be evaluated. If you know what the training is supposed to achieve, you can design an evaluation study to determine if the goals were met. Suppose a manufacturing company is selling too many defective

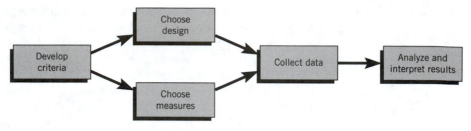

FIGURE 7-5
The five steps in evaluating a training program.

products. It might set as a training objective teaching employees to reduce errors in their manufacturing tasks. The criterion could be a specified reduction in the number of defective products. When the criterion is specific, such as a reduction of 10%, it is relatively easy to evaluate the effectiveness of the training program.

Training criteria are classified into two levels, both of which are important in evaluating training: training level and performance level. **Training-level criteria** are concerned with what people are able to do at the end of training in the training environment itself rather than on the job. **Performance level criteria** are concerned with the person's performance on the job rather than in the training setting. In other words, performance criteria are concerned with transfer of training. Thus training level is concerned with what the person learned, whereas performance level is concerned with the effects of the training on the job itself.

Performance- and training-level criteria are individually deficient in evaluating the effectiveness of training. The performance level is important because it shows whether or not the training has had the intended effects on the job. Because most training is intended to affect job performance, a training program without effects at the performance level is ineffective. On the other hand, it is important to know what the employees learned in the training. The best criterion for this is at the training level. Someone might learn a great deal and for some reason not apply it to the job. Failure to have an effect on the job might be due to other factors. For example, a person might know what to do and how to do it, but the opportunity to apply the knowledge might never occur. Employees might be given a first aid course to help them better handle work accidents. If no accidents occur, the employees will not show any effects at the performance level.

Another useful way of classifying criteria is to divide them into four types, two of which can be placed in the performance level and two in the training level (Kirkpatrick, 1977; see also Alliger & Janak, 1989):

Reactions	Behavior
Learning	Results

Reactions criteria refer to how much each trainee liked the training and how much they believed they got out of it. It is assessed with a questionnaire given to trainees at the end of the training session. **Learning criteria** refer to what the person learned in training—what the trainee is able to demonstrate behaviorally in terms of knowledge and skills acquired in training. It might be assessed with an examination given at the end of training. Both of these criteria types relate to the training level. They are frequently used in colleges and universities. Student evaluations are reaction criteria, and exam scores are learning criteria.

Behavior criteria concern the trainee's behaviors on the job that might have been due to training. This type of criterion looks at whether or not the person is doing the things he or she was taught. **Results criteria** deal with whether or not the training affected what it was intended to. Did the training reduce costs or increase productivity? This final type of criterion serves as the bottom line for the effectiveness of a training program. Both behav-

RESEARCH IN DETAIL

SOMETIMES EVENTS OCCUR IN ORGANIZATIONS that produce the equivalent of an experiment. Such was the case with the study by Campion and Campion (1987) when the availability of training for only some employees allowed the researchers to conduct a naturally occurring experiment to evaluate the effects of training. Employees were assigned to be either trained or untrained merely because the organization had insufficient resources and time for everyone to be trained. After the training was completed, the researchers assessed everyone to compare criteria between the trained and untrained employees.

This study took place in an electronics company that needed to move a large number of employees from manufacturing jobs to marketing jobs. Many of the employees lacked interview skills. The managers of the organization were concerned that their employees would be unable to perform well enough in an interview to transfer to another job. To remedy the deficiency, an interview skills training program was developed and implemented.

Roughly half of the eligible employees were given training and half were not. The training was evaluated with each of the four types of criteria: reaction, learning, behavior, and results. The reaction criterion was assessed, with a questionnaire at the end of the training. The majority of participants believed the training was worthwhile. Learning was assessed, with a test given to the trained employees at the beginning and end of training. This knowledge test showed that the participants learned about proper interview behavior during the training.

The behavior criterion was assessed by having the interviewers who later interviewed all employees rate how well they performed. According to this criterion, the trained group performed the same as the untrained group. Finally, the results criterion was assessed by noting the number of job offers each employee received. Here again there were no differences between the trained and untrained individuals.

These results suggested that the training was effective in teaching the employees interview skills but ineffective in helping them perform better in an actual job interview. From the organization's point of view, the training did not meet its objectives. The reasons for this failure are not clear. Perhaps the training was unnecessary because most employees already had good interview skills. Perhaps the training included the wrong material. In either case, this study demonstrates why it is important for organizations to assess different types of criteria when evaluating a training program.

Source: Campion, M. A., & Campion, J. E. (1987). Evaluation of an interviewee skill training program in a natural field experiment *Personnel Psychology, 40,* 675–691.

ior and results criteria are performance level because they focus on what happens on the job rather than on the training setting.

All of these criterion types are important because each is a partial indicator of the training success. A recent meta-analysis of 34 training studies showed that most criteria assessed within the same study were only slightly correlated with one another (Alliger, Tannenbaum, Bennett, Traver, & Shotland, 1997). Furthermore, in any given training program, only some of the criteria may show the desired results. Campion and Campion (1987) conducted a study in which they evaluated a training program against four different criteria. Their results showed that the training was effective at the training level but not at the performance level. These results demonstrate that one must be careful to include criteria at both levels to evaluate the effectiveness of a training program (see Research in Detail).

Choose Design

A *design* is the structure of a study that specifies how data are collected, whether it is a study of training or some other phenomenon. With a training evaluation, the type of criterion sets limits on the designs that can be used. For reaction criteria, the only feasible design is one that assesses participants once at the end of training. It makes no sense to assess nonparticipants or to assess participants before they go through training. People who have not been trained cannot have a reaction to what they have not experienced. People who have not yet been trained cannot have a reaction to what they are about to experience.

Other criteria can be assessed with many different types of designs. The two most popular are: pretest–posttest and control group. The *pretest–posttest design* assesses trainees before and after training. The *control group design* compares trainees with a group of employees who have not received the training. Each design has its advantages and limitations in evaluating a training program.

Pretest–Posttest. The **pretest–posttest design** is intended to provide information about how much the trainees gained from the training. It can be used to assess the amount learned in the training itself or the amount of change in behavior back on the job. To conduct a study with this design, the measures of interest are assessed before the training begins (pretest) and again after it has been completed (posttest). Figure 7-6 illustrates the structure of this design. Both pretest and posttest measures are part of the training program. It is not unusual for a training program to begin with a test to see what trainees know and conclude with a test to see what they have learned. Assessments can also occur on the job well before and well after training. For example, if a training program is intended to improve productivity, measures of productivity could be taken for the six months prior and the six months after training. Some training may not show effects on the job for a long period of time. Thorough evaluation would not be possible immediately after training.

The pretest–posttest design is popular because it is a practical design to use in organizations. It is usually easy to build in an assessment at the beginning and end of a training program. The assessment can also be used as a means of providing feedback. The major drawback of this design is that it is difficult to attribute changes to the training itself rather than other events in the organization. This is particularly true for performance criteria. If a training program is designed to improve job performance, gains in performance

FIGURE 7-6
Structure of a pretest-posttest training evaluation design.

from before to after training might have occurred for many reasons. Just making supervisors aware that performance is a problem could motivate them to put pressure on subordinates to perform. This increased attention on performance would coincide with the training and might be the cause of the performance gains. To find out if the training itself was the cause of the improvement would require a research design with a control group.

Control Group. A control group design compares employees who receive training to equivalent employees who have not been trained. Figure 7-7 illustrates the structure of this design. To conduct a control group study, a group of employees is selected for the study. Half are assigned at random to the trained group, and the other half are the controls who receive no training. At the end of the training program, all employees in the study are assessed on the measures of interest. The comparison between the two subgroups of employees indicates the effects of the training.

This design is more difficult to use in an organization because it is not always possible to assign employees at random to the two groups. In addition, there can be contamination as the trained employees tell the untrained control group employees what they have learned. However, this design is an improvement over the pretest–posttest when you wish to determine the effects of training. It helps control for the possibility that it was something other than training that caused the changes that you observed in employees.

Choose Measures of the Criteria

Once criteria have been chosen, the actual measures of those criteria need to be selected. The criterion of interest determines to a great extent what sorts of measures can be used to assess it. Reaction criteria require the use of a questionnaire that trainees can complete to give their reactions. The specific design of the questionnaire must be decided. There are many ways to ask people their reactions to training. For example, questions can ask how much the trainee learned or if the training was enjoyable.

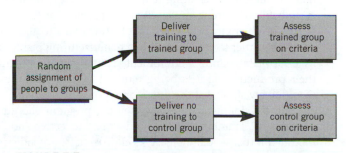

FIGURE 7-7
Structure of a control group training evaluation design.

Learning criteria usually involve some sort of test given at the end of training. Training intended to increase knowledge about a topic can be evaluated with a knowledge test, much like an examination given in school. Training to enhance other types of skills would require a different approach, such as a role play or simulation test. Assessment of performance criteria would require measuring trainee behavior or results in the job setting rather than in training.

Collect Data

Although the underlying logic of an evaluation study is simple and straightforward, carrying out the study can be a difficult undertaking because collecting the data poses many practical problems. People are not always cooperative, and many things can and do go wrong. It is difficult to perform pure random assignment in an organization, so that compromises have to be made. Often this means that the trained group comes from one department and the control group from another. Differences between the trained and untrained employees might then be caused by department differences on the criteria of interest.

The best possible design should always be planned. Every researcher knows that the plan might not be carried out without problems. This means that modifications might have to be made during the study. A good researcher is able to deal effectively with problems that occur during the data collection step of the study. If this step is conducted properly, it will be possible to draw conclusions about the effectiveness of the training program.

Analyze and Interpret Data

The data from evaluation studies are analyzed with inferential statistics. With a pretest–posttest design, the statistics will indicate how much the trainees changed from the pretest to the posttest. With a control group study, the statistics should show how much difference exists between the trained and untrained employees. In both cases, the statistic used could be as simple as a t test.

If all four prior steps of the training evaluation have been well done, it will be possible to reach a confident conclusion about the effectiveness of the training program. It is always a good idea to evaluate training, and it should be evaluated at both performance and training levels. Training will often be effective at only one of the two levels, so assessment of both will give useful information about the effects the training might have had.

If training works at both levels, it can be considered effective and should continue. Training that does not work at either level should be considered ineffective and eliminated or modified. Training that is effective at the training but not the performance level is probably the wrong approach to the problem or is an incomplete solution to the problem. A productivity problem might be due to inadequate knowledge or skill, but it can be caused by other factors as well. In a manufacturing plant, poor productivity can be caused by poor maintenance of equipment. Training of equipment operators is unlikely to affect their productivity if it is being reduced by faulty equipment. An evaluation of training would likely show that the operators learned, but productivity stayed the same.

The development of a new training program should always include an evaluation component. Training that is found to be ineffective should not continue but should be modified if that would increase its effectiveness. A good strategy for developing training is to pilot test it before implementation. A small group of employees could be put through the training, and the training would be evaluated at several levels. It would not be implemented throughout the organization until it has been found to be effective during pilot testing. This approach also allows for the modification of training so that it can be improved before full implementation throughout the organization. This strategy for developing training programs should result in making the most of training resources.

FUTURE ISSUES AND CHALLENGES

In their summary of future trends that affect the field of organizational training, Goldstein and Gilliam (1990) noted that changes in the nature of the workplace over the next few decades would require new training strategies in organizations. These workplace trends include

Changing demographics of the workforce

Increased use of technology

Internationalization

Shifts from manufacturing to service jobs

These trends will require more training by organizations.

It has been projected that the workforce in the United States will become older and that a larger proportion of the workforce will be comprised of minorities (Goldstein & Gilliam, 1990). This will occur while the level of necessary skills is increasing as a result of technological changes that affect how work is done. The relatively low-skilled manufacturing jobs of the past are being replaced by service jobs and technical jobs that require greater skill. In addition, organizations are becoming global in their operations and perspectives.

All of these changes will increase the need for organizational training. Older employees will have to be retrained to take on different sorts of jobs that might not have existed when they were initially hired. Underskilled workers will have to be given the necessary skills on the job that they might not have gotten in school. In addition, organizations will have to find ways to overcome the vestiges of discriminatory practices of the past. Training might focus on enhancing the skills of minorities to take on jobs they were denied even a few years ago.

The projected shortages of technically trained people may require that the emphasis in organizations shift from selection to training. This trend is one in which the United States may lag behind other countries that are less selection oriented. Organizations may have to be prepared to hire based on potential to learn rather than on present level of skills. They may also have to train and then retrain employees as their skills are made obsolete by technological change.

During the 1992 presidential campaign, President Clinton noted that no young person today can count on finding a job that will require the same skills throughout his or her entire career. Training will become an increasingly important activity to both individuals and the organizations that employ them. Hesketh (1997) argued that with rapid job changes brought on by technology, organizations need not only do more training, but also training in transferable skills rather than immediate tasks; otherwise employees will experience constant retraining. Rather than training a person to do one particular task, he or she should be taught the underlying principles that will allow for easy transfer to new tasks. For example, computer system training is often no more than showing a person a series of steps to accomplish a task, such as printing a document. If the software changes, new training must be done. However, someone who understands the principles underlying printing and software design can easily use a new system with little or no retraining. Jobs today can change so quickly that training quickly becomes obsolete

CHAPTER SUMMARY

Training is one of the most important activities of large organizations. The design of effective training programs in organizations is a five-step process:

Determine training needs through needs assessment

Set objectives for training

Design training

Deliver training

Evaluate training

The first step of a training program is to determine the need for training. This includes not only what should be trained but also who should be trained. Once the training need is established by a needs assessment, the objectives for the training should be decided. From the objectives a series of training criteria should be developed by which to judge the effectiveness of the training.

The design of effective training should consider characteristics of trainees. Different individuals might have different training needs. It should also incorporate the principles of good training and the methods that will be used. Many principles determine whether or not a particular training program will be effective:

Feedback

General principles

Identical elements

Overlearning

Sequencing of training sessions

Many training methods can be used. Each has its strengths and limitations, and no one method is necessarily better than the others. Choice of method depends on what and who are trained.

Training evaluation is done by conducting a research study to determine if the training was effective. The evaluation process includes five steps:

Select criteria

Choose a research design

Choose measures

Collect data

Analyze data and interpret results

A well-conducted evaluation study can provide valuable information about whether or not a training program is having its intended effects on individuals and organizations. A training program that is ineffective should be eliminated or modified so that it is effective. In the long run, a policy of evaluating training will lead to better use of training resources and a more effective workforce.

I/O PSYCHOLOGY IN PRACTICE

THIS CASE CONCERNS the development of management skills in high-level corporate executives, which is one of the major responsibilities of Dr. Charles Evans, who is an I/O psychologist working for an international consulting firm, RHR International, in Toronto, Canada. Dr. Evans received his Ph.D. in I/O psychology from the University of Guelph in Canada in 1994. Since then, he has been a consultant for RHR. His responsibilities are to work on projects for client organizations, which are some of the largest corporations in the world. Most of his work is in the areas of employee assessment and performance appraisal. His work is somewhat unusual because it focuses on the development of managerial skills rather than on employee selection, even though he uses many tools generally used for selection.

One of Dr. Evans' major functions is to provide assistance and feedback to executives who need to enhance their managerial skills. Often people who are promoted to high levels in organizations find that success on the job requires new approaches of dealing with people than they had used effectively at lower levels. A common problem is that executives are too autocratic and focused on results. Although subordinates at lower levels might have responded constructively to direct orders, middle and higher level managers do not. Instead, executives need to use skills in communication and persuasion. One must gain support for taking actions that require cooperation from many people for success. Individuals who lack these skills must develop them or they will remain ineffective.

Dr. Evans addresses these and other problems by collecting information about the individual and then giving feedback based on that information. He conducts a structured interview to assess the individual's background and interpersonal skills. A 360 degree feedback (see Chapter 4) is conducted, and the results are discussed with the person to let him or her know how he or she comes across to peers, subordinates, and supervisors. Dr. Evans assists the person in coming up with a development plan to address deficiencies and improve management skills. He serves as a coach to the person in helping figure out ways to do a better job.

Dr. Evans does this work mainly in North America, but his firm works with executives throughout the world. Companies pay executives very high salaries, and they are willing to spend a lot on their development, including hiring a private coach to help enhance their management skills. Such efforts can help organizations function better because their executives are more effective in dealing with people.

Discussion Questions

1. Why would a high-level executive want to enhance management skills?

2. How do you tell a person who has risen to the top of an organization that he or she needs to handle people more effectively?

3. Which of the training methods would be most effective here?

4. How would you go about evaluating what Dr. Evans does?

Part Four

THE INDIVIDUAL
AND THE ORGANIZATION

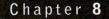

THEORIES OF
EMPLOYEE MOTIVATION

ill Gates, the founder and head of Microsoft Corporation, is known for his arduous work schedule. He typically spends 12 hours a day at the office and works several hours more at home. He does not own a television set because he says it is too distracting. At the present time, Gates is the richest person in the United States. Yet he still continues to work harder than almost anyone, even though he does not need more money. What drives Gates to work so hard? He says that he is motivated by challenges and the desire to learn new things.

Few people work as hard as Bill Gates. Furthermore, not everyone works for the challenge as he does. A variety of factors motivate people to work hard. The necessity to make money is certainly one of them. But there are others, which can be tangible, such as an insurance benefit, or intangible, such as a sense of accomplishment. Theories of motivation explain why people work hard. They also explain other types of work behavior that do not involve job performance. Most of the theories, however, have focused on job performance because job performance has been a central variable for the I/O field.

This chapter discusses job performance in terms of several popular theories, with a focus on motivation rather than ability. (In Chapter 10 we will explore other things that affect performance.) It also covers explanations for other forms of work behavior, such as turnover. The chapter begins by defining motivation in the context of the work environment. It then introduces work motivation theories and briefly overviews each of the eight theories to be covered. Each theory is next discussed in greater detail, along with the research evidence for its validity.

<u>Objectives</u>   **The student who studies this chapter should be able to:**
1. Define motivation.
2. List the major work motivation theories that are discussed in this chapter.
3. Describe how each of the major work motivation theories explains work behavior.
4. Compare and contrast the major work motivation theories.

WHAT IS MOTIVATION?

Motivation is a concept in psychology that has been discussed at great length for at least a century, but it is still difficult to define. **Motivation** is generally defined as an internal state that induces a person to engage in particular behaviors. From one perspective, it has to do with the direction, intensity, and persistence of behavior over time. *Direction* refers to the choice of specific behaviors from a large number of possible behaviors. For example, an employee might decide to go to work on a particular day instead of calling in sick and doing something else, such as watch television, go shopping, or visit a friend. *Intensity* refers to the amount of effort a person expends at doing a task. If an employee is asked to sweep a floor, the person can exert a lot of effort by sweeping hard and fast or exert a little effort by sweeping softly and slowly. *Persistence* refers to the continuing engagement in a behavior over time. Employees might work extra hours in order to accomplish tasks that they are motivated to complete.

From another perspective, motivation is concerned with the desire to acquire or achieve some goal. That is, motivation derives from a person's wants, needs, or desires. Some people, for example, are highly motivated to acquire money. It is presumed that a high level of motivation to have money would affect the behavior relevant to acquiring it.

WORK MOTIVATION THEORIES

Work motivation theories are most typically concerned with the reasons, other than ability, that some people perform their jobs better than others. Depending on the situation, these theories can predict people's choice of task behavior, their effort, or their persistence. Presuming that people have the necessary ability and that constraints on performance are relatively low, high levels of motivation should lead to good job performance. (See the discussion of job performance in Chapter 10.)

The theories covered in this chapter view employee motivation from very different perspectives. Two popular need theories that are discussed are concerned with categories of things that people are motivated to get such as food or recognition. Both need hierarchy theory and ERG (existence, relatedness, and growth) theory classify all human needs into a small number of categories. Both presume that people's behavior is directed toward fulfilling their needs. Two-factor theory says that various aspects of work address one of two categories of need. One category concerns the nature of the job itself, and the other concerns rewards such as pay.

Reinforcement theory views behavior as the result of rewards or reinforcements. As opposed to need theories, reinforcement theory describes motivation as the result of envi-

© 1997 United Feature Syndicate, Inc.

ronmental influences rather than internally generated motives. Expectancy theory, like reinforcement theory, attempts to relate environmental rewards to behavior. Unlike reinforcement theory, it is concerned with human cognitive processes that explain why rewards can lead to behavior.

Self-efficacy theory is concerned with how people's beliefs about their own capabilities can affect their behavior. According to this theory, motivation to attempt a task is related to whether or not the person believes he or she is capable of successfully accomplishing the task.

Equity theory is quite different from the other theories in that it is concerned with people's values rather than needs, beliefs, or reinforcements. The theory presumes that people universally value fairness in their social relations at work. Situations in which unfairness or inequity exists are presumed to motivate employees to fix it.

Goal-setting theory explains how people's goals and intentions can result in behavior. Like need theories, it notes that motivation begins inside the person, but it also shows how environmental influences can shape motivation and behavior.

Even though these various theories view motivation from different perspectives, they do not necessarily lead to different predictions about behavior. Portions of some of these theories can be complementary, and efforts have been made to integrate features of some of them. For example, Locke and Latham (1990) combined aspects of expectancy and self-efficacy theories with their goal-setting theory. In the remainder of this chapter, the various motivation theories will be discussed in detail.

NEED THEORIES

The three need theories discussed here view motivation as deriving from people's desires for certain things. It is implied that needs can differ both within the same person over time and across different people. The need hierarchy and ERG theories are concerned with variations in needs within individuals over time. Need theories were quite popular in the psychological literature at one time. In recent years, I/O researchers have turned their attention to more cognitively oriented theories, such as the goal-setting and self-efficacy theories. Perhaps the major reason for the declining interest in need theories is that research on needs has failed to find strong relations with job performance, possibly because needs are "distal" constructs (Kanfer, 1992) that are far removed from job performance.

That is, the rather general needs in these theories can be satisfied in many ways and with many different behaviors. Thus, a particular need is not likely to be strongly associated with any particular behavior. A person who has a high need to accomplish challenging tasks, for example, can fulfill that need either on or off the job. Nevertheless, need theories have contributed to our understanding of work motivation by showing how people can vary in the rewards they want out of work.

Need Hierarchy Theory

Maslow's **need hierarchy theory** (Maslow, 1943) states that fulfillment of human needs is necessary for both physical and psychological health. Human needs are arranged in a hierarchy that includes physical, social, and psychological needs. Figure 8-1 illustrates the need hierarchy from the lowest level physical needs to the highest level psychological needs. The lowest level physiological needs include the physical necessities for survival, such as air, water, and food. The second level consists of safety needs, those things that protect us from danger. This level includes the need for security and shelter. The third level are the love needs, which include the need for love, affection, and affiliation with others. The fourth level are esteem needs, which involve self-respect and the respect of others. Finally, there is self-actualization, which Maslow did not define precisely. It refers to the fulfillment of personal life goals and reaching one's potential, or as Maslow did state, "the desire to become . . . everything that one is capable of becoming" (Maslow, 1943, p. 382).

According to Maslow, a need must be unmet to be motivating, and people are motivated by the lowest level need that is unmet. That is, if two levels of needs are unmet, the lower level need will dominate. Thus, a hungry person would not be concerned with danger and might risk stealing food even though the punishment for theft is severe. A person with unmet safety needs would not be concerned about going to a party and having a good time with friends. Maslow recognized, however, that there can be exceptions to the hierarchy and that some individuals can find certain higher order needs to be more important than lower level ones. Furthermore, many individuals in Western society have the first four needs met and may never have experienced deprivations of one or more of them, especially food. Therefore, the basic needs are not motivating.

Research on need hierarchy theory has not been very supportive. Locke and Henne (1986) have noted that at least part of the difficulty is that Maslow's statement of the the-

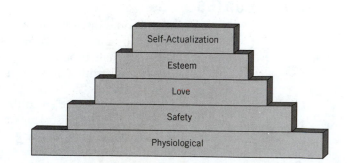

FIGURE 8-1
Maslow's needs hierarchy.

ory is rather vague, making it difficult to design good tests of it. Despite its lack of empirical support, need hierarchy theory has had a positive impact on organizations. It continues to be taught to both current and future managers. This helps focus attention on the importance of meeting employees' needs at work.

ERG Theory

Alderfer's (1969) **Existence, Relatedness, Growth (ERG) theory** was an attempt to fix some of the difficulties in Maslow's need hierarchy. In this theory there are three as opposed to five needs, which are arranged on a continuum rather than a hierarchy. The idea is that people can move back and forth from one category of need to another, and lack of fulfillment of needs in one category can affect needs in another category.

The three needs are shown in Figure 8-2. *Existence needs* involve material objects as well as those that address physiological desires and the necessities for basic survival, such as food and water. *Relatedness needs* are similar to Maslow's social needs and involve relationships with "significant" other people, such as family members, friends, co-workers, and supervisors. *Growth needs* concern creativity or productivity within the self or in the environment. Growth implies that the person is fully utilizing his or her capabilities or is even developing additional capabilities.

Alderfer's three needs are arranged in a continuum in order of their concreteness. Existence needs are most concrete because they involve physical objects. Relatedness is next because it involves people in terms of social relationships, which are not manifestations of the physical world. Finally, growth is least concrete because it does not have to involve physical aspects of the environment at all, although physical objects can be the end product, for example, a painting or a novel.

In contrast to Maslow, Alderfer allows for the flow of need strength back and forth through the continuum. When a need is fulfilled, the person experiences a lessened desire for that need and a greater desire for a less concrete need. After a big meal, for example, a person would experience an increased need to socialize with others. The concept of **frustration-regression** explains that when people are frustrated in their attempts to fulfill needs at one level, they will regress to needs at a more concrete level. For example, suppose a person fails at a personally important task that would fulfill his or her growth needs. That person might regress back to a relatedness need and affiliate with other people. There are two exceptions to this pattern. Failure to fulfill an existence need leads to greater existence need, and fulfillment of growth needs leads to greater growth need.

Research evidence has been somewhat more supportive of Alderfer than of Maslow, but the evidence is somewhat mixed. For example, Wanous and Zwany (1977) asked em-

FIGURE 8-2
Alderfer's need continuum of existence, relatedness, and growth.

ployees to rate their extent of satisfaction and fulfillment and the importance of 23 individual work needs. They used complex statistical methods to determine if people's reported level of work need fulfillment would conform to existence, relatedness, and growth. They found good support for the growth category, moderate support for the existence category, and only weak support for the relatedness category. They next tested the idea that need satisfaction at one level would affect need importance at another. Only partial support was found for this theory. Two findings did support it: The higher the growth satisfaction, the higher was the need for growth; and the higher the relatedness satisfaction, the higher was the need for growth. On the other hand, two findings failed to support the theory: Existence satisfaction was unrelated to relatedness satisfaction; and the greater the relatedness satisfaction, the greater (not less) was relatedness importance. As with Maslow, however, the content of the need categories is not very precise, particularly for the growth needs, and measurement of need satisfaction and importance is difficult. This makes empirical testing problematic because the important concepts of the theory might not be adequately measured.

Two-Factor Theory

Herzberg's (1968) **two-factor theory** states that motivation comes from the nature of the job itself, not from external rewards or job conditions. The human needs that work addresses are divided into two categories—those deriving from the animal nature of human beings, such as the physiological needs, and those relating to the higher level, uniquely human ability for psychological growth. Job aspects relevant to the animal needs are called **hygiene factors** and include pay, supervision, co-workers, and organizational policies. Job aspects relevant to growth needs are called **motivator factors** and include achievement, recognition, responsibility, and the nature of the work itself.

According to Herzberg, the way to motivate employees is to provide appropriate levels of motivator factors. Hygiene factors, no matter how favorable, cannot lead to motivation. Furthermore, Herzberg argues that job satisfaction and dissatisfaction are separate and unrelated constructs rather than opposite ends of the same continuum. Motivator factors can lead to satisfaction, but their absence can lead only to lack of satisfaction and not dissatisfaction. Hygiene factors can lead to dissatisfaction, but at best they can produce only lack of dissatisfaction rather than satisfaction.

Most researchers consider Herzberg's theory to be invalid (Locke & Henne, 1986). The major problem with the theory is that the two-factor structure of job satisfaction versus dissatisfaction has not been supported by research. The research conducted by Herzberg is considered flawed because it relied on employee descriptions of satisfying and dissatisfying events. In describing such events, people tend to note things they did themselves as satisfying and things done by others as dissatisfying. This makes it seem that satisfaction and dissatisfaction are caused by different factors.

Despite shortcomings in the theory, Herzberg has been influential. His work helped focus the field on the important issue of providing meaningful work to people. It led to the application of job enrichment in many organizations. It also was the basis for Hackman and Oldham's (1976) job characteristics theory, which is discussed in Chapters 9 and 10.

REINFORCEMENT THEORY

Reinforcement theory describes how rewards or reinforcements can affect behavior. The theory does not deal with internal states such as motivation, so in a sense it is a nonmotivational theory. It explains behavior as a function of prior reward experiences or "reinforcement history." Behavior is seen as a response to the environment.

The major tenet of reinforcement theory is the *law of effect* (Thorndike, 1913). This states that the probability of a particular behavior increases if it is followed by a reward or reinforcement. Conversely, the probability of a behavior decreases if it is followed by a punishment. Behaviors become established through the pairing or associating of behavior with reinforcement. In other words, rewards are *contingent* on a particular behavior occurring. In a job context, this means that performance-relevant behaviors will increase in frequency if they are rewarded.

Rewards can be tangible (money) or intangible (praise). They can be given by the organization or be a byproduct of tasks themselves. Thus, the organization can provide a bonus for good performance, or good performance can provide a sense of accomplishment by itself. Both can be equally reinforcing and lead to continued good performance.

This rather simple idea that behavior increases if it is rewarded is the basis of incentive systems, such as piece rates for factory workers or commissions for salespeople. With **incentive systems**, rewards are contingent on individual units of productivity, such as attaching the door of a refrigerator or selling an automobile. For jobs with countable

It requires a tremendous amount of motivation to win a marathon. Most jobs require far less effort than running a marathon.

output, it can be relatively easy to institute incentive systems. For other jobs there can be specific, measurable performance-relevant behaviors that could be quantified. For example, telephone operators can be rewarded for answering the phone within a specified number of rings. With many jobs, however, it is not feasible to develop incentive systems as discussed here. For example, it would be quite difficult to design a piece-rate system for public school teachers. Good performance for a teacher is not easy to divide into individual units of productivity or individual behaviors that can be rewarded.

Research has shown that rewards can be effective in enhancing job performance. Stajkovic and Luthans (1997) conducted a meta-analysis of 19 studies of the effects of rewards, both monetary and nonmonetary, on job performance. They found that on average reward systems result in a 17% increase in performance. However, not every study has found an increase in performance (e.g., Coch & French, 1948). Although rewards can enhance job performance under some conditions, such conditions do not always exist in organizations. Additional influences by other employees, constraints in the environment (e.g., inadequate equipment), and the indifference of individuals to particular rewards can result in the failure of incentive systems.

Many organizations have applied reinforcement theory principles to influence the behavior of employees. These efforts have involved not only job performance but other behaviors as well. The control of employee absence has been the focus of reinforcement programs. Some organizations allow employees a certain number of sick leave days in a year. To encourage attendance, employees are paid for the sick leave days they do not use. Other organizations reward each employee who meets a criterion of attendance for a given period of time (e.g., no absences in a month). A rather unusual absence control program was a lottery system studied by Pedalino and Gamboa (1974). With this system all employees present at work each day were allowed to draw a card from a standard deck of playing cards. At the end of a week, employees with perfect attendance would have a five-card poker hand. The eight employees with the best poker hands won a prize of $20. This system was found to reduce absence frequency by about 18%.

Although the principles of reinforcement theory can be useful, the theory itself has fallen somewhat out of favor among most I/O psychologists. The major reason is probably that reinforcement theory gives little insight into motivational processes (Locke, 1980). It merely describes relations between reinforcement and behavior. In addition, some people object to the idea of using rewards to regulate behavior. They believe that these programs represent an unethical form of manipulation. Many of those who hold this position are assuming that the technique of reinforcement has more power over people than it actually does. Under the proper circumstances, people will voluntarily work harder for rewards that they want. Reinforcement theory says nothing about whether or not a person will want a reward. This issue is addressed by expectancy theory, which we discuss next.

EXPECTANCY THEORY

Expectancy theory attempts to explain how rewards lead to behavior by focusing on internal cognitive states that lead to motivation. Reinforcement theory states that reinforcement will lead to behavior; expectancy theory explains when and why this will occur. The basic idea is that people will be motivated when they believe that their behavior will lead to rewards or outcomes that they want. If they do not believe that rewards will be contingent on their behavior, they will not be motivated to perform that behavior. If they do not want the contingent rewards, they will not be motivated to perform a behavior.

Several somewhat different versions of expectancy theory have been adapted to the I/O domain. The oldest and most well known is Vroom's (1964). Vroom's theory posits that motivation or force is a mathematical function of three types of cognitions. The equation relating force to cognitions is:

Force = Expectancy × Σ(Valences × Instrumentalities)

In this equation **force** represents the amount of motivation a person has to engage in a particular behavior or sequence of behaviors that are relevant to job performance. It could be thought of as the motivation to perform. **Expectancy** is the subjective probability that a person has about his or her ability to perform a behavior. It is similar to self-esteem or self-confidence in that a person believes he or she can perform the job at a particular level. *Subjective probability* means that people can vary in the certainty of their beliefs. A subjective probability of zero means that the person is certain that he or she is incapable of performing successfully. A subjective probability of 1.0 means that the person is absolutely convinced, without the slightest doubt, that he or she can perform successfully. A subjective probability of .50 means that the person believes there is a 50/50 chance of success.

Valence is the value of an outcome or reward to a person. It is the extent to which a person wants or desires something. In the job setting, money is a frequent reward that can have different valence levels for different people. **Instrumentality** is the subjective probability that a given behavior will result in a particular reward. For any given situation, there can be more than one reward or outcome for a behavior. For each possible outcome, a valence and instrumentality are multiplied. Then each valence-instrumentality product is summed into a total, and the total is multiplied by expectancy to produce a force score. If the force score is high, the person will be motivated to achieve the outcomes of the job. If the force score is low, the person will not be motivated to achieve the outcomes.

Table 8-1 shows how possible combinations of values for expectancy, valence, and instrumentality are combined into a force score. This case presumes that there is a single outcome. As the table shows, only when all three components are high will force be high.

TABLE 8-1
The relation of expectancy, valence, and instrumentality to force

EXPECTANCY SCORE	VALENCE SCORE	INSTRUMENTALITY SCORE	FORCE SCORE
High	High	High	High
High	High	Low	Low
High	Low	High	Low
High	Low	Low	Very low
Low	High	High	Low
Low	High	Low	Very low
Low	Low	High	Very low
Low	Low	Low	Very very low

If any one of the three components is low, force will be low. If any one of the three components equals zero, there will be no motivation.

In most situations more than one outcome is possible, so that the situation is somewhat more complex because the valence-instrumentality for each outcome is combined. The way this works is best illustrated with an example. Suppose you are at work on a Friday afternoon and your boss asks for a volunteer to work overtime for extra pay. Suppose further that you find your job rather boring and would find the prospect of working extra hours somewhat aversive. In this case there are two outcomes—receiving extra money and enduring several hours of boredom. If you believe that you are capable of working overtime, your expectancy will be high. Assuming that you believe both that you will get the overtime pay and that you will be bored, both instrumentalities will be high. The final factor that determines your motivation to work overtime will be the relative valences of the two outcomes. If the positive valence or desire for money is greater than the negative valence or desire to avoid the boredom, then you will be motivated to volunteer. If the positive valence for money is less than the negative valence for boredom, then you will be motivated to avoid volunteering.

Expectancy theory can also predict a person's choice of behavior from two or more options. Suppose that you have a dinner date, and you must choose between working overtime or going on the date. For each possible course of action, there will be an expectancy, valences, and instrumentalities. Thus, there will be a force to work overtime and a force to go on the date. The course of action with the greater force is the one, in theory, that you will take.

There has been research support for the predictions of expectancy theory. Studies have shown that performance is related to the individual components of expectancy theory, as well as for the multiplicative combination (Van Eerde & Thierry, 1996). In the typical study, a sample of employees is surveyed and asked to indicate their expectancies that they can perform the job, as well as their valences and instrumentalities for each of a number of possible outcomes. In addition, supervisors are asked to provide job performance ratings for each employee. The total force score is then correlated with performance. Hackman and Porter (1968), for example, conducted such a study and found that force predicted performance as assessed by both objective production data and supervisor ratings.

Fox, Scott, and Donohue (1993) assessed the valence of pay and job performance of production employees who worked on an incentive pay system. These employees worked for a clothing manufacturer. The performance measure was the number of garments produced and was taken from company records. In this study those individuals who valued pay the most had the highest levels of job performance. Consistent with expectancy theory, valence of rewards related to performance when performance was tied to rewards.

Van Eerde and Thierry (1996) conducted a meta-analysis of expectancy theory studies that looked not only at predictions of job performance, but at effort and preferences as well. Although the study showed that the force score related to measures of job performance as expected, it related more strongly to measures of effort. Similarly, the force score related more strongly to an individual's preference for something other than their actual choice, for example, wanting to quit a job versus actually quitting. These findings demonstrate that motivation is only one element in processes that lead to behavior at work. A person might be motivated to work harder, but this doesn't necessarily produce better job performance. Having a preference for something is not the same as making an actual choice, for other factors can be important, such as not being able to find another job when you want to quit your present one.

SELF-EFFICACY THEORY

Self-efficacy theory states that motivation and performance are determined in part by how effective people believe they can be (Bandura, 1982). In other words, people with high **self-efficacy** believe they are capable of accomplishing tasks and will be motivated to put forth effort. People with low self-efficacy do not believe they can accomplish tasks; they will not be motivated and will not put forth the effort. In a way, this is like a self-fulfilling prophecy in which a person behaves in a manner that fulfills his or her initial belief. This theory presumes that the person has the necessary ability and that constraints on performance are not insurmountable.

The self-efficacy concept itself is concerned with specific tasks or courses of action, and people vary in their self-efficacy across different tasks. Thus, a student might have high self-efficacy for taking essay exams and low self-efficacy for taking multiple-choice tests. This can explain why many students complain that they are good at one type of test and not the other. The theory would predict that students would exert greater effort when taking the type of test for which their self-efficacy was higher.

Self-efficacy is much like the concept of expectancy. The major difference is that expectancy is concerned with a specific activity at a particular point in time, whereas self-efficacy is concerned with the general feeling that a person is or is not capable in some domain of life, such as playing tennis. For example, a person might have a high level of expectancy that if he or she makes the effort he or she can win a tennis game. A high level of self-efficacy is the belief that one is a good player. Obviously, these two concepts are closely related, for the person with high self-efficacy should have a high expectancy, but they are not the same. The person who believes he or she is good at tennis might not be confident about winning if he or she is playing one of the best professional players in the world. Self-efficacy theory and expectancy theory are compatible in predicting that people will do well at tasks when they believe they can succeed. Expectancy theory also considers the influence motivation has on rewards, a subject that is not addressed by self-efficacy theory.

The theory of self-efficacy has been well tested, and research has been quite supportive. Studies in the training domain have shown that self-efficacy for particular tasks relates to performance in training on those tasks. For example, McIntire and Levine (1991) conducted a longitudinal study of self-efficacy and performance among students taking college-level typing courses. They assessed self-efficacy before the course began and at the end of the course. They also assessed the number of words per minute typed and the grade at the end of the course. Finally, each student was asked to set a goal for the number of words typed by the end of the course. The results were that self-efficacy before the class predicted the number of words per minute typed at the end of the course, but not the grade in the course. Self-efficacy was also related to the goal set with greater self-efficacy associated with setting a higher goal. These results suggest that self-efficacy can be a factor in future performance. The results with goals suggest that self-efficacy might operate through the setting of goals, such that students with high self-efficacy set harder goals, which resulted in better performance. Goal setting is discussed in detail later in this chapter.

Similar results with self-efficacy have been found in other training studies. Mathieu, Martineau, and Tannenbaum (1993) found that self-efficacy assessed before a bowling class was related to students' subsequent performance at the end of class. Locke and Latham (1990) conducted a meta-analysis of 13 studies relating self-efficacy to performance in both laboratory and field settings. They found a mean correlation of .39, with correlations as high as .74.

Whereas at least some of the relation between people's self-efficacy and their performance can be attributed to motivation, some of the relation might also be due to ability. One of the ways in which high self-efficacy develops is through success. Individuals who have high levels of ability are likely to have experienced success in the past and thus are likely to be high in self-efficacy. In the McIntire and Levine (1991) study, course grade related to self-efficacy at the end of the class but not the beginning, suggesting that students who achieved better grades enhanced their self-efficacy. Karl, O'Leary-Kelly, and Martocchio (1993) found that positive feedback on a speed reading task raised the self-efficacy of people who were initially low in self-efficacy.

Dov Eden and his associates have conducted a series of studies in the workplace in which they manipulated self-efficacy to see its effects on job performance. These experimental studies controlled for ability and initial motivation by randomly assigning subjects to have their self-efficacy raised or not by providing information or training. Eden refers to this as the **Galatea effect** in which people's beliefs about their own capabilities lead them to perform better, as in a self-fulfilling prophecy. Eden and Aviram (1993) successfully applied this approach to increase the job search success of unemployed people. Similarly, Eden and Zuk (1995) used this technique to convince naval cadets in the Israel Defense Forces that they were unlikely to get seasick. This illness creates significant problems for all navies because it can interfere with job performance at sea. Eden and Zuk conducted an experiment in which cadets were randomly assigned to one of two groups—a briefing that assured them seasickness was unlikely and would not interfere with their performance, or a control group that was given no such briefing. While at sea, the briefed cadets had less seasickness and performed better than the control group. This very simple technique to enhance self-efficacy was quite effective.

Self-efficacy theory is a useful theory with implications for the work setting. It suggests that motivation and performance can be enhanced by raising the self-efficacy of employees. Bandura (1982) discussed how self-efficacy can develop through a series of successes with increasingly difficult tasks. An organization could apply this principle by structuring the assignments of employees in such a way that they succeed at increasingly challenging tasks. This strategy can be particularly important with new employees, who may take some period of time to become adept at all aspects of the job. Relatively simple assignments could be given to new employees, with more difficult tasks introduced slowly to allow the person to experience few, if any, failures. As the person experiences success on more and more difficult tasks, his or her self-efficacy should increase. Karl et al. (1993) suggested using this approach in training programs. Dov Eden and his associates have shown that training can be successful for raising self-efficacy.

EQUITY THEORY

Equity theory (Adams, 1965), states that people are motivated to achieve a condition of equity or fairness in their dealings with other people and with organizations. According to

Adams (1965), employees who find themselves in inequitable situations will experience dissatisfaction and emotional tension that they will be motivated to reduce. The theory specifies conditions under which inequity will occur and what employees are likely to do to reduce it.

Inequity is a psychological state that arises from employees' comparisons of themselves with others. What is specifically compared are ratios of outcomes to inputs. **Outcomes** are the rewards or everything of personal value that an employee gets from working for an organization, including pay, fringe benefits, good treatment, enjoyment, and status. **Inputs** are the contributions made by the employee to the organization. They include not only the work that the employee accomplishes, but the experience and talents that he or she brings to the job as well. Thus, an employee with many years of job experience would have greater inputs than an employee just starting out in a career.

The theory posits that employees form psychological comparisons of their own outcome/input ratios to those of other employees. That is, employees will psychologically evaluate how much they receive from the job (outcomes) in relation to their contributions (inputs), which is represented as the ratio:

OUTCOMES/INPUTS

Each employee compares his or her ratio to the ratios of people chosen for comparison. These comparison people or *others* might be employees doing the same job inside or outside the organization. They might also be people who have different types of jobs. Talk show host Sally Jessy Raphael has publicly complained that she makes less money than another host, Oprah Winfrey. Raphael might have chosen to compare herself with other hosts or other television personalities, such as actors or newscasters. It is likely that she chose Winfrey because of the close similarity of their jobs.

The comparison involves the entire ratio and not the individual outcomes or inputs. Thus, a person may believe a situation is equitable even though his or her outcomes are less than inputs. It is only when the employee believes that his or her ratio is different from other people's that inequity exists. This difference can be in either direction. That is, an employee can experience *underpayment* inequity if he or she believes that other people get more outcomes for their inputs. *Overpayment* inequity exists when an employee believes he or she is getting more outcomes for his or her inputs than other people are getting.

Figure 8-3 illustrates several possible comparison situations. In each case it is presumed that the employee's ratio is 10/20. That is, the employee receives one unit of outcome for each two units of input. Note that the outcome and input scores do not have to be equal. It is the comparison that is important, not the ratio itself. In the first two cases, the comparison other also has a ratio that reduces to one outcome per two inputs, so equity is achieved. In the first case the outcomes are half of the target person's (5) but the inputs are half as well (10). In the second case, both the outcomes and inputs are double (20 and 40, respectively). The next two cases illustrate underpayment inequity. That is, the employee's ratio is lower than the comparison other's, resulting in a feeling of underpayment. In the third case the comparison other is getting the same outcomes but is giving only half the inputs (10/10), and in the fourth case the comparison other is getting double the outcomes for the same inputs. The last two cases involve overpayment inequity. That is, the employee is receiving more outcomes per unit of input than the comparison other. In case 5 the comparison other receives half the outcomes for the same inputs, and in case 6 the comparison other receives the same outcomes for double the inputs.

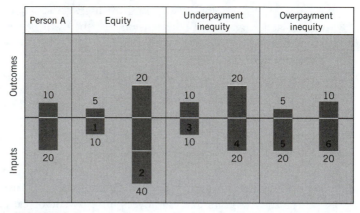

FIGURE 8-3

An illustration of equity and inequity. Person A has twice as many inputs as outcomes (see bars in first column). The other six bars represent comparison other's inputs and outcomes. Person A will experience equity or inequity depending on who he or she chooses as a comparison. Cases 1 and 2 illustrate equity, where both inputs are double outcomes. Case 3 represents underpayment because the outcomes are the same as Person A's, but inputs are only half. Case 4 is underpayment because inputs are the same as Person A's, but outcomes are double. Case 5 is overpayment because inputs are the same as Person A's, but outcomes are half. Case 6 is overpayment because outcomes are the same as Person A's, but inputs are double.

According to Adams (1965), underpayment inequity induces anger and overpayment inequity induces guilt. In either case, the employee will be motivated to reduce the inequity through several possible mechanisms. Three of these mechanisms are particularly relevant to the organizational setting—changing inputs, changing outcomes, or withdrawal from the situation. An employee can change inputs by either increasing or decreasing productivity, depending on whether the inequity is over- or underpayment. An employee can change outcomes by seeking additional rewards from work. For example, he or she can ask for a raise or file a formal grievance. Withdrawal can be temporary, as in lateness or absence, both of which can be a means of reducing inputs. It can also be permanent turnover.

Much of the research that has tested equity theory has been conducted in laboratory settings. In the typical laboratory study, subjects are asked to complete a task for some reward, and inequity is experimentally induced. In general, these studies have provided support for the expected underpayment effect of lowered performance, but not the overpayment effect of raised performance (Locke & Henne, 1986). A study conducted by Greenberg (1990) showed that a pay cut was associated with increased stealing by factory workers. Greenberg explained his results as being consistent with equity theory. That is, employees who experienced inequity because of the pay cut increased their outcomes by stealing.

In an Australian study, Iverson and Roy (1994) found that employee perceptions of inequity correlated with their intentions to quit the job and with job search behavior. Both of these variables have been found to predict turnover (e.g., Blau, 1993b), as we discuss in Chapter 10.

Although equity theory was quite popular among I/O researchers at one time, interest in it has declined over the past decade. Locke and Henne (1986) believe that this decline is caused by the fact that the theory does a better job of explaining past behavior than predicting future behavior. Part of the difficulty is that the theory is not able to predict how employees choose their comparison others. Without knowing this, it is difficult to make predictions about how a particular organizational policy or action will be perceived by employees. Nevertheless, equity theory has directed attention to the importance of treating employees fairly and to the possible negative effects of not doing so.

Recent research on fairness in the workplace has replaced equity theory with a somewhat different perspective. Equity theory deals with fair allocation or distribution of rewards. By contrast, recent theories of **procedural justice** in the workplace are concerned with the fairness of the reward distribution process (Kanfer, 1992). It might be more important that employees believe that the process was fair rather than that the distribution was equitable. Sweeney and McFarlin (1997), for example, found that perceptions of fair processes for allocation of rewards was related to employee attitudes and intention of quitting the job. Future research will probably focus on both the distribution and process for distribution of rewards.

GOAL-SETTING THEORY

The theory of motivation that probably has been the most useful for I/O psychologists is **goal-setting theory** (Locke & Latham, 1990). Principles of goal setting have been widely used in organizations, although it is not necessarily based on the theory. For example, Yearta, Maitlis, and Briner (1995) noted that 79% of British organizations use some form of goal setting. Various goal-setting programs have been widely used throughout the industrialized world.

The basic idea of this theory is that people's behavior is motivated by their internal *intentions*, *objectives*, or *goals*—the terms are used here interchangeably. Goals are quite "proximal" constructs, for they can be tied quite closely to specific behaviors. For example, a salesperson might have the goal of selling a certain amount of product in a given month. Because goals can be tied closely to particular behaviors relevant for performance, goal-setting theory has been strongly tied to behavior.

According to the theory, a goal is what a person consciously wants to attain or achieve. Goals can be specific, such as "receive an 'A' on the next exam," or general, such as "do well in school." General goals such as doing well in school are often associated with a number of more specific goals such as receiving an "A." Locke and Henne (1986) note four ways in which goals affect behavior. First, goals direct attention and action to behaviors that the person believes will achieve the goal. A student who has the goal of making an "A" on an exam would be expected to engage in studying behavior, such as reading the assigned material and reviewing class notes. Second, goals mobilize effort in that the person tries harder. The student with the goal of an "A" will concentrate harder to learn the material. Third, goals increase persistence, resulting in more time spent on the behaviors necessary

TABLE 8-2
Important factors for goal setting to improve job performance

1. Goal acceptance by the employee
2. Feedback on progress toward goals
3. Difficult and challenging goals
4. Specific goals

Source: "Work Motivation Theories," by E. A Locke & D. Henne, 1986. In C. L. Cooper & I. T. Robertson (Eds.). *International Review or Industrial and Organizational Psychology 1986.* Chichester, UK: John Wiley.

for goal attainment. The student who wants an "A" will spend more time studying. Finally, goals can motivate the search for effective strategies to attain them. The conscientious student will attempt to learn effective ways of studying and good test-taking strategies.

Goal-setting theory predicts that people will exert effort toward accomplishing their goals and that job performance is a function of the goals set. From an organizational standpoint, goal setting can be an effective means of maintaining or increasing job performance, and many organizations have used goal setting to do so. According to Locke and Henne (1986), several factors are necessary for goal setting to be effective in improving job performance (Table 8-2). First, employees must have *goal commitment*, which means that they accept the goal. An organizational goal is not necessarily an individual employee goal, and only goals of the individual person will motivate behavior. Second, *feedback* is necessary because it allows people to know whether or not their behavior is moving them toward or away from their goals. It is difficult for goals to direct behavior unless the person receives feedback. Third, the more difficult the goal, the better the performance is likely to be. A goal of a 4.0 grade point average is likely to result in better performance than a goal of 3.5, which is likely to result in better performance than a goal of 3.0. Although people will not always reach their goals, the harder the goal, the better the performance, at least until the point at which the person is working at the limit of his or her capacity. Finally, specific hard goals are more effective than vague "do your best" goals. Vague goals can be effective, but specific goals that allow the person to know when they are met are best.

Goal-setting theory is well supported by research (Locke & Latham, 1990) and is currently the most popular theory of motivation in the I/O domain. Not only have its propositions been the subject of considerable research, but goal setting is a popular means of increasing job performance as well. The theory and research surrounding it have underscored several important factors that are essential for a successful goal-setting program. For example, all four of the factors in Table 8-2 are necessary if a goal-setting program is to be effective.

Although research has shown that goal-setting can be effective, some researchers have begun to note its limitations. Yearta et al. (1995) noted that most goal-setting studies involved single goals, such as increased production in a factory. They showed that with more complex jobs and multiple goals, performance was lower when goals were difficult. Doerr, Mitchell, Klastorin, and Brown (1996) showed that group goals were better than individual goals for increasing speed of production in a fish processing plant (see the Research in Detail box).

RESEARCH IN DETAIL

THERE HAS BEEN a trend in large organizations toward the use of work groups and teams rather than individuals to accomplish work. Thus, it is important that we understand how groups and individuals differ in their behavior and reactions. One area of concern is how to motivate people who work in groups. Goal-setting can be an effective motivational technique for individuals, but will it be equally effective with groups?

This study was conducted in a fish processing plant in the northwestern United States with a workforce consisting entirely of non-Americans. These employees worked two to three hours per day cleaning and dressing salmon that arrived by boat. During the course of the study, 39 employees participated in an experiment with goal-setting. Three conditions were created—group goal, individual goal, and no goal. An initial baseline measure of production speed was taken to serve as the standard against which to set goals. The goals represented working at a consistent pace that was faster than typically maintained. Employees were given feedback as well as an incentive of state lottery tickets for goal achievement.

To meet the group goal, the output of everyone combined had to achieve the predetermined amount. For the individual condition, each person had his or her own goal. Results showed that productivity was significantly higher for both conditions than for the no goal control condition, although the group goal productivity was even higher than the individual. Mean time to process 50 fish was 538 versus 570 seconds for group and individual goals, respectively. The no goal mean was 702 seconds.

These results demonstrate that in production situations, goal-setting can be quite effective. Furthermore, groups might respond even more favorably than individuals. As discussed in Chapter 12, groups can have powerful effects on members, and conditions that motivate groups can have enhanced effects on individuals in those groups. However, it should be recognized that this study involved single goals with very simple tasks. These effects might not occur in situations where things are more complex. Nevertheless, goal-setting can be a powerful motivational tool if applied appropriately in the proper setting.

Source: Doerr, K. H., Mitchell, T. R., Klastorin, T. D., & Brown, K. A. (1996). Impact of material flow policies and goals on job outcomes. *Journal of Applied Psychology, 75*, 142–152.

Action Theory

Although goal-setting theory is the most popular goal theory in I/O, several variations have been developed (Farr, Hofmann, & Ringenbach, 1993). Most are more explicit in describing the process by which people tie goals to behaviors. Perhaps the most extensive, which goes far beyond our American theories, is German **action theory**, which describes a process linking goals to actions (Frese & Zapf, 1994). This theory proposes that work motivation theories focus mainly on goal-oriented behaviors called actions. Such actions are the product of a conscious intent to accomplish something, which can be as small as finishing one piece on an assembly line to achieving a promotion at work. The major focus of this theory is on the actions themselves and on the processes leading to actions.

In the workplace where we are performing tasks to accomplish objectives, whether imposed by the organization or the person, actions predominate.

Action theory describes a process involving a hierarchy of cognitions from an initial desire to have something to specific actions designed to acquire it. In simplified form, the process involves the following four steps:

A person wants something.

A goal to acquire it is set.

A plan to achieve the goal is accepted.

Actions are engaged to carry out the plan.

For example, you might want to make a lot of money, so you set the goal of landing a well-paying job when you graduate college. Your plan might be to major in a field in which such jobs are plentiful and to have a high grade point average. Actions will address these aspects of the plan, such as investigating job opportunities of various majors and studying for classes. This approach sees the individual as the initiator of action, or the cause of his or her own behavior, as opposed to reinforcement and other motivation theories that emphasize how a person responds to the environment.

FUTURE ISSUES AND CHALLENGES

There are two major challenges to the field in the area of motivation. First, research is needed to adequately test theories of motivation. Second, organizations need to know how employees can be motivated to do their jobs well. These two areas are not mutually exclusive, for adequate theory testing can provide ideas for effective organizational interventions aimed at improving motivation. On the other hand, the development and implementation of programs to enhance motivation can provide evidence relevant to the testing of theories.

Many studies have tested the various motivation theories discussed in this chapter. Methodological limitations have made it difficult to provide strong tests for several of them. Perhaps the most troublesome problem is that of adequately measuring the constructs of the theories, particularly theories involving cognitions or needs. Studies of needs have used self-reports. Thus, people are asked to indicate how well their needs have been met or to estimate the current level of needs. The underlying assumption in using self-reports is that people are aware of their levels of need and that they are willing to reveal them. Maslow (1943) noted that people are not necessarily aware of their needs, making their reports inaccurate. If Maslow is correct, self-reports do not provide good data to test need theories.

Difficulties have also been noted with assessing the components of expectancy theory (e.g., Campbell & Pritchard, 1976). People in these studies are asked to estimate their valences and subjective probabilities, but it is not clear how accurate these estimates are. More work is needed to develop better ways to assess these internal states and cognitions.

As discussed in this chapter, motivation theories have led to several effective strategies for changing employee behavior. Perhaps the most effective have been interventions based on reinforcement principles and goal setting, as we have already seen. There is the need, however, to better understand how to implement principles, including the advantages and drawbacks to various practices. For example, a goal-setting program can focus employee attention on certain job aspects to the exclusion of others. If a typist has the goal of increasing speed, he or she might sacrifice accuracy. The conditions under which motivation interventions are effective and ineffective need additional study.

CHAPTER SUMMARY

This chapter discussed nine theories that consider motivation from very different perspectives. The three need theories—need hierarchy, ERG, and two-factor—view motivation as arising from internal needs. The need hierarchy and ERG theories attempt to classify all human needs into five and three categories, respectively. With both theories, needs are rather broad; and although they predict that needs direct behavior in a general direction, they cannot specify what behaviors are likely to arise. A person with a high level of achievement need, for example, might work hard on the job to achieve success. On the other hand, he or she might direct most of his or her efforts to achievement outside work. Two-factor theory states that motivation comes from two categories of needs that are addressed by work.

Reinforcement theory takes an environmental view and states that behavior is a function of a person's reinforcement history. According to this view, job-relevant behaviors that are rewarded are likely to be repeated in the future. Expectancy theory attempts to explain how rewards lead to behavior. It states that people will perform well if they believe their efforts will lead to performance, that performance will lead to rewards, and that they want the rewards.

Self-efficacy theory states that people's beliefs about their own capabilities are an important component of motivation. A person who believes that he or she is incapable of performing on the job is not likely even to try. A high level of self-efficacy or belief in one's own capability is a necessary component in work motivation and subsequent job performance.

Equity theory states that people value fair and equitable treatment by their organizations. A situation that is inequitable will motivate an employee to take action to make that situation equitable. This can be achieved in the work setting by changing the level of contribution to the organization, by changing the rewards obtained from work, or by quitting.

Goal-setting theory posits that people's behaviors are directed by conscious goals and objectives. The theory underscores several factors that are important determinants of how well goal setting can improve job performance. Four are particularly important: goal commitment by employees, feedback about progress toward goals, high goal difficulty, and specificity of goals.

Although these various theories view motivation from different perspectives, they are not necessarily incompatible, and in fact elements of various theories have been integrated. Locke and Latham (1990) discuss consistencies between features of expectancy theory, self-efficacy theory, and goal-setting theory. In particular, they see self-efficacy as an important ingredient in goal commitment. A person with low self-efficacy concerning the achievement of a goal is not likely to become committed to that goal.

Perhaps the best way to summarize the current status of each of the eight theories is to indicate how well each has been supported by research findings in the organizational domain. Figure 8-4 shows ratings for each theory on a scale from 1 to 5, where 1 represents less validity evidence and 5 represents more validity evidence. (These ratings were taken from Locke and Henne, 1986, for all but ERG and reinforcement theory.) As can be seen,

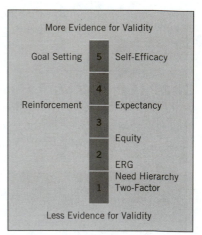

FIGURE 8-4

Validation evidence for the eight motivation theories. According to this scale, 1 represents little or no empirical support for the theory and 5 represents strong and consistent empirical support. *Source:* Based on "Work Motivation Theories," by E. A. Locke and D. Henne, 1986, in C. L. Cooper and I. T. Robertson (Eds.), *International Review of Industrial and Organizational Psychology 1992.* Chichester, UK: John Wiley.

need hierarchy, ERG, and two-factor theory have had little support, although the first two have had a few good tests of their predictions. Equity theory has had somewhat better support. Expectancy and reinforcement theory have had good support, although not all research findings have been consistent. Self-efficacy and goal-setting theories have had very strong support in the research literature.

I/O PSYCHOLOGY IN PRACTICE

THIS CASE CONCERNS a goal-based theft control program that Dr. Lynn Summers helped design. Dr. Summers received his Ph.D. in I/O psychology in 1977 from the University of South Florida. He is vice president of Mediappraise Corporation, a company that provides I/O services via the internet. One of its specialties is 360 degree feedback (see Chapter 4) done online. The peers, subordinates, and supervisors of an employee can complete an assessment about him or her on a webpage. After viewing feedback about themselves from these various perspectives, an employee prepares an improvement plan by interacting with an online program. Mediappraise also does other types of assessments and opinion surveys using the internet. It is one example of how I/O psychologists can use this new communication medium. Before helping to found the company, Dr. Summers had his own consulting practice. One of his projects was helping an organization deal with employee theft.

Dr. Summers was asked by a national fast-food chain to devise a program to control theft in its restaurants. In the restaurant industry, internal theft is a much larger problem than theft due to robbery. This chain wanted to do something about employees who were either stealing food for themselves or giving food to friends for free. Dr. Summers investigated the situation and helped a team of employees representing dif-

(Continued next page)

ferent restaurants come up with six different interventions. Of interest here is a goal-setting procedure, which turned out to be the most effective.

The goal-setting procedure was quite simple. In each restaurant the manager assigned a small group of employees responsibility for control of the theft of a particular item, such as chicken breasts. The group was shown how to figure out the number of chicken breasts that were "missing" each day. It was also assigned a specific goal for reducing the number.

The company found that the goal-setting program was quite effective in that thefts were reduced. What no one is certain about is why it worked. The employees were not instructed about how they should go about reducing the theft—they were only given a goal. It is possible that members of the group had been stealing, and they merely stopped. It is also possible that the group members knew which people were stealing and put pressure on them to stop. At the very least, the program directed employee attention to the problem, and as we discussed previously, this is one of the ways goal-setting enhances performance. No matter why it worked, this case illustrates that goal-setting can be an effective means of affecting behavior. Often managers need only set a goal and then allow their subordinates the latitude to figure out how to achieve it.

Discussion Questions

1. What factors cause employees to steal?
2. Why did the goal-setting program reduce stealing?
3. What other interventions might have reduced stealing?
4. How widespread do you think employee theft is in large organizations?

Chapter 9

JOB SATISFACTION AND ORGANIZATIONAL COMMITMENT

very few years the Gallup Organization conducts a poll to find out how Americans feel about their jobs. Over the years the majority of those polled have indicated that they like their jobs. In a 1997 national poll, 86% of working people liked their jobs overall (Gallup Poll, 1997). In 1991, 73% of the employed said they would continue to work even if they no longer needed the money (Hugick & Leonard, 1991), although only a little over half of the respondents said they would stay on the same job. Although most people were satisfied with their job overall, they were not necessarily happy with all aspects of their jobs. If you are now working, or have held a job in the past, you certainly had feelings about different aspects of your job, such as your co-workers, your pay, the nature of the work, and your supervisor. *Job satisfaction* refers to people's feelings about the different aspects of their job.

One of the major tasks I/O psychologists perform is assessing employee job satisfaction so that organizations can take steps to improve it. I/O researchers have extensively studied the causes and consequences of job satisfaction since the beginning of the I/O field itself. It is undoubtedly the most studied variable in I/O psychology, despite the seeming greater importance of job performance to organizational functioning. Much of this popularity, as we will see, derives from the relative ease with which it can be assessed.

Another reason for the popularity of the study of job satisfaction is that it is a central variable in many theories that deal with organizational phenomena, such as the nature of work, supervision, and the job environment. Job satisfaction has been posited as a cause of important employee and organizational outcomes ranging from job performance to health and longevity.

In this chapter we cover the nature of job satisfaction, including how it is measured, its potential causes, and possible consequences. As perhaps the most popular variable in I/O psychology, job satisfaction is frequently included in studies of all sorts of organizational phenomena. You will see it frequently mentioned throughout most of the remaining chapters of this book.

In addition, this chapter reviews the research on organizational commitment. *Commitment* is an attitudinal variable that concerns people's attachment to their jobs and is important because it relates to behavior at work. For example, commitment is a precursor to employee turnover (Mathieu & Zajac, 1990).

Objectives   **The student who studies this chapter should be able to:**
1. Define job satisfaction and organizational commitment.
2. Characterize the differences between job satisfaction and organizational commitment.
3. Explain how job satisfaction and organizational commitment are measured.
4. Summarize the findings on possible causes and effects of job satisfaction and organizational commitment.

THE NATURE OF JOB SATISFACTION

Job satisfaction is an attitudinal variable that reflects how people feel about their jobs overall as well as various aspects of them. In simple terms, job satisfaction is the extent to which people like their jobs; job dissatisfaction is the extent to which they dislike them.

There have been two approaches to the study of job satisfaction—the global approach and the facet approach. The *global approach* treats job satisfaction as a single, overall feeling toward the job. Many studies assess people's overall satisfaction, and many of the findings discussed in this chapter reflect that variable.

The alternative approach is to focus on job **facets** or different aspects of the job, such as rewards (pay or fringe benefits), other people on the job (supervisors or co-workers), job conditions, and the nature of the work itself. A list of the most often studied facets appears in Table 9-1.

The facet approach permits a more complete picture of job satisfaction. An individual typically has different levels of satisfaction with the various facets. He or she might be very dissatisfied with pay and fringe benefits but at the same time be very satisfied with the nature of the work and supervisors. This is a typical pattern for Americans, as we will see in the next section.

HOW PEOPLE FEEL ABOUT THEIR JOBS

The Gallup Organization frequently conducts surveys of Americans' feelings about work, as we discussed earlier (Gallup, 1997; Hugick & Leonard, 1991). The results generally find that most Americans like their jobs overall. Satisfaction with 16 different facets of

TABLE 9-1
Common job satisfaction facets

Pay	Job conditions
Promotion opportunities	Nature of the work itself
Fringe benefits	Communication
Supervision	Security
Co-workers	

TABLE 9-2

Sixteen features of jobs listed from most to least important for Americans
and the percentage of people satisfied with each one

FEATURE	PERCENTAGE
Having good health insurance and other benefits	67
Having interesting work	88
Having job security	79
Having the opportunity to learn new skills	88
Being able to take vacations of a week or more during the year	88
Being able to work independently	89
Having your accomplishments recognized by the people you work with	76
Having a job in which you can help others	83
Limiting the amount of on-the-job stress	62
Having regular hours, that is, not being scheduled to work nights and weekends	86
Earning a high income	66
Working close to home	87
Doing work that is important to society	83
Chances for promotion	60
Having a lot of contact with people	91
Having flexible hours	83

Source: From "Job Dissatisfaction Grows; 'Moonlighting' on the Rise," by L. Hugick and J. Leonard, 1991, The Gallup Poll News Service, 56.

work, however, was variable in the 1991 survey (Hugick & Leonard, 1991). The respondents indicated both the importance of and their satisfaction with each of the facets. Table 9-2 lists these 16 facets with the most important at the top and the least important at the bottom. The second column is the percentage of people who were satisfied with each one. As you can see, the largest percentage of people were satisfied with aspects that involved the nature of the work itself. Most people were satisfied with how interesting the work is and the amount of contact with other people. Far fewer were satisfied with rewards, such as fringe benefits and promotion opportunities.

The typical American pattern of facet satisfaction is also shown in Figure 9-1 with data from the norms of the Job Satisfaction Survey (JSS) (Spector, 1985). The JSS assesses nine job satisfaction dimensions, eight of which evaluate popular facets. The norms are based on the job satisfaction scores of 24,713 employees from dozens of organizations throughout the United States. The figure shows that Americans are typically very satisfied with their supervisors, co-workers, and nature of the work they do. They are less satisfied with rewards, such as pay, promotion opportunities, and fringe benefits. The pattern of the JSS norms is consistent with the Gallup results.

This rather consistent profile of facet satisfaction is not universal, for differences have been found across countries. For example, Marion-Landais (1993) found that Dominicans were more satisfied than Americans who worked for branches of the same company in their own countries, while several studies have shown that Japanese workers are less satisfied than Americans (e.g., Smith & Misumi, 1989). Griffeth and Hom (1987) found that Latin American managers were less satisfied than European managers. Spector and

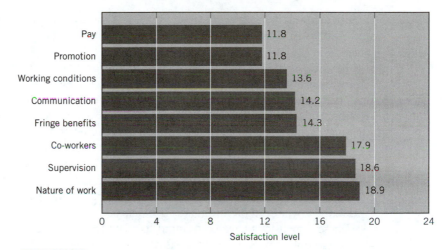

FIGURE 9-1

Mean satisfaction levels for various facets of the Job Satisfaction Survey (Spector, 1985). Satisfaction level is indicated on the horizontal axis. The numbers next to the bars are the means for each facet. They range from a low of 11.8 for pay and promotion to a high of 18.9 for nature of work.

Wimalasiri (1986) found that Americans and Singaporeans did not differ in their global job satisfaction. However, Americans were significantly more satisfied with supervision, co-workers, and the nature of the job, and Singaporeans were significantly more satisfied with pay and promotion opportunities. Finally, while Gallup polls consistently find that most Americans like their jobs, a 1996 survey found that only 55% of Indians were happy with their jobs.

Although these studies show that people in different countries have different feelings about work, they don't shed much light on the reasons. One explanation for these job satisfaction differences involves basic values that vary across countries. Hofstede (1984) assessed four important values in 40 countries. Although individuals differed on values within each country, there were mean differences that relate to important variables in the workplace. The culture values are:

Individualism/Collectivism

Masculinity

Power distance

Uncertainty avoidance

Individualism is the extent to which people focus on their own interests and needs rather than those of others; **collectivism** is the opposite, which is a focus on other people. Australia, Canada, Great Britain, and the United States were highest on individualism, while Hispanic countries, such as Venezuela and Colombia, were lowest according to Hofstede (1984). **Masculinity** reflects the extent to which organizations focus on achievement and job performance as opposed to the health and well-being of employees. Scandinavian countries were low on this value, which is reflected in their strong emphasis on health and well-being at work (note Erez's 1994 study showing Scandinavian interest in these topics in Chapter 1), while high countries include Japan and Austria. The United States is in the upper third.

Power distance is the tolerance people have for power and status differences among levels of an organization. Countries with high power distance tend to produce managers who demand obedience from subordinates. Hispanic countries tended to be high, such as Philippines and Mexico, while Austria and Israel were lowest. The United States was in the lower half of the scale. **Uncertainty avoidance** reflects the level of comfort in situations that are unpredictable. In organizations people can maintain predictability by adhering to formal procedures and rules; thus, in countries high on this dimension, organizations tend to be very rule oriented. Countries highest on this dimension were Greece and Portugal, while the lowest were Singapore and Denmark. The United States was in the lower third on uncertainty avoidance.

These dimensions have been found to relate to many organizational variables. In the job satisfaction area, Hui, Yee, and Eastman (1995) showed that individualism/collectivism scores for a country significantly related to satisfaction with social aspects of work. People from collectivist countries were more satisfied. This can be explained by the better social relations existing in countries in which such relationships are more valued. People make more effort to get along with others and are less concerned with their own well-being. Additional research is needed to see if the other dimensions also relate to job satisfaction.

THE ASSESSMENT OF JOB SATISFACTION

Job satisfaction is almost always assessed by asking people how they feel about their jobs, either by questionnaire or interview. Dozens of scales can be administered in a questionnaire, and satisfaction is usually assessed in this way. Sometimes, more often in practice than research, employees are interviewed about their satisfaction. A few cases can be found in which job satisfaction was assessed by asking supervisors (e.g., Spector, Dwyer, & Jex, 1988) or observers (Glick, Jenkins, & Gupta, 1986) to estimate another person's satisfaction. One study even asked elementary school children to estimate the satisfaction of their parents (Trice & Tillapaugh, 1991), and in another study husbands were asked about their wives' satisfaction with being working mothers (Barling & MacEwen, 1988). In this study, husbands agreed quite well with their wives' reports of their own satisfaction.

Job Descriptive Index (JDI)

Of all the job satisfaction scales available, the **Job Descriptive Index (JDI)** (Smith, Kendall, & Hulin, 1969) has been the most popular with researchers. It is also the most thoroughly and carefully validated. This scale assesses five facets:

Work	Supervision
Pay	Co-workers
Promotion opportunities	

Many users of the scale have summed the scale into an overall job satisfaction score. However, this practice is not recommended by one of the scale's developers (Ironson, Smith, Brannick, Gibson, & Paul, 1989), as we will discuss after we cover satisfaction scales.

Table 9-3 contains a sample of the scale's 72 items and their respective subscales. Each item is an adjective or short phrase that is descriptive of the job. Responses are "yes," "uncertain," or "no." For each subscale, a brief explanation of the facet is provided, followed by the items concerning that subscale.

The JDI has been used frequently by organizational researchers. Cook, Hepworth, Wall, and Warr (1981) listed over 100 published studies that used the JDI. The extensive body of research using the scale provides extensive evidence for its validity. The

TABLE 9-3
Sample items from the Job Descriptive Index (JDI)

Think of the work you do at present. How well does each of the following words or phrases describe your work? In the blank beside each word below, write

__Y__ for "Yes" if it describes your work
__N__ for "No" if it does NOT describe it
__?__ if you cannot decide

WORK ON PRESENT JOB
_____ Routine
_____ Satisfying
_____ Good

Think of the pay you get now. How well does each of the following words or phrases describe your present pay? In the blank beside each word below, write

__Y__ for "Yes" if it describes your pay
__N__ for "No" if it does NOT describe it
__?__ if you cannot decide

PRESENT PAY
_____ Income adequate for normal expenses
_____ Insecure
_____ Less than I deserve

Think of the opportunities for promotion that you have now. How well does each of the following words or phrases describe these? In the blank beside each word below, write

__Y__ for "Yes" if it describes your opportunities for promotion
__N__ for "No" if it does NOT describe them
__?__ if you cannot decide

OPPORTUNITIES FOR PROMOTION
_____ Dead-end job
_____ Unfair promotion policy
_____ Regular promotions

Think of the kind of supervision that you get on your job. How well does each of the following words or phrases describe this? In the blank beside each word below, write

__Y__ for "Yes" if it describes the supervision you get on your job
__N__ for "No" if it does NOT describe it
__?__ If you cannot decide

SUPERVISION
_____ Impolite
_____ Praises good work
_____ Doesn't supervise enough

Think of the majority of the people that you work with now or the people you meet in connection with your work. How well does each of the following words or phrases describe these people? In the blank beside each word below, write

__Y__ for "Yes" if it describes the people you work with
__N__ for "No" if it does NOT describe them
__?__ if you cannot decide

CO-WORKERS (PEOPLE)
_____ Boring
_____ Responsible
_____ Intelligent

Source: The Job Descriptive Index, which is copyrighted by Bowling Green State University. The complete forms, scoring key, instructions, and norms can be obtained from Dr. Patricia C. Smith, Department of Psychology, Bowling Green State University, Bowling Green, OH 43403.

biggest limitation of the scale is that it has only five facets. There has been some criticism that particular items might not apply to all employee groups (e.g., Buffum & Konick, 1982; Cook et al., 1981), but this criticism is probably true of all job satisfaction scales.

Although the scale has been well validated, efforts have continued to improve the JDI. Roznowski (1989) has used sophisticated statistical techniques to develop new items that would improve the scale's reliability and validity. Smith and her colleagues have updated and improved the scale by replacing some of its items (Balzer, Smith, Kravitz, Lovell, Paul, Reilly, & Reilly, 1990). They also added a sixth scale of overall satisfaction called the Job in General Scale, which we discuss later.

Minnesota Satisfaction Questionnaire (MSQ)

Another popular job satisfaction scale is the **Minnesota Satisfaction Questionnaire (MSQ)** (Weiss, Dawis, Lofquist, & England, 1966). This scale comes in two forms, a 100-item long version and a 20-item short version. Both versions have items that ask about 20 facets of job satisfaction, but facet scores are computed only for the long form. The short form is used to assess either global satisfaction or intrinsic and extrinsic satisfaction. *Intrinsic satisfaction* refers to the nature of job tasks themselves and how people feel about the work they do. *Extrinsic satisfaction* concerns other aspects of the work situation, such as fringe benefits and pay. Both intrinsic and extrinsic satisfaction are the combination of several facets.

The 20 dimensions of the MSQ are shown in Table 9-4. Each of the MSQ items is a statement that describes a facet. The employee is asked to indicate how satisfied he or she is with each one. For example, an item for the Activity facet is "Being able to keep busy all the time." The overall scale has been shown to have good reliability and evidence for validity. Several researchers have questioned how the items have been classified into the intrinsic and extrinsic groups (Cook et al., 1981; Schriesheim, Powers, Scandura, Gardiner, & Lankau, 1993).

TABLE 9-4
Dimensions from the Minnesota Satisfaction Questionnaire (MSQ)

Activity	Ability utilization
Independence	Company policies and practices
Variety	Compensation
Social status	Advancement
Supervision (human relations)	Responsibility
Supervision (technical)	Creativity
Moral values	Working conditions
Security	Coworkers
Social service	Recognition
Authority	Achievement

Source: "Instrumentation for the Theory of Work Adjustment," by D. J. Weiss, R. Dawis, L. H. Lofquist, & G. W. England, 1966, Minnesota Studies in Vocational Rehabilitation: xxi, University of Minnesota.

TABLE 9-5
Three items from the Job in General Scale (JIG)

Think of your job in general. All in all, what is it like most of the time?
In the blank beside each word or phrase below, write

__Y__   for "Yes" if it describes your job
__N__   for "No" if it does NOT describe it
__?__   if you cannot decide

JOB IN GENERAL

_____   Undesirable
_____   Better than most
_____   Rotten

Source: The Job in General Scale, which is copyrighted by Bowling Green State University. The complete forms, scoring key, instructions, and norms can be obtained from Dr. Patricia C. Smith, Department of Psychology, Bowling Green State University, Bowling Green, OH 43403.

Job in General Scale (JIG)

Ironson et al. (1989) developed a scale of global job satisfaction that contains items that do not reflect the various facets of the job. The **Job in General Scale (JIG)** was patterned on the JDI. It contains 18 items that are adjectives or short phrases about the job in general. Three of the items are shown in Table 9-5. The scale has good reliability and correlates well with other scales of overall job satisfaction. Because it is a relatively new scale, it has not yet been used in many research studies.

Is Global Satisfaction the Sum of Facets?

Researchers have debated whether global job satisfaction is the sum of facets or something different. Patricia Cain Smith, the developer of the JDI, has argued that they are separate (Ironson et al., 1989). Many researchers, however, have treated the sum of facet scores as an indicator of overall job satisfaction. Each MSQ item reflects a specific facet so that the total score is a sum of facets. This is justified by the fact that facets often correlate well with overall job satisfaction. For example, Ironson et al. (1989) found a .78 correlation of the JIG with the JDI Work scale. On the other hand the summing of subscale scores presumes that all facets have been assessed and that each makes an equal contribution to global satisfaction. It seems unlikely that each facet has the same importance to every individual. Thus, the sum of facets is an approximation of overall job satisfaction, but it may not exactly match the global satisfaction of individuals.

ANTECEDENTS OF JOB SATISFACTION

What makes people like or dislike their jobs? This question has been addressed in hundreds of research studies. Most of them have taken an environmental perspective. They have investigated features of jobs and organizations that lead employees to be satisfied or dissatisfied. Several studies have shown, however, that people with the same jobs and highly similar job conditions can vary considerably in their satisfaction (see Spector,

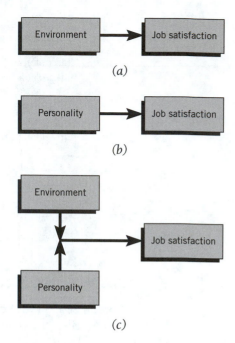

<u>FIGURE 9-2</u>

Three models illustrating (a) the impact of the job environment on job satisfaction, (b) the impact of personality on job satisfaction, and (c) the joint influence of the environment and personality on job satisfaction.

1992). Findings such as these have led some researchers to take a personality perspective. Their purpose has been to show that certain types of people are inclined to like or dislike their jobs. Still other researchers have taken the interactionist perspective of person–job fit, which combines the environmental and personality approaches. Person–job fit recognizes that different people prefer different features of a job. It attempts to learn which sorts of people are satisfied with which sorts of job conditions. Job satisfaction, according to this view, is the product of appropriately matching the individual to the job. All three perspectives—environment, personality, and interactionist—are illustrated in Figure 9-2.

Environmental Antecedents of Job Satisfaction

Several prominent theories suggest that various features of the job environment are causes of job satisfaction. These features include characteristics of jobs and job tasks, as well as various aspects of the organization. Indeed, many studies have supported the idea that certain job environment variables relate to job satisfaction.

Job Characteristics. In the 1960s the hypothesis that simple, routine factory work was inherently boring and dissatisfying became widely accepted (see Hulin & Blood, 1968). Modifying the job to be more complex and meaningful was thought to be a way to enhance job satisfaction. Frederick Herzberg (1968; Herzberg, Mausner, & Snyderman, 1959) was a leader in the movement to enrich jobs to make them more meaningful and satisfying to people by focusing on key characteristics of jobs.

Job characteristics refer to the content and nature of job tasks themselves. There are only a few different characteristics studied as contributors to job satisfaction (Wall & Martin, 1987). Five are part of Hackman and Oldham's (1976) influential job characteristics theory (see Chapter 10 for details of the theory):

Skill variety	Autonomy
Task identity	Job feedback
Task significance	

(See Table 9-6 for definitions of the core characteristics.) The core characteristics can be modified to make simple jobs larger in scope. **Scope** is the complexity and challenge of a job.

Dozens of studies across many different types of jobs have shown that each of the five characteristics relates to job satisfaction. Fried and Ferris (1987) conducted a meta-analysis of studies relating the Hackman and Oldham characteristics to global satisfaction. As discussed in Chapter 2, meta-analysis is a quantitative procedure for combining results of different studies. Table 9-6 contains Fried and Ferris's mean correlations across various studies of the relations between job characteristics and global job satisfaction. You can see that correlations ranged from .20 for task identity to .45 for job scope. Scope was assessed by combining scores on all five core characteristics.

Although the relation between job characteristics and job satisfaction is consistent across samples in the United States and other Western countries, it might not be universal. Pearson and Chong (1997) were unable to find the same results in Malaysia. The five core characteristics were unrelated to job satisfaction in a sample of nurses. The researchers argue that in this Asian culture, it might be more important to focus on relationships among co-workers and supervisors as a means of achieving high job satisfaction than on the nature of job tasks. However, a study conducted in more developed and westernized Hong Kong found relations quite similar to the United States between job characteristics and job satisfaction (Wong, Hui, & Law, 1998). Clearly, we need to be careful

TABLE 9-6
Dimensions of job characteristics and their mean correlations with job satisfaction from the Fried and Ferris (1987) Meta-Analysis

CHARACTERISTIC	MEAN CORRELATION	DESCRIPTION OF CHARACTERISTIC
Skill variety	.29	The number of different skills necessary to do a job
Task identity	.20	Whether or not an employee does an entire job or a piece of a job
Task significance	.26	The impact a job has on other people
Autonomy	.34	The freedom employees have to do their jobs as they see fit
Job feedback	.29	The extent to which it is obvious to employees that they are doing their jobs correctly
Job Scope	.45	The overall complexity of a job, computed as a combination of all five individual characteristics

Source: "The Validity of the Job Characteristics Model: A Review and Meta-Analysis," by Y. Fried and G. R. Ferris, 1987, *Personnel Psychology, 40,* 287–322.

about generalizing results from one country to another, and not assume that what works here will work everywhere.

One limitation of most studies that have addressed the influence of job characteristics on job satisfaction is that the job characteristics were assessed with questionnaires given to the employees themselves. As discussed in Chapter 2, merely demonstrating that variables are correlated does not mean that one necessarily causes the other. For example, people who like their jobs are likely to describe them in more favorable terms than people who dislike them, thereby reporting higher levels of job scope. Thus, job satisfaction might be the cause rather than the consequence of job characteristics as reported by employees on questionnaires. Although the Fried and Ferris (1987) results are consistent with the view that certain job characteristics can lead to job satisfaction, more evidence is needed to give confidence to this conclusion.

Unfortunately, studies that have used different methodologies have been less supportive of the idea that these five job characteristics lead to job satisfaction. For example, Spector and Jex (1991) used both questionnaires and job analysis techniques to assess job characteristics in a sample of employees who represented a wide range of jobs. Whereas the questionnaire measure of job characteristics correlated with job satisfaction, the job analysis data did not.

Griffin (1991) conducted a longitudinal quasi-experiment in an organization that changed the characteristics of jobs. He found that job satisfaction increased immediately following the change in characteristics. It returned to the level found before the change in jobs by the time of a two-year followup. His results suggest that changes in job satisfaction may have been due to a Hawthorne Effect rather than the job characteristics themselves.

On the other hand, Melamed, Ben-Avi, Luz, and Green (1995) were able to show relations between job analysis ratings of job characteristics and job satisfaction. In this study of Israeli factory workers, two characteristics were assessed—cycle time and underload. Cycle time is the amount of time it takes to complete a task, such as attaching a wheel to a car. Underload refers to a passive task, such as watching a dial, in which there is little to do. Short cycle times of under a minute and underload were associated with job dissatisfaction. Perhaps job satisfaction is affected by job characteristics but not the five core characteristics.

Role Variables. Another popular set of variables grew from research and theory on role stress. Two specific variables have been prominent in this research—role ambiguity and role conflict. **Role ambiguity** is the extent to which employees are uncertain about what their job functions and responsibilities are. Many supervisors fail to provide clear guidelines and directions for their subordinates, leading to ambiguity about what the employee is supposed to do.

Role conflict arises when people experience incompatible demands either at work (intrarole) or between work and nonwork (extrarole). *Intrarole conflict* arises from multiple demands on the job. For example, two supervisors might ask the person to do incompatible tasks. One might ask the person to take more care in doing the work, and the other might ask the person to work faster. These demands are incompatible in that the employee would have to work more slowly to be more careful. The incompatibility would be reflected in role conflict.

Extrarole conflict occurs between demands from work and nonwork domains. Such conflict commonly occurs when employees have children and the needs of children conflict with the demands of the job. When a child is sick, a parent may have to stay home from work, thus experiencing role conflict. This particular type of role conflict is discussed in the next section on work–family conflict.

As with job characteristics, many studies have shown correlations between the role variables as assessed by employee questionnaires and job satisfaction. Jackson and Schuler (1985) meta-analyzed these studies and reported mean correlations with global satisfaction of $-.30$ and $-.31$ for role ambiguity and role conflict, respectively. Correlations of role ambiguity and role conflict varied across job satisfaction facets, with the strongest being for supervision satisfaction ($r = -.36$ for both role variables). This makes sense because role ambiguity and conflict arise to a great extent from the behavior and practices of supervisors. Correlations were weakest with pay satisfaction ($r = -.17$ and $-.20$ for ambiguity and conflict, respectively).

These correlational results are consistent with the idea that role variables are antecedents of job satisfaction. Very few studies, however, have attempted to confirm these findings using more conclusive methodologies. One of the few attempts to study objective role ambiguity was a laboratory simulation by Hall (1990). In this study, college students completed in-basket exercises in which role ambiguity was manipulated by providing or withholding information about the subject's role in the exercise. No effects of objective role ambiguity were found on satisfaction with the task. Thus, again we are not certain why perceived role ambiguity and conflict relate to job satisfaction.

Work–Family Conflict. **Work–family conflict** is a form of role conflict in which the demands of work and the demands of family life conflict. The problem can be particularly acute for two-career couples with children and for single parents. With both parents working or with single parents, role conflicts are certain to arise over issues such as staying home with sick children and participating in school functions.

The 1991 Gallup survey found that 34% of Americans experience a considerable amount of work–family conflict (Hugick & Leonard, 1991). The survey included a question that asked what people believed to be the best family–work situation for people with children. Thirty-nine percent of respondents, both men and women, believed that one parent should work and the other should stay home with the children. Only 14% believed that both parents should work full-time outside of the home. Again there were no differences in the responses of men and women.

Several studies have found that employees who report high levels of work–family conflict had lower job satisfaction than their counterparts with low levels of conflict (e.g., Bedeian, Burke, & Moffett, 1988; Frone, Russell, & Cooper, 1994; Netemeyer, Boles, & McMurrian, 1996; Rice, Frone, & McFarlin, 1992). This pattern was found for both men and women (Kossek & Ozeki, 1998), suggesting again that both genders respond similarly to work–family conflict.

Although having both a parent and work role can have detrimental effects, particularly for women who usually assume the major responsibility for children, dual roles can have positive effects as well (Langan-Fox, 1998). Work can provide enhanced self-esteem and social support from others, which for some people counteracts the more negative effects of dual roles. As Langan-Fox (1998) points out, what is most critical is the quality of each role, rather than their number. An individual who has a good family and work situation will likely be satisfied with both.

Organizations that are concerned with work–family conflict have taken steps to help their employees. Two of the most frequently used approaches are flexible work schedules

"Heads we take your job offer and move to L.A. Tails we take my promotion and head for Denver."

and onsite child care in the workplace. Both make it easier for employees with children to manage both family and work responsibilities. Flexible schedules allow an individual to take time off to deal with nonwork demands, such as taking a sick child to the doctor. Onsite child care makes it easier for parents by enabling them to take their children with them to work. Parents can visit their children during breaks, and they are nearby in case of illness. Scandura and Lankau (1997) surveyed male and female managers about flexible hours and their job attitudes. Flexible hours was associated with greater job satisfaction for both men and women who had children living with them, but not for men and women without children.

Pay. You might think that pay would be a strong determinant of global job satisfaction. Although pay itself is associated to some extent with global satisfaction, it relates more strongly with the facet of pay satisfaction. Furthermore, it is the fairness with which pay is distributed or equity (see Chapter 8) that determines pay satisfaction rather than the actual level of pay itself. You can find people making minimum wage who are satisfied with pay, whereas professional athletes and entertainers might be dissatisfied with six- and even seven-figure salaries. For example, Sally Jessy Raphael, who hosts a popular afternoon television talk show, was quite vocal in her dissatisfaction with a salary of over $300,000 per year. Her dissatisfaction grew from her comparison with Oprah Winfrey, who makes several times more. Raphael believed that because they both had the same job they should have the same salary.

All this leads to the hypothesis that if we compare the pay and pay satisfaction of people across different jobs, we will find little or no correlation. People who make more money are not necessarily more satisfied when they have different jobs. On the other hand, if we have a sample of people who all do the same job, those who make more money should be more satisfied. In other words, Oprah Winfrey will probably have less to complain about than Sally Jessy Raphael, who makes far less money. Research support for this hypothesis comes from two studies. Spector (1985) found a mean correlation of only .17 between salary level and pay satisfaction in three samples of employees who held different jobs. Rice, Phillips, and McFarlin (1990) found a much larger .50 correlation between pay and job satisfaction in a sample of mental health professionals holding the same jobs. Pay satisfaction is affected by how an individual's salary compares to others in the same job rather than people in general.

Personal Antecedents of Job Satisfaction

The majority of studies of the causes of job satisfaction have taken an environmental perspective. In recent years, I/O psychologists have become interested in the possibility that personal characteristics might also be important. Some have gone as far as to suggest that job satisfaction might be caused in part by genetic predispositions. Arvey, Bouchard, Segal, and Abraham (1989) compared the job satisfaction of identical twins who were reared apart and discovered that their satisfaction levels were related. Although this single study provides only tentative evidence for the role of genetics, many studies have shown a link between personal characteristics and job satisfaction (e.g., Brush, Moch, and Pooyan, 1987; Staw, Bell, and Clausen, 1986).

Personality. The idea that job satisfaction may be caused in part by personality can be traced back to the Hawthorne studies. The Hawthorne researchers noticed that certain individuals, whom they called the *chronic kickers*, were continually complaining about the job (Roethlisberger, 1941). No matter what the researchers did for them, the chronic kickers always had new complaints. More recently, Schneider and Dachler (1978) noted in a longitudinal study that job satisfaction seemed very stable over time, and they speculated that it might be the product of personality traits.

Staw and Ross (1985) further explored the satisfaction stability idea by studying the job satisfaction of people who change types of jobs or employers. They found that the job satisfaction of these individuals was correlated across jobs and organizations. In other words, the job satisfaction of people on one job correlated with their satisfaction on another. Staw and Ross concluded that job satisfaction was caused in part by underlying personality. Some people are predisposed to like their jobs, whereas others are predisposed not to like them.

Other researchers have also found correlations across assessments of job satisfaction as people change jobs or organizations (Gerhart, 1987; Gupta, Jenkins, & Beehr, 1992). Newton and Keenan (1991) found evidence that personality, as well as the job environment, is important. They studied a group of British engineers during their first four years on the job after college. They found similar consistency in job satisfaction over time as that found in the prior studies. In addition, they found that engineers who changed jobs increased their satisfaction. Thus, although personality may have contributed to satisfaction, changing jobs tended to increase it as well.

Even stronger evidence for dispositions than consistency across time was provided by Staw et al. (1986) who studied people's job satisfaction over the span of decades (see the Research in Detail box). They found that personality assessed in adolescents predicted job satisfaction up to 50 years later.

A limitation of all of these personality studies is that they demonstrate that personality is important without specifying the nature of the many specific personality traits that relate to job satisfaction (Judge, 1992). Particular attention has been given to two, however—negative affectivity and locus of control.

Negative affectivity (NA) is the tendency for an individual to experience negative emotions, such as anxiety or depression, across a wide variety of situations. Watson, Pennebaker, and Folger (1986) extended the NA idea to the workplace, hypothesizing that high NA individuals would respond to their jobs negatively and would be likely to be dissatisfied. A number of studies have found relations between NA and job satisfaction (e.g., Cropanzano, James, & Konovsky, 1993; Judge, 1993; Moyle, 1995; Schaubroeck, Ganster, & Fox, 1992).

RESEARCH IN DETAIL

ONE OF THE limitations of many I/O studies is that data are collected at a single point in time. The study by Staw, Bell, and Clausen (1986) stands out as a rare example of a long-term longitudinal study of job satisfaction. The study spanned 50 years, comparing the personality of adolescents with their later job satisfaction.

The study made use of data from the Intergenerational Studies begun at the University of California, Berkeley, during the 1920s. Three groups of subjects were assessed using interviews and questionnaires several times during their lives. Staw et al. had several judges, who were either clinical psychologists or psychiatric social workers, read the extensive material in each subject's file and make ratings about them on several personality characteristics. Scores on 17 characteristics were combined into affective disposition scores. Examples of the characteristics include thin-skinned, punitive, condescending, hostile, distrustful, irritable, and moody.

Results showed that affective disposition assessed as young as early adolescence correlated significantly with job satisfaction assessed up to 50 years later. For the 46 subjects who had data at adolescence and decades later on the job, the correlation between disposition and satisfaction was .37. This is larger than many of the correlations found between job conditions and job satisfaction.

There are several explanations for these results, as noted by Staw et al. First, it may be that affective disposition, as assessed here, relates to a person's view of the world. People with a negative disposition might perceive all aspects of their lives, including their jobs, as worse than people with a more positive disposition. Alternatively, disposition might lead to job choice, with negative people seeking out worse jobs than positive people. Although this study cannot answer these questions, it demonstrates that through some as yet to be determined mechanism, personality is a likely precursor to job satisfaction. These results suggest that organizations should carefully consider characteristics of individuals when implementing job changes intended to enhance job satisfaction.

Source: Staw, B. M., Bell, N. E., & Clausen, J. A. (1986). The dispositional approach to job attitudes: A lifetime longitudinal test. *Administrative Science Quarterly, 31,* 56–77.

Locus of control refers to whether or not people believe they are in control of reinforcements in life. People who believe that they control reinforcements are termed *internals*. People who believe that fate, luck, or powerful others control reinforcements are termed *externals*. Internals have been found to be more satisfied with their jobs than externals (O'Brien, 1983; Spector, 1982).

Although the research on these personality traits has shown a connection with job satisfaction, the reasons are not well delineated. Watson et al. (1986) suggested that NA relates to job satisfaction because the high NA person perceives and experiences the job negatively, regardless of the actual conditions. It is possible that externals experience their jobs in a similar way. There are other mechanisms that are equally plausible. For example, Spector (1982) hypothesized that one reason for the higher satisfaction of internals is their higher job performance. Individuals who perform better might be better rewarded and thus like their jobs better. Personality might also be related to job choice. Perhaps people with certain personality traits choose better jobs and therefore have higher satisfaction. Clearly, research is needed to determine why personality relates to job satisfaction.

Gender. More and more women have entered the workforce in jobs that have been traditionally held by men. It has become important to understand how men and women might differ in their job attitudes. Most studies that have compared men and women in their global job satisfaction have found few differences. Meta-analytic studies involving multiple samples and thousands of employees have failed to find gender differences (Brush et al., 1987; Witt & Nye, 1992). Greenhaus, Parasuraman, and Wormley (1990) found no significant gender differences in their study, even though the distribution of jobs was not the same in their sample for both genders—males were more likely to have managerial/profes-

Most Americans say that they like their jobs.

sional jobs, and females were more likely to have clerical jobs. This suggests that women may be happier with less on the job than men, although reasons for this are not clear.

Age. The workforces in many countries have been getting older because of both the changing demographic makeup of the population (there are more elderly people) and legislation that has made age discrimination illegal. A question that has been of interest to I/O psychologists concerns possible changes in job satisfaction over a person's life span. Many studies have shown that older workers are more satisfied with their jobs than younger workers. Brush et al. (1987) calculated a mean correlation between age and job satisfaction of .22 in their meta-analysis of 21 studies.

Two large sample surveys, one conducted in England (Clark, Oswald, & Warr, 1996) and the other in nine countries including the United States (Birdi, Warr, & Oswald, 1995), found a curvilinear relation between age and job satisfaction. For these countries, job satisfaction at first declines with age, reaching the lowest level at around age 26 to 31, and then increasing through the rest of the working career. Some of this difference might be attributable to better adjustment to work through experience. However, Birdi et al. found evidence that older workers have better conditions and greater rewards at work.

Cultural and Ethnic Differences. Another trend in the composition of the workforce in the United States and other countries is that it is becoming increasingly multicultural. In addition, large organizations frequently have facilities in multiple countries and employ people from those countries. For example, American automobile manufacturers have plants outside the United States. Japanese automobile manufacturers such as Toyota have plants in the United States. If organizations are to deal appropriately with a diverse workforce, then they must understand how people of various ethnic, racial, and cultural backgrounds view and feel about their jobs.

Several studies have compared the job satisfaction of black and white employees in the United States. Some of these studies have found that blacks have slightly lower satisfaction (e.g., Greenhaus, Parasuraman, & Wormley 1990; Tuch & Martin, 1991), although Brush et al. (1987) reported no racial differences in their meta-analysis of 21 studies. Studies that have found differences in satisfaction have also noted differences in other variables, suggesting that job experiences might differ in at least some organizations. For example, blacks had lower mean performance ratings than whites in the Greenhaus, et al. (1990) study. Perhaps the factors leading to lower ratings resulted in lowered job satisfaction. In the Tuch and Martin (1991) study, blacks perceived their jobs to have fewer rewards than whites, thus possibly accounting for satisfaction differences in this particular study.

Person–Job Fit

Most researchers have tended to treat the environmental and personal factors as independent influences on job satisfaction. In other words, they have studied characteristics of jobs or of individuals that may lead to satisfaction. Another approach, however, is to look at the interaction of both factors. The person–job fit approach states that job satisfaction will occur when there is a good match between the person and the job (Kristof, 1996).

Much of the research on person–job fit has looked at the correspondence between what people say they want on a job and what they say they have. For example, employees could be asked how much autonomy they have and how much they want. The difference between having and wanting represents the amount of fit of person to job. Studies have been quite consistent in showing that the smaller the discrepancy between having and wanting, the greater the job satisfaction (Edwards, 1991).

Another approach to studying the interplay of the job and person is to look at the interaction of person and job factors in predicting job satisfaction. That is, person factors are used as moderators of the relation between job variables and job satisfaction. A **moderator variable** affects the relation between two other variables. One might find that a particular job variable relates to job satisfaction for people at one level of a person variable, and not for people at another level. For example, males might react differently than females to a job condition. Thus there might be a positive correlation between the job condition and job satisfaction for males, and no correlation for females. We would say that gender moderated the relation between job condition and job satisfaction. It determines whether or not the two variables are correlated.

In the job characteristics area, many studies have attempted to find the sorts of people who would react positively to high-scope jobs (i.e., those high on the Hackman & Oldham, 1976, five job characteristics). One personality characteristic that comes from Hackman and Oldham's (1976) theory is **growth need strength (GNS)**. This characteristic refers to a person's desire for the satisfaction of higher order needs, such as autonomy or achievement. Meta-analyses of studies that have addressed the effects of growth need strength have shown that it moderates the relation between job characteristics and job satisfaction (e.g., Loher, Noe, Moeller, & Fitzgerald, 1985). Correlations between these two variables were greater for individuals who were high in growth need strength than for individuals who were low.

This relation is illustrated in Figure 9-3. The horizontal axis of the graph represents the scope of the job; the vertical axis represents job satisfaction. One line is for high GNS

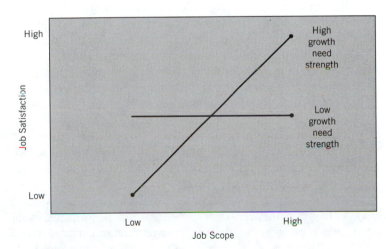

FIGURE 9-3

The moderating effect of growth need strength on the job scope—job satisfaction relation. Scope is represented by the horizontal axis of the graph. Job satisfaction is on the vertical axis. For people high in growth need strength, satisfaction is high when scope is high and low when scope is low. For people who are low in growth need strength, satisfaction is unaffected by level of job scope.

people, and the other line is for low GNS people. As the graph shows, people who are high in GNS will be satisfied with high-scope jobs and not with low-scope jobs. The scope of the job is not important for people low in GNS. Their satisfaction stays constant regardless of job scope.

POTENTIAL EFFECTS OF JOB SATISFACTION

A number of organizationally relevant behaviors are thought to be the result of job satisfaction or dissatisfaction. Many I/O psychologists have felt compelled to justify their interest in job satisfaction to managers by showing that it is relevant to behaviors that have an important impact on the well-being of organizations. Three of these behaviors have been prominent in the literature: job performance, turnover, and employee absence. In recent years, job satisfaction has been seen as important because of its potential effects on variables that are of more concern to employees than organizations. Of particular interest is the relation of job satisfaction to health and well-being.

Job Satisfaction and Job Performance. Two meta-analyses have related job performance to job satisfaction. Both suggest that the correlation between global job satisfaction and job performance is in the middle .20s (Iaffaldano & Muchinsky, 1985; Petty, McGee, & Cavender, 1984). The correlation with individual facets, however, is variable, ranging from .054 for pay satisfaction to .196 for satisfaction with intrinsic aspects of the job in the Iaffaldano and Muchinsky (1985) study.

At least part of the reason for the relatively small mean correlations found in these meta-analyses may have to do with the measures of job performance available in many studies. Most studies rely on supervisor ratings of performance, which suffer from several limitations, as discussed in Chapter 4. Supervisors frequently exhibit rating errors, especially when ratings are for organizational purposes. This can produce inaccuracy in performance ratings, which introduces extra error into the statistics. Relations of satisfaction with performance would likely be stronger if more accurate measures of performance were used.

Although it is clear that performance and satisfaction are related, there are two opposite explanations. First, satisfaction might lead to performance. That is, people who like their jobs work harder and therefore perform better. Second, performance might lead to satisfaction. People who perform well are likely to benefit from that performance, and those benefits could enhance satisfaction. A well-performing person might receive more pay and recognition, which might increase job satisfaction. Both of these explanations are illustrated in Figure 9-4. In the top part of the figure, satisfaction leads to effort, which in turn leads to performance. In the bottom part, performance leads to rewards and rewards lead to satisfaction.

Jacobs and Solomon (1977) conducted a study that supports the second explanation. They hypothesized that satisfaction and performance would be related more strongly when performance leads to rewards. The rationale is that employees who perform well will be more satisfied because they have received rewards. Jacobs and Solomon (1977) found support for their hypothesis that a performance-reward linkage leads to stronger satisfaction-performance relations.

Job Satisfaction and Turnover. Quitting the job or turnover has been tied to job satisfaction. Many studies have shown that dissatisfied employees are more likely than satis-

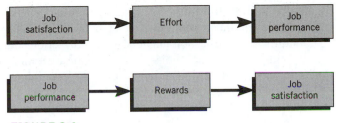

FIGURE 9-4

Two possible models illustrating why job performance relates to job satisfaction. In the first model, job satisfaction leads to increased effort on the job, which leads to job performance. In the second, job performance leads to rewards, which lead to job satisfaction. As noted in the text, evidence exists to support the second model.

fied employees to quit their jobs (e.g., Crampton & Wagner, 1994; Dickter, Roznowski, & Harrison, 1996).

Correlations between job satisfaction and turnover have been interpreted as indicating the effects of satisfaction on behavior. One reason that it has been possible to demonstrate such a linkage between job satisfaction and turnover has to do with the designs of turnover studies and the nature of turnover. Most turnover studies are predictive, assessing job satisfaction in a sample of employees and then waiting some period of months or years to see who quits. The predictive nature of these studies allows the conclusion that dissatisfaction is a factor that leads employees to quit their jobs.

Job Satisfaction and Absence. Conventional wisdom suggests that absence from work is the byproduct of employee job dissatisfaction. People who dislike their jobs will be more likely to miss work than people who like their jobs. Several meta-analyses have looked at this question, and they show that the connection between job satisfaction and absence is inconsistent and usually quite small. For example, Farrell and Stamm (1988) found correlations of 2.13 and 2.10, respectively, between absence and global job satisfaction using two different measures of absence. These are typical correlations found in absence studies. Tharenou (1993), however, found correlations as high as 2.34 between absence and job satisfaction in a sample of Australian blue-collar workers. Perhaps absence and satisfaction are more strongly related under some conditions.

Hackett and Guion (1985) found that absence correlated more strongly with some satisfaction facets than others. Satisfaction with the nature of the work itself correlated most strongly with absence.

One possible reason for the small relation between satisfaction and absence is that a person can be absent for many reasons (Kohler & Mathieu, 1993), including employee illness, family member illness (especially children), personal business, and fatigue, as well as just not feeling like going to work. Whereas some of these reasons might be associated with job satisfaction, others probably are not. For example, satisfaction might be associated with absence caused by not feeling like going to work, but it is not likely to be associated with absence caused by serious illness. Thus, overall absence is not likely to have a strong relation with job satisfaction. If reasons for absence are considered, however, relations might be stronger (Kohler & Mathieu, 1993).

Health and Well-Being. A number of I/O psychologists have been concerned that job dissatisfaction might be related to employee health and well-being. Indeed, claims can be found that job satisfaction might be a factor in serious illness and even death.

Some correlational studies show that job satisfaction relates to health variables. Studies have found that dissatisfied employees reported more physical symptoms, such as sleep problems and upset stomach, than their satisfied counterparts (Begley & Czajka, 1993; O'Driscoll & Beehr, 1994). Dissatisfaction has also been found to correlate with negative emotions at work, such as anxiety and depression (Jex & Gudanowski, 1992; Thomas & Ganster, 1995). These negative affective states could be considered indicators of emotional well-being at work. Evidence relating job satisfaction to more serious health problems, such as heart disease, has been harder to produce.

Job and Life Satisfaction. Another important issue concerns the contribution of job satisfaction to overall **life satisfaction**—how satisfied a person is with his or her life. It is considered to be an indicator of overall happiness or emotional well-being. According to a 1991 Gallup poll, 87% of Americans are satisfied with their lives (Hugick & Leonard, 1991). Studies of life satisfaction have found that it correlates with job satisfaction (e.g., Adams, King, & King, 1996; Judge & Watanabe, 1993; Lance, Lautenschlager, Sloan, & Varca, 1989; Weaver, 1978).

Three hypotheses have been proposed about how job and life satisfaction might affect one another (Rain, Lane, & Steiner, 1991). The *spillover hypothesis* suggests that satisfaction (or dissatisfaction) in one area of life affects or spills over to another (Weaver, 1978). Thus, problems and dissatisfaction at home can affect satisfaction with work, whereas problems and dissatisfaction at work can affect satisfaction with home. The *compensation hypothesis* says that dissatisfaction in one area of life will be compensated for in another. A person with a dissatisfying job will seek satisfaction in other aspects of life. A person with a dissatisfying home life might seek satisfaction in work. The *segmentation hypothesis* states that people compartmentalize their lives and that satisfaction in one area of life has no relation to satisfaction in another.

The three hypotheses lead to contradictory predictions about the correlation between job and life satisfaction. Spillover predicts a positive correlation in that satisfaction at work will affect satisfaction in other areas of life. Compensation predicts a negative correlation because dissatisfaction in one area of life will be compensated for by satisfaction in another. Segmentation predicts no correlation because people keep satisfaction with different areas of life separated. Rain et al. (1991) point out that because research has consistently found a positive correlation between job and life satisfaction, the spillover hypothesis is the only one supported by studies.

Assuming that the spillover hypothesis is correct, the next question of concern is why job satisfaction and life satisfaction are correlated. Explanations have been advanced that life satisfaction causes job satisfaction and that job satisfaction causes life satisfaction. Judge and Watanabe (1993) conducted a longitudinal study over a five-year span that suggests that both explanations are correct. That is, job satisfaction and life satisfaction affect one another in that satisfaction or dissatisfaction in either will affect the other.

Nevertheless, too little attention has been given to the interplay of work (e.g., job characteristics) and nonwork (e.g., family problems) factors in the experiences of and reactions to jobs. A complete understanding of either the work or nonwork domain will not likely be possible without a better understanding of how they affect one another.

ORGANIZATIONAL COMMITMENT

Organizational commitment is another popular attitudinal variable in the work domain. It is strongly related to job satisfaction, but it is distinctly different (Tett & Meyer, 1993). There have been several somewhat different definitions of commitment, but all involve the attachment of the individual to the organization. The most often studied conception is based on the work of Mowday, Steers, and Porter (1979), which considers organizational commitment to consist of three components:

1.   An acceptance of the organization's goals
2.   A willingness to work hard for the organization
3.   The desire to stay with the organization

More recently a three-component conception of commitment has been developed (Meyer, Allen, & Smith, 1993). The three types of commitment are:

Affective

Continuance

Normative

Affective commitment occurs when the employee wishes to remain with the organization because of an emotional attachment. *Continuance commitment* exists when a person must remain with the organization because he or she needs the benefits and salary or cannot find another job. *Normative commitment* comes from the values of the employee. The person believes that he or she owes it to the organization to remain out of a sense that this is the right thing to do.

Meyer et al. (1993) discuss the nature and origins of the three components of commitment. Figure 9-5 shows the major influences on each. As you can see, there are different

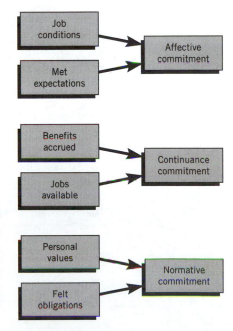

FIGURE 9-5

Antecedents of the three components of organizational commitment. Each type of commitment has different antecedents. Affective commitment arises from favorable experiences on the job. Continuance is produced by the investments in the job and the difficulty in finding another job. Normative comes from a sense of obligation either because of the person's values or from favors done for the person by the organization.

TABLE 9-7
Four items from the Mowday, Steers, and Porter (1979)
Organizational Commitment Questionnaire

I find that my values and the organization's values are very similar.
I am proud to tell others that I am part of this organization.
I could just as well be working for a different organization as long as the type of work was similar.
This organization really inspires the very best in me in the way of job performance.

Source: "The Measurement of Organizational Commitment," by R. T. Mowday, R. M. Steers, and L. W. Porter, 1979, *Journal of Vocational Behavior, 14,* 224–247.

factors involved in each component. Affective commitment arises from job conditions and met expectations. That is, did the job provide the rewards that the employee expected? Continuance commitment is produced by the benefits accrued from working for the organization and by the lack of available alternative jobs. Normative commitment comes from the employee's personal values and from the obligations that the person feels toward the employer. These obligations come from favors that the organization has done, such as paying the person's school expenses.

Assessment of Organizational Commitment

Organizational commitment is measured with self-report scales, not unlike those used to assess job satisfaction. Four items from the most popular scale, developed by Mowday et al. (1979), are shown in Table 9-7. The items tap the three aspects of commitment—acceptance of goals, willingness to work hard, and intention to stay with the organization. All three components relate strongly to one another, and combined they indicate commitment.

The three components in the Meyer et al. (1993) conception of commitment can be assessed with a scale they developed. Table 9-8 contains two of the items for each component. As opposed to the Mowday et al. (1979) scale, the components in the Meyer et al. (1993) scale produce separate scores. Research with the scale has found support for the

TABLE 9-8
Six items from the Meyer, Allen, and Smith (1993) Three-Component Organizational Commitment Scale

Affective Commitment
I would be very happy to spend the rest of my career with this organization
I really feel as if this organization's problems are my own
Continuance Commitment
Right now, staying with my organization is a matter of necessity as much as desire
It would be very hard for me to leave my organization right now, even if I wanted to
Normative Commitment
I do not feel any obligation to remain with my current employer
Even if it were to my advantage, I do not feel it would be right to leave my organization now

Source: "Commitment to Organizations and Occupations: Extension and Test of a Three-Component Conceptualization," by J. P. Meyer, N. J. Allen, and C. A. Smith, 1993; *Journal of Applied Psychology, 78,* 538–551.

idea that the three types of commitment are separate variables (Dunham, Grube, & Castañeda, 1994; Meyer, Bobocel, & Allen, 1991). Hackett, Bycio, and Hausdorf (1994) noted that the Mowday et al. (1979) scale assesses mainly affective commitment. It correlates strongly with the affective commitment subscale but not with the continuance or normative subscales.

Organizational Commitment and Other Variables

Organizational commitment has been prominent in a number of models involving many organizational variables. Turnover in particular has been a focus of much commitment research (e.g., Bluedorn, 1982; Williams & Hazer, 1986). Because commitment refers to the attachment of people to jobs, it should be related to turnover. Those with low commitment should be more likely to quit the job than those with high commitment. Cohen (1993) conducted a meta-analysis of 36 studies correlating overall commitment with turnover. He found an average correlation of -.24 between commitment and turnover. All three commitment components (affective, continuance, and normative) have been shown to correlate with turnover (Hackett, Bycio, & Hausdorf, 1994; Jaros, Jermier, Koehler, & Sincich, 1993). For all three components, low commitment was associated with quitting the job.

Commitment has been studied in relation to many organizational and personal variables. A meta-analysis summarized the results of over 200 studies that reported correlations of commitment with dozens of different variables (Mathieu & Zajac, 1990; see also Cohen, 1992). Table 9-9 contains a sample of their findings. Included are the variables that have been discussed in this chapter in relation to job satisfaction. There are many parallels between commitment and job satisfaction. This should not be surprising because there is a strong correlation ($r = .49$) between organizational commitment and global job satisfaction.

TABLE 9-9
Mean correlations of organizational commitment with several work variables

VARIABLE	MEAN CORRELATION
Skill variety	.14
Autonomy	.15
Job scope	.38
Role ambiguity	−.24
Role conflict	−.27
Job satisfaction (global)	.49
Job performance (supervisor ratings)	.13
Absence	.12
Turnover	−.25
Age	.20
Gender	−.09[a]

[a]Females were slightly lower in commitment.

Source: "A Review and Meta-Analysis of the Antecedents, Correlates, and Consequences of Organizational Commitment," by J. F. Mathieu and D. M. Zajac, 1990, *Psychological Bulletin, 108,* 171–194.

Table 9-9 shows that organizational commitment is related to age with about the same correlation that job satisfaction relates to age. There was little relation with gender, indicating that men and women displayed about the same level of commitment.

Organizational commitment relates to several work environment variables, including job scope, role ambiguity, and role conflict, as well as work–family conflict (Netemeyer et al., 1996). It also relates to absence and turnover, with about the same magnitude of correlation as does job satisfaction. Commitment had a very small correlation with job performance ($r = .13$). This finding is surprising because a major component of commitment is a willingness to work hard for the organization. Meyer and Allen (1997) noted that different components of commitment relate differently to performance. Affective and normative commitment are associated with better job performance, but continuance commitment is associated with lower performance (Hackett et al., 1994; Shore, Barksdale, & Shore, 1993). Individuals who believe they must keep their jobs tend to perform more poorly than individuals who believe they are free to quit. It is possible that people who feel trapped in their jobs respond with reduced effort, but it is equally likely that poor performers are less marketable and feel they cannot easily find another job.

The idea of commitment has been extended from the organization to other work-related domains. Barling, Wade, and Fullagar (1990) developed a union commitment scale, and Meyer et al. (1993) developed an occupational commitment scale. Occupational commitment concerns the occupation rather than a particular organization. People might be very committed to their occupation, such as accounting or law, and uncommitted to their current employer. The focus of a person's commitment is important in determining their responses. For example, Keller (1997) found that occupational commitment among engineers and scientists related to an objective measure of performance (number of articles published), but organizational commitment did not. Success in publication may have been relevant to how individuals viewed their occupations but not their organizations. On the other hand, Cropanzano, Howes, Grandey, and Toth (1997) found that occupational commitment was less strongly related than organizational commitment to intention of quitting the job. We might expect that occupational commitment will relate to behaviors relevant to success in that occupation. Organizational commitment will relate to behaviors and variables relevant to the present job.

FUTURE ISSUES AND CHALLENGES

Several important questions in the domain of job attitudes need to be addressed in the future. Our understanding of the factors that lead to job satisfaction is incomplete. Results of studies that use employee reports of job conditions are consistent in showing relations with job satisfaction. The reasons for these correlations have not been adequately addressed in our research. It seems most likely that satisfaction arises from complex interactions of jobs and people. A focus on just jobs or people will not likely shed much light on the question.

In addition, the reasons for correlations between personality characteristics and job satisfaction are not understood. Research needs to determine why personality relates to job satisfaction. Watson, Pennebacker, & Folger (1986) hypothesized that certain types of people are simply more satisfied than others, regardless of the situation. Again, satisfaction seems to be caused by the interplay of job and person. Understanding personality will require looking at both the individual and the job conditions. Studying the fit of the person to the particular job is likely to help us understand satisfaction.

The role of job satisfaction in health and well-being is an important question that needs attention. The possibility exists that enhancing satisfaction might lead to healthier and better adjusted people. If this is the case, it will become even more important to determine how job satisfaction can be improved. It seems likely that the answer will involve providing different job conditions for different people.

CHAPTER SUMMARY

Job satisfaction is the most frequently studied variable in I/O psychology. It is the extent to which people like or dislike their jobs (global satisfaction) or aspects of their jobs (facet satisfaction). It is usually measured with questionnaires administered to employees. Several popular job satisfaction scales are available:

Job Descriptive Index (JDI)

Minnesota Satisfaction Questionnaire (MSQ)

Job in General Scale (JIG)

Research has linked job satisfaction to a number of job environment variables. It has been shown to correlate with job characteristics, role variables, and pay. Job satisfaction has also been found to correlate with personal characteristics, including age; and various personality variables, such as negative affectivity and locus of control.

Research has also linked job satisfaction to several employee behaviors. Lack of satisfaction seems to be a cause of employee turnover. It is related modestly to job performance and slightly to absence, although it is not clear that satisfaction is the cause of either. There is evidence that performance may be the cause of satisfaction. Job satisfaction has even been linked to employee health, but we will need future research to tell us specifically how job attitudes might affect health.

Organizational commitment is another attitudinal variable that has been popular among I/O researchers. Commitment concerns the employee's attachment to the organization. It correlates strongly with job satisfaction, but it is conceptually different. Three components of commitment have been identified as affective, continuance, and normative. Organizational commitment has many of the same correlates as job satisfaction, including job characteristics, role variables, turnover, absence, and age.

I/O PSYCHOLOGY IN PRACTICE

THIS CASE IS a job satisfaction project carried out by Dr. Charles E. Michaels. Dr. Michaels received his Ph.D. in industrial/organizational psychology in 1983 from the University of South Florida. He is currently an associate professor of management at the University of South Florida. As a professor he divides his time between teaching, research, and consulting for local and national organizations. Dr. Michaels is an expert in job satisfaction, and much of his consulting and research is in this area.

One consulting project was a job satisfaction survey done for a county fire department. What makes this project unusual is that Dr. Michaels was hired by the firefighters' union rather

(Continued next page)

I/O PSYCHOLOGY IN PRACTICE

than the management of the department. Although most I/O psychologists work for management, occasionally they work for unions as well. Union representatives approached Dr. Michaels to conduct a satisfaction survey because there was considerable unrest among the union's members. The combination of a new fire chief and a two-year wage freeze led to widespread dissatisfaction among the firefighters. The union representatives were hopeful that a study would provide an impetus for change on the part of management.

Dr. Michaels began this project by interviewing several groups of employees. From the interviews he was able to develop a satisfaction questionnaire appropriate to the issues of the organization. He surveyed all of the firefighters using the questionnaire and found that satisfaction was quite low. In particular, there was dissatisfaction with both pay and communication. The results of the study were compiled into a report that was given to the union representatives. They used the report in a successful campaign for higher wages and improved communication. One year later Dr. Michaels repeated the survey and found that job satisfaction had significantly increased. Furthermore, the largest increases were in the facets of pay and communication satisfaction. This case illustrates that job satisfaction surveys can be used to improve the conditions of work for employees.

Discussion Questions

1. What sorts of things would you expect to raise the job satisfaction of firefighters?

2. Do you think the results of this project would have been different if Dr. Michaels had been hired by management?

3. What effects would you expect if the city management had ignored the results of this study?

4. Can you think of another way Dr. Michaels could have assessed job satisfaction?

Chapter 10

PRODUCTIVE AND COUNTERPRODUCTIVE EMPLOYEE BEHAVIOR

On May 6, 1993, a U.S. postal service employee brought two guns to work and opened fire on his co-workers. One person was killed and two were injured before he shot and killed himself as well. His reason was apparently anger over not being given a promotion. In reaction to this and similar incidents, the postal service has implemented an employee assistance program to offer counseling services to troubled employees. This program is designed to deal with emotional problems and involves clinical rather than I/O psychologists.

The postal service is not the only organization in which such incidents of violence have occurred. Furthermore, most violence in the workplace has less dramatic results, and so the news media pay little attention. Fights among employees are not unusual events, and most go unreported to police. As we will see later in this chapter, employees sometimes assault one another or those they are supposed to protect as part of their jobs.

Violence and other forms of counterproductive behavior, such as sabotage and theft, are a tremendous problem for organizations. The postal service, as well as other organizations, has asked I/O psychologists to help reduce this kind of employee behavior.

Although violence at work is an important problem, two other behaviors have dominated the attention of I/O practitioners and researchers: employee withdrawal (absence and turnover) and job performance. Other important behaviors have received far less attention. In this chapter, we discuss both productive and counterproductive behavior. Productive behavior includes job performance and organizational citizenship behaviors (OCB), such as helping co-workers. Counterproductive behaviors include aggression, sabotage, theft, and withdrawal.

<u>Objectives</u>   **The student who studies this chapter should be able to:**
  1. Discuss how environmental and personal characteristics impact job performance.
  2. Explain how the principles of human factors can be used to enhance job performance.
  3. Summarize the research on the causes of employee withdrawal.
  4. Discuss how counterproductive behavior can result from environmental and personal factors.
  5. Summarize the research on organizational citizenship behavior.

PRODUCTIVE BEHAVIOR: JOB PERFORMANCE

In order for an organization to achieve its purposes, individual employees must perform their jobs at some reasonable level of proficiency. This is as true for government organizations, in which poor performance means a failure to provide mandated public services, as it is for private companies, in which poor performance can mean bankruptcy. From a societal standpoint, it is in everyone's best interest for organizations to have employees who perform their jobs well. Good performance enhances organizational productivity, which directly enhances the national economy.

People can perform their jobs well only if they have both the necessary ability and motivation. Organizational practices and job conditions can enhance these personal characteristics or serve as constraints that interfere with job performance. These three factors—ability, motivation, and organizational constraints—are illustrated in Figure 10–1. The figure shows how ability and motivation lead to performance but can be blocked by constraints.

Ability and Performance

Most selection efforts by I/O psychologists focus on identifying the necessary abilities for specific jobs and finding people who have those abilities. First, worker-oriented job analysis methods (as discussed in Chapter 3) are used to determine the necessary KSAOs (knowledge, skill, ability, and other personal characteristics) for a job. Once the KSAOs are identified, selection procedures are implemented to find individuals who have the appropriate characteristics. Although KSAOs deal with a variety of attributes, most selection devices (as discussed in Chapter 5) are designed to assess abilities. Finally, in addition to what employees bring with them, additional knowledge and skills can be developed through training. If an organization is to have a workforce with the necessary abilities for good job performance, all three steps must be followed.

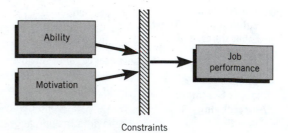

<u>FIGURE 10-1</u>
Good job performance requires both ability and motivation. Organizational constraints, such as inadequate training, can interfere with good performance.

It has been well established that various measures of ability relate to job performance (see Chapters 5 and 6). As might be expected, the nature of the job determines the mix of specific abilities necessary. For example, Gutenberg, Arvey, Osburn, and Jeanneret (1983) showed that cognitive ability predicts performance for most jobs. The more mentally demanding the job, however, the stronger was the relation between cognitive ability and job performance. In other words, cognitive ability is more important for mentally demanding jobs (e.g., an engineer) than for simple jobs (e.g., a file clerk). Caldwell and O'Reilly (1990) demonstrated that matching people's abilities to the KSAO requirements from a job analysis can be a useful strategy for enhancing job performance. They also found that employees whose abilities matched their jobs were more satisfied. These results are consistent with the notion that job performance might lead to satisfaction (see Chapter 9). Employees who have the characteristics necessary for good performance will be more successful on the job and will be more satisfied.

Motivation and Performance

Motivation is an individual characteristic, but it can arise from both within the worker (e.g., personality) and environmental conditions. Organizational attempts to enhance motivation in the workforce have focused more on environmental interventions than on individual selection. In theory, one might assess motivation in job applicants and hire those with the highest levels. I/O psychologists, however, have directed most of their selection attention to the assessment of ability rather than motivation. Attempts to enhance motivation have been concerned primarily with the structure of jobs, with incentive systems, or with the design of technology, all of which are discussed in this chapter.

Personal Characteristics and Performance

Several employee characteristics are relevant to job performance and may affect ability to do the job. Others affect employee motivation to work hard. In most cases, it is difficult to disentangle the effects of ability from the effects of motivation on job performance. For example, people with high levels of ability can also have high levels of motivation. As their ability leads to good performance and associated rewards, their motivation to perform may be enhanced. High-ability people might perform better because they are more skilled or because they put forth more effort, or both.

Cognitive ability (mathematical and verbal reasoning) has been found to predict job performance over a wide variety of jobs (e.g., Pearlman, Schmidt, & Hunter, 1980; Schmitt, Gooding, Noe, & Kirch, 1984). In Chapters 3 and 5 we discussed how specific measures of ability are related to job performance, so ability will not be discussed again here. This chapter is concerned with the "Big Five" personality characteristics which many researchers believe represent the basic dimensions of human personality. We also discuss how locus of control and age relate to performance.

The "Big Five" and Performance. Many psychologists today believe that human personality can be described by five dimensions, called the **Big Five**: extraversion, emotional stability, agreeableness, conscientiousness, and openness to experience (Barrick & Mount, 1991). Table 10-1 presents a brief description of each dimension.

TABLE 10-1
Description of the "big five" dimensions of personality

DIMENSION	DESCRIPTION
Extraversion	Sociable, gregarious, assertive, and talkative
Emotional stability	Anxious, depressed, angry, worried, insecure
Agreeableness	Courteous, flexible, good-natured, cooperative
Conscientiousness	Dependable, responsible, hardworking, achievement oriented
Openness to experience	Imaginative, curious, broadminded, intelligent

Source: "The Big Five Personality Dimensions and Job Performance: A Meta-Analysis," by M. R. Barrick and M. K. Mount, 1991, *Personnel Psychology, 44,* 1–26.

Two meta-analyses have summarized relations between each of the five dimensions and job performance (Barrick & Mount, 1991; Tett, Jackson, & Rothstein, 1991). In general, the two studies concluded that personality is associated with job performance, although they were not completely consistent. Barrick and Mount found that conscientiousness was the strongest correlate of job performance, whereas Tett et al. found that it was agreeableness. Furthermore, Barrick and Mount discovered that certain personality dimensions were correlated more strongly with performance for some jobs than others. Although mean correlations were not large, these studies provide evidence that personality might be an important factor for job performance. As noted in Chapter 5, some of the reason for the small correlations between personality and performance can be attributed to choosing personality variables that are irrelevant for performance. The type of performance measure and the type of job are also important factors in how well a particular trait relates to performance.

Locus of Control and Performance. *Locus of control* concerns people's beliefs about their ability to control reinforcements in their environment (see Chapter 9). Research has shown that *internals*, those who believe they can control reinforcements, have higher levels of job motivation than *externals*, those who do not believe they control reinforcements (see reviews by O'Brien, 1983; Spector, 1982). Although greater motivation might be expected to result in better job performance in general, the effects of motivation can be more complex. Blau (1993a) studied how locus of control related to two different job performance aspects of bank tellers (see Research in Detail). Blau noted that internals have been shown to have higher levels of work motivation, which should lead them to display more initiative on the job. Externals, on the other hand, have been shown to be more conforming and would be expected to respond better to highly structured tasks that allow for little personal initiative. This is exactly what he found. Internals performed better in developing important job skills, whereas externals performed better on the routine clerical tasks that were highly structured. Blau's study suggests that relations between personality and job performance can depend on the particular dimension of performance.

Age and Performance. Many people would undoubtedly predict that job performance declines with age. The stereotype of the nonproductive older worker probably has roots in the fact that many physical abilities decline with age. For example, professional athletes almost always retire before they reach 40 years of age. Research has shown that the stereo-

RESEARCH IN DETAIL

MOST OF THE research on job performance has failed to consider that different aspects of performance might be influenced by different factors. Blau's (1993) study is an exception in that it studied the relation of locus of control with three different measures of performance. Blau hypothesized that internals would do better in some areas of performance, but externals would do better in others. Specifically, internals would perform better at tasks requiring independence and initiative. Externals would perform better at tasks that required compliance to rules and supervisory directives.

Subjects for this study were 146 bank tellers. Locus of control in the work domain and three performance measures (productivity, dollar shortages, and self-development) were assessed. Productivity was an objective measure of the volume of work processed by each teller, and it represents a highly structured part of the job. Dollar shortage was an objective measure of accuracy in accounting, which is also a highly structured part of the job. Self-development, assessed by supervisors, was the extent to which employees enhanced their skills through their own initiative and independent action.

As Blau predicted, the correlations with locus of control differed across the different performance measures. The correlations were .27, .05, and −.30 for productivity, dollar shortages, and self-development, respectively. Externals performed significantly better than internals in productivity, but internals performed significantly better in self-development. The correlation between locus of control and dollar shortages was not significant. The correlation between productivity and self-development was negative, suggesting that the employees who had the highest levels of productivity had the lowest levels of self-development.

These results suggest that different people can do well at different aspects of the same job. The tellers who were the most productive were the poorest at self-development. Perhaps this shows that individuals differed in how much time and effort they put into different aspects of the job. Externals may have focused on the day-to-day requirements for productivity. Internals, on the other hand, put effort into learning new tasks, perhaps with the personal objective of receiving future promotions. This study emphasizes that job performance can be quite complex. Organizations should recognize that there can be more than one way to be a productive employee.

Source: Blau, G. (1993). Testing the relationship of locus of control to different performance dimensions. *Journal of Occupational and Organizational Psychology, 66,* 125–138.

type is incorrect, however. Older workers in many jobs are as productive as their younger co-workers.

McEvoy and Cascio (1989) conducted a meta-analysis of 96 studies relating age to job performance. Rather than job performance declining with age, their study found no relation. The performance of older workers is no worse than that of younger colleagues. Although some abilities might decline with age, other skills and a level of job wisdom that may lead to greater efficiency may increase with experience. What older workers lack in physical ability they may more than compensate for by better task strategies, better management of time, and more efficient approaches. The physical demands of the majority of jobs are well within the ability range of most older workers, unless they are in poor health. Of course, poor health can adversely affect the job performance of even the youngest workers.

Environmental Conditions and Job Performance

The job environment can affect job performance in many ways. The environment can have a positive or negative influence on employee motivation, leading to an increase or decrease in employee efforts. Similarly, the environment can be structured to facilitate performance by making it easier for individuals to accomplish their jobs, or it can contain constraints that interfere with performance. One study showed that something as simple as allowing employees to listen to music over stereo headsets improved job performance, apparently by reducing tension (Oldham, Cummings, Mischel, Schmidtke, & Zhou, 1995). In this chapter we will look at somewhat more complex factors of incentive systems, technology design, and organizational constraints.

Job Characteristics and Performance. One of the most influential theories that relate the nature of jobs to performance is Hackman and Oldham's job characteristics theory (Hackman & Oldham, 1976, 1980). This theory is based on the presumption that people can be motivated by the intrinsic nature of job tasks. When work is interesting and enjoyable, people will like their jobs (as discussed in Chapter 8), be highly motivated, and perform well.

Job characteristics theory is illustrated in Figure 10-2. This theory states that features of jobs induce psychological states that lead to satisfaction, motivation, and job perfor-

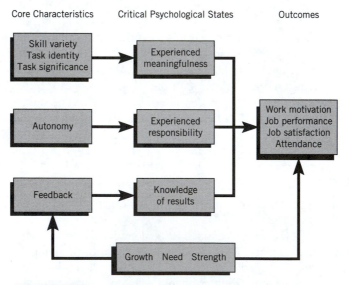

FIGURE 10-2

Hackman and Oldham's (1976) job characteristics model. *Source:* "Motivation Through the Design of Work: Test of a Theory," by J. R. Hackman and G. R. Oldham, 1976, *Organizational Behavior and Human Performance, 16,* 250–279.

mance. The job features, or core characteristics (described in Table 9-5), lead to three psychological states. Skill variety, task identity, and task significance lead to experienced meaningfulness of work; autonomy leads to feelings of responsibility; and feedback leads to knowledge of results. These three states are critical to the satisfaction and motivation of employees. When jobs induce them, individuals will be motivated and satisfied and will perform better.

The levels of the core characteristics determine how motivating a job is likely to be. Hackman and Oldham (1976) noted that the **Motivation Potential Score (MPS)** of a job can be calculated by combining scores on the core characteristics. Specifically, the following formula is used:

$$MPS = (SV + TS + TI)/3 \times Auton \times Feed$$

where SV = skill variety, TS = task significance, TI = task identity, $Auton$ = autonomy, and $Feed$ = feedback. Note that the three characteristics leading to experienced meaningfulness are averaged. The average is multiplied by autonomy and feedback, which lead to experienced responsibility and knowledge of results, respectively. The multiplicative nature of the formula implies that a job cannot be motivating if it leads to low levels of even one of the three psychological states. If one of the three multiplied terms equals zero, the MPS will be zero.

There is one last piece of the theory: the moderator effect of growth need strength (GNS). As noted in Chapter 9, GNS is a personality variable that concerns the need for fulfillment of higher order needs, such as personal growth, autonomy, or achievement. According to Hackman and Oldham (1976), the connection from job characteristics to psychological states to outcomes holds mainly for individuals who are high on GNS. This means that this is a person–job fit theory, in which only certain types of people will respond well to high MPS jobs. Hackman and Oldham had little to say about low GNS people and what might motivate them.

Studies that used employee self-reports as measures of the core characteristics have supported their relation with motivation and performance (Fried & Ferris, 1987), as well as the moderating effect of GNS (Loher, Noe, Moeller, & Fitzgerald, 1985). Research using other methods has been more equivocal. Although studies can be found demonstrating that changing or redesigning jobs to be higher in MPS result in better job performance, other studies show no effect from job redesign. An interesting longitudinal study by Griffin (1991) showed that the effects of job redesign were a temporary increase in job

satisfaction and a delayed increase in job performance. These results suggest that the connection among job conditions, satisfaction, and performance is more complex than the job characteristics theory would lead us to expect.

Incentive Systems and Performance. A possible way of increasing job performance, at least performance quantity, is incentive systems that reward employees for each unit of work performed (see Chapter 8's discussion of reinforcement theory). Such systems are common with salespeople who receive commissions or with factory workers who are on **piece-rate systems** that pay them for each unit of production. Incentive systems work through motivation by rewarding employees for behavior beneficial to the organization. Most such systems reward job performance, although examples can be found that reward employees for other behaviors such as attendance.

Although incentive systems can increase productivity, they have not been universally successful. Yukl and Latham (1975), for example, found that a piece-rate system increased the productivity of only two of three groups with which it was implemented. In their classic study of factory workers, Coch and French (1948) documented how peer pressure within work groups could undermine the effects of a piece-rate system. The productivity of one factory worker was cut in half by pressure from co-workers.

In order for an incentive system to be effective, three elements must be in place. First, the employees must have the ability to increase productivity. If they are presently working at the limit of their capability, introducing an incentive system will not improve performance. Second, employees must want the incentives. Not everyone is willing to work harder for money or other rewards. For an incentive system to work, the incentive must be something that people want. Finally, an incentive system will not work if there are physical or psychological constraints on performance. A salesperson in a store cannot sell if there are no customers. Figure 10-3 shows how the three elements combine to determine the effectiveness of an incentive system.

Design of Technology. The Hawthorne studies showed that social factors can be more important than the physical environment in job performance. There is no doubt, however, that the physical features of job settings can affect performance. The field of **human factors** (also called **ergonomics**) or **engineering psychology** is concerned with the inter-

FIGURE 10-3
Incentives can lead to improved performance if employees are able to perform better, if they want the incentives, and if there are few constraints.

face between people and the physical environment, including tools, equipment, and technology. Human factors psychologists are involved in the design of the physical environment to make jobs safer and easier to accomplish. Through their work over the past few decades, human factors psychologists have developed sound design principles and procedures. The influence of the field can be found in the design of everything from automobiles and consumer appliances to military aircraft and nuclear power plants.

Displays and Controls. The major focus of human factors is on the interaction between people and tools, machines, or technology. Two major areas of concern are the presentation of information to the person and the manipulation of the tool or machine by the person.

In an automobile the driver must be given information about speed. He or she also must control the speed and direction of the vehicle. Human factors principles tell engineers how best to present information and design controls.

A machine can provide information to a person in many ways. The nature and use of the information determine how it should best be presented. Most machine information is provided through either the visual or auditory channel, or sometimes both. For danger or warning signals, such as at a railway crossing, it is best to use both, such as a bell and flashing lights.

With machines most information is provided in a visual display. Two different types of visual displays for quantitative information (airplane altitude) are shown in Figure 10–4. The upper display in the figure is a two-point style, which is like a traditional clock with the shorter and heavier hand representing altitude in thousands of feet and the longer and thinner hand representing hundreds of feet. The lower display is a digital display, which indicates the altitude by showing the numerals. Obviously, in an airplane there is a need to be able to both determine altitude quickly and accurately because errors can lead to disaster. The digital display is superior to the two-point display because it is easy to mix up the two hands (Buck, 1983). For example, 2,100 feet can be misread as 1,200 feet, which could present a problem for anyone attempting to fly over a 2,000-foot-high mountain.

The manipulation of the machine by the person, often in response to information provided by a display, is accomplished through controls. The design of the best control is also determined by the particular purpose and situation. Most controls are worked with either the hand or foot, although other possibilities can be found (e.g., the knee or elbow). Hand controls are best when fine or precise motions are necessary, such as steering an automobile. Foot controls are best when force is more important than precision, such as with a brake pedal for an automobile.

FIGURE 10-4

Types of altitude displays for an aircraft. *Source:* "Control and Tools" (p. 214) by J. R. Buck, 1983, in B. H. Kantowitz and R. D. Sorkin (eds.), *Human Factors*, New York: John Wiley.

<u>FIGURE 10-5</u>

Examples of shift knobs that can be discriminated by touch alone. *Source: Human Factors: Understanding People–System Relationships* (p. 311), by B. H. Kantowitz and R. D. Sorkin, 1983, New York: John Wiley.

There are a number of important design considerations with controls. First, they should be found in a logical place, with controls for the same function together. A well-designed automobile console, for example, will place the lighting controls together, the windshield wiper and washer controls together, the heater and air conditioner controls together, and so on. A control to work a front window should be in front of a control to work a back window, and a control to work a feature on the right side of the car should be to the right of a control to work the same feature on the left side.

Second, vital controls that can produce important consequences should be recognizable by touch. This is not important for the volume control on a car radio, but it is vital for the landing gear on an airplane. Figure 10–5 illustrates several different knobs for stick-type levers, such as the shift lever of an automobile. Each of these can be discriminated by touch alone. Knobs such as these are used in airplanes.

Third, controls should provide appropriate feedback so that the person knows that the function has been accomplished. With an on/off switch, the person might hear a click and feel a tactile sensation indicating that the switch has been activated or deactivated. Some switches use springs so that the switch lever can only be in the on or off position, and the person can feel the lever lock into place. Finally, the directions in which controls are moved should logically match the directions in which the machine will move. For example, an increase in some factor should involve moving a switch either clockwise, up, or to the right, as opposed to counterclockwise, down, or to the left. This is the general rule followed with most equipment with volume controls, such as radios and televisions. Levers to move a device to the right should move clockwise or to the right, as in most vehicles.

Computer–Human Interaction. These principles of displays and controls have been available for many years, but relatively little research is being conducted on them today. Instead human factors psychologists have turned their attention to computer–human interaction. *Computer-human interaction* is the interplay of people with computers and associated technologies that have led to tremendous changes in the workplace for both blue- and white-collar work. Although automation and computerization have in some cases replaced people, computers are fast becoming common and necessary parts of many people's jobs. It has been estimated that as many as half of American workers will be using computers at work by the end of the century (Giuliano, 1982).

A major issue for computer–human interaction is communication between human and machine. That is, how best should computers provide information to people, and how best can people tell computers what they wish done? In order for people to communicate effectively with computers, they must develop a conceptual understanding or **mental model** of how the computer operates (Frese, 1987). A person who knows how to drive an automobile, for example, has a mental model of how the operation of the controls results in the appropriate movement of the vehicle.

Frese (1987) noted that efficient use of computers by people can arise by focusing on two essential elements: training people and appropriate system design. Training is necessary because in many jobs people are hired without all the necessary skills for the computer system they must use. Even when people do have the necessary skills, computer systems and software are constantly changing, requiring a continued training effort to maintain proficiency. Research on computer training has suggested ways in which it can enhance performance. Augustine and Coovert (1991), for example, have shown that the use of animated models can be quite effective in enhancing performance of computer tasks. Animated models show the computer system in action rather than giving a written description or instructions. This approach is similar to the demonstration portion of a video (e.g., Nintendo or Play Station) game that shows the game in action.

System design is essential, for many existing systems are poorly designed and inefficient. Research on computer–human interaction has provided many insights about how best to design systems that people can learn and use efficiently. Coovert (1990) argues that the best systems represent problems in a way that matches how people who use them represent problems. Systems that require people to adopt new ways of looking at familiar problems are difficult to learn.

The Apple Macintosh computer is an example of a system that was designed with the user in mind. Different elements are represented with small pictures or icons that represent what they are. The icon that represents a file looks like a file folder. To delete a file, you place its icon on an icon that looks like a trash can. Figure 10-6 is a picture of a Macintosh screen that shows these icons. The Macintosh system can be easier to learn than alternatives that rely on written commands: To delete a file you might have to enter the command "DELETE" followed by the name of the file.

The principles of human factors can be used to design tools and equipment so that people can perform their tasks more easily and efficiently. Whether or not this translates into better overall job performance depends on many other factors. If employees are not motivated to perform well, making their job tasks easier through better equipment design might mean that they do the same work with less effort. Furthermore, constraints in the work environment, which we discuss next, may prevent better performance, even though certain tasks might be accomplished more efficiently.

From a human factors perspective, the goal is to design technology that will be helpful to people. However, technology can come with a price, and not all effects are positive. The introduction of computers in manufacturing has changed jobs but not always for the better. Although new factory systems might be more efficient, they can increase employee boredom and stress (Wall & Davids, 1992). Often the person who used to be an active

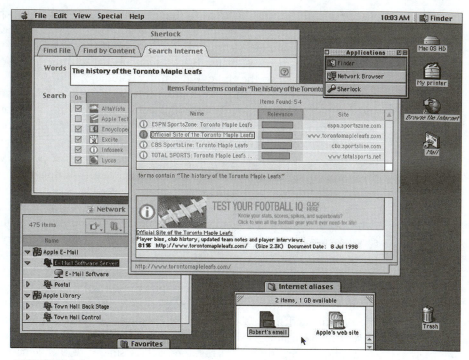

FIGURE 10-6
An Apple Macintosh screen.

participant on the assembly line is relegated to passively watching a machine operate. The loss of control over tasks to the machine can be associated with job dissatisfaction and poor emotional well-being (Mullarkey, Jackson, Wall, Wilson, & Grey-Taylor, 1997).

Organizational Constraints

Organizational constraints are aspects of the work environment that interfere with or prevent good job performance. They can arise from any aspect of the job, including the physical environment; supervisory practices; and the lack of needed training, tools, equipment, or time. Peters, O'Connor, and Rudolf (1980) outlined eight different areas of constraints, which they derived from critical incidents. They asked 62 employed people to describe an incident in which something at work interfered with their job performance. From an analysis of the incidents, they came up with the constraint areas. Each is shown in Table 10-2, along with a brief description.

According to Peters and O'Connor (1980), organizational constraints have a detrimental effect on job performance, especially for the most capable and highly motivated. Support for this idea comes from a study by Spector, Dwyer, & Jex (1988), in which high levels of employee-reported constraints were associated with low levels of supervisor-rated performance. Klein and Kim (1998) found that salespeople's reports of constraints were correlated with their actual sales performance. Individuals who scored highest on constraints sold the least amount. O'Connor, Peters, Rudolf, and Pooyan (1982) further

TABLE 10-2
Eight organizational constraint areas

Job-related information: Data and information needed for the job.

Tools and equipment: Tools, equipment, instruments, and machinery necessary for the job, such as computers or trucks.

Materials and supplies: Materials and supplies necessary for the job, such as lumber or paper.

Budgetary support: Money necessary to acquire resources to do the job.

Required services and help from others: Help available from other people.

Task preparation: Whether or not the employee has the KSAOs necessary for the job.

Time availability: The amount of time available for doing job tasks.

Work environment: The physical features of the job environment, such as buildings or weather.

Source: "Situational Constraints and Work Outcomes: The Influence of a Frequently Overlooked Construct," by L. H. Peters and E. J. O'Connor, 1980, *Academy of Management Review, 5,* 391–397.

demonstrated that constraints can be potentially detrimental to employees themselves, as well as their performance. They found that high levels of situational constraints, as reported by employees, were associated with job dissatisfaction and frustration. Jex and Gudanowski (1992) found similar results, as well as a tendency for employees reporting high levels of constraints to be more likely to intend to quit their jobs. Intentions have been shown to be an important precursor of turnover (Mobley, Griffeth, Hand, & Meglino, 1979; Steel & Ovalle, 1984). Thus, it seems that organizational constraints can have detrimental effects not only on job performance, but on employee satisfaction, frustration, and possibly turnover as well. This conclusion must be tempered by the fact that most constraint measures have relied entirely on employee self-reports for all the data. Studies using other methods will be necessary to determine the importance of the job environment.

ORGANIZATIONAL CITIZENSHIP BEHAVIOR (OCB)

Organizational citizenship behavior (OCB) is generally defined as behavior that goes beyond the formal requirements of the job and is beneficial to the organization. OCB is usually assessed by having supervisors rate their subordinates on OCB behaviors. Sample items from the Smith, Organ, and Near (1983) popular OCB scale are shown in Table 10-3. Note that while some of these items fit the definition of going beyond requirements (e.g., makes suggestions), others do not (e.g., being punctual).

TABLE 10-3
Four items from the Organizational Citizenship Behavior Scale

Assists supervisor with his or her work

Makes innovative suggestions to improve department

Is punctual

Gives advance notice if unable to come to work

Source: "Cognitive Versus Affective Determinants of Organizational Citizenship Behavior," by D. W. Organ and M. Konovsky, 1989, *Journal of Applied Psychology, 74,* 157–164.

Organ and Konovsky (1989) divided OCB into these two categories of behaviors that are specifically required and those that are not. *Altruism* is helping another employee or supervisor with a problem, even though it is not required. It might involve helping a co-worker who has been absent or making suggestions to improve conditions. *Compliance* is doing what needs to be done and following rules, such as coming to work on time and not wasting time.

OCB can be an important aspect of an employee's behavior that contributes to overall organizational effectiveness. Individuals who are high on OCB are not necessarily the best performers in other areas, however. MacKenzie, Podsakoff, and Fetter (1991) assessed OCB and objective sales performance of salespeople. They found little relation between the two types of behavior. Employees who had the best sales record were no different from those with the poorest in terms of their OCB. In some cases, salespeople who performed poorly in sales may have made significant contributions to the organization through their OCB. Evidence exists that this does occur. Podsakoff, Ahearne, and MacKenzie (1997) studied 40 work crews in a paper mill, assessing the OCBs of individual members in relation to the crew's overall performance rather than individual employee performance. Results showed that higher levels of OCB among crew members were associated with higher total crew productivity and fewer defects.

Several factors have been suggested as the cause of organizational citizenship behavior (Schnake, 1991). Job satisfaction and supportive behavior by the supervisor are two of them. Support for their possible role in OCB has been provided by studies that have found correlations between measures of OCB and both of these variables. Becker and Billings (1993) found that job satisfaction correlated with OCB in the United States. Farh, Podsakoff, and Organ (1990) discovered that OCB correlated with job satisfaction and employee perceptions of supervisor supportive behavior in Taiwan.

McNeely and Meglino (1994) found that different types of OCB were related to different variables. Actions that benefited other employees were correlated with concern for others. Actions that benefited the organization correlated with perceived equity. These authors concluded that each type of OCB had different causes, although both were related to job satisfaction.

Organizational citizenship behavior is a new area of study. This kind of behavior makes important contributions to organizational functioning, but more research needs to be done to enhance our understanding about how it does so. We also need to know how to encourage people to engage in these behaviors at work. The focus on OCB has expanded the scope of behavior that the I/O field has studied.

COUNTERPRODUCTIVE BEHAVIOR: WITHDRAWAL

On any given day in almost any large organization, some people will come to work late; some people will miss the entire workday; and some people will quit the job permanently. All of these *withdrawal* behaviors involve employees not being at work when scheduled or needed, either temporarily as in tardiness or absence or permanently as in turnover. Most of the research on withdrawal behaviors has considered them to be related phenomena. As noted by Mitra, Jenkins, and Gupta (1992), some researchers have considered absence and turnover to be alternative reactions to job dissatisfaction. Both may reflect attempts by employees to escape, either temporarily or permanently, from situations they find unpleasant.

In their meta-analysis Mitra et al. (1992) found that absence and turnover were moderately correlated. In other words, employees who quit the job were likely to have had relatively high levels of absence before they quit. In a similar meta-analysis Koslowsky, Sagie, Krausz, and Singer (1997) found that lateness (not getting to work on time) correlated with both absence and turnover. Late people are often absent people and are likely to quit. Although correlations among withdrawal measures might mean that they have similar causes, other explanations are possible. For example, individuals who plan to quit their jobs might use up their sick leave rather than forfeit it upon leaving. On the other hand, people planning to quit might be absent to engage in job hunting.

Most of the withdrawal research in the I/O literature has been directed to understanding absence and turnover. Whereas both forms of withdrawal might share some similar causes, they are both distinct behaviors that can arise for many reasons.

Absence

Absence—employees not showing up for work when scheduled—can be a major problem for organizations. Many jobs require someone's presence even when the scheduled person is not there. Absence requires that organizations either overstaff so that enough people will be available each day or have substitutes on call. Whereas the idea of substitutes for teachers is undoubtedly familiar to everyone, many organizations, especially factories, have substitutes available for other types of work as well. Often the on-call substitutes are other employees who may be asked to work an extra shift to fill in, frequently at higher overtime salary rates.

The major approach to understanding why absence occurs has focused on withdrawal as a response to dissatisfying jobs and job conditions. Absence and job satisfaction are related, but research has found quite small correlations between them. Farrell and Stamm (1988) conducted a meta-analysis of 72 absence studies and noted that the two best predictors were prior absence history and the organization's absence policy rather than job satisfaction. People who have frequently been absent in the past are likely to be absent in the future. Organizations that have policies designed to control absence by either rewarding attendance or punishing absence have less absence. Individual-level variables, such as gender, age, or job attitudes, have shown small or no consistent relation with absence.

One complication in the study of absence is that it is a complex variable that can arise from many causes. Goff, Mount, and Jamison (1990) found that having primary responsibility for child care predicted absence with a correlation considerably higher than that typically found with job satisfaction. Presumably, absence can be caused by having to take care of children whether or not the employee likes his or her job.

Dalton and Mesch (1991) asked subjects to classify their absence into one of two categories: due to illness or due to other circumstances. They found that the two types of absence had different correlates. Absence due to illness, but not other circumstances, was related to job satisfaction and gender. (The dissatisfied and women were ill more frequently.) Absence due to other circumstances was related to job tenure and absence policy. (Organizations with longer tenured employees and less restrictive policy had more absence.) These results suggest that the different types of absences have different causes that might be reduced with different procedures.

Nicholson and Johns (1985) have taken a different approach to the explanation of absence. They note that absence can be caused by the absence culture of a work group or

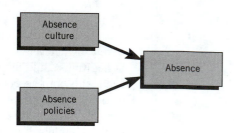

FIGURE 10-7
Both the absence culture of the work group and organizational absence policies contribute to employee absence.

organization. That is, in any work group or organization there will generally be accepted social rules governing the appropriate amount and reasons for absence. One organization might have a culture that encourages absence whenever one does not feel like coming to work. Another might encourage employees to come to work unless it is absolutely impossible for them to do so.

Research evidence supports the idea of an absence culture in organizations. Martocchio (1994) asked employees to indicate their perceived benefits and costs of being absent from work. He combined the data for each work group. Results found that a person was absent more frequently if his or her co-workers believed that being absent carried many benefits and few costs.

Harrison and Shaffer (1993) found that employee absence was significantly correlated with employee estimates of their work group level of acceptable numbers of absences. On average, employees were absent less than what they perceived the acceptable level to be. Mathieu and Kohler (1990) found that work group absence predicted individual-level absence. Employees whose co-workers were absent frequently were absent more often than employees whose co-workers were seldom absent.

Figure 10-7 illustrates that absence culture and absence policies are the two biggest factors in absence. Although job satisfaction has been the focus of most absence research, it seems that its potential effects are overshadowed by culture and policies. A dissatisfied individual who might want to escape work by calling in sick is not likely to do so if absence is punished. Job satisfaction might be a factor in absence only under conditions of an accepting culture and a liberal absence policy.

Turnover

In every organization employees will quit their jobs from time to time. The quitting of employees is called **turnover**. The percentage of the workforce that quits in a given period of time is called the *turnover rate*. When the rate becomes excessive, the organization's workforce can become too inexperienced and untrained, resulting in inefficiency and difficulties in achieving the organization's objectives. Dalton and Todor (1993) discussed factors that determine if turnover creates problems, including performance level of quitters and replacement costs.

Turnover is not a problem if the quitters are people who perform poorly. Trevor, Gerhart, and Boudreau (1997) studied the relation between job performance and turnover. They found a curvilinear relation in that the best and worst employees were most likely to quit. For the best performers, good salary raises reduced turnover. Thus, turnover can have beneficial results if better replacements can be found for poor performers. However, good performers might also quit because often the best people are those who are the most attractive to other organizations.

Poor performers will quit for several reasons. They know they are not doing well on the job, or they want to find jobs for which they are better suited. Alternatively, it is not uncommon for supervisors to "encourage" turnover by targeting individuals for harassment. Poor performers might be denied rewards, be given distasteful work assignments, and be treated unkindly in order to get them to quit.

Serious difficulties can arise from this approach to creating turnover and can produce more problems than it solves. It can affect employees who are not the intended target. The harassment of one employee can create a hostile and uncomfortable work environment for everyone. Legal ramifications are also possible, for harassed employees might file lawsuits. If the supervisor and target of harassment are of a different gender or ethnic backgrounds, a discrimination case might be filed. Finally, harassment is an unethical behavior, and even poorly performing employees should be dealt with in a fair and honest manner.

The second issue that determines the costs of turnover to organizations concerns the expense involved in replacing people who have quit. For some jobs, recruiting and hiring can be costly and time consuming. Hiring high-level executives can take months of searching for applicants, conducting extensive and expensive out-of-town interviews, and offering expensive bonuses and benefits. Other jobs might require a long period of training before an employee is able to be fully productive. In the armed services, it can take more than a year to fully train a fighter pilot. If there is a high level of pilot turnover, the cost to the government will be very high.

Job satisfaction has been a central variable in the research on turnover (Maertz & Campion, 1998). Figure 10-8 illustrates how the turnover process is thought to work. It shows that job satisfaction leads to intention to quit, which leads to turnover. Furthermore, the relation between intention to quit and turnover is moderated by the unemployment rate. People who are dissatisfied with their jobs are likely to intend to quit them. Intentions are often precursors to behavior that leads to quitting. It is unlikely, however, that people will quit their jobs unless they have another job available. As shown in the model, the unemployment rate, which reflects the availability of alternative employment, affects whether or not dissatisfaction and intentions are translated into turnover.

There is good support for the propositions in this model. First, job satisfaction and intention of quitting correlate quite well (Blau, 1993b), which is consistent with the idea that satisfaction leads to intention. Second, Blau found that both job satisfaction and in-

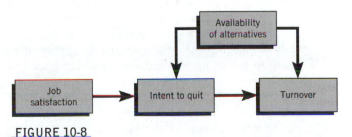

FIGURE 10-8
Employee turnover as a function of job satisfaction and unemployment rate.

tention of quitting correlated with job search behaviors, such as applying for another job and going on a job interview.

Third, Carsten and Spector (1987) found in their meta-analysis that both job satisfaction and intention to quit predict future turnover, with satisfaction having a smaller magnitude of correlation ($r = -.23$) than intention ($r = .38$). The predictive nature of these studies supports the idea that job satisfaction and intention are precursors of turnover. Finally, two studies have shown that the unemployment rate moderates the relation between job satisfaction and turnover and between intention and turnover (Carsten & Spector, 1987; Gerhart, 1990). These studies show that when the unemployment rate is low and alternative job opportunities are plentiful, there is a strong relation of satisfaction and intention with turnover. When the unemployment rate is high and alternative job opportunities are scarce, however, there is little predictability of turnover by intention and job satisfaction. In other words, dissatisfied people may wish to quit their jobs, but they can only do so when alternative employment is available.

Dickter, Roznowski, and Harrison (1996) tracked the quitting of individuals, who either liked or disliked their jobs, over several years. For both groups, likelihood of turnover increased from the time of hiring until about two years on the job, after which it declined. Dissatisfied individuals were more likely to quit than their satisfied counterparts until about four years on the job. After four years differences disappeared. Apparently, the effects of job satisfaction on turnover are time limited, as perhaps those who wish to quit eventually give up and make the best of the situation.

Mitra et al. (1992) found that the unemployment rate also moderated the relation between absence and turnover. When the unemployment rate is low, there is a larger correlation between absence and turnover than when unemployment is high. In other words, absence is a precursor to turnover when people can find alternative employment relatively easily. When jobs are hard to find, absence does not relate well to turnover.

Although many employees quit their jobs because they are unhappy with them, there are other reasons for turnover. First, a person might quit for health reasons. Heart attack survivors will often make drastic changes in their lifestyles, which can include quitting their jobs. Sometimes people get injured on the job and cannot continue to do certain tasks. Overuse injuries, such as **carpal tunnel syndrome,** which is a serious wrist injury, are becoming more and more frequent with certain types of jobs. These painful conditions can lead to employees' quitting to find work that does not continue to aggravate their physical problems. Second, people will sometimes quit jobs they like to pursue other life interests. These might include child rearing, continuing their education, or training for athletic pursuits, such as the Olympics. Third, people might quit because of family problems, such as the illness of a family member or divorce. Finally, people might quit because their spouse has been offered a better job in another location.

Some of these reasons go beyond the workplace, but organizations can do a great deal to address some of these causes of turnover. An organization can create a safer work environment to reduce injuries and can encourage healthy behavior to reduce illness. Many organizations have instituted employee wellness programs, which can include exercise programs, smoking and weight control classes, and stress management workshops. Organizational policies and practices can help employees pursue other interests while continuing to work. For example, on-site child care can make it easier for employees with young children to continue their jobs. With such programs, child care is provided at the place of employment so that employees can take their children to work and spend breaks and lunch periods with them. Having their children nearby can provide peace of mind that makes it easier for employees to focus attention on work. Flexible work schedules that allow employees to work at times that do not interfere with other interests can keep some employees from quitting their jobs.

COUNTERPRODUCTIVE BEHAVIOR: AGGRESSION, SABOTAGE, AND THEFT

Instances of irate employees shooting their co-workers and often themselves have brought national attention to the issue of employee aggression. Although these relatively rare (Neuman & Baron, 1997) but extreme examples fall more within the domain of clinical psychology or criminology, the issue of employee behavior that is damaging to organizations is an important one for the I/O field. Most instances of aggression and other counterproductive behaviors are not spectacular enough to appear in the news media. Aggression against others at work, sabotage (the destruction of organizational property), and theft of organizational property, however, can directly or indirectly result in tremendous monetary and personal costs for employees and their organizations.

Geddes (1994), for example, reported that supervisors in her study were frequent targets of aggressive responses by subordinates who received negative performance appraisals. Although a relatively small percentage were physically attacked, Geddes points out that nationally there could be several million supervisors who have been assaulted during their careers.

Sabotage has also resulted in large monetary cost to organizations. Direct costs come from damage to tools, equipment, and property. Indirect costs arise from the loss of productivity that occurs, for example, when an assembly line is shut down for repairs or when employees must wait while a piece of equipment is repaired or replaced. Many acts of sabotage are blatant, such as burning down a building. Other acts can be surreptitious and difficult to prove. It is often impossible to determine if an equipment-damaging accident was really accidental. For example, an employee might purposely ignore warning signals on a piece of equipment, such as the indicator light that a truck is low on oil or water. In some cases, employees might remove the oil or water, knowing that it will damage the equipment. If the employee is careful, it will be difficult to prove that he or she purposely sabotaged the equipment.

Employee theft has been estimated to cost American businesses billions of dollars per year (Greenberg & Barling, 1996). In a national survey of retailers, employees were found to be responsible for more theft than shoplifters (Hollinger, Dabney, Lee, Hayes, Hunter, & Cummings, 1996). Organizations spend considerable money and resources to control theft. Many organizations have tried to weed out potential thieves with the use of paper-and-pencil "honesty tests" (see Chapter 5). Others have resorted to lie detector tests, either for job applicants or current employees.

Counterproductive behaviors have been studied as reactions to frustration and dissatisfaction at work. Figure 10-9 shows how such reactions occur. It begins with organizational constraints that prevent not only job performance as discussed earlier but also attainment of employee personal goals. These constraints might involve the areas shown in Table 10-2 that interfere with good job performance. They might also involve organizational practices, supervisor behavior, or other factors that prevent employees from getting the rewards they want from work. For example, an employee might be denied a desired

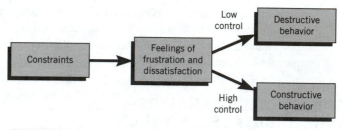

FIGURE 10-9

Constructive and destructive employee behavior as a result of frustration and employee control.

raise or promotion. It was believed that this was the reason for the post office shooting we discussed earlier ("Three Die," 1993). Constraints induce feelings of dissatisfaction and frustration. The feelings in turn lead to behaviors that can be constructive, such as developing more effective strategies to overcome obstacles, or destructive, such as sabotage, aggression, or theft.

Beliefs about control determine in part whether individuals choose constructive or destructive responses. An employee who believes that constructive efforts can overcome obstacles is likely to attempt to do so. An employee who believes that he or she cannot control obstacles might resort to counterproductive behaviors. This could result in aggression against other people or property.

The illegal nature of many counterproductive behaviors has made research difficult to conduct (Giacalone & Rosenfeld, 1987). Support for the model presented earlier comes mainly from questionnaire studies that ask employees to report (usually anonymously) about their jobs and reactions. These studies have shown that employee reports of organizational constraints are correlated with job satisfaction and feelings of frustration. Individuals who report high levels of constraints also report low levels of satisfaction and high levels of frustration (e.g., Jex & Gudanowski, 1992). Feelings of job dissatisfaction and frustration have been shown to relate to destructive behaviors (e.g., Chen & Spector, 1992; Storms & Spector, 1987). Finally, employee locus of control has been found to moderate the relation between feelings of frustration and destructive behaviors. Individuals with an external locus of control showed a correlation between frustration at work and destructive behaviors. Their internal counterparts showed little or no correlation between frustration and destructive behavior (Storms & Spector, 1987). Thus, when people with external control beliefs were frustrated, they were more likely to engage in counterproductive behavior.

Although these studies are consistent with the model in Figure 10-9, their reliance on employee questionnaires is a major limitation. Perlow and Latham (1993), however, conducted a study of employee aggression that used a stronger methodology. They administered a locus of control scale to employees of a residential retardation facility and found that it could predict which employees would later abuse clients. Employees with an external locus of control were more likely than employees with an internal locus of control to be caught assaulting residents of the facility. This study supports the idea that control has an important influence on aggressive behavior.

Greenberg (1990) conducted a study that showed how theft can be a reaction to perceived inequity or unfairness among employees. Employees of a manufacturing company had their pay cut 15% for a 10-week period. Thefts increased during the period of the pay cut and returned to precut levels when pay levels were restored. Greenberg explained these results as being caused by employee feelings of inequity over having to work just as hard for less pay. One might also presume that the pay cut was a constraint that would induce frustration on the part of employees, thus lending support to the constraints model. Skarlicki and Folger (1997) also found a link between a variety of counterproductive behaviors, including sabotage and theft, and perceived fairness of treatment. Employees who perceived unfair treatment were more likely to be said by co-workers to engage in 17 counterproductive behaviors than employees who felt fairly treated.

Labor Unrest and Strikes

Another area in which we see counterproductive behavior as a response to frustration or unfair treatment is in labor–management disputes. The history of organized labor contains many acts of violence on both sides. A tactic often used by unions is to "attack" the organization by withholding output. Work slowdowns and stoppages are counterproductive from the organization's perspective. In addition, sabotage can be quite common during union actions, such as strikes.

Labor unrest and strikes can occur for many reasons. Often these actions are accompanied by frustration among employees who believe that they are not treated fairly. These beliefs can lead to a variety of counterproductive behaviors such as work slowdowns or sabotage. Frustration and perceptions of unfair treatment have been associated with strikes (Bluen, 1994; Giacalone & Knouse, 1990).

FUTURE ISSUES AND CHALLENGES

Over the past few years there has been increasing discussion in the media about worker productivity, particularly in the United States. As foreign competition has increased, so has the concern with staying competitive. Much of this concern revolves around the job performance of workers and ways in which it can be enhanced. Such enhancement has always been a major focus for the field of I/O psychology, and it is addressed by many of the activities of the field. Of particular concern in the future will be the appropriate ways in which technology can enhance productivity without harming the health or well-being of employees. Research has already pointed to the positive and negative sides of new computer advances. Computers can facilitate the performance of many tasks, and robotic devices have freed people from many dangerous and unpleasant jobs. On the other hand, jobs that require the excessive use of computers have been associated with certain physical injuries, such as carpal tunnel syndrome.

A second issue concerns the understanding and control of destructive behavior. Organizations over the past decade have put considerable effort into reduction of theft, but they have given little attention to sabotage or aggression. Additional research is needed to provide procedures that organizations can implement to reduce destructive behavior. The limited research to date suggests that enhancing people's control at work might well reduce their destructive behaviors.

CHAPTER SUMMARY

The productive and counterproductive behavior of employees at work is a vital area of concern to the I/O field. Job performance, absence, and turnover have been a major focus of attention for both research and practice. Destructive behaviors, such as sabotage, aggression at work, and theft, are also important. Recent attention has also been given to organizational citizenship behavior (OCB).

Job performance is a central variable for the I/O field. Much of the research and practice of I/O psychologists is concerned with understanding, assessing, or enhancing job performance. Performance results from the interplay of ability and motivation. Both environmental and personal factors are important influences. Personality characteristics, such as the Big Five and locus of control, have been shown to relate to performance. Job characteristics, incentive systems, and technology are important environmental influences.

One of the major objectives of the human factors field is to enhance job performance through the design of tools and equipment. Although the Hawthorne studies suggested that the social environment was more important than the physical, the physical environment can still influence job performance. Physical aspects, such as lighting and sound levels, as well as the design of equipment and the ways in which information is presented all have important influences on performance.

Organizational constraints are features of the work environment that interfere with good job performance. Such conditions can lead to lower job satisfaction and employee turnover.

Organizational citizenship behavior (OCB) is behavior that goes beyond the formal requirements of the job and is beneficial to the organization. It involves both altruistic (helping others) and compliance (following rules) behavior. OCB is important because it can contribute to organizational well-being. Both job satisfaction and supportive supervisory behavior are correlated with how much employees engage in organizational citizenship behavior.

Withdrawal behavior—absence and turnover—can create tremendous problems for organizations. Most of the research on both of these variables has considered them to be reactions to job dissatisfaction. This seems to be more true for turnover, at least during times of plentiful jobs, than for absence, which correlates only slightly with job satisfaction. Furthermore, withdrawal can arise from many causes, with only some related to job attitudes.

The counterproductive behaviors of sabotage, aggression at work, and theft can produce tremendous costs to organizations. The limited research conducted on these behaviors suggests that they are reactions to feelings of frustration and dissatisfaction. Furthermore, employees who believe they have little control at work are more likely to engage in destructive behavior.

I/O PSYCHOLOGY IN PRACTICE

THIS CASE CONCERNS a turnover project carried out by Dr. Jeanne M. Carsten. Dr. Carsten received her Ph.D. in I/O psychology in 1987 from the University of South Florida. Since then, she has been employed by Chase Manhattan Bank in New York City, one of the largest financial institutions in the world. Her current job title is Vice President for Measurement, Evaluation, and Administration. Her responsibilities cover many areas of I/O, including attitude surveys, employee development, selection, and training. One of her major functions is to carry out projects designed to address specific organizational problems.

The first major project she was assigned was to find a solution to an excessive turnover rate among bank tellers. Although high turnover is normal and expected with these employees, the management of the bank believed that its rate had become excessive. Dr. Carsten was charged with finding out why and suggesting solutions.

The first phase of this project was to collect information. Interviews were conducted with tellers and their supervisors to find out why they were quitting. Tellers were asked about problems they encountered on the job. In addition, a salary survey was conducted to see if other banks were paying their tellers more, which they were.

The second phase was to prepare and present an action plan to the management of the bank. There were 12 recommendations, including raising salaries, training teller supervisors to provide better assistance to their subordinates, clarifying job performance standards, and offering additional teller training.

During the final phase of the project, almost all of the recommendations were implemented. Afterward the turnover rate declined by almost 50%. Without a control group, one cannot be certain what caused improvement in the turnover rate. During the course of the project, the national unemployment rate increased, which would have reduced turnover. Dr. Carsten points out that the turnover rate became lower than that at other banks, however, lending support to the idea that the changes were effective. Furthermore, many of the changes, such as improving supervisory practices and clarifying performance standards, may have been of benefit for reasons other than turnover reduction. This case illustrates how an I/O psychologist who works for an organization can help improve working conditions for employees.

Discussion Questions

1. Why do you think the bank tellers quit their jobs?

2. What factors would encourage you to stay on a job that you did not like?

3. Do you think Dr. Carsten's interventions did anything else besides reduce turnover?

4. Might employees at this bank have engaged in other forms of withdrawal behavior?

EMPLOYEE HEALTH AND SAFETY

Does work contribute to the health and emotional well-being of employees? Illness and mortality rates vary considerably among people in different occupations (Fletcher, 1988). For example, Violanti, Vena, and Marshall (1986) found that police officers were more likely than a matched sample of municipal workers to die from certain types of cancer, ulcers, and suicide. They speculated that police officers experience elevated risks for these causes of death because they are exposed to high job stress, have irregular sleeping and eating schedules, engage in poor health habits, and get little exercise.

As the Violanti et al. (1986) study illustrates, the work environment contributes to the physical health and emotional well-being of employees in many ways. The impact of the workplace is often direct and immediate: An employee can be injured or killed on the job. Other times the workplace affects health over a long period of time: A person can be exposed to a toxic substance that may lead to cancer only after many years on the job. Finally, the effects of the job are sometimes indirect. For example, Violanti et al. (1986) discussed how police officers frequently use alcohol to cope with the stress of police work, and alcohol consumption has been associated with illnesses that police officers are more likely to contract. Thus conditions at work, such as stress, can affect behavior that is relevant to physical health, although the conditions themselves might or might not directly affect health.

Table 11-1 lists some frequent sources of illness and injury on the job, along with some common occupations for which each is particularly problematic. These sources represent concrete physical conditions at work, such as equipment or toxic substances, and they are more likely to affect physical health rather than emotional well-being. The effects of these sources tend to be direct, although for some people exposure over a long period of time must occur for illness or injury to develop. For example, it can take years to become injured or disabled from repetitive motions, such as typing. Certain occupations are more likely than others to exhibit each of these sources, although employees on most jobs might encounter any of them. Those who work outdoors, such as park rangers or roofers, are most likely to encounter either extremely hot or extremely cold conditions; but even office

TABLE 11-1
Frequent sources of illness and injury for workers in some common occupations

SOURCE	OCCUPATION
Infectious disease	Dentist, nurse
Loud noise	Airline baggage handler, musician
Physical assault	Police officer, prison guard
Repetitive actions	Data entry clerk, typist
Temperature extremes	Park ranger, roofer
Toxic substances	Exterminator, farmer

workers might encounter extremes of temperature if their buildings do not have adequate heating or air conditioning. Whereas police officers and prison guards are more likely to be victims of assault, virtually anyone might be assaulted at work, although for most jobs the chances are remote.

In addition to the physical conditions listed in Table 11-1, certain nonphysical conditions might affect physical health and emotional well-being. Nonstandard work schedules, such as night shift work, have been implicated as causes of both physical and psychological problems. Several nonphysical work conditions are frequently discussed in the literature under the general topic of job stress. Such conditions as workload, lack of control, role ambiguity, role conflict, and organizational constraints have all been associated with physical health or emotional well-being.

In this chapter we are concerned with employee health and well-being at work. We discuss the physical and nonphysical conditions that affect health, as well as accidents, which can arise from employee behavior or work conditions. Finally, we cover burnout, a psychological state thought to be the result of stressful work conditions.

Objectives **The student who studies this chapter should be able to:**
1. List the major physical work conditions that affect employee health.
2. Explain how work schedules can affect employee health and well-being.
3. Discuss the nature of job stress, including its causes and effects.
4. Describe the causes of accidents and the steps that can be taken to prevent them.
5. Define burnout and state how it relates to employee health and well-being.

PHYSICAL CONDITIONS AFFECTING HEALTH AND SAFETY

Physical work conditions tend to have direct physical effects on people. Sometimes the effects are immediate, but often they occur over long periods of time. When it takes a long time for an illness or injury to develop, it can be difficult to determine exactly what caused it. In addition, there can be effects on emotional well-being. Serious illness and injury are almost certainly associated with some level of psychological distress and trauma, particularly when the person has been disabled.

In this section, we discuss the effects of six physical work conditions:

Infectious disease

Loud noise

Physical assaults

Repetitive actions

Temperature extremes

Toxic substances

Exposure to any of these conditions may cause either minor or major health problems.

Infectious Disease

Employees who must deal with the public (e.g., hairstylist, police officer, sales clerk, or teacher) may be exposed to infectious disease, although most such cases result in relatively minor illnesses, such as cold or flu. Exposure to serious infectious diseases is of particular concern to people in the health care professions who must deal with seriously ill and dying patients. The National Safety Council (1992a) estimated that 12,000 people per year are infected on the job with hepatitis B, a serious disease that affects the liver. Wallack (1989) found that the majority of health care workers feel at risk of contracting AIDS from patients. Murphy, Gershon, and DeJoy (1996) noted that AIDS exposure is a major source of job stress, frequently leading to anxiety and distress. The concern with AIDS has had considerable impact on safety practices in the health professions. In the United States the Centers for Disease Control and Prevention (CDC) recommends that all health care workers comply with the **Universal Precautions**, which is a set of safety procedures, such as:

Disposing of sharp objects in a special container

Wearing disposable gloves when handling blood or body fluids

Immediately cleaning all bodily fluid spills with disinfectant

Recapping needles that have been used

Unfortunately, large numbers of health care workers fail to follow them even though research shows that these procedures are highly effective (Murphy et al., 1996). Those who follow them can dramatically reduce their chances of becoming seriously ill.

Loud Noise

Loud noise occurs at many jobs, particularly those involving heavy equipment or machinery. Airports, construction sites, factories, and mines can all be noisy places, exposing employees to conditions that can affect both their health and their job performance.

The intensity of noise is measured in **decibel (dB)** units. The decibel scale is a logarithmic scale, meaning that the relation between decibel level and sound intensity is not linear. Increasing the sound level by 10dB is an increase of 10 times in sound intensity, and by 20dB it is an increase of 100 times. The decibel levels of several common sounds found in the workplace are shown in Figure 11-1.

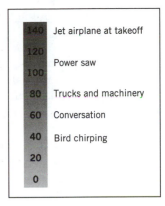

FIGURE 11-1
Sound intensity levels in decibels for some common sounds. *Source: Sound Sense,* by National Safety Council, 1992, Itasca, IL: Author.

Exposure to extremely loud noises, such as explosions, can severely damage a person's sense of hearing, sometimes permanently. Noise of this magnitude is painful and most people will avoid places where such noises occur. Of even more concern at work is continuous exposure to moderately loud noise that exceeds 85 decibels (National Safety Council, 1992b). If continued over a period of months or years, moderately loud noise can lead to permanent hearing loss, particularly in the higher frequencies. Because noise of this intensity is not typically painful, however, many employees will do nothing to avoid it. It is quite common for employees in noisy work environments to suffer from hearing loss. Hearing damage can also be caused by exposure to loud music. Listening to headphones at high volume levels can be particularly dangerous because the dB level in the ear can be quite high.

Because of the potential for hearing damage, many countries have laws governing the legal levels of noise to which an employee can be exposed. Employees who work in noisy environments are given hearing protection to prevent hearing loss. It is common, for example, to see airline employees wear such protection when they are around jets that have their engines running.

Besides hearing damage, there is evidence suggestive of a link between noise exposure at work and cardiovascular disease. Though not conclusive, studies have found that employees exposed to high levels of noise are more likely than employees not exposed to have heart problems (Cohen & Weinstein, 1981). Cohen and Weinstein (1981) also note the possibility (not very well studied) that noise at work might lead to other diseases as well.

Physical Assaults

When you mention workplace assault, most people think of the U.S. postal service, where in the past decade the news media have reported several cases of irate employees shooting co-workers and supervisors, many fatally. The U.S. Bureau of Labor Statistics (1996) reports that homicide was the second leading cause of workplace fatalities overall in 1996. Although it was the leading cause for women, more men were victims (740) than women (172). This is because far more men are killed at work than women, and for men traffic accidents are the leading cause of death. Despite the media attention paid to postal shootings, only 8% of homicides at work are committed by co-workers. Most (80%) are the re-sult of robberies or other crimes.

For many jobs assault is a fairly common occupational hazard. For example, people who work with psychiatric inpatients, particularly adolescents, are at considerable risk of assault, although rarely is this fatal to the employee. To control violence at these facilities, it is common to medicate patients. Specialized training is also offered at many institutions to help employees avoid assaults and defend themselves from patients.

Police officers can also be targets of attacks, and officers in most large cities experience occasional assaultive situations in arresting or subduing people. However, differences in assault frequencies can be dramatic across countries. For example, in the American city of Tampa, Florida, there were 581 reported assaults on 934 total police officers in 1997, ac-cording to police department officials. During the same year, the 5,000-officer force in Toronto, Canada, a city about 10 times the size of Tampa, was assaulted only 395 times, according to their police service officials. Clearly, policing is far more dangerous in Amer-ican than Canadian cities.

Convenience store clerks in the United States have become targets of violent crime, particularly in large cities. During 1992 in the state of Florida alone there were 15 mur-ders of clerks, which was the same as the number of murders of police officers ("Slaying Was Store's 176th Call," 1993).

Assaults of employees can be carried out by animals as well as by people. In many jobs dog bites can be a significant problem. Meter readers, phone installers, and door-to-door salespeople can all have problems with dogs. People who work directly with animals can also be targets of animal assault. Veterinarians, zoo keepers, and farm workers can be injured on the job by animals.

Repetitive Actions

Many jobs require repeated physical actions of various body parts. Employees who use computers at work often spend their entire day typing. Traditional assembly-line work re-quires that an employee perform the same operation over and over. Such repetitive ac-tions can result in **repetitive strain injuries**, in which the body parts involved can become inflamed and sometimes permanently damaged. The U.S. Department of Labor has estimated that repetitive strain injuries cost $20 billion in 1993 for workers' compen-sation claims in the United States, as well as indirect costs to employers of as much as $100 billion a year (Occupational Safety and Health Administration, 1997).

Perhaps the most well known of these injuries is **carpal tunnel syndrome**, which is a wrist injury that causes pain, numbness, and weakness in the fingers and hands. It is brought on by repeated use of the fingers and wrist. Perhaps the most well-known cause is from using a computer keyboard, but other repetitive hand motions can also cause it. In 1995 it was estimated that 3.9 out of every 10,000 workers had this injury (U.S. Bureau of Labor Statistics, 1995), which works out to more than 50,000 people in the United States. Although mild cases can be alleviated with rest, severe cases can result in perma-nent damage. Surgery can sometimes repair the injury but not always.

Repetitive strain injuries can be reduced with two often very inexpensive strategies. First, the proper design of tools and equipment can go a long way to reducing the strain on the body that can result in these injuries. Figure 11-2 shows a wrist rest that can help prevent carpal tunnel syndrome in people who use computer keyboards. It is a bar that helps keep the typist's wrists straight so that the strain on the wrist is reduced.

FIGURE 11-2
A device that helps reduce strain on a person's wrist when using a computer keyboard.

A second strategy is to allow employees to take frequent rest breaks. In Sweden there are laws governing the maximum amount of time an employee can be asked to use a computer keyboard without a break and the maximum amount of time he or she can type in a day. In the United States similar legislation has been debated. A combination of both equipment design and rest breaks can be successful in reducing the likelihood that employees will contract debilitating repetitive strain injuries.

Temperature Extremes

People who work outdoors can be subject to extremes of hot and cold weather, depending on the climates in which they live. Such conditions can be threats to health, and employees have been known to die of extreme weather conditions. Illness and death will occur in humans if their core or internal body temperature deviates too much from 37° Celsius (98.6° Fahrenheit). Core temperatures above 45°C (113°F) or below 25°C (77°F) will quickly lead to death, often from heart failure (Bell, 1981).

Ambient or surrounding air temperature has a lot to do with maintaining core temperature. It is important when employees work in extreme weather conditions that appropriate steps be taken to ensure that they do not become over- or underheated. In cold conditions employees should have sufficiently warm clothing to maintain body temperature. Under very extreme conditions, exposure to the outside air should be limited to brief time periods. In hot conditions, people should be given sufficient liquids to prevent dehydration, for sweating is the primary means by which the body maintains its core temperature.

Research concerning the effects of temperature on performance has been mixed, with some studies showing that heat improves performance and some showing that it decreases it (Bell, 1981). Extreme conditions such as intense heat will eventually lead to physical exhaustion and heat stress that will certainly interfere with performance. Under less extreme conditions, job performance is not necessarily compromised. The use of appropriate clothing and intake of fluids (in hot environments) can allow employees to remain productive under adverse conditions.

Toxic Substances

The exposure of employees to toxic substances has been given more and more attention as research has begun to show how such substances can affect health. The problem with exposure to many substances is that adverse health effects such as cancer can take years or decades to develop. Furthermore, not every person exposed will develop symptoms. This makes it difficult to determine the effects of exposure, because many things might contribute to a particular person contracting an illness.

Employees in many jobs can be exposed to toxic substances, often in unexpected places. Employees in chemical plants or exterminators and farm workers who use insecticides can expect to be exposed. Office workers in enclosed buildings, however, can be exposed to various chemicals, such as toners from copying machines or solvents that might be used to clean ink. Reactions to exposure can range from fairly minor symptoms such as headaches or nausea to serious conditions that can permanently damage vital organs such as the kidneys or liver. At times only a few sensitive individuals will exhibit symptoms, but it is not unusual for most of the individuals in an office to become ill, leading to what has been termed the *sick building* phenomenon, which can arise from toxic substances or microorganisms.

Organizations that expose their employees to toxic substances run the risk of lawsuits by ill or disabled employees. In the United States, the Occupational Safety and Health Administration (OSHA) is charged with seeing that workplace safeguards are used to protect workers. Many countries have laws to protect employees from toxic substances and other conditions that affect health. Even so, each year thousands of workers are injured or killed on the job because of toxic substance exposure (National Safety Council, 1992c).

WORK SCHEDULES

Whereas most employed people work standard schedules of approximately eight daylight hours per day during weekdays, the use of nonstandard schedules involving longer work shifts, nights, and weekends is spreading. Of particular interest to I/O psychologists have been three types of schedules: night shifts, long work shifts, and flextime.

Night Shifts

Many organizations, such as hospitals and police departments, run 24 hours per day, requiring the use of two or three shifts of workers to cover the entire day. A typical three-shift sequence is

8 A.M. to 4 P.M.

4 P.M. to 12 A.M.

12 A.M to 8 A.M.

referred to as the day, evening, and night or graveyard shifts, respectively. Some organizations hire people to work a fixed shift; that is, they work the same shift all the time. Other organizations use rotating shifts: Employees work one shift for a limited length of time, say a month, and then switch or rotate to another shift. According to a U.S. Bureau of Labor Statistics (1998) study, 16.8% of American workers had some sort of nonstandard work schedule in 1997, requiring evening, night, or rotating shifts.

The major health problem with working night shifts is that the typical sleep/waking cycle is disturbed. Associated with this cycle are the *circadian rhythms* of physiological changes that occur throughout the day. These include body temperature changes and changes in hormone levels in the bloodstream. It has been suggested that disruption of the natural rhythm of sleep can cause health problems.

The most obvious health problem in working night shifts is sleep disturbance—either being unable to fall asleep or having a poor quality of sleep (Daus, Sanders, & Campbell, 1998). Several studies have found that people who work night shifts are more likely than day shift workers to experience sleep problems (e.g., Koller, Kundi, & Cervinka, 1978), although not all studies have found this effect. Barton and Folkard (1991) found that employees on temporary night shifts had greater sleep problems than employees who worked permanent night shifts, but the permanent night shift workers were no more likely to have sleep problems than the day shift workers. The researchers argued that in their sample of nurses each employee working the permanent night shift volunteered to do so. These volunteers were able to adjust to night work and not experience sleep problems.

Long-distance drivers sometimes work long shifts that can interrupt sleep patterns.

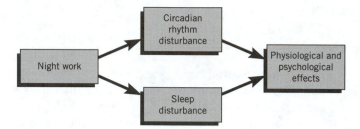

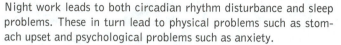

FIGURE 11-3

Night work leads to both circadian rhythm disturbance and sleep problems. These in turn lead to physical problems such as stomach upset and psychological problems such as anxiety.

Sleep problems might arise from disruption of the circadian rhythms, but another simple explanation has been advanced. Koller et al. (1978) believe that night shift workers get worse sleep because there is more noise during the day when they are trying to sleep. In their study of Austrian oil refinery workers, they found that 62.6% of night workers who slept during the day complained of having their sleep disturbed by noise. Only 15.8% of day workers who slept at night had the same complaint.

Sleep disturbance is not the only health problem that has been associated with night shift work. Digestive system problems have been shown to be more frequent in night shift workers (e.g., Koller et al., 1978). Akerstedt and Theorell (1976) studied physiological changes in workers before, during, and after a period of night shift work. In this study the blood levels of the hormone gastrin, which is related to stomach acid secretion, was assessed twice a day over a period of five weeks. Results showed a decrease in gastrin during the time the workers were on the night shift. Although this study shows that night shift work can have physiological effects, it is not clear why they occurred. Was it the disruption of the circadian rhythm that upset the secretion of gastrin, or was it lack of sleep (Figure 11-3)? Whatever it was, at least one solution to night shift effects is to allow several consecutive days of rest per week (Totterdell, Spelten, Smith, Barton, & Folkard, 1995).

In addition to health problems, shiftwork can cause social problems as well. Having to work nights and sleep days can isolate a person from family and friends. Bohle and Tilley (1998) surveyed hospital nurses concerning their feelings about shiftwork. The best predictor of dissatisfaction was conflict between work and nonwork activities. Individuals who reported high levels of conflict tended to report the greatest dissatisfaction with shiftwork.

One final potential health problem for night shift workers in some jobs is assault. Budd, Arvey, and Lawless (1996) conducted a survey of employed people in one American city and found that assaults were most commonly experienced at night.

Long Shifts

The typical full-time work shift is 8 hours. Many organizations, however, have implemented longer shifts, and many employees have jobs that do not have fixed shifts but can require long work days. For example, truck and bus drivers may have routes that cannot be completed in an 8-hour day. The most popular alternative long work schedule is the 4-

day 10-hour shift, or 4/40. Some organizations that operate 24 hours per day have gone to two 12-hour shifts per day.

One important difficulty with the long work day is fatigue (Ronen & Primps, 1981). A 10-to-12-hour day can be quite tiring if the work is mentally or physically demanding. On the other hand, many employees like the longer days because it gives them more usable free time per week and reduces commuting costs (Breaugh, 1983). Pierce and Dunham (1992) compared 8-hour rotating shifts with 12-hour rotating shifts in a sample of police officers. The officers preferred the longer shifts and reported less fatigue. They also reported fewer health problems and less stress. The longer day gave them more days off, which may have produced the positive effects.

Raggatt (1991) conducted a study of Australian bus drivers that showed that long shifts might have serious health effects (see the Research in Detail box in this chapter).

RESEARCH IN DETAIL

ONE OF THE limitations associated with questionnaire studies of job conditions and job stress is that most of the variables assessed are rather abstract theoretical constructs such as autonomy or role ambiguity. The present study (Raggatt, 1991) was somewhat different. The major job condition variable was the number of hours worked over the past month. The study was designed to determine if working long hours would be associated with a number of psychological, physical, and behavioral strains, as well as accidents.

Subjects for this study were 93 Australian bus drivers. Each driver was asked to complete a questionnaire that asked about job satisfaction, psychological distress, health symptoms, sleeping problems, speeding, pill taking, alcohol consumption, and number of prior accidents. They were asked to indicate the number of hours they had worked over the prior four weeks. Many of the drivers worked very long shifts, with most exceeding 40-hour workweeks. Twelve- to 14-hour workdays were not unusual.

Results indicated that working long shifts was associated with taking pills (e.g., stimulants), drinking alcohol, and having difficulty sleeping. These strains were associated with health symptoms, psychological distress, job dissatisfaction, and accidents. The drivers also reported significantly more health symptoms, depression, anxiety, and fatigue than people in general.

Raggatt presented a model suggesting that the demands of the job, particularly long driving shifts, resulted in fatigue and sleep disturbance. The coping strategies used by the drivers often involved the use of stimulants to stay awake and depressants and alcohol to sleep. The combination of fatigue brought on by driving and poor sleep and the use of pills and alcohol contributed to psychological and physical strains. Raggatt recommended that many of these important health-related problems could probably be reduced by giving drivers more rest breaks and shorter work shifts. Organizations need to pay attention to the health consequences of requiring long work shifts.

Raggatt, P.T.F. (1991). Work stress among long-distance coach drivers: A survey and correlational study. *Journal of Organizational Behavior, 12,* 565–579.

The length of work shift was associated with sleep problems, alcohol consumption, and use of stimulants. These outcomes were also associated with job dissatisfaction and poor health. Thus long work shifts can have detrimental effects for some jobs. For other jobs, such as police officers, long shifts can be beneficial.

It is not only long shifts, however, that can have detrimental effects on people. Working in excess of 48 hours per week has been shown to relate to health, including heart disease (Sparks, Cooper, Fried, & Shirom, 1997). These detrimental effects seem only to occur in people who work long hours nonvoluntarily, which is often the case in organizations that have downsized or reduced their number of employees. Survivors usually wind up working more hours to cover tasks of colleagues who have been fired. The European Council adopted rules in the mid-1990s restricting work hours in member countries, including maximum hours worked per day and week (13 and 48, respectively).

Flexible Work Schedules

Fixed daily work schedules are still the norm, but increasingly organizations have been trying flexible schedules, known as **flextime**, that allow workers to determine, at least in part, the hours of the day that they work. In 1997, 27.6% of American workers had flextime, which was more than double the percentage a decade earlier (U.S. Bureau of Labor Statistics, 1998). There are many varieties, from systems requiring only that employees work their allotted hours per day to systems that allow employees the option of starting their shift an hour early or an hour late. As mentioned in Chapter 9, flextime can be part of a family friendly policy that allows working parents more flexibility to take care of child care responsibilities.

From the organization's perspective, an advantage of a flexible work schedule is that it allows employees to take care of personal business on their own time rather than on work time. Thus, an employee could have a doctor's visit in the morning and begin the shift late. Research has confirmed that there is less absence (Krausz & Freibach, 1983; Pierce & Newstrom, 1982) and tardiness (Ralston, 1989) with flextime than with fixed work schedules.

Other outcomes of flexible work schedules, such as job performance and satisfaction, have been difficult to determine because of the inconsistencies in results across studies. At least part of the reason for the inconsistent results might be the varying methodologies used. For example, Pierce and Newstrom (1982) found that both job performance and job satisfaction were better with flexible than fixed schedules. They compared the job performance and satisfaction of employees in one organization using a fixed schedule with those of employees of three other organizations using flexible schedules. However, it is possible that organizational differences other than schedules were responsible for the differences.

Ralston (1989) used a somewhat more rigorous research design, comparing two government offices, one that implemented a flexible schedule and one that did not. An advantage of this design is that it assessed employees one month prior to and one year after implementation of the flexible work schedule. Ralston found that job satisfaction but not job performance was improved in the flextime group; however, a limitation to this study is that job satisfaction and job performance were not assessed directly. Rather, employees were asked to indicate if high levels of each were a benefit of a flexible work schedule. It is difficult to directly compare these results with those of Pierce and Newstrom (1982).

TABLE 11-2
The results of three studies of flexible work schedules[a]

OUTCOME VARIABLE	KRAUSZ & FREIBACH (1983)	PIERCE & NEWSTROM (1982)	RALSTON (1989)
Attendance	Yes	Yes	Yes
Health symptoms	No	N/A	No
Job performance	N/A	Yes	No
Job satisfaction	No	Yes	Yes

[a]"Yes" indicates significant relation of work schedule and outcome variable. "No" indicates a nonsignificant relation.

Source: "Effects of Flexible Working Time for Employed Women upon Satisfaction, Strains, and Absenteeism," by M. Krausz and N. Freibach, 1983, *Journal of Occupational Psychology, 56,* 155–159; "Employee Responses to Flexible Work Schedules: An Inter-Organization, Inter-System Comparison," by J. L. Pierce and J. W. Newstrom, 1982, *Journal of Management, 8,* 9–25; and "The Benefits of Flextime: Real or Imagined?" by D. A. Ralston, 1989, *Journal of Organizational Behavior, 10,* 369–373.

A third study had perhaps the strongest research design of the three because it compared multiple departments of the same organization in which some had adopted a flexible schedule and some had not (Krausz & Freibach, 1983). The authors noted that the implementation of flexible schedules occurred for convenience and that there were few differences between the flexible and fixed schedule departments. There were no job satisfaction differences found between them. An obvious difference between this and the prior two studies is that this study was conducted in Israel and the other two were conducted in the United States. It is possible that Americans respond more favorably than Israelis to flexible work schedules.

The results of these three studies are summarized in Table 11-2. Also included are results concerning physical symptoms such as headaches or stomach distress. The results for attendance (absence and tardiness) were consistent across the three studies. Similarly, the two studies that included a measure of health symptoms found no effect. Unfortunately, results were inconsistent for job performance and job satisfaction. This makes it difficult to reach a definitive conclusion about these two variables. Flexible work schedules may indeed have these benefits, but it would be premature to draw this conclusion. Additional research will be needed to resolve this question.

JOB STRESS

Everyone has experienced **stress** at one time or another. Taking an exam is a situation that is stressful for most students, particularly for those who want good grades. On most jobs there are situations that employees find stressful. Being reprimanded by a supervisor, having too little time to complete an important assignment, or being told that you might be fired are all situations that almost anyone would find stressful. Warr and Payne (1983) asked a random sample of British workers if they had been emotionally upset by something at work the prior day. Fifteen percent of the men and 10% of the women said they had been. Whether or not being upset at work has long-term health consequences is not clear; however, most job stress researchers believe that unfavorable job conditions can affect employee health and well-being (Cooper & Cartwright, 1994). In this section we review what is known about the effects of job stress.

© 1996 United Feature Syndicate, Inc. (NYC)

The Job Stress Process

To understand job stress, you must first understand several concepts that are involved in the stress process. A **job stressor** is a condition or situation at work that requires an adaptive response on the part of the employee (Jex & Beehr, 1991). Being reprimanded, having too little time, and being told about the possibility of being fired are all examples of job stressors. A **job strain** is a potential aversive reaction by an employee to a stressor, such as anxiety, frustration, or physical symptom such as a headache (Jex & Beehr, 1991). Jex and Beehr (1991) categorize strains into

Psychological reactions

Physical reactions

Behavioral reactions

(See Table 11-3.) Psychological reactions involve emotional responses such as anxiety or frustration. Physical reactions include symptoms such as headaches or stomach distress and illnesses such as cancer. Behavioral reactions are responses to job stressors and include substance use, smoking, and accidents.

Models of the job stress process presume that job stressors lead to job strains. It is generally recognized, however, that the process is not automatic and that the employee's perception and appraisal of the stressor are essential parts of the process. Appraisal is the extent to which a person interprets an event or situation to be personally threatening. Not everyone will see the same situation as a job stressor. One person who is given an extra work assignment sees it as an opportunity to make a good impression on the supervisor, while another sees it as an unfair imposition on their free time.

Figure 11-4 (based on Frese & Zapf, 1988) illustrates how job stressors lead to job strains. In this model, job stressors (step 1) are objective conditions or situations in the work environment. For example, there might be a fire at work. In order for the fire to become a stressor, the employee must be aware of its existence. This leads to step 2, which is perception of the stressor. Perception alone, however, is not sufficient to lead to strain. The employee must appraise the stressor as aversive or threatening (step 3). If a building is on fire, virtually anyone would appraise the situation as threatening. If it is only an ashtray that is on fire, it is doubtful that many would find it a threat. If the location is filled

<u>TABLE 11-3</u>
Examples of job strains from each of the three categories of job strains

JOB STRAIN	*EXAMPLES OF SPECIFIC OUTCOMES*
Psychological reactions	Anger
	Anxiety
	Frustration
	Job dissatisfaction
Physical reactions	Physical symptoms
	Dizziness
	Headache
	Heart pounding
	Stomach distress
	Illness
	Cancer
	Heart disease
Behavioral reactions	Accidents
	Smoking
	Substance use
	Turnover

Source: "Emerging Theoretical and Methodological Issues in the Study of Work-Related Stress," by S. M. Jex and T. A. Beehr, 1991, *Research in Personnel and Human Resources Management, 9,* 311–365.

with flammable materials, however, even a lit match would be dangerous. It is the interpretation or appraisal of the situation that determines if it will lead to the next steps, which involve strain. Strains in this model are divided into short term (step 4) and long term (step 5). Short-term strains occur immediately. Upon seeing a fire, an employee might experience fear (psychological reaction), become nauseated (physical reaction), and jump out a window (behavioral reaction). If the person experienced a severe enough trauma from the experience, he or she might develop post-traumatic stress disorder, which would be a long-term strain.

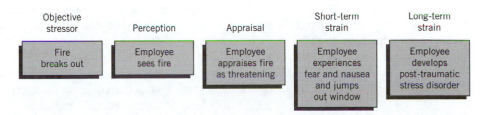

<u>FIGURE 11-4</u>
A five-step model of the job stress process (based on Frese & Zapf, 1988). An objective stressor (step 1) leads to its perception (step 2), and it is appraised by the individual (step 3). If it is appraised to be a challenge or threat, it can lead to short-term strains (step 4) and eventually long-term strains (step 5).

Job Stressors

Although many different conditions at work might serve as job stressors, relatively few have been studied. Five in particular have been given significant research attention as possible causes of employee strains. Existing research provides at least some evidence that each is associated with strains. We will see, however, that popularity is not necessarily associated with how important these stressors might be.

Role Ambiguity and Role Conflict. Role ambiguity and role conflict, often referred to as role stressors, have been popular topics of study in job stress research. As defined in Chapter 9, *role ambiguity* is the extent to which employees are unclear about what their job functions and responsibilities are supposed to be. Role conflict occurs when there is incompatibility between demands at work or between work and nonwork. Role ambiguity would be experienced by a manager who is put in charge of a department store and given no instructions or directions. He or she might not know who sets prices for items, who determines what to order, or who sets store policy. This same person would experience role conflict if his or her boss asked for an appointment at the same time that a staff meeting was scheduled with subordinates.

The research on role ambiguity and role conflict has focused primarily on psychological strains. The results of Jackson and Schuler's (1985) meta-analysis showed that high levels of both role stressors were associated with low levels of job satisfaction and high levels of anxiety/tension and intention to quit the job. Correlations with behavioral strains, such as absence and job performance, were quite small in most studies. It should be kept in mind that most studies of job performance use supervisor ratings which (as discussed in Chapter 4) can be quite inaccurate. Fried, Ben-David, Tiegs, Avital, and Yeverechyahu (1998) improved on the typical job performance measure by asking specific questions about performance (e.g., "the employee is assigned the most difficult tasks in the department" and "the employee is capable of reading technical drawings"), rather than the more typical ratings of work quality and quantity. Relations of role ambiguity and role conflict with this measure of job performance were considerably higher than typically found, suggesting that researchers need to pay more attention to the quality of performance measures in future studies. Of course, we must be careful in awaiting replication before drawing firm conclusions.

Most of the research on role stressors has used self-report scales completed by employees. This means that in the five-step model, role stressors were assessed at the level of appraisal (step 3). It is unclear to what extent objective job conditions were responsible for these appraisals or whether those conditions resulted in psychological strains. Jex and Beehr (1991) wondered if role ambiguity and role conflict were perhaps not very important stressors. Their lack of importance is underscored by a study in which engineers were asked to indicate a stressful incident that occurred at work during the prior month (Keenan & Newton, 1985). Incidents that reflected role ambiguity or role conflict were quite rare.

Workload. Workload concerns the work demands that the job places on an employee and can be of two types: quantitative and qualitative. *Quantitative workload* is the amount of work that a person has. A heavy quantitative workload means that a person has too much to do. *Qualitative workload* is the difficulty of work relative to a person's capabilities.

A heavy qualitative workload means that the employee is not capable of doing job tasks because they are too difficult for him or her. It is possible for a person to experience only one type of workload in a job. He or she might have a lot of work to do that is not necessarily difficult, or difficult work to do that is not necessarily plentiful.

Workload research has found that it relates to all three types of strains—psychological, physical, and behavioral (Jex & Beehr, 1991). This research has involved a variety of methodologies that allow us to draw more definitive conclusions about the possible outcomes of this stressor.

Questionnaire studies have shown that employee reports of their workloads correlate with a variety of strains. Spector, Dwyer, and Jex (1988) found significant correlations of workload with the psychological strains of anxiety, frustration, job dissatisfaction and intention of quitting and the physical strains of health symptoms. Jamal (1990) found significant correlations of workload with the strains of job dissatisfaction, intention of quitting, and health symptoms. Karasek, Gardell, and Lindell (1987) found that workload was associated with the strains of depression, exhaustion, job dissatisfaction, health symptoms, and heart disease. These three studies were quite geographically diverse, having been conducted in the United States, Canada, and Sweden, respectively.

Studies have shown that workload can also affect physiology. It has been associated with blood pressure (Fox, Dwyer, & Ganster, 1993) and adrenaline secretion in the bloodstream (Johansson, 1989). In these studies, it is not clear whether or not the physiological changes result in either psychological or physical strain. Fox et al. (1993) failed to find that their objective measure of workload correlated with health symptoms or job satisfaction.

Although research has shown that workload alone can be associated with strains, the effects of workload can involve the action of other variables, most notably control. We will discuss the joint effects of workload and control after we discuss the effects of control.

Control. Control is the extent to which employees are able to make decisions about their work. Such decisions involve all aspects of work, including when to work, where to work, how to work, and what tasks to do. Employees with a high level of control are able to set their own work schedules, choose their own tasks, and decide how to complete those tasks. In a low-control job the work schedule is set, tasks are assigned, and often even the procedures for accomplishing tasks are specified. College professors have a high level of control because they decide what courses they teach, how they will teach them, and often even when and where they will teach them. Factory workers usually have little control because they work a fixed schedule, are given a specific task to do, and may be told exactly how to do that task. In many factories the work is paced by machine. In other words, the work comes down a conveyor belt at a fixed rate, and the worker must keep up with the machine.

Control appears to be an extremely important component of the job stress process. It is also a component of job characteristics theory (see Chapters 9 and 10). Studies have found that employee perceptions of control are associated with all three categories of strain, although results are most consistent with psychological strain. Table 11-4 shows the mean correlations of perceived employee control with several strains reported in Spector's (1986) meta-analysis. As you can see from the table, high levels of control are associated with high levels of job satisfaction, organizational commitment, job involvement, and

TABLE 11-4

Mean correlations of perceived control with job stressors
from Spector's (1986) meta-analysis

STRESSOR	MEAN CORRELATION
Job satisfaction	.30
Organizational commitment	.26
Job involvement	.41
Emotional distress	−.25
Intent to quit	−.17
Health symptoms	−.25
Absence	−.19
Job performance	.20
Turnover likelihood	−.22

Source: "Perceived Control by Employees: A Meta-Analysis of Studies Concerning
Autonomy and Participation at Work," by P. E. Spector, 1986, *Human Relations, 11,*
1005–1016.

performance. Low levels of control are associated with high levels of emotional distress, intent to quit the job, health symptoms, absence, and turnover.

The control studies summarized in Spector's (1986) meta-analysis concerned employee perceptions about how much control they had at work. In most of these studies, control and strains were assessed with questionnaires given to employees. This sort of study makes it difficult to know if job strains are the result of perceived control or if perceived control is the result of strains. Perhaps employees who dislike their jobs, or employees who have low commitment, or employees who are in poor health perceive their jobs to be low in control, even though the job may not be. As noted previously, there is evidence that how people feel about work affects their perception of the job, including the amount of control they have (Spector, 1992). In other words, the supposed strain might cause the supposed stressor, rather than the reverse. To make things even more complicated, it has been found that employees who perform well on the job are given more control (Dansereau, Graen, & Haga, 1975), suggesting that performance affects the amount of control the employee has. Perhaps the extra control given to good performers raises their job satisfaction. Rather than the strain being caused by the stressor, the stressor is caused by the strain. Perceived control is an important variable in job stress. More research is needed to expand our understanding of how it affects strains.

Machine Pacing. Studies of objective or actual control help solve the problem of inferring the effects of control on strains because they do not rely on employee reports about control. That is, they allow us to draw conclusions about the actual effects of low control. One area in which objective control has been studied is *machine-paced work*, which means that a machine controls when the worker must make a response. Factory work is the best example when the conveyor belt controls the speed at which the employee works. Computer technology has introduced machine pacing into nonfactory work as well. Millions of people worldwide sit at computer terminals all day doing what is not much different from simple factory work. They respond to information that comes on the screen at a pace that is set by the machine.

The effects of machine pacing and other work conditions have been studied for several years by a research group at the University of Stockholm in Sweden. A major focus of this research is to understand how human physiology is affected by job stressors, such as machine pacing. Two types of stress-related hormones have been studied—catecholamines (adrenaline and noradrenaline) and cortisol. These substances help prepare the body for action when danger or challenge occurs. Adrenaline is often said to help energize the performance of athletes during competition. Its actions can be felt as "butter-flies" in the stomach. Cortisol helps control swelling during injury (Sarafino, 1990).

The University of Stockholm research has shown that both control and workload affect physiological responses. In a series of studies of employees, these researchers assessed the level of hormones by analyzing urine samples at home and at work. They found that as workload increased, the amount of adrenaline and noradrenaline increased (Frankenhaeuser & Johansson, 1986). When people work hard, their bodies may use these two hormones to help energize performance. Control also had an effect on these two catecholamines. Employees who were machine paced had higher levels of adrenaline and noradrenaline than employees who were self-paced (Johansson, 1981). The effects of control on cortisol were somewhat different. With machine pacing (low control), the cortisol level increased from home to work. With self-pacing (high control), however, the cortisol level decreased from home to work (Frankenhaeuser & Johansson, 1986). The researchers hypothesized that distress was the important component in these results. Lack of control was presumed to increase the level of cortisol because it distressed the employees, and distress is associated with the secretion of cortisol.

In addition to physiological reactions, machine pacing has been associated with psychological strains and health symptoms. Compared to self-paced work, machine-paced work has been found to be associated with anxiety (Broadbent & Gath, 1981), dissatisfaction, and health symptoms (Smith, Hurrell, & Murphy, 1981). All of these studies combined have provided reasonably convincing evidence that job stressors can have both physiological and psychological effects. They have not demonstrated, however, that these effects lead to illness. Johansson (1989) points out that frequent high levels of catecholamines and cortisol have been associated with heart disease. Thus, we might speculate that working under conditions that caused distress would increase chances of later illness. The evidence to connect job stressors and illness is as yet circumstantial.

The Demand/Control Model. The **demand/control model** (Karasek, 1979) states that the effects of job stressors are a complex interplay of demands and employee control. Demands are stressors such as workload that require adaptation. Put another way, a demand taxes an employee's ability to cope with the environment. According to the theory, demands lead to strain only when there is insufficient control. Stated another way, having control reduces the negative effects of demands. Figure 11-5 illustrates how control affects the relation between demands and strain. It shows that when control is high, demands (stressors) do not lead to strain. When control is low, however, strains increase as stressors increase. The model implies that giving people control at work can be a successful strategy for reducing the negative effects of job stressors.

Research support for the demands/control model has been mixed, with only some studies finding the hypothesized effect (Ganster & Schaubroeck, 1991). At least some of the reason for the inconsistent results may be the measures of demands and control, which have differed across studies. Wall, Jackson, Mullarkey, and Parker (1996) showed

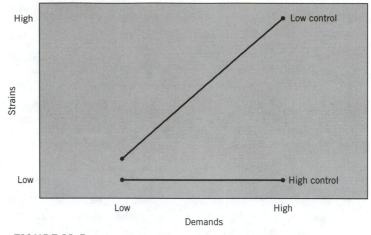

FIGURE 11-5

The demands/control model. When control is high, there is no relation between demands and strain. When control is low, strain increases as demands increase.

that the nature of control mattered in their test of the model. They found support for the model with a measure that focused on control over employees' immediate tasks, but not with a measure of more general control. Two of the studies that found the effect used objective measures of demands (Dwyer & Ganster, 1991; Fox, Dwyer, & Ganster, 1993). Another possible factor is the type of job studied. Westman (1992) found support for the demand/control model for clerks but not managers in an Israeli bank. Additional research will be necessary to more fully explore this important model.

ACCIDENTS

Accidents are the leading cause of death among Americans from 1 to 37 years old and the fourth leading cause of death for all ages (National Safety Council, 1992c). One of the major accomplishments of the twentieth century in the United States was reducing the workplace accident rate by 90% to where today most accidents occur off the job. However, in 1996 there were still 4,800 workplace fatalities and 3.9 million disabling injuries in the United States alone (National Safety Council, 1996). Figure 11-6 shows the major types of fatal workplace accidents in the United States in 1996. As you can see, motor vehicles were the leading cause, accounting for 42%. Figure 11-7 shows the accident rates for eight categories of jobs. Agriculture and mining are the most dangerous, whereas manufacturing, trades (working in a store), and services (accounting, banking, legal work, and real estate) are the safest.

Preventing accidents has been a major concern of organizations because of both organizational and employee costs. It has been estimated that American workplace accidents cost a total of $121 billion in 1996 (National Safety Council, 1996), much of the cost paid by employers and their insurance companies. In order to prevent accidents, we need to understand their causes and how these causes can be eliminated. Table 11-5 lists employee and organizational factors that have been associated with accidents. Employee fac-

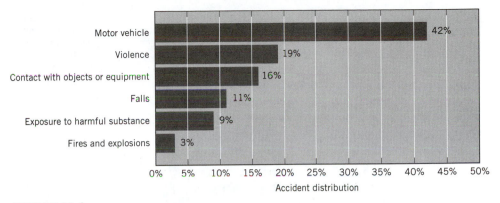

FIGURE 11-6

Major types of fatal work accidents for 1996 in the United States. *Source:* U.S. Bureau of Labor Statistics (1996). *National Census of Fatal Occupational Injuries, 1996,* [Online] Available: http://stats.bls.gov/news.release/cfoi.nws.htm [1998, February 18].

tors include personality characteristics (e.g., neuroticism), experiences (e.g., recent death in the family), and behaviors (e.g., alcohol consumption or smoking). Savery and Wooden (1994) surveyed Australian workers from 61 different organizations. They found that frequency of stressful events (e.g., divorce) was related to work accidents. Organizational factors include everything from the selection and training of personnel to the design of the workplace.

As Sheehy and Chapman (1987) point out, the evidence for several of these factors does not allow us to conclude that they are a cause of accidents. For example, although personality characteristics and exposure to stressful events have been shown to be associ-

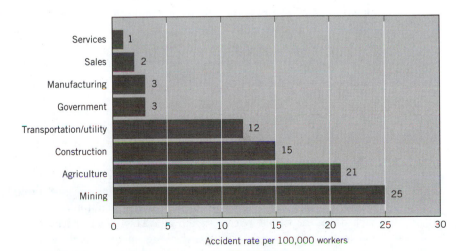

FIGURE 11-7

Fatal accident rates for several categories of jobs for 1996 in the United States. *Source:* National Safety Council (1996). *Accident Facts.* [Online] Available: http://www.nsc.org/lrs/statinfo/afp48.htm [1998, February 18].

TABLE 11-5
Both individual and organizational factors associated with work accidents

Individual Employee Factors
    Alcohol and drug use on the job
    Exposure to stressful life incidents (e.g., death in the family)
    Personality characteristics (e.g., aggressiveness and neuroticism)
    Smoking
Organizational Factors
    Employee selection
    Equipment design
    Low turnover and absence
    Management commitment to safety
    Safety training

Source: "Industrial Accidents," by N. P. Sheehy and A. J. Chapman, 1987, in C. L. Cooper and I. T. Robertson (Eds.), *International Review of Industrial and Organizational Psychology 1987*, pp. 201–228, Chichester, UK: John Wiley.

ated with accidents, most studies assessed these variables after the accident occurred. One cannot be certain if the personality variable or the level of job stress was the result rather than the cause of the accident. One exception is a study by Iverson and Erwin (1997) who showed that negative affectivity (the tendency to experience negative emotions) predicted subsequent work injuries a year later. Individuals who were high on this personality variable were more likely to experience an injury. The existing findings provide a good starting point for devising strategies to reduce accidents. Such strategies might focus on selection of appropriate people, training, control of behavior such as alcohol consumption at work, or the appropriate design of the work environment and equipment.

Many different approaches have been tried to prevent accidents. Some involve design of equipment, whereas others focus on employees. The best strategy depends on the particular situation and an analysis of accident causes. Often solutions can be fairly simple, such as having employees wear protective goggles to prevent eye injuries. The application of human factors can be effective when equipment is poorly designed from a safety standpoint. An example is the push lawnmower, which can be a dangerous device. At one time the design allowed an operator to get a hand or foot caught in the revolving blade. All new lawnmowers now sold in the United States must be designed with a handle release switch that turns off the engine (or blade) when the operator lets go of the handle. Such a system makes it difficult for a person to accidentally stick a hand or foot into a moving blade.

A major difficulty in preventing workplace accidents is getting the cooperation of employees to use the appropriate safety equipment and engage in safe behaviors. People can often find safety devices inconvenient and safety equipment uncomfortable. Some people tape down the handle release switch on a lawnmower because they find it annoying and fail to use safety goggles because they are uncomfortable. Accepted workplace practices among employees might preclude the use of particular practices because they are thought to waste time, take too much effort, or even reflect on a person's lack of courage in facing dangerous situations. An organization might have to take stern measures to deal with these problems, including the disciplining or firing of employees who refuse to work safely.

Hoyos (1995) analyzed workplace hazards from 400 jobs in western Germany and concluded that one reason for unsafe behavior was lack of knowledge. He conducted an experiment in which blue-collar employees were given either an explanation of the nature of hazards and their prevention or a list of safety rules with no explanation. Subsequently, the former group was observed to use safer approaches in their work than the latter group. This study demonstrates how training can be effective in encouraging safety.

Another approach that has at times been successful is the use of an incentive system for safe behavior. Fox, Hopkins, and Anger (1987) reported on the use of this approach for the reduction of accidents in a mining organization. Mining is a dangerous occupation with accident frequencies exceeding those associated with most other forms of work. To control accidents, Fox et al. (1987) introduced a *token economy* at two mining companies whereby employees received trading stamps for safe behavior. The stamps could be exchanged for items at a redemption store. This system was not unlike the token economies used in prisons, schools, and treatment facilities to control behavior. The project was highly successful. Accident rates, injury rates, and costs resulting from accidents were reduced by as much as 50 times and were maintained over the 11-year span of the study. Use of the incentive approach is not appropriate for every situation, but it can be an effective tool when unsafe behavior is the problem.

Ludwig and Geller (1997) successfully used goal setting (see Chapter 8) to encourage safer driving behavior in a sample of pizza deliverers. They asked drivers to set goals concerning the percentage of time they would come to a complete and safe stop before pulling into traffic. The goal setting improved not only the targeted behavior, but also other safety behaviors for which goals had not been set, such as seatbelt use. Goals can be an effective means of improving not only job performance, as we discussed in Chapter 8, but safety, as well.

BURNOUT

Burnout is a distressed psychological state that an employee might experience after being on the job for a period of time. A person suffering from burnout is emotionally exhausted and has low work motivation. In a sense, it involves being depressed about work and having little energy and enthusiasm for the job. Originally, the concept was developed to explain the reactions of many employees in the helping professions, such as psychotherapists and social workers. The early burnout researchers believed that burnout was the result of working intensely with other people. More recently, however, the idea

TABLE 11-6
The three burnout components and expected results of each

COMPONENT	RESULTS
Emotional exhaustion	Absence
	Fatigue
Depersonalization	Callous and uncaring treatment of clients and other people
	Hostility toward other people
Reduced personal accomplishment	Low motivation
	Poor performance

FIGURE 11-8

Job stressors and job strains that have been associated with burnout. *Source:* "A Review and an Integration of Research on Job Burnout," by C. L. Cordes and T. W. Dougherty, 1993, *Academy of Management Review, 18,* 621–656.

has been extended to workers in all sorts of jobs, even those who have little contact with others.

Burnout is assessed with scales administered to employees. The most popular scale, the Maslach Burnout Inventory (MBI) (Maslach & Jackson, 1981), measures three components of burnout:

Emotional exhaustion

Depersonalization

Reduced personal accomplishment

Emotional exhaustion is the feeling of tiredness and fatigue at work. *Depersonalization* is the development of a cynical and callous feeling toward others. *Reduced personal accomplishment* is the feeling that the employee is not accomplishing anything worthwhile at work. Table 11-6 lists some of the byproducts of each burnout component. For example, emotional exhaustion should lead to fatigue and absence.

Feelings of burnout have been found to correlate with many job stressor and job strain variables and might be considered a type of strain (Cordes & Dougherty, 1993; Lee & Ashforth, 1996). High levels of burnout have been associated with low levels of perceived control and job satisfaction and high levels of role conflict, health symptoms, intention of quitting the job (Shirom, 1989), and work overload (Bacharach, Bamberger, & Conley, 1991).

Figure 11-8 shows some of the job stressors and strains that correlate with burnout. These stressors are possible causes of burnout. Some researchers believe that poor job performance may be caused by burnout (Cordes & Dougherty, 1993).

As we have seen in many other areas of I/O psychology, research in the burnout domain has also been dominated by self-report survey methods. From these studies we know many of the variables that are correlated with burnout. We are not yet certain about the causes of burnout and how organizations can prevent it. One study, however, has shown that burnout can be reduced by taking a vacation (Westman & Eden, 1997). Unfortunately, in their study the "vacation effect" was short-lived and disappeared after a couple of weeks back on the job.

FUTURE ISSUES AND CHALLENGES

As we have seen in this chapter, the workplace can have significant effects on the health and well-being of employees. We know many of the conditions at work that cause adverse health effects, such as exposure to extremes of temperature, loud noise, and toxic substances, but there are many more about which we are unsure. For example, does lack of employee control, as happens with machine pacing, lead to serious illness, such as heart disease? Do the health symptoms associated with high workloads result in serious illnesses? The answer to such questions will tell us how we should intervene in the workplace. If conditions themselves are the cause of illness, then the job environment should be redesigned. This might involve giving employees more autonomy and control over their work. If, on the other hand, the cause of illness is in the person rather than the work, interventions should be directed toward helping people cope with job demands. It seems likely, however, that the answer will lie in the interaction of the person with the work environment. Frankenhaeuser and Johansson (1986) hypothesized that the physiological effects of work are determined by how people feel about their jobs. If that is so, then the proper matching of people to jobs that they like will do much to increase the healthfulness of work.

A second important challenge for the future is finding ways to help people cope with new technologies. Automation is certainly not new, but as computerization continues to spread throughout both blue-collar and white-collar jobs, new health-related problems will arise. We are already seeing that the widespread use of computers is producing repetitive strain injuries. Research has also shown that machine pacing, which occurs with many automated systems, may have serious health consequences. We need to understand better the physical and psychological effects of working with computerized technologies and how to reduce any negative effects that may be found.

CHAPTER SUMMARY

Work can be a dangerous place, not only for blue-collar workers who must use hazardous equipment and substances, but for white-collar workers as well. Many hazards have immediate consequences, such as an injury from an accident. Often, however, the effects of work conditions do not show up for many years, such as a cancer that is produced from years of exposure to a carcinogenic chemical.

Physical work conditions tend to have effects that are primarily physical. Exposure to extremes of temperature can cause injury and death; exposure to infectious disease can cause illness; exposure to loud noise can cause hearing loss; repetitive actions can cause hand and wrist problems; and exposure to toxic substances can cause cancer. Nonphysical conditions can have effects that are both physical and psychological. Work schedules, for example, have been associated with job satisfaction and physical symptoms.

Many researchers believe job stress to be a factor in both physical illness and psychological strain. Although most of the research is circumstantial, there is evidence accumulating to support the idea that work demands and control have important health implications. Some of the effects of job stressors, however, may be indirect. For example, research has associated job conditions with health-related behaviors such as smoking and substance use.

Accidents are a major cause of death for people of working age. The causes of accidents involve both employee and organizational factors. Programs directed toward both eliminating physical hazards in the workplace and encouraging safe behavior seem most effective in reducing accidents.

Burnout is a psychological state involving fatigue and lack of motivation for work. Research on burnout has found that burnout is associated with many job stressors and strains and may itself be considered a psychological strain.

I/O Psychology in Practice

This case concerns a study of job stress by Dr. Kerry Bunker, who received his Ph.D. in I/O psychology in 1976 from the University of South Florida. As supervisor of Human Resources Research at AT&T, where he worked for over 10 years, he conducted applied research on the identification and development of management talent. He is now a senior program associate in leadership development at the Center for Creative Leadership in Greensboro, NC, developing training tools to enhance the skills of managers.

At AT&T, Dr. Bunker was involved in a 9-year study of stress among company managers, begun because of the impending breakup of AT&T's monopoly on long-distance telephone service. The U.S. government's threat to break up the company was causing widespread anxiety and discomfort among AT&T managers.

The major purpose of the study was to understand the ways in which AT&T managers coped with stress at work and in life. A sample of employees was given questionnaires and in-depth interviews, repeated over time. As the study progressed, it became apparent that there were beneficial effects. Employees began reporting that discussions with the interviewers gave them insights into the sources of stress and how they dealt with them. Participants reported that they believed these insights led to better strategies for dealing with stress. When they realized that the project was helping people, interviewers offered feedback to participants about their coping strategies. Much of the interviewing was done by clinical rather than I/O psychologists.

Considering the design of this study, it is difficult to determine exactly what the effects of the project were. However, one participant told Dr. Bunker that the experience saved his life by convincing him not to commit suicide. This project illustrates that studies carried out in organizations can have effects beyond those intended. A project designed as a research study of stress wound up unintentionally being a stress management intervention.

Discussion Questions

1. Why do you think that the breakup at AT&T stressed the managers?

2. Are most employers as concerned as AT&T with the job stress of employees?

3. Are AT&T managers more or less stressed than employees of other organizations?

4. What other techniques could AT&T have used to help its managers cope?

Part Five

THE SOCIAL CONTEXT OF WORK

Chapter 12

WORK GROUPS AND WORK TEAMS

On July 3, 1988, the U.S. Navy guided missile cruiser *Vincennes* shot down an Iranian airliner, killing all 290 persons onboard. Responsibility for firing the fatal missile was shared by several members of the Anti Air Warfare Team. This team is supposed to be able to identify hostile aircraft correctly and to shoot only when threatened. Obviously something went wrong, and much of the blame can be placed on poor teamwork. Someone mistakenly identified the airliner as hostile, and over the next few stressful minutes no one corrected the mistake. The Navy has spent considerable time and effort since the tragedy trying to determine how best to prevent similar mistakes in the future. I/O psychologists have been very much involved in this effort (see this chapter's "I/O Psychology in Practice").

The Navy is not the only organization in which people work in teams. Teams can be found in factories, hospitals, schools, and stores. Any job that requires the coordinated actions of more than one person can involve teams. In many work settings, we find groups of people who work relatively independently but still come in contact with one another. College professors, salesclerks, security guards, and teachers often do most of their work alone, although many other people in their organizations may be doing similar work. Even the most independent employees are affected by the behavior of others with whom they interact at work.

In this chapter we turn our attention from the individual employee to groups of employees. We will see how the behavior of individuals is very much affected by the behavior of other people in the work environment. It would be correct to say that one cannot fully understand the behavior of individuals without considering the influence of others because people rarely work totally alone and unaffected by others.

We begin this discussion by distinguishing work groups from work teams. Four important group concepts will be discussed:

Roles

Norms

Group cohesiveness

Process loss

Next the chapter covers the effects of groups on job performance. Techniques for enhancing group and team performance are included.

<u>Objectives</u>   **The student who studies this chapter should be able to:**
1. Define work groups and work teams, and note the distinction between them.
2. Explain the four important group concepts.
3. Summarize the findings on group performance.
4. Discuss the procedures that can be used to enhance work group performance.

WORK GROUPS VERSUS WORK TEAMS

A **work group** is a collection of two or more people who interact with one another and share some interrelated task goals. These two characteristics, interaction and interrelatedness, distinguish a group from just a collection of people. A university department faculty is a work group. The members of the faculty interact with one another from time to time, and they have interrelated goals involving the education of students. Each faculty member teaches courses that taken together constitute the requirements for the major course of study. On the other hand, all of the students of the university are not a group because they do not all interact with one another, although subsets of them do, and they do not all share interrelated goals. Rather, each student has an individual goal that is unrelated to the goals of other students.

A **work team** is a type of work group, but a team has three specific properties (West, Borrill, & Unsworth, 1998):

1. The actions of individuals must be interdependent and coordinated.
2. Each member must have a particular, specified role.
3. There must be common task goals and objectives.

For example, each person on a surgical team has a specific role. A surgeon does the cutting and sewing; a surgical nurse assists and provides instruments; and an anesthesiologist keeps the patient unconscious and monitors vital signs. The actions of these people are coordinated. The cutting cannot begin until the person is asleep. The surgeon cannot sew unless the nurse gives him or her the tools. There is a common goal of successfully completing the surgery without losing the patient.

The distinction between a group and a team is an important one. All teams are groups, but not all groups are teams. A group consists of people who work together but can do their jobs without one another. A team is a group of people who cannot do their jobs, at least not effectively, without the other members of their teams. For the remainder of this chapter, all group principles will apply to teams as well.

IMPORTANT GROUP CONCEPTS

To understand groups and teams, you must understand four important group concepts. The first three (roles, norms, and group cohesiveness) describe important aspects of groups and teams that help us understand how they operate. The fourth (process loss) is concerned with what sorts of things happen in work groups and teams that prevent people from putting all of their efforts into job performance.

Roles

The concept of **role** implies that not everyone in a group or team has the same function or purpose. Instead, different individuals have different jobs and responsibilities in the group or team. In a surgical team one person has the role of surgeon, another of nurse, and another of anesthesiologist. In a well-running work team, each role is clearly defined, and all team members know exactly what their roles are.

Formal roles are specified by the organization and are part of the formal job description. In a surgical team each person's job title—surgeon, nurse, or anesthesiologist—defines the role in a formal way. There may even be organizational documents, such as written job descriptions and job analyses, that define the roles. **Informal roles** arise from group interaction rather than the formal rules and specifications of organizations. Groups can invent roles that do not exist formally, or the group's informal roles can supersede the formal ones.

An example of an invented role is someone in a work group taking on the role of greeting card sender. It is common in a work group for employees to send cards to one another during special occasions, such as birthdays and family deaths. A group member might take on the role of buying and sending cards at the appropriate times. An example of the informal superseding the formal occurs when one person has the formal title of supervisor, but another person is the actual and informal leader. This can occur in combat teams when the members consider the lower ranking experienced sergeant rather than the higher ranking but inexperienced lieutenant to be the leader.

Groups vary considerably in the extent to which roles are specialized among members. In a surgical team, for example, the training and credentials are such that little overlap in roles can occur among the surgeon, nurse, and anesthesiologist. With other groups or teams, members can change roles or rotate responsibilities over time. In an academic department of a university, it is common for faculty to take turns at being the chairperson.

Norms

Norms are unwritten rules of behavior accepted by members of a work group. These rules can cover everything from style of dress and manner of speech to how hard everyone works. Norms can exert powerful influences on individual behavior because many groups will strenuously enforce them. In order to be a group member in good standing, one must conform to norms. Violation of norms will bring pressure to bear on the violator. Initially, group members will remind the deviate that his or her behavior violates the norm: "I thought you should know that we don't do that sort of thing around here." Continued violation can bring with it increasingly more severe forms of enforcement that can even result in violence. Assaults on persons and property are not uncommon when important norms are violated. Finally, when all attempts to enlist conformity with norms have failed, the violator will be ostracized by members of the group. No one will talk to the person or have anything to do with him or her. This process is illustrated in Figure 12-1.

It is common for work groups to adopt production norms that dictate how much each person will produce, especially in manufacturing plants where production is countable, although it can occur in almost any type of organization. People who work too hard (rate

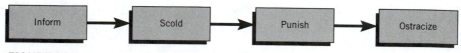

FIGURE 12-1

Norm violators are informed, scolded, punished, and then ostracized from the group.

busters) or do not work hard enough (gold bricks) will be pressured by their groups to conform. This typically begins with a friendly explanation that "we don't work this hard around here" and can escalate in some organizations to violence. A good illustration of production norms can be found in Coch and French's (1948) classic study of a pajama factory with a piece-rate system. In this factory, employees assembled pajamas and could work at their own pace. Coch and French documented the output of a worker who began to exceed the 50-unit per hour production norm of her work group. When group members pressured her, she restricted her output to about 45 units per hour. A short time later the group was disbanded, and within a matter of days, the worker's output more than doubled.

Work group norms can have a bigger impact on member behavior than supervisors or organizational practices. In the Coch and French (1948) study, production was restricted, even though a piece-rate system was in place. Employees would sacrifice the opportunity to make extra money to keep from violating group norms. Clearly, norms could prove quite useful as a means of enhancing productivity if they could be appropriately directed. The changing of group norms can be difficult for the management of an organization, which must structure the changes so that it is in the best interest of the group to adopt them. For example, group incentive systems can be an effective means of getting groups to adopt high production norms. With such a system all members of the group are given rewards, such as a monetary bonus, if the group achieves some specified level of performance. As demonstrated by Coch and French (1948), incentive systems will not always motivate groups to perform well.

Sundstrom, De Meuse, and Futrell (1990) suggest that goal setting can be an effective means of getting groups to adopt norms that are consistent with good organizational functioning. This approach differs from individual goal setting in that the entire group has a goal rather than each person. The trick to an effective goal-setting program is to get group members to commit themselves to the goals. Participation by group members in the goal-setting process can be an effective means of accomplishing this commitment. Managers and group members can negotiate the group's goals. Participation has been found to be a powerful technique for achieving commitment by employees within organizations (Coch & French, 1948).

Group Cohesiveness

Group cohesiveness is the sum of forces attracting group members and keeping the group together. It is a group phenomenon; and for a group to be highly cohesive, most if not all members must have strong motives to remain in the group. A high level of group cohesiveness has important implications for group behavior. Norms tend to be strongly enforced only in groups that are highly cohesive. The violation of a norm, particularly an important one, can be threatening to a group's existence. If group continuation is vitally important to group members, the conformity to norms will be a critical issue. In the workplace, people are often dependent on their jobs for their economic survival, and the work group can be as important as the family. Threats to the well-being of the group are taken seriously.

Because cohesive groups strongly enforce their norms and work groups might adopt norms for high or low productivity, one might expect that there would be no consistent relationship between cohesiveness and job performance in groups. This is exactly the case: Some studies within organizations have found that highly cohesive groups perform better (e.g., Keller, 1986; Tziner & Vardi, 1983), and others have found no significant relation (George & Bettenhausen, 1990; Greene, 1989). Greene's (1989) results are consistent with this view in that goal acceptance was related to productivity but group cohesiveness was not.

Group cohesiveness, on the other hand, is related to job satisfaction within the group. Members of highly cohesive groups tend to be more satisfied than members of minimally cohesive groups. This has been found in both classroom settings (e.g., Colarelli & Boos, 1992) and work settings (e.g., Keller, 1986).

Process Loss

Much of the time and effort of work group members is devoted to accomplishing organizational objectives through the performance of individuals. Much effort, however, goes into other group functions that have little to do with job performance, including time spent in group maintenance functions such as norm enforcement and conflict resolution among members. It can also involve social activities, such as meals or conversation, that enhance group cohesiveness, which can be important for efficient group functioning. All the time and effort expended on activities not directly related to production or task accomplishment are referred to as **process loss**.

Groups vary tremendously in the amount of time they devote to maintenance activities. Some groups have problems with norm violators and interpersonal conflicts that can consume a great deal of time and energy. Other groups run smoothly with little friction and few internal distractions. In the next section on group performance, we will see that groups do not always perform as well as we might expect. Process loss can have a lot to do with the inefficiency that sometimes occurs in groups. Nevertheless, a certain amount of process loss is necessary and may lead to better future performance by the group.

© 1996 United Feature Syndicate, Inc. (NYC)

GROUP PERFORMANCE

There is a widespread belief that group performance is superior to individual performance for many tasks. This belief is based on the notion that something emerges in the interaction among people that enables a group to be better than the sum of its members. In other words, people inspire one another to be better than they would have been alone. It is true that for some tasks the coordinated efforts of two or more people are necessary because a single individual could not accomplish them alone. For example, several people are needed to build a house. Some tasks may require more than two hands, and others may require the lifting of objects that one person cannot do alone. For many tasks, however, groups are not necessarily better than individuals. Part of the reason is process loss—group members distract and keep one another from concentrating solely on the task at hand. There are additional reasons that we discuss as we compare the performance of individuals with groups.

Performance in the Presence of Others

One of the earliest known group phenomena in psychology is that task performance is affected by the presence of others. In the late 1800s, Norman Triplett noted that the performance of bicycle riders was faster when they were racing against other people than when they were racing alone (Triplett, 1897). Subsequent research with laboratory tasks, however, did not always find that people performed better in the presence of others. Performance was better in the presence of others in some studies but worse in other studies.

The most widely accepted explanation for these results was put forth by Zajonc (1965), who noticed that the type of task determined if performance was enhanced or inhibited by the presence of others. He suggested that the presence of others increases phys-

Performing in front of an audience raises arousal, as this person will certainly experience.

iological arousal, which has effects on task performance. Performance is improved (the **social facilitation** effect) by other-induced arousal when the task is simple or well learned, such as bicycle riding. On the other hand, performance is decreased or inhibited by other-induced arousal when the task is complex or new to the individual, such as solving a complex mathematics problem. These results suggest that for complex tasks, people should be given private space that allows them to keep their arousal levels relatively low. For simple tasks, the arousal produced by the presence of others can enhance performance, but other people can also be a distraction in the workplace, leading to poorer performance.

Group Versus Individual Performance on Additive Tasks

When researchers compare individuals to groups on task performance, they are usually concerned with an **additive task**. The output of the task is countable, and the total output is the sum of the individual group member outputs. The total output for a group of cashiers in a supermarket would be additive because the total sales are the sum of all the individual cashiers' sales. The effects of group process on additive task performance can be seen by comparing the output of an interacting group of people with an equal number of individuals who do not interact. The noninteracting individuals are referred to as a **nominal group**. Their output reflects the output of a given number of individuals. The output of the interacting group, by comparison, reflects how well the same number of people will perform in a group.

Research dating back to the nineteenth century has consistently shown that nominal groups do as well and usually better than interacting groups (Davis, 1969). This finding is well illustrated by research done over 100 years ago by an agricultural engineer in France named Ringelmann. Kravitz and Martin (1986) described Ringelmann's research in which he compared the task performance of groups and individuals. Ringelmann noted that the sum of individual efforts often surpassed the effort of an equal number of people working in a group. Table 12-1 summarizes how group and individual efforts compare. It shows the results across several different types of tasks involving the pulling and pushing of objects. The first column shows the number of people in the group. The second column shows the expected output of a group, which was calculated as the number of people in the group times the average individual performance. In other words, a group of two people should produce double the output of a single person, and a group of four people

TABLE 12-1
Strength of object pulling and pushing as a function of group size

SIZE OF GROUP	EXPECTED PULL (KGS)	ACTUAL PULL (KGS)	PERCENTAGE OF ACTUAL TO EXPECTED PERFORMANCE
1	1	1	100
2	2	1.86	93
4	4	3.08	77
8	8	3.92	49

Source: "Ringelmann Rediscovered: The Original Article," by D. A. Kravitz and B. Martin, 1986, *Journal of Personality and Social Psychology, 50,* 936–941.

should produce four times the output of a single person. The third column shows the actual performance of the group. As the table illustrates, the actual interacting group output is considerably less than the nominal group output. The percentage that the interacting group output is of the nominal group output declines as the group size increases (see column 4). Clearly, something is happening with the interacting group that is inhibiting performance.

There are at least two explanations for the group effect on additive task performance. The first explanation is the possibility of process loss. Group members might interfere with one another's task performance, or they might spend time and effort on group maintenance activities rather than on the task at hand. This might explain inhibited performance in some studies, but with the rope-pulling task this does not seem likely. The nature of the task required that all group members concentrate their efforts on pulling the rope at the same time when a signal was given. Group members could not have been doing something else at the time.

A second and more likely explanation is a phenomenon called **social loafing**—people do not put forth as much effort in a group as they would if they were working alone, and the larger the group, the less effort each person exerts. Latané, Williams, and Harkins (1979) found this phenomenon to be widespread in both laboratory and field settings. Freeman, Walker, Borden, and Latané (1975) observed that the more people in a party in a restaurant, the smaller was the percentage of the tip. Individuals alone tipped an average of 19%, whereas parties of five or more tipped an average of less than 13%.

The social loafing effect can be diminished when group members believe that their individual output is being assessed. In one study, the social loafing effect was reduced by telling subjects that their individual performance was being measured (Williams, Harkins, & Latané, 1981). The phenomenon may also be limited to individualistic cultures, such as Australia, Canada, England, and the United States (see the discussion of culture values in Chapter 9), where emphasis is placed on the self rather than on society. Earley (1989) found that Chinese management trainees who came from a collectivist culture, where emphasis is placed on the group and society, did not demonstrate social loafing. Wagner (1995) found that group size and identifiability of individual output did not affect the cooperativeness of collectivist Americans, thus supporting the hypothesis that the collectivism of the Chinese trainees explained why they did not social loaf.

Brainstorming

Groups are said to be superior to individuals in generating ideas or solutions to problems (Osborn, 1957). The theory is that group members inspire one another to generate ideas that they would not have thought of alone. **Brainstorming** is a group technique that is supposed to result in improved performance with this type of task. A group is given instructions to generate ideas without being critical or judgmental in any way. Ideas will be evaluated and modified later.

Unfortunately, research has failed to find that the performance of groups that brainstorm is superior to that of nominal groups (Gallupe, Bastianutti, & Cooper, 1991). Rather than inspiring one another, group members often inhibit one another. Part of the difficulty is undoubtedly attributable to process loss. The group may not spend as much time as individuals generating ideas. Perhaps even more important, individuals can be reluctant to share ideas in the group because of shyness or social anxiety. Alone a person might be more confident and secure in generating ideas.

Electronic brainstorming has been shown to enhance performance in an idea-generation task with the use of computers (Dennis & Valacich, 1993; Gallupe et al., 1991). Individuals are asked to enter ideas into a computer rather than writing them down. This technique was found to produce equal or better performance than that of nominal groups (the combined output of individuals who worked alone) and better performance than groups of individuals who shared their ideas. In the Gallupe et al. (1991) study, computer brainstorming subjects were aware that several people were working on the same task at the same time and that as ideas were entered onto the computer, they would be seen by everyone. Individuals were not known to one another, which may have reduced the social anxiety that could have inhibited performance in an interacting group. In a similar study, however, Valacich, Dennis, and Nunamaker (1992) found that anonymity made no difference in the performance of brainstorming individuals linked by computer. This study suggests that social anxiety is not the reason for the poorer performance of interacting groups.

Gallupe, Cooper, Grisé, and Bastianutti (1994) conducted a study that showed how electronic brainstorming produces better performance in part because people do not have to wait their turn for others to speak. They can type their responses as they think of them. When electronic brainstormers had to wait their turn to enter their responses onto the computer, performance was about the same as that for the interacting groups. This suggests that process loss is responsible for the poorer performance of interacting groups compared to computer or nominal brainstorming groups.

Group Decision Making

Groups within organizations frequently make decisions ranging from the relatively unimportant (e.g., the color of the new stationery) to those that significantly affect the lives and well-being of thousands (e.g., closing a plant and laying off all the workers). Organizations differ tremendously in the extent to which important decisions are made by individual managers (the autocratic approach) or by groups (the democratic approach). Even in the most autocratic organizations, however, it is common for individuals to make decisions only after consultation with a group or committee. The president of the United States consults the cabinet for important decisions, and the presidents of corporations usually have their "inner circles" of associates who serve the same purpose.

Evaluating the quality of a decision is not always an easy or straightforward undertaking. Often the evaluation depends on the values of the person doing the determination and the criterion chosen for comparison. If a government decides to go to war, the decision might be considered good by one person because the war was won and bad by another because many people were killed. Although most Americans supported President Bush's decision to use military force against Iraq during the Gulf War, many believed it was a bad decision that cost too many lives. Similarly, if a company president decides to downsize and lay off thousands of employees, it might be considered a good decision by stockholders whose stock might go up in value and a poor decision by employees who might lose their jobs. A solution to this dilemma is to evaluate a decision against the objective that it was meant to obtain. The Gulf War would be considered a good decision because it accomplished the objective of liberating Kuwait. If the objective was removing Saddam Hussein from power, our evaluation of the decision would be different. A layoff might be a good decision if it results in a financially healthier company, but a bad decision if it does not.

We review two areas of group decisions in this section. First is the issue of whether groups take more risks or are more conservative in their decisions than individuals. As we will see in our discussion of group polarization, this question has no simple answer. The second issue concerns how groups sometimes make inappropriate decisions, even though most of the group members knew the decision was a poor one. This is the phenomenon of groupthink, which we also discuss.

Group Polarization. If a group of people decides on one of several possible courses of action, will the choice involve greater or lesser risk than the choice made by an individual? In other words, are groups riskier or more conservative than individuals in their decisions? This question has been addressed by hundreds of studies comparing group decisions to the decisions of individuals. The answer is that group decisions often differ from the decisions of individuals, but whether they are riskier or more conservative depends on the nature of the decision.

The typical risky decision study asks individuals and groups to choose one option from a series of options that vary in risk. For example, a decision task might involve deciding the acceptable odds of survival for undergoing elective surgery. Table 12-2 is one of the choice-dilemmas (Kogan & Wallach, 1964) that have been used in many risk studies. In these studies subjects are first asked to make an individual decision. The subjects are then placed into groups and are asked to come to a group decision. In most studies, the group decisions are more extreme than the mean of the individual decisions. For example, suppose that five subjects choose the following acceptable odds for the surgery problem: 20, 20, 20, 60, and 80 chances out of 100 of dying in surgery. The mean of their choices is 40. When placed in a group, however, the same people are likely to choose lower odds, closer to the majority position of 20.

Typically, in groups the majority position holds more weight than the minority position, and the shift of the group is toward the majority view. If the majority of the group members make a risky choice, the group decision is likely to be riskier than the mean of its individuals. If the majority make a conservative choice, the group is likely to shift its decision in a conservative direction. This deviation from the group mean is called **group polarization** (Lamm & Myers, 1978), meaning that the group is more extreme (closer to one pole or the other) than the mean of its individuals.

A number of explanations have been offered for the group polarization phenomenon. One likely explanation is that the members who hold the minority view will likely conform to the majority, especially if one member's choice is far from the choices of the other

---

TABLE 12-2
A risk-related choice task used in group decision research

Mr. B, a 45-year-old accountant, has recently been informed by his physician that he has developed a severe heart ailment. The disease would be sufficiently serious to force Mr. B to change many of his strongest life habits—reducing his workload, drastically changing his diet, giving up favorite leisure-time pursuits. The physician suggests that a delicate medical operation could be attempted which, if successful, would completely relieve the heart condition. But its success could not be assured, and in fact, the operation might prove fatal.

Source: Risk Taking: A Study in Cognition and Personality, by N. Kogan and M. A. Wallach, 1964, New York: Holt, Rinehart and Winston.

group members. The individuals who find that others made the same choice that they did are likely to be convinced that theirs was the best choice. Most of the group discussion will be directed to convincing the minority that they should adopt the "correct" majority viewpoint. Although most of the group decision shift research has concerned risk-related decisions, this phenomenon probably holds for any type of choice situation. For example, decision shift would be expected in deciding how much money to spend on an item.

Groupthink. High-level decision-making groups in corporations and governments typically are comprised of experts who should be able to make good decisions. Unfortunately, something can happen to decision-making processes when groups of people get together, leading them to make decisions that any reasonably bright, informed individual would probably never make. Irving Janis (1972) has conducted in-depth analyses of decision fiascoes and has developed a theory of what can go wrong when groups make decisions. **Groupthink** is a phenomenon that can occur when groups make decisions that individual members know are poor ones (Janis, 1972). Janis notes as examples the Ford Motor Company's decision to produce the Edsel, an automobile that lost $300 million; the Kennedy administration's decision to invade Cuba at the Bay of Pigs, an invasion that was

The decision that led to the *Challenger* disaster was likely caused by groupthink. (Moorhead, Ference, & Neck, 1991)

a total failure; and the Johnson administration's decision to escalate the Vietnam War, which the United States never won (Janis, 1972). Moorhead, Ference, and Neck (1991) analyzed the decision to launch the space shuttle *Challenger* in 1986. Despite warnings that cold weather could cause serious mechanical failures, NASA officials decided to launch the shuttle in freezing temperatures, producing the worst disaster in American space flight history.

According to Janis, groupthink is likely to occur in highly cohesive groups with strong leaders when the social pressures to maintain conformity and harmony in the group take precedence over sound decision making. The likelihood of groupthink is increased when decision-making groups isolate themselves from outside ideas and influences. Note the following sequence of events: Suppose that the leader of the group presents a bad idea at a meeting. Each member might initially suspect that the idea is a poor one but is reluctant to be the one to say so. Much like the story of the Emperor's New Clothes, no one wants to stick his or her neck out and question the leader's decision. As each individual looks around the room and notices that everyone is silent, he or she may begin to doubt his or her initial judgment. After all, if everyone else seems to be going along, perhaps the idea is not so bad. As the group process gets rolling, any criticism is quickly rationalized away, and pressure is put on individual members to conform to the group point of view. Some of the factors leading to groupthink are illustrated in Figure 12-2.

Janis (1972) offers several suggestions for avoiding groupthink. Two major themes appear throughout these suggestions. First, group leaders should serve as impartial moderators in group meetings rather than attempting to control the decision alternatives that are recommended. Second, group members at every stage of the decision-making process should critically evaluate decision alternatives and continually seek information that might support or refute the wisdom of a decision. Janis discusses specific actions that groups should take to maintain a critical and objective frame of mind. For example, groups should periodically break into smaller subgroups to discuss critical issues, and members of the decision-making groups should discuss issues with subordinates. These actions can help groups avoid getting caught in a cycle of groupthink that can result in making the wrong decision.

Aldag and Fuller (1993) reviewed the research on groupthink. They noted that few good tests of its propositions exist; those that do exist support only part of the theory. For example, group cohesiveness does not seem to be necessary for groupthink to occur. Janis

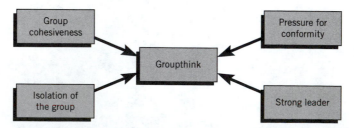

FIGURE 12-2

Several factors can lead to groupthink. Of the four shown here, group cohesiveness seems unnecessary according to Aldag and Fuller (1993).

(1972), however, offers sound advice about how to avoid bad group decisions by soliciting a variety of views. This is a potential advantage of having diversity in the backgrounds of group members. A diverse group is likely to have different perspectives on a problem and its solution.

INTERVENTIONS WITH WORK GROUPS IN ORGANIZATIONS

Most organizations consist of a network of interrelated work groups. In order for the organization to function effectively, individuals must coordinate their efforts within their own groups, and groups must coordinate their efforts with one another. In this section, we discuss three techniques that can be used to improve group functioning. The autonomous work group is an alternative to the traditional organization of a factory. Items are assembled by small groups of employees rather than by all production employees. The autonomous work group idea has been adapted for nonmanufacturing organizations as well. Quality circles are groups of employees who are assembled to provide suggestions to management. Team building is a family of procedures used to improve the functioning of teams.

Autonomous Work Groups

In the traditional factory, the assembly of a product is broken down into many small operations. For large, complex products, like an automobile, there can be hundreds or thousands of operations, each done by a separate employee. Because assembling a product requires the coordinated effort of a large number of people, many resources must be devoted to supervision. The autonomous work group is an alternative system whereby an entire product is assembled by a small group of employees. A factory will be comprised of

Autonomous work groups at Butler Corporation assemble entire grain dryers, which is the cylinder surrounded by steam.

TABLE 12-3
Distinguishing features of autonomous work groups at Butler Corporation

1. Employees frequently rotated jobs.
2. After about 18 months, most employees knew the entire production process.
3. Groups designed and purchased their own tools.
4. Group members went on service calls to do warranty repairs.
5. Quality control inspection was done by group members.
6. There were few supervisors.
7. Group members participated in hiring and firing.
8. Supervisors served as coaches providing counseling and training.
9. There were weekly group meetings and monthly plant meetings.
10. There were employee advisory groups to management.

Source: Work Redesign, by J. R. Hackman and G. R. Oldham, 1980, Reading, MA: Addison-Wesley.

many work groups, each assembling an entire product. Because assembly of a product involves only the coordination of group members, relatively few resources are necessary for supervision. Groups are relied on to manage themselves, requiring far fewer supervisors.

The details of how autonomous work groups operate vary to some extent from organization to organization. One such system, described by Hackman and Oldham (1980), was implemented by the Butler Corporation when it opened a new grain dryer plant. A grain dryer is a large piece of farm equipment that contains over 3,000 parts (see photograph). At Butler each dryer is assembled by an autonomous work group. Each group is responsible for managing itself and for product assembly. Ten distinguishing characteristics of the groups at Butler are listed in Table 12-3. As you can see, each member of the group learns each operation, so that after about 18 months on the job every employee can assemble an entire dryer. The group is responsible for the quality of the finished product, which it must test before sending it out of the plant. If a dryer is defective, a group member might have to make a service call to fix it. The role of supervisors is different at Butler. There are few of them, and their major function is to offer advice and training to team members. The approach is participative, with frequent staff meetings and an advisory committee comprised of members from different groups.

Research has shown that autonomous work groups benefit employees and organizations. Job satisfaction is typically higher with autonomous work groups than more traditional approaches (Cordery, Mueller, & Smith, 1991; Pearce & Ravlin, 1987). Job performance has been found to be the same in manufacturing organizations (Wall, Kemp, Jackson, & Clegg, 1986) or better (Banker, Field, Schroeder, & Sinha, 1996). However, the decreased need for supervisory personnel can result in an overall greater efficiency for these autonomous work groups even when productivity is the same (see the Research in Detail box in this chapter). Autonomous work groups have been found to have better performance than traditional work groups in nonmanufacturing organizations (Cohen & Ledford, 1994).

Quality Circles

A **quality circle** is a group intervention that gives employees the opportunity to have greater input into issues at work. Quality circles are groups of employees who meet periodically to discuss problems and propose solutions relevant to their jobs. Typically, the

RESEARCH IN DETAIL

IT IS RARE in field settings to be able to do a true experiment in which two or more experimental conditions are created and subjects are randomly assigned to them. Wall, Kemp, Jackson, and Clegg (1986) conducted a *quasi-experiment*, meaning that the design of the study was an approximation to an experiment. Two factories that represented the two experimental conditions of interest were compared, but employees were not randomly assigned to work at each factory. It is therefore possible that the observed effects were due to differences in the two factories rather than the autonomous work group treatment.

The study was conducted at a candy manufacturing company in England. Officials of the company decided to experiment with autonomous work groups by trying them at one factory. The researchers were enlisted to evaluate the effects of the new system. The productivity, job satisfaction, and mental health of employees at the autonomous work group factory were compared to those factors for employees at a matched factory that used the traditional assembly-line approach. Data were collected 6 months, 18 months, and 30 months after the new factory began operation.

The results showed that employees in the autonomous work group factory were more satisfied with their jobs than employees in the traditional factory. Their productivity, however, was not better. In fact, during the first 6 months of operation, the productivity of the autonomous work groups was quite disappointing. Much of the difficulty was attributed to problems with new equipment and the time needed for training employees in the new production procedures. By the 30-month time period, performance in both factories was equivalent. Because the autonomous work group factory had fewer supervisors, however, it was found to be more cost efficient.

One finding illustrates the difficulties in drawing conclusions from quasi-experimental studies. The turnover rate was found to be higher in the autonomous work group factory than the traditional factory. This finding was surprising because employees of the former factory were more satisfied with their jobs than employees of the latter factory. The authors noted that the unemployment rate in the area of England where the autonomous work group factory was located was lower than it was where the traditional factory was located. They speculated that the unemployment rate may have been the cause of the turnover rate differences, rather than the type of factory. Because of the design of the study, we cannot be certain why the difference occurred. This study does provide evidence to support the idea that autonomous work groups can be more cost efficient than traditional factory structures. Organizations should be aware, however, that extra effort and time may be needed for successful implementation of the system.

Source: Wall, T. D., Kemp, N. J., Jackson, P. R., & Clegg, C. W. (1986). Outcomes of autonomous workgroups: A long-term field experiment. *Academy of Management Journal, 29,* 280–304.

groups are comprised of people who have similar jobs in manufacturing organizations, and discussions revolve around issues of product quality and production efficiency. As with autonomous work groups, quality circles have been attempted in all types of organizations.

In theory, quality circles have benefits for both employees and organizations. They allow individual employees to enjoy greater participation, which many find stimulating and enjoyable. It can be a welcome break from routine work to spend time discussing work problems with colleagues. For the organization, it should mean better production procedures because the people who do the work are often the most knowledgeable about what the problems are and how they can be solved.

Too little research has been done on quality circles to draw any firm conclusions about their effects on employees or organizations (Van Fleet & Griffin, 1989). The few studies that have investigated quality circle benefits have yielded somewhat mixed results (Bettenhausen, 1991). Marks, Mirvis, Hackett, and Grady (1986) conducted one of the few studies that compared participants with nonparticipants in the same organization. They found that employees who participated in the quality circle program were more productive and had fewer absences than employees who did not.

These results are quite promising, but they need to be replicated in other organizations before we can conclude that quality circles will increase productivity and reduce absence. Nevertheless, quality circles have become very popular in organizations in part because they are easy to implement and consume few resources.

Team Building

Team building refers to any of a number of activities designed to enhance the many different aspects of the functioning of work groups or teams. Some team-building efforts are task oriented—they attempt to help team members improve how they accomplish their team tasks. Other efforts are interpersonally oriented—they are concerned with how well team members communicate and interact. This approach presumes that teams will perform better when their members can communicate and interact with one another effectively (Buller, 1986).

There is no one particular way in which team building is done, but three factors characterize team-building efforts (Buller, 1986). First, team building is a planned activity; that is, it consists of one or more exercises or experiences that are designed to accomplish a particular objective. Second, team building is typically conducted or *facilitated* by a consultant or trainer who is an expert in the particular form of team building that is being done. It would be difficult for a team to run itself through team building, for the trainer is an integral part of the experience. Third, team building usually involves an existing work team. Individuals are trained in team building to enhance their individual team skills within their work teams.

Team building often involves team members discussing problems and coming up with solutions. The role of the team trainer is to facilitate the discussion by getting team members talking to one another. This might involve directing questions at individuals:

"Tom, what sorts of problems have you been having with product quality?"

"Ellen, why don't you seem to get the information that you need?"

Or summarizing and reflecting back to the group the points that have been made:

"It sounds like everyone is concerned that there are too many defective parts."

"I guess everyone feels uninformed about decisions."

The trainer's job is to get people to raise issues, identify problems, and discuss possible solutions. The trainer might also have to mediate conflicts if the discussion leads to arguments among team members.

Dov Eden has used team building with Israeli army artillery teams like this one.

The results of studies designed to show the positive effects of team building have been inconsistent. For example, Dov Eden conducted two team-building studies with units of the Israeli army (see photograph) and found positive effects for one (Eden, 1986) and no effects for the other (Eden, 1985). Buller (1986) reported that team building had positive effects on job performance for six of the nine studies he reviewed. He pointed out that the wide variety of interventions that are considered team building across different studies has made it difficult to draw firm conclusions about its effectiveness.

FUTURE ISSUES AND CHALLENGES

One by-product of complex technology in the workplace is the necessity for coordinated team effort among employees. Complicated equipment in both civilian and military organizations can require several people to operate. On a guided missile cruiser like the U.S.S. *Vincennes*, for example, it takes several people to operate the tracking equipment that distinguishes hostile from friendly aircraft. When teamwork breaks down, as it did when the *Vincennes* shot down an Iranian airliner, the consequences can be severe. The challenge for I/O psychology in the future is to find ways to improve the functioning of teams.

Autonomous work groups are becoming increasingly popular ways of organizing manufacturing organizations. Part of the motivation at the present time is the necessity for downsizing that requires the elimination of supervisory personnel. Although autonomous work groups can have advantages, expanding the scope of the factory worker's job poses several challenges. Most important, as factory jobs become more complex, they will require a higher level of ability and initiative. People with more skills and motivation will have to be either hired or developed on the job. For the I/O psychologist, this means the introduction of selection procedures to find the best people, training to enhance their skills, and systems to increase motivation.

Team-building techniques have been in use for many decades, but the kind of intervention that is effective remains unclear. It is likely that the most effective approaches will be determined by the situation. Military teams, for example, must deal with the stress of combat. This might require different team behaviors than those for teams that operate complex machinery.

CHAPTER SUMMARY

Much of the work done today in organizations is performed by work groups or work teams. Work groups are collections of individuals who interact at work and share interrelated task goals. Work teams are a type of work group, but the tasks of individual members are coordinated and interrelated; the team members have different roles; and the team has a common objective or task goal.

Four concepts relate to work groups. *Roles* distinguish the specific positions and functions of individuals in a group or team. *Norms* are group rules of behavior that in many groups are rigidly enforced. *Group cohesiveness* is the sum of forces holding the group together. Highly cohesive groups rigidly enforce their norms. *Process loss* is the time and effort that group members spend keeping the group operating rather than working on tasks.

The presence of other people affects task performance. Simple or well-learned tasks are facilitated by the presence of others; complex or new tasks are inhibited by the presence of others. Group performance is often inferior to the combined performance of an equal number of individuals working alone. For additive tasks (the total performance is the sum of each individual's performance), the phenomenon of social loafing explains that the larger the group, the less effort each individual expends.

Group polarization explains that, depending on the situation, group decisions can be riskier or more conservative than individual decisions. Groupthink explains how groups of highly talented decision makers can make bad decisions when placed in decision groups.

Three interventions have the potential for improving group functioning and performance. Autonomous work groups are given the responsibility for entire jobs, such as assembling whole products like appliances or automobiles. Quality circles are groups of employees who meet periodically to come up with solutions to work problems. Team building is one of a number of interventions designed to improve the functioning of work teams.

I/O PSYCHOLOGY IN PRACTICE

THIS CASE CONCERNS a U.S. Navy team development training program created and carried out by Dr. Janis Cannon-Bowers. Dr. Cannon-Bowers received her Ph.D. in I/O psychology in 1988 from the University of South Florida. Since then she has been working at the Naval Air Warfare Center Training Systems Division in Orlando, FL, where she holds the title of Research Psychologist. Her major responsibility is to do research on team performance and training to develop new, more effective approaches. As a result, she has become involved in training naval officers in team development.

Two naval tragedies in the late 1980s led to much research into team performance. In 1987 the U.S.S. *Stark* was hit by an Iraqi missile. In 1988 the U.S.S. *Vincennes* shot down an Iran-

(Continued next page)

ian airliner. An investigation of both incidents revealed poor teamwork was a major factor. This led to the U.S. Navy's effort to improve the performance of teams. Dr. Cannon-Bowers' efforts have involved this research and also interventions aimed at improving team performance on navy ships.

Many different teams on combat ships carry out complex and dangerous functions, often under the severe stress of combat. There is no time for group deliberation because all functions must be carried out quickly and efficiently, with life-and-death decisions being made in seconds. It is vital that teams develop into well-functioning units that do their jobs efficiently. On a combat ship the commanding officer (C.O.) must see to it that the various teams develop into effective units. To do so, the C.O. must have skills in team development.

Dr. Cannon-Bowers and her colleagues designed a team development training program for C.O.s that she conducts at the Navy's Surface Warfare School. The program is intended to give the C.O.s insights into team functioning and sound training principles. It covers the ways to

1. Give feedback
2. Accept criticism by subordinates
3. Create a climate for learning
4. Develop a "shared mental model" or common understanding of the team's functions
5. Avoid groupthink

The response to the training by the C.O.s has been positive. From the perspective of participant reaction criteria, it is successful. Research is now under way to determine the effects of the program on the more important criterion of team performance at sea. Preliminary findings are quite favorable.

Discussion Questions

1. Do you think Dr. Cannon-Bowers' program will prove to be effective?
2. What steps could the Navy take to improve team performance on ships?
3. Is awareness of the causes of groupthink enough for team members to avoid it?
4. How would you go about giving feedback to subordinates if you were a ship's C.O.?

Chapter **13**

LEADERSHIP AND POWER
IN ORGANIZATIONS

What makes a person a good leader? Has President Clinton been a good leader? During both of his terms the media reported constant rumors and scandals. He was sued for sexual harassment and was the target of unrelenting hostile jokes. His opponents attacked his character constantly, arguing that he was morally unfit for the job. Yet in the midst of serious charges of immoral behavior and perjury, and an impeachment trial in the United States Senate, poll after poll found that the overwhelming majority (two-thirds) of Americans approved of his performance in office. The U.S. economy was the strongest in decades with the stock market breaking records, the federal budget was balanced, serious crime was on the decline, and welfare reform seemed to be successful. Are these signs of his effectiveness? How would you go about determining how effective he was? Is good leadership a matter of character or a matter of being able to get important things done? Will the same person be a good leader in all situations? These are important questions to both government and nongovernment organizations. The answers tell us whom to choose as our leaders, and they tell leaders how they must act to be effective.

In this chapter we deal with the important domain of leadership in organizations. We discuss the nature of leadership and how leaders influence followers. We summarize what is presently known about the personal characteristics that relate to good leadership performance and the effects of leader behavior on subordinates. We see how good leadership is the result of leader behavior, leader characteristics, and the leadership situation. Finally, we discuss women in leadership positions.

Objectives **The student who studies this chapter should be able to:**
1. Define leadership.
2. Explain the five sources of power and three sources of political power.
3. Summarize the major approaches and theories of leadership.
4. Compare and contrast the major approaches and theories of leadership.
5. Discuss the barriers to women's advancement in the workplace.

WHAT IS LEADERSHIP?

You probably have an intuitive idea of what leadership is. A *leader* is the one in charge or the boss of other people. Just because you are in charge, however, does not mean that people will listen to you or do what you say. What at first seems simple is quite complex, as we discuss in this chapter. Leadership scholars have come up with many different definitions of leadership, and no one definition has been universally accepted (Yukl, 1989). A common idea that runs through various definitions is that leadership involves influencing the attitudes, beliefs, behaviors, and feelings of other people. Even nonleaders influence others, but leaders exert a disproportionate influence; that is, a leader is more influential than a nonleader.

Within an organization, leaders are often associated with supervisory positions; however, being a supervisor does not guarantee that you will be able to influence others. Furthermore, many leaders in organizations have no formal organizational title. Informal leaders often arise in work groups and may be more influential over the behavior of group members than the actual supervisors. Formal and informal leadership is an aspect of formal and informal roles that we discussed in Chapter 12. An organization assigns the role of leader (e.g., manager or supervisor) to a person. An individual develops the informal leader role through interaction with colleagues. A person who is particularly skilled might find that others look to him or her for guidance, perhaps more so than to their own supervisors. The amount of influence that a person has over others is determined by several personal and organizational factors, which we discuss next.

SOURCES OF INFLUENCE AND POWER

French and Raven's (1959) Bases of Power

French and Raven (1959) described how the influence or **power** one person has over another, such as a supervisor over a subordinate, is based on five factors. These factors, listed in Table 13-1, involve both individual characteristics and organizational conditions and concern the relationship between leader and follower, or supervisor and subordinate. Although these bases of power are discussed as characteristics of the supervisor, power arises from the interaction between subordinate and supervisor. The supervisor makes an influence attempt, but it is the behavior of the subordinate that determines whether or not it is effective. Table 13-1 indicates how supervisors can use each power base.

Expert power is based on the knowledge and expertise that the supervisor has. A subordinate is likely to follow the directives of a person who he or she believes has special knowledge or expertise about the issue at hand. Note that it is the expertise the subordi-

TABLE 13-1

The five French and Raven (1959) bases of interpersonal influence and power and how they can be used

BASES	USE
Expert	Give information
Referent	Get subordinates to like you
Legitimate	Get a high level position or rank
Reward	Give rewards for compliance
Coercive	Give punishments for noncompliance

Source: "The Bases of Social Power," by J.R.P. French, Jr., and B. Raven, 1959, in D. Cartwright (Ed.), *Studies in Social Power* (pp. 150–167), Ann Arbor, MI: Institute for Social Research.

nate believes the supervisor to have that is important, rather than the actual expertise. Although actual expertise affects perceived expertise, some people are better than others at appearing to be experts. Titles (doctor), college degrees (Ph.D.), certifications (certified public accountant), and distinctions (Nobel Prize winner) can enhance the perceived expert power of an individual. Expert power can be particularly effective because the subordinate is likely to be convinced that the supervisor's directive is correct and should be followed.

Referent power is the extent to which the subordinate likes and identifies with the supervisor. A person is likely to be influenced by another whom he or she admires or likes. This source of power can be developed through personal relationships with other people. It can also be enhanced by raising the status of the supervisor. A person with celebrity status is likely to have a high level of referent power. CEOs of several large companies have become national celebrities, such as Michael Eisner of Disney Corporation and Ted Turner of Turner Broadcasting.

Legitimate power is the power inherent in a supervisor's job title. It is derived from the subordinate's belief that the supervisor has the legitimate right or authority to be in charge. Much of the strength of this power derives from the subordinate's values about the rights of supervisors. If the subordinate refuses to recognize the authority of the supervisor, there will be no power in the supervisor's title.

Reward power is the ability of the supervisor to reward subordinates with bonuses, desirable job assignments, promotions, or raises. **Coercive power** is the ability of the supervisor to punish subordinates with disciplinary actions, fines, firing, or salary reductions. Organizations differ in the extent to which supervisors can give out punishments and rewards. In private companies it is not unusual for a supervisor to be able to give raises and promotions to a subordinate. In government organizations, an individual supervisor might not be able to do so because these rewards are determined by legislative action.

All five types of power can be effective if used properly. The major limitation of reward power is that subordinates might become accustomed to it and comply only when the reward is available. Coercive power can have detrimental effects because subordinates might become angry and strike back, either directly or indirectly. Reliance on coercive power can lead to counterproductive behavior by subordinates (see Chapter 10). Aguinis, Nesler, Quigley, Suk-Jae-Lee, and Tedeschi (1996) showed that expert, referent, and reward power were associated with good relations between college professors and their students. On the other hand, coercive power was associated with poor relations.

Yukl's (1989) Sources of Political Power

French and Raven's bases of power are concerned with the influences people have on one another in any setting. Yukl's (1989) sources of political power are concerned specifically with power in organizations. According to Yukl, *political action* is the process by which people gain and protect their power within the organization. He outlined three means by which political power is achieved and maintained in organizations (Figure 13-1).

Control over decision processes involves controlling and influencing important decisions in the organization, such as the allocation of resources. This sort of power can be achieved by serving on appropriate committees (e.g., finance) or taking on the right tasks (preparation of the budget). Influence in the U.S. Congress is based largely on being on the most powerful committees.

Forming coalitions means entering into agreements with others to support your position in return for support of the others' position. Again this is often seen in legislative bodies when different factions agree to support each other in favored positions. Senators who support an important issue such as equal employment opportunity might agree to help those who support the issue of gun control in return for support of their issue.

Co-optation involves trying to diffuse another faction's opposition by allowing its members to participate in the decision. The hope is that this will make it difficult for them to remain in opposition. For example, a local government that wishes to take action to reduce the pollution produced by local industry is sure to run into opposition. A political approach to reducing or co-opting that opposition would be to assign the task to a committee that included industry representation.

These sorts of political actions are quite common in both government and nongovernment organizations. Gaining influence in large organizations can be more a matter of achieving political rather than individual power. Even the president of the United States does not have the personal power to get laws enacted that might solve the nation's worst problems. Since Jimmy Carter, every U.S. president has campaigned on a promise to get Congress to pass a balanced federal budget. It wasn't until three administrations later that President Clinton was able to fulfill this promise.

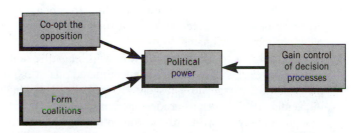

FIGURE 13-1
Yukl (1989) discusses how political power tactics can be a means of achieving political power in an organization. *Source: Leadership in Organizations* by G. A. Yukl, 1989, Englewood Cliffs, NJ: Prentice Hall.

ABUSE OF SUPERVISORY POWER

When used appropriately, the various forms of power can provide tools to enhance the functioning of organizations. They can also be used to help individuals to have positive feelings about work and to perform their jobs well, but there is a potentially negative side to power. Some supervisors will use their power to mistreat subordinates because the supervisor believes that punitive measures are necessary to get people to perform well. In other cases, it is done because the supervisor enjoys wielding power over others.

Supervisors who enjoy abusing others might do so in any number of ways. Employee harassment occurs when supervisors are free to demand that their subordinates do exactly what they are told regardless of the appropriateness of demands. Thus, an individual might be required to do personal favors or be punished. Some supervisors use a harsh and punitive style and may belittle subordinates for even minor mistakes. This produces an intimidating and uncomfortable work environment for subordinates.

Perhaps the best known form of power abuse is **sexual harassment**, which is behavior of a sexual nature that

Is unwanted

Can adversely affect a person's employment

Interferes with a person's job performance

Creates a hostile and intimidating work environment

The sorts of behaviors that comprise sexual harassment include

Unwelcome sexual advances and requests

Unwanted physical contact or touching

Use of offensive language

Repeated requests for a date

Threats of punishment for noncompliance with requests

Sexual harassment is illegal in the United States and many other countries. In the United States it is covered by civil rights legislation and is considered a form of discrimination. Many cases have resulted in lawsuits, with companies having to pay damages to employees in excess of $100,000. Although sexual harassment is the act of an individual, organizations have been held accountable for the behaviors of their employees. Thus, organizations are expected to prevent their supervisors from engaging in sexual harassment of their subordinates.

It is difficult to know exactly how widespread sexual harassment might be. Several surveys have asked women if they encountered one or more instances of behaviors that fit the definition (Fitzgerald, Drasgow, Hulin, Gelfand, & Magley, 1997; Schneider, Swan, & Fitzgerald, 1997), such as crude comments or jokes, or unwanted requests for a date. Although as many as two-thirds of women report experiencing such incidents, Fitzgerald et al. caution that these behaviors do not necessarily constitute harassment. Many of these behaviors only become harassment when they are unwanted and are repeated often enough to create a hostile or intimidating work environment. An isolated comment or simple request for a date is not harassment, so one should not interpret such surveys as indicating that most women have been victims.

Terpstra and Cook (1985) studied the nature of sexual harassment complaints filed with the Illinois Department of Human Rights over a two-year period beginning in 1981. There were 81 cases filed, 76 by women and 5 by men. Most cases involved what the researchers classified as the less serious behaviors of date requests, unwanted advances, unwanted physical contact (touching), and offensive language. The authors were surprised that there were relatively few cases of more serious behaviors, such as sexual extortion (threats of punishment for noncompliance). They concluded that the more serious behaviors are far less frequent than the less serious ones. Even the least serious can be devastating to an employee who must endure repeated uncomfortable interactions with a supervisor. Furthermore, most cases are unreported, so the 81 cases are likely only a fraction of the total number of incidents that undoubtedly occurred during that time.

Sexual and other forms of employee harassment are serious matters that organizations should attempt to control. When supervisors and other employees engage in certain forms of harassment, they can get their organizations into legal difficulties. The costs of legal problems, however, are probably quite small in comparison to the hidden costs to organizations. Terpstra and Cook (1985) noted that sexual harassment can lead to job stress, poor performance, absence, and turnover. The costs of these effects may be hard to measure, but they can have a tremendous detrimental impact on organizational functioning. In addition, these behaviors can be harmful to the well-being of employees. Organizations would be wise to make efforts to safeguard their employees from victimization by supervisors as well as others who abuse their power.

APPROACHES TO THE UNDERSTANDING OF LEADERSHIP

Many approaches to the study and understanding of leadership have been taken. The trait approach is concerned with determining the personal characteristics of good leaders. It asks the question,

"Who will make a good leader?"

The behavior approach is concerned with finding out which leader behaviors are effective. It asks the question,

"What do good leaders do?"

The contingency approach (Fielder's and path-goal) assumes that good leadership is a function of the interplay of the person, his or her behavior, and the situation. It asks the question,

"Under a given condition, who will be a good leader and what behavior is likely to be effective?"

The leader–member exchange theory and the charismatic/transformational approaches focus on the relationships between subordinates and supervisors. They ask the question,

"How does the interaction between subordinate and supervisor affect the subordinate's behavior?"

All of these approaches have contributed to our understanding of leadership, and we discuss them in this section. We also cover the Vroom–Yetton model for deciding how to approach decision-making tasks in work groups.

The Trait Approach

The oldest approach to the study of leadership is the *trait approach*. It is based on the presumptions that some people make better leaders than others and that it is possible to determine the traits of good leaders. Some proponents of this approach would argue that good leadership is a function of the person and that a person who is a good leader in one situation would be a good leader in any situation. It would follow that various leaders, such as Alexander the Great, Winston Churchill, Martin Luther King, Jr., and George Washington, could have been great leaders in other times and situations. This does not seem likely, however, since each man had different attributes and adopted a different approach to leadership that was appropriate to his circumstances.

Most of the research studies that have attempted to uncover the traits of good leaders have used one of two approaches. One approach used a methodology similar to employee selection studies, which were discussed in Chapter 6. A sample of leaders, typically supervisors in an organization, is identified for study. A criterion for leadership performance, typically job performance, is chosen. The supervisors are assessed on the criterion and on the personal traits of interest. These might include measures of various abilities, job experiences, motivation, and personality. Relationships between the personal characteristics and performance are interpreted as the effects of traits on leader performance.

Various studies have used many different measures of personal characteristics, as well as different measures of performance. Randle (1956), for example, assessed about 100 different traits of managers. Although many studies have used well-validated measures, many have used untested instruments developed for the particular study. Some of these measures were not of good quality, especially in early studies conducted before we fully understood some of the biases that affect psychological measurement. This has contributed to inconsistency of results across studies in predicting leader performance. Nevertheless, research on manager performance has shown that personal traits such as cognitive ability can predict managerial performance (Hogan, Curphy, & Hogan, 1994).

The second approach is concerned with *leader emergence*, that is, who in a group will become the leader. These studies had groups of people work on a laboratory task, and the criterion was who became the leader of the group. The performance of the leader would not usually be assessed. It is possible that the personal characteristics that resulted in an individual's becoming the leader (for example, physical attractiveness) would not necessarily result in that person's being a good leader.

It should come as no surprise that results across many of these studies have been inconsistent. Some studies found that certain characteristics were associated with leader emergence, whereas others did not. To make sense out of an inconsistent literature, Lord, de Vader, and Alliger (1986) conducted a meta-analysis to combine results across studies statistically. They found that intelligence, aggressiveness, decisiveness, and dominance were associated with leader emergence.

The Leader Behavior Approach

The *leader behavior approach* is concerned with what leaders do rather than what their personal characteristics might be. Although leader behavior studies have dealt with specific behaviors, most have concentrated on leadership styles. A *leadership style* is a cluster of related behaviors that represent an approach to dealing with subordinates. For example, some supervisors prefer to allow subordinates to have input into decisions that affect them. Such a style of asking advice and having discussions about issues is called *participative*. Other supervisors do not involve subordinates in decisions. Rather, they make the decision and announce it to the group. This style in which subordinates are given little input is called *autocratic*.

The most influential research program to study leader behaviors is the Ohio State Leadership Studies, which were begun in 1945 (Stogdill, 1963). This series of studies was designed to uncover the effects of specific supervisory behaviors on subordinates. The Ohio State researchers began by collecting about 1,800 critical incidents that represented either very good or very bad instances of supervisory behavior. They used these incidents as the basis for developing a 150-item questionnaire on leader behavior. The questionnaire was administered to several samples of employees, who answered each item about their supervisors. A complex statistical procedure called *factor analysis* was used to see if the 150 items could be reduced to a smaller number of underlying dimensions of leadership. The dimensions, which were based on the intercorrelations among the 150 items, showed that two aspects of leadership were represented, which they called consideration and initiating structure.

Consideration is the amount of concern that supervisors show for the happiness and welfare of their subordinates. It includes friendly and thoughtful behavior that makes the workplace pleasant for subordinates. **Initiating structure** is the extent to which the supervisor defines his or her own role and makes clear what is expected of subordinates. It includes assigning tasks to subordinates and scheduling the work. One of the major contributions of the Ohio State Leadership Studies was development of scales to assess these dimensions. The most widely used is the **Leader Behavior Description Questionnaire (LBDQ)**, which is completed by subordinates about their supervisor. Table 13-2 contains four items that assess consideration and four items that assess initiating structure.

Many studies have used the LBDQ in an attempt to discover the effects of leader behavior on subordinates. A good example is Fleishman and Harris's (1962) study of pro-

---

TABLE 13-2

Eight items from the consideration and initiating structure scales of the Leader Behavior Description Questionnaire (LBDQ), Form XII

Consideration Items
He or she is friendly and approachable.
He or she does little things to make it pleasant to be a member of the group.
He or she puts suggestions made by the group into operation.
He or she treats all members of the group as his or her equals.

Initiating Structure Items
He or she lets group members know what is expected of them.
He or she encourages the use of uniform procedures.
He or she tries out his or her ideas in the group.
He or she makes his or her attitudes clear to the group.

Note: Items were modified to eliminate the generic "he."

Source: *Manual for the Leader Behavior Description Questionnaire—Form XII* by R. M. Stogdill, 1963, Columbus: Ohio State University.

duction workers in a truck manufacturing plant. Data were collected from subordinates of 57 supervisors with the LBDQ. The grievance and turnover rates were also collected for each supervisor's work group. Grievances can be considered behavioral measures of dissatisfaction with conditions of work. In unionized and government organizations, grievances require hearings that can consume considerable employee time. An excessive grievance rate can destroy the efficiency of a work group because people are spending time in unproductive ways.

Fleishman and Harris (1962) found that the mean LBDQ scores for the supervisors were related to the grievance and turnover rates in their departments. Supervisors with low scores on consideration and high scores on initiating structure had higher turnover rates and more grievances among subordinates than supervisors who were high on consideration and low on initiating structure. The lowest scoring supervisors on consideration had a turnover rate that was about four times higher than the highest scoring supervisors (Figures 13-2 and 13-3).

Although it is tempting to interpret these results as a demonstration of the effects of leader behavior on important subordinate behaviors, there are two major difficulties in doing so. First, the LBDQ might not be a good indicator of supervisory behavior and may be telling us as much about subordinates as their supervisors. Several studies have attempted to find out what subordinate reports about their supervisors really mean. It has been found that the reports are affected by biases and stereotypes of the subordinate. In a series of studies, college students were asked to view a videotape of a supervisor interacting with subordinates. At random all subjects who watched the same tape were told that the supervisor was rated either high or low in performance. Subjects who were told that the supervisor was a good performer rated him differently on the LBDQ than subjects

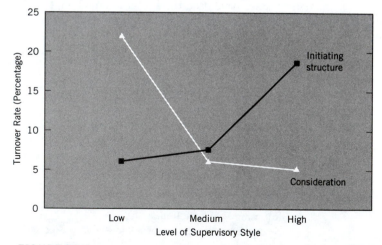

FIGURE 13-2

Turnover rate as a result of both the consideration and initiating structure of supervisors. *Source:* Adapted from "Patterns of Leadership Behavior Related to Employee Grievances and Turnover," by E. A. Fleishman and E. F. Harris, 1962, *Personnel Psychology, 15,* 43–56.

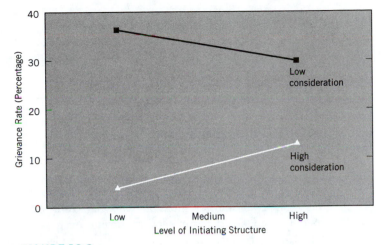

FIGURE 13-3

Grievance rate as a result of both the consideration and initiating structure of supervisors. *Source:* Adapted from "Patterns of Leadership Behavior Related to Employee Grievances and Turnover," by E. A.
Fleishman and E. F. Harris, 1962, *Personnel Psychology, 15,* 43–56.

who were told he was a poor performer (e.g., Lord, Binning, Rush, & Thomas, 1978;
Phillips & Lord, 1982).

The second problem concerns drawing causal conclusions from data collected at one
time in a cross-sectional research design (see Chapter 2). We cannot be certain from a
study such as Fleishman and Harris's (1962) if the grievance and turnover rates are
caused by supervisor behavior or if supervisor behavior is caused by the grievance and
turnover rate. Studies have shown that supervisor behavior can be affected by subordinate
behavior (e.g., Lowin & Craig, 1968), particularly job performance. Yukl (1989) concluded that a reciprocal relationship probably exists between supervisor style and subordinate behavior. A supervisor whose subordinates are filing many grievances might
become angry and reduce consideration behavior. This might make subordinates more
angry and lead them to file more grievances, which will lead to even less consideration,
and so on. These sorts of reciprocal processes have rarely been studied in I/O psychology.

At the present time it seems that supervisory styles can have effects on subordinates.
Participatory practices have been linked to both job performance and job satisfaction, but
these linkages are not always strong (Wagner, 1994). Part of the reason for small effects
might have to do with the areas in which employees are allowed to participate. Sagie and
Koslowsky (1994) found larger relations between perceived participation and job satisfaction when the participation involved deciding how to implement a change at work rather
than whether or not to implement it. They concluded that it is important to consider the
kinds of decisions appropriate for subordinate participation.

Participation has been shown to work in several studies. In others, however, it has not
had positive effects. For example, Bragg and Andrews (1973) conducted a study in which
participation worked in two of three departments. At the beginning of the study, the supervisor of a hospital laundry department changed from an autocratic to a participative

style. Over the next 18 months there were positive effects on attendance, job performance (a 42% increase), and job satisfaction. The supervisory approach was successfully introduced in the medical records department but not in the nursing department. The reasons why participatory styles sometimes succeed and sometimes fail are complex and may relate to the situations under which they are tried. This brings us to the basic idea of contingency theory: The situation interacts with leader characteristics and leader behavior.

Fiedler's Contingency Theory

The trait approach assumes that certain characteristics of people will make them good leaders. The behavior approach presumes that certain leader behaviors will be effective regardless of the situation. **Fiedler's contingency theory** states that leadership is a function of both the person and the situation. One characteristic of the leader and three characteristics of the situation determine leadership effectiveness.

The theory begins with the characteristic of the leader, which Fiedler (1978) refers to as the *motivational structure* of the leader. The motivation structure is assessed with a self-report instrument called the **Least Preferred Coworker (LPC) scale**. Although the name implies that it assesses the co-worker, the scale actually measures a characteristic of the leader, not the subordinate. The LPC asks the leader to think about the person with whom he or she has had the most trouble working, that is, the co-worker with whom he or she would least like to work. The leader then describes his or her least preferred co-worker using a semantic differential type scale (Osgood, Tannenbaum, & Suci, 1957). The LPC consists of 18 bipolar adjective items, which are scales in which a person indicates which of two words with opposite meaning best describes someone, such as pleasant versus unpleasant or friendly versus unfriendly. (Examples from the LPC scale appear in Table 13-3.)

Fiedler's theory is also concerned with the situational variable of leader situational control. *Situational control* concerns the amount of power and influence the leader has over subordinates. It is the extent to which the supervisor's actions will predictably lead to subordinate behavior. There are three characteristics of the leadership situation that comprise situational control. *Leader-member relations* is the extent to which subordinates get along with and support their supervisors. *Task structure* is the extent to which subordinate job tasks are clearly and specifically defined. *Position power* refers to the amount of power and influence that the supervisor has, including the ability to give out rewards and punishments. A supervisor with good leader–member relations, highly structured tasks for subordinates, and high position power will be in a situation of high control. A supervisor

TABLE 13-3
Four items from Fiedler's (1978) Least Preferred Coworker Scale (LPC)

Pleasant	- -	Unpleasant
Friendly	- -	Unfriendly
Rejecting	- -	Accepting
Tense	- -	Relaxed

Source: "The Contingency Model and the Dynamics of the Leadership Process" (pp. 59–112), by F. E. Fiedler, 1978, in L. Berkowitz (Ed.), *Advances in Experimental Social Psychology, 11,* New York: Academic Press.

with poor leader–member relations, low task structure for subordinates, and low position power will be in a situation of low control.

According to Fiedler's (1978) theory, the LPC of the supervisor determines the situations in which he or she will perform well. Individuals who are low on LPC do well under both very high and very low situational control. Individuals who are high on LPC will do best under conditions of moderate situational control. Take, for example, the situation in which the leader doesn't get along well with subordinates, the subordinates have unstructured tasks, and the leader has little power. This is an unfavorable situation, and the LPC leader would be expected to be more effective than the high LPC leader. However, if the situation is moderately favorable, where relations are poor, but task structure is high and the leader has moderate power, the high LPC person should be more effective than the low LPC person. Figure 13-4 illustrates how supervisor performance is a function of situational control for individuals high and low in LPC.

Research on contingency theory has provided mixed support for its validity, and Fiedler certainly has his critics. Two meta-analyses combined the results of many tests of the theory (Peters, Hartke, & Pohlmann, 1985; Strube & Garcia, 1981). Both found that leader performance was a joint function of LPC and situational control, although the predictions of the theory were not completely upheld. What is not clear at the present time is exactly why LPC and situational control interact. The major difficulty is that no one, not even Fiedler, is quite sure what LPC represents. LPC was intended to measure something about leader motivation, but it is not clear that motivation is assessed. Fiedler (1978) states that low LPC leaders are more concerned with getting tasks done than with having good relationships with subordinates, whereas high LPC leaders have the opposite motivations, being more concerned with having good relationships with subordinates than

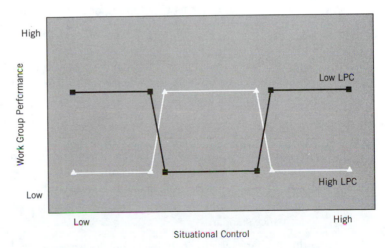

FIGURE 13-4

Group performance as a result of both situational control and LPC of the leader. *Source:* Adapted from "The Contingency Model and the Dynamics of the Leadership Process," by F. E. Fiedler, 1978, in L. Berkowitz (Ed.), *Advances in Experimental Social Psychology, 11,* New York: Academic Press.

with getting the job done. At this time, all we can say for sure is that the LPC assesses some unknown but important characteristic of leaders.

Although the theory states that the situation determines the best leader characteristics, Fiedler does not believe that a supervisor should attempt to adapt his or her style to the particular situation. He believes that supervisors should modify the situation to be appropriate to their own leadership style. To this end he has developed a training program called **Leader Match**. Fiedler (1978) summarized the results of several field experiments comparing Leader Match-trained supervisors with untrained controls. The results showed better group performance for the trained supervisors. Some question has been raised, however, about whether Leader Match training results in leaders changing the situation according to theory, or if the results of the Leader Match research are due to other factors (Jago & Ragan, 1986).

Despite the criticisms of the theory, Fiedler has been one of the most influential people in the study of leadership. His major contribution has been to show us that leadership involves the complex interaction of leader characteristics with the leadership situation. His work has been extended by theorists who have developed more complex contingency theories. One of these is path-goal theory, which we discuss next.

Path-Goal Theory

Path-goal theory (House & Mitchell, 1974) is another contingency theory that is more complex than Fiedler's. It posits that subordinate job performance and satisfaction result from the interplay of situational characteristics, subordinate characteristics, and supervisor style. The basic idea, which is based on expectancy theory, is that the supervisor can enhance the motivation and satisfaction of subordinates by providing rewards for good job performance and by making it easier for subordinates to achieve their task goals. Supervisors can accomplish this by adopting one of four supervisory styles, the efficacy of which is determined by situational and subordinate characteristics.

The four supervisory styles are

Supportive style. This style is similar to the Ohio State Leadership Studies' style of consideration. It involves showing concern for the needs and welfare of subordinates.

Directive style. This style is similar to the Ohio State Leadership Studies' style of initiating structure. It involves the structuring of job tasks for subordinates and letting them know what is expected.

Participative style. This style involves seeking input from subordinates and allowing them to participate in decision making.

Achievement style. This style involves emphasizing achievement and good performance. It includes the setting of challenging task goals and emphasizing high performance standards.

Subordinate characteristics include personality variables, such as locus of control and self-perceived ability. Locus of control is the extent to which subordinates believe that they can control rewards in their lives. A person with an internal locus of control believes that he or she is able to control rewards. A person with an external locus of control believes that rewards are controlled by others or by outside forces. Self-perceived ability is the extent to which the subordinate believes he or she is capable of doing the task well. It is similar to self-efficacy, which was discussed in Chapter 8, but it is specific to the particular task at hand. Situational characteristics include aspects of tasks, such as dangerousness, repetitiveness, and structure.

House and Mitchell (1974) derived a series of hypotheses based on the basic ideas of the theory. These hypotheses describe how certain supervisory styles will affect subordinates under certain conditions. For example,

1. When tasks are boring, dangerous, stressful, or tedious, a supportive style will be the most appropriate. Subordinates who must deal with these situations will have their anxiety lowered and their self-esteem raised by a supportive supervisor.

2. When tasks are unstructured and subordinates are inexperienced, a directive style will be most appropriate because subordinates will be uncertain about what to do. A directive supervisor will increase subordinates' effort and satisfaction by telling them what is expected and what they should do.

Unfortunately, researchers have focused attention on only a few of the several hypotheses of path-goal theory, particularly the second hypothesis given here. Although some of this research has supported the theory (Podsakoff, MacKenzie, Ahearne, & Bommer, 1995), many of the findings are inconsistent (Wofford & Liska, 1993). In part, the inconsistency may be due to methodological weaknesses in some of the studies. Another possibility is that some of the propositions are not quite correct.

Keller (1989) noted that not all individuals are bothered by lack of structure on a job and in fact some people might prefer it. People who prefer unstructured tasks should be

RESEARCH IN DETAIL

ONE OF THE hypotheses of path-goal theory is that when task structure is low, initiating structure by the supervisor will result in subordinate satisfaction. In other words, when subordinates are unsure about what is expected, clarification by the supervisor will be appreciated. Keller (1989) noted that research support for this hypothesis has been inconsistent across studies. He reasoned that a mistake of path-goal theory was assuming that all employees would find lack of structure unpleasant. His hypothesis was that the subordinate's need for clarity would determine his or her reaction to initiating structure in a job with low structure.

In this study, a survey was conducted among professionals in research and development (R&D) organizations. Because this work involves discovering new knowledge and technologies, an R&D job can have little structure. Respondents to the survey completed scales to assess the extent to which they need and prefer clarity on the job, the initiating structure of their supervisor, and their job satisfaction.

Data analyses showed that Keller's hypothesis was correct. Those individuals with a high need for clarity were more satisfied with high-initiating structure than low-initiating structure. Individuals with a low need for clarity were more satisfied with low-initiating structure than high-initiating structure. This study suggests that supervisors should consider the personality of each subordinate in deciding the most appropriate supervision method.

Source: Keller, R. T. (1989). A test of the path-goal theory of leadership with need for clarity as a moderator in research and development organizations. *Journal of Applied Psychology, 74,* 208–212.

more satisfied with a low-structure job and would respond negatively to a directive supervisory style. Samples of employees from four organizations were assessed on subordinate need for structure, job performance, job satisfaction, and supervisor directive style (Keller, 1989). The results were consistent with predictions that subordinates who had a high need for structure would respond favorably to directive supervision (see the Research in Detail box in this chapter). Keller's study suggests that one of the propositions should be modified to take subordinate personality into account.

Future research will be needed to show which of the original House and Mitchell (1974) hypotheses can be supported. It seems likely, in light of Keller's (1989) findings, that new hypotheses involving the interplay of situations, subordinates, and supervisors will be developed. One implication of Keller's findings is that different supervisory approaches might be necessary with different subordinates. This brings us to the leader–member exchange theory of leadership, which is concerned with the interactions of each subordinate-supervisor dyad or pair.

Leader–Member Exchange (LMX) Theory

The **leader–member exchange (LMX) theory** (Dansereau, Graen, & Haga, 1975) focuses on the subordinate–supervisor dyad rather than on the subordinate and work group. Dansereau et al. argue that one of the major limitations of most leadership research is its implicit assumption that each supervisor's group of subordinates is sufficiently homogeneous to justify studying it as a unit and that each supervisor adopts the same style across all subordinates. On the contrary, they propose that supervisors will treat individual subordinates differently, and that over time the relationships between supervisors and subordinates will evolve.

Dansereau et al. (1975) discussed two types of relationships that develop between supervisors and subordinates. The **cadre** or **in-group** consists of subordinates who are trusted and influential members of the work group. The supervisor treats them with consideration and adopts a participative style with them. The **hired hands** or **out-group**, by contrast, are subordinates who are supervised with a directive style and are given little input into decisions. These relationships evolve over time, with characteristics of subordinates affecting the category in which they find themselves. To become part of the cadre, a subordinate must be perceived as dependable and hard working. In return for cadre status, a subordinate must be prepared to exert effort on the job beyond the minimum expected.

In their research, Dansereau et al. (1975) found that within work groups supervisors had two distinct groups in terms of how much participation was allowed. Members of the cadre were more satisfied with their jobs, believed they had better relations with supervisors, and were less likely to quit than the hired hands. Care must be taken, however, in concluding that the satisfaction and turnover differences were the result of supervisor treatment. It is likely that supervisor behavior toward each subordinate was as much a function of the subordinate's job performance as it was a cause of that performance (Bauer & Green, 1996).

One contribution of the leader–member exchange approach is that it focused attention on the importance of individual relationships within each supervisor–subordinate dyad. The idea was the basis of an intervention study in which supervisors were trained to enhance their relationships with each subordinate. Graen, Novak, and Sommerkamp

(1982) conducted a field experiment in which one group of supervisors was trained in leader–member exchange. The training was intended to help supervisors improve their relationships with subordinates. Each trained supervisor had meetings with each subordinate to discuss work issues and the working relationship between them. The subordinates of the trained supervisors subsequently had better job performance and higher job satisfaction than a control group in which supervisors were not trained.

Research has shown that the quality of LMX relationships, as perceived by subordinates, is associated with several important variables. Wayne, Shore, and Liden (1997) found that quality of LMX correlated with several subordinate outcomes. Those with good relationships with supervisors were less likely to intend to quit and more likely to be good performers, engage in organizational citizenship behavior, and have high organizational commitment. Wilhelm, Herd, and Steiner (1993) found that good relationships with supervisors was associated with high levels of job satisfaction. In their meta-analysis of 79 studies, Gerstner and Day (1997) showed that individuals who had good relationships with their supervisors tended to perform better, had higher job satisfaction, were more committed to their employers, and perceived the job as less stressful than individuals with poor relationships with supervisors.

There have been criticisms and limitations noted about the LMX theory of leadership. First, differential treatment of subordinates within a work group can be destructive (Yukl, 1989). Equity theory, as discussed in Chapter 8, describes how employees can react negatively to unequal treatment. The higher turnover rate and lower job satisfaction of the hired hands in the Dansereau et al. (1975) study might well be interpreted as a response to inequity. Schriesheim (1980) points out that supervisors often direct influence attempts at entire work groups at one time, rather than treating each individual differently. She believes that a focus on both work groups and individual dyads makes the most sense for understanding leadership. LMX theory helped focus attention on the relationship between subordinate and supervisor. It also led to an understanding that supervisors do not act the same way with all subordinates.

Transformational Leadership Theory

Transformational leadership theory deals with leaders who have considerable and unusual influence over their followers, or in other words are **charismatic**. It is in some ways a return to the trait approach, by focusing on characteristics of leaders in relation to effectiveness. However, it differs from prior approaches in going beyond linking traits to performance, and it attempts to determine how leaders affect their followers. Furthermore, where other theories of leadership explain the relationships between most supervisors and subordinates, the focus here is specifically on charismatic or **transformational leaders** who are unusual in how their followers become devoted to them. Many examples of charismatic and transformational leaders can be found throughout our history. They include Abraham Lincoln, Winston Churchill, John F. Kennedy, and Martin Luther King, Jr. In more recent times, Presidents Ronald Reagan and Bill Clinton have been often noted as being charismatic to their followers, although one is charismatic to conservatives and the other to liberals.

Several theories are considered transformational theories (Yukl, 1989), as they are variations on the same underlying theme. A leader who is charismatic and has a profound effect on followers is transformational. Such a leader can transform followers' aspirations, needs, preferences, and values, by providing a vision of something worthwhile to achieve. Followers become motivated to make personal sacrifices to reach the goals set forth by the leader. These goals might be positive, such as John F. Kennedy's call for a successful manned mission to the moon before the end of the 1960s. It can also be something negative, such as the call to go to war.

Charisma can be thought of as a relationship between a leader and follower. Gardner and Avolio (1998) explain that certain leaders are able to convince followers of their competence and the importance of a vision. They engage in behaviors that make them appear to be creative, innovative, powerful, and trustworthy. Much of the leader's influence derives from beliefs by the followers that only by following the leader will they be able to achieve the vision, such as making the company profitable.

Although there is a danger in transformational leaders convincing followers to engage in unacceptable behavior, a leader's power can be a tool to accomplish positive goals. In organizations, transformational leaders can convince followers to make extraordinary efforts to achieve worthwhile objectives, such as producing a superior product, providing an important service, solving a social problem, or finding a cure for a disease. These leaders can help provide direction for an organization through their vision and can help motivate employees to pursue that vision. Such leaders can be highly effective.

Research on transformational leadership shows that it relates to several subordinate variables that are important for organizational functioning. For example, individuals who perceive their supervisors to be transformational tend to be high on organizational citizenship behavior and satisfaction with supervision (Koh, Steers, & Terborg, 1995). They also report less intention of quitting and more organizational commitment (Bycio, Hackett, & Allen, 1995). Furthermore, although it might seem that transformational leadership is innate, researchers have been successful at training people to exhibit the behaviors. For example, Kirkpatrick and Locke (1996) trained two actors to assume the role of a transformational leader, which observers were able to accurately detect. Barling, Weber, and Kelloway (1996) were able to successfully train bank managers to be more transformational, and showed that training had an impact on the performance of their branches.

Relatively little research has been conducted on transformational leadership. However, existing studies are quite suggestive that this leadership approach has considerable potential for application. If transformational leaders have happier and more productive subordinates, and if it can be trained, organizations would benefit by encouraging supervisors to adopt this approach. More studies like Barling et al. (1996) are needed to confirm their promising results.

Vroom–Yetton Model

The **Vroom-Yetton model** (Vroom & Yetton, 1973) is a different kind of leadership theory from theories we have discussed so far. Rather than describing how the leadership process works, Vroom–Yetton is a prescriptive model that indicates the supervisory approach to use in a given situation. The model is based on psychological principles that specify the likely outcomes of the style that a supervisor uses when a work group decision needs to be made. These principles were placed into a decision tree (Figure 13-5) that a supervisor can use to decide how to approach a decision-making task with his or her work group.

The model specifies five approaches to making a decision that range from the auto-

A. Does the problem possess a quality requirement?
B. Do you have sufficient information to make a high-quality decision?
C. Is the problem structured?
D. Is acceptance of decision by subordinates important for effective implementation?
E. If you were to make the decision by yourself, is it reasonably certain that it would be accepted by your subordinates?
F. Do subordinates share the organizational goals to be attained in solving this problem?
G. Is conflict among subordinates over preferred solutions likely?

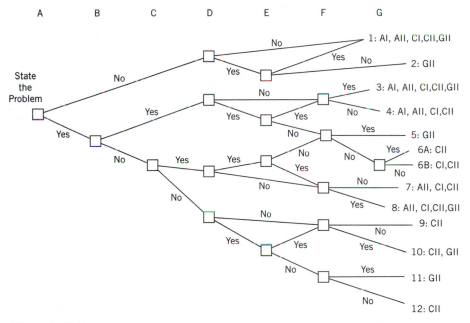

FIGURE 13-5

The Vroom–Yetton decision tree for group decisions, and the seven lettered questions that determine the approach that should be used. *Source: Leadership and Decision-Making* by V. H. Vroom and P. W. Yetton, 1973, Pittsburgh: University of Pittsburgh Press. Reprinted by permission of the University of Pittsburgh Press.

cratic (supervisor makes decision alone) to the democratic (supervisor and work group make the decision together). It also specifies seven problem attributes, which are phrased as questions, such as,

"Does the problem possess a quality requirement?"

and

"Do you have enough information to make a high-quality decision?"

Answers to the seven questions determine the best decision-making approach to use. All five approaches are shown in Table 13-4, and the problem attribute questions are shown in Figure 13-5.

Vroom and Yetton (1973) provided decision trees that can easily be used to follow the answers to all seven questions to the recommended decision-making approaches. The

TABLE 13-4
The five Vroom–Yetton (1973) approaches to making a group decision

AI	Make the decision yourself.
AII	Get information from subordinates and then make the decision yourself.
CI	Share the problem with selected subordinates individually, get their input, and then make the decision yourself.
CII	Share the problem with subordinates in a meeting, get their input, and then make the decision yourself.
GII	Share the problem with subordinates in a meeting, and the group makes the decision.

Source: Leadership and Decision-Making, by V. H. Vroom and P. W. Yetton, 1973, Pittsburgh: University of Pittsburgh Press.

specific approach taken depends on whether you wish to minimize the time necessary for a decision or the likelihood of group acceptance of the decision. The letters over the top of the decision tree shown in Figure 13-5 represent the seven questions, which are shown at the top of the figure. Each square in the tree represents the answer to the question that is associated with the letter. For example, the leftmost square at the beginning of the tree represents the answer to the question, "Does the problem possess a quality requirement?" If the answer is yes, you follow the lower line with "yes" written above it. If the answer is no, you follow the upper line with "no" written above it. You trace through the tree from left to right, answering each question when you get to a square and following the yes/no answer until you reach the end of a branch. Here you will find the recommended approach, AI to GII.

A limited number of studies have tested the Vroom–Yetton model. For the most part the findings support the recommendations of the theory. Vroom and Jago (1988) compiled results across six studies that compared the effectiveness of decisions that conformed with those that failed to conform to the theory's advice. The success rate for decisions made in accordance with the theory was higher than for decisions made in violation of it—62% versus 37%, respectively. On the other hand, Field and House (1990) provided only mixed support for the theory. They had a sample of supervisors and their subordinates report on the process and effectiveness of a decision. Although the supervisor data supported the Vroom–Yetton model, the subordinate data did not. Field and House were hesitant to conclude that the theory was invalid and called for additional research to test it.

Vroom and Jago (1988), noting limitations to the Vroom–Yetton model, presented a revised version, which was more complex. They added problem attribute questions and provided equations whereby answers to questions could be combined mathematically. Perhaps most helpful for a practicing manager who wishes to use the advice of the theory is a computer program that they developed. The program asks a number of questions and outputs specific advice.

The Vroom–Yetton model and now the Vroom–Jago model have the potential to be the most useful of the leadership theories from the perspective of the practicing manager who wishes to use the latest findings to guide his or her supervisory approach. At the present time the research findings have been promising, but too few studies have been conducted in field settings to test whether or not following the theory always leads to better decision outcomes.

WOMEN IN LEADERSHIP POSITIONS

Women have made considerable strides in achieving management and supervisory positions in organizations. It has been estimated that by 1990, about 40% of all management jobs in the United States were held by women (Morrison & Von Glinow, 1990). Despite their success at the lower levels of management, women are still underrepresented at the higher levels of organizations. Although estimates vary, it appears that women hold somewhere between 2% and 4% of high-level management and executive jobs (Morrison & Von Glinow, 1990; Snyder, Verderber, Langmeyer, & Myers, 1992). Furthermore, a study of manager career progression in Fortune 500 companies found that, although women were as likely as men to be promoted, their salary progression lagged significantly behind that of their male colleagues (Stroh, Brett, & Reilly, 1992). A more recent study of high-level executives in a financial services corporation found little difference between men and women's compensation (Lyness & Thompson, 1997), offering hope that the discrepancies are declining at higher organizational levels .

What do these two women have in common? They were both leaders of their countries. Although the United States has never had a woman as president, other countries have had female leaders. Both Golda Meir of Israel (left) and Margaret Thatcher of England (right) were prime ministers of their countries.

Although women are having more difficulty than men achieving high-level positions in most organizations, this problem is not found in all organizations. Powell and Butterfield (1994) found that females who applied for promotion were more (not less) likely than men to be promoted to top management in the U.S. civil service. In part, the gender difference was attributed to better job performance by the female applicants. The lack of bias against women may have been due to fairer promotion practices and commitment to equal employment opportunity in government agencies.

Many explanations have been advanced for the **glass ceiling** phenomenon that symbolizes women's difficulty in getting beyond the lower levels of management. Some of these explanations have focused on differences between men and women in their career preparation and their attitudes. Although gender differences might account for some of the glass ceiling effect, they do not even approach being a complete explanation (Morrison & Von Glinow, 1990). For example, Snyder et al. (1992) compared male and female employees of a social service agency on variables that have been hypothesized as explanations for women's poor career progression. They found no gender differences on organizational commitment or self-ratings of perceived work competence.

A more likely explanation has to do with the attitudes and stereotypes of those at the top levels of organizations who make decisions about hiring. Research by Virginia Schein and her colleagues (Schein, Mueller, Lituchy, & Liu, 1996) demonstrated how subtle stereotypes about characteristics of men and women put women at a disadvantage for management selection. They asked people to describe the characteristics of managers, men, and women and found that the description of managers overlapped with descriptions of men but not descriptions of women. It was concluded that the reason a woman might have difficulty getting promoted is that she is not seen as having the characteristics necessary for the position. It is not that the decision maker is consciously discriminating against women. Rather, the male candidates seem to fit the requirements for the job better than the female candidates. According to this view, equal access to high-level management jobs will require attitude change on the part of those who do the hiring. Furthermore, this phenomenon seems to be universal, for they found similar results in China, England, Germany, Japan, and the United States.

Somewhat more encouraging findings can be found in a study by Heilman, Block, Martell, and Simon (1989). When their subjects were asked about the characteristics of successful female managers, rather than just females, they were seen as being very much like managers in general. These researchers noted that views of a woman change when she is a successful manager. As the number of women in management increases, these results predict that they will be seen as having the appropriate characteristics.

Powell and Butterfield (1994) suggested that the federal government may be a model of how to eliminate the glass ceiling. Important factors include a strong management commitment to equal employment opportunity and uniform selection procedures that reduce subjectivity in decisions.

Gender and Leadership Style

Do men and women in leadership positions differ in their supervisory styles? Our stereotypes of men and women suggest that women would be more concerned with the feelings and emotional well-being of subordinates (consideration) and men would be more concerned with getting the job done (initiating structure). Research on gender differences in leadership suggests that the answer is complex.

Eagly and Johnson (1990) conducted a meta-analysis of studies that compared the leadership styles of men and women. They combined the results of over 160 leadership studies and arrived at several conclusions. One is that the stereotypic styles of men being high in structure and women being high in consideration have been found in laboratory research but not in field studies with actual leaders. They had two explanations for this finding. First, in an organizational setting, there are environmental constraints and requirements that may force male and female supervisors to adopt similar styles. Second, organizations may select women who have leadership styles similar to men's. In laboratory studies, subjects are selected more randomly, and there are fewer constraints on the leader behaviors that the subject adopts. Thus, whereas females may be inclined to supervise differently than men do, organizational settings do not allow them to express that inclination.

On the other hand, when men and women were compared on their autocratic or democratic tendencies, gender differences were found in both the laboratory and field. Men have been found to be more autocratic and women more democratic in their styles. Eagly and Johnson (1990) pointed out that each style will probably be more effective under different organizational circumstances. They noted that research is needed to determine whether there are gender differences in actual supervisory performance.

Men and women have also been compared in the extent to which their subordinates see them as transformational. Bass, Avolio, and Atwater (1996), based on three samples, found that women were either the same or higher on transformational leadership than men. Unfortunately, their study does not permit conclusions about effectiveness. Nevertheless, it suggests that there are gender differences in leadership style.

FUTURE ISSUES AND CHALLENGES

One of the biggest challenges for the future of leadership in organizations concerns the increasing diversity of the workplace. In most large organizations the workplace is becoming increasingly female and multicultural, from both the hiring of increasing numbers of minority members and the globalization of the world economy. Leadership is affected in two areas.

First, more divergent and flexible methods need to be developed for supervisors to deal with a more varied group of subordinates. This might involve education in appropriate behaviors for different countries and cultures and increased sensitivity to issues that might not have existed with more homogeneous groups. For example, the introduction of women into formerly male-dominated jobs has produced conflicts that supervisors must be prepared to mediate. Sexist language that might once have been the norm in an all-male work group will now offend many female co-workers. Supervisors need to find ways to deal with such issues in a constructive and effective way.

Second, the problem of the glass ceiling, which exists for minorities as well as women, needs to be addressed in the future. At present minorities and women have a difficult time progressing in their careers for many reasons. Few effective solutions have been implemented, resulting in limited progress for these groups. It is imperative from the perspective of both employees and organizations that ways be found to ensure that the best people are placed in leadership positions.

CHAPTER SUMMARY

Leadership is an important function in organizations in which the efforts of many individuals must be coordinated and directed. Leadership refers to the disproportionate influence that one person has over others, and in organizations it is typically associated with management and supervisory positions. Leaders' influence over their followers is based on a number of factors. French and Raven (1959) provided five bases of power and influence

Expert

Referent

Legitimate

Reward

Coercive

Yukl (1989) added the political influence tactics of

Controlling decisions

Coalition formation

Co-optation

There have been many approaches to the study of leadership. The trait approach attempts to find characteristics that make people good leaders. The leader behavior approach, represented by the Ohio State Leadership Studies, views leadership from the perspective of behaviors that are and are not effective. Contingency theories, such as Fiedler's and path-goal, state that leadership is a complex interaction of leader characteristics and the leadership situation. The leader–member exchange theory points out that leadership can be fully understood only by focusing attention on the often unique interactions of a supervisor with each subordinate. Charismatic and transformational leadership theories look at the way some leaders are able to have a profound influence on the attitudes, beliefs, behaviors, and values of subordinates. Finally, the Vroom–Yetton model and its successor the Vroom–Jago model are prescriptive theories that tell a supervisor how best to approach a decision situation.

Although women have made great strides in the workplace, they still have a difficult time breaking through the glass ceiling into high-level management positions. Perhaps the best explanation for this phenomenon has to do with the stereotypes of women's behavior. It is interesting that research has found few differences in the consideration and initiating structure styles of men and women managers, but women seem to be more democratic than men.

THIS CASE IS about a project carried out by Dr. Kathleen McNelis to identify the characteristics her organization would require for the manager of the future. Dr. McNelis received her Ph.D. in I/O psychology in 1985 from Ohio State University. She is currently the director of human resource development at Florida Progress Corporation, St. Petersburg, FL, an electric utility company. Her main job responsibilities are executive assessment for selection, executive education, organizational development, and planning and selection for international assignments. During her tenure with the company, she has been involved with conducting surveys of employee attitudes, developing and validating tests, running an assessment center, and training.

The future manager project is part of an organizational effort to respond to rapid social and technological change. The effort involves planning for the future human resource needs of the company, including figuring out what sorts of competencies and skills future managers will need.

Assessing the competencies (KSAOs from Chapter 3) requires a form of job analysis that considers the future requirements of the job. Dr. McNelis used several procedures, including group interviews, individual interviews, and questionnaires. Managers at all levels were asked to identify competencies for jobs that would be produced by a plan developed for the future of the company.

Specific competencies that were identified included the abilities to make independent decisions and to innovate, the ability to manage and handle change, identification with management values such as ethics, and effective leadership. The next step of the project was to develop a special assessment center (see Chapter 5) to assess the competencies of present managers. Individuals who were assessed got a summary of their improvement areas. Individual training plans were developed for each person, allowing the person to build skills in needed areas. Rather than developing a manager training program, skill development was done individually, mostly through self-study. For example, the company created a self-development learning center that was stocked with appropriate materials to learn these competencies. Computer-based training, much of it on the internet, was also available. The goal was to have company managers ready for the future by enhancing skills that will be needed at a later time.

Discussion Questions

1. Will managers of the future need different skills than the managers of today?

2. What are the major skills necessary for good managerial performance today?

3. Do power company managers need different skills than managers of other organizations?

4. How well does a self-study approach work with managers in a company, and what elements are necessary for success?

ORGANIZATIONAL DEVELOPMENT AND THEORY

So far our focus in this book has been on the individual employee or small groups of employees in the context of the organization. In this last chapter, we change our perspective from the individual to the organization itself. We deal with two important topics—organizational development and organizational theory.

Organizations in the modern industrialized world find themselves in a rapidly evolving environment that requires appropriate changes in both their structure and function. The field of *organizational development* helps organizations make changes that are rationally planned and implemented. Organizational change is often forced by circumstances and crises that are beyond the control of those in charge, which result in hurried changes in response to an emergency. Such precipitous changes can be damaging to the organization in the long term.

For example, many organizations today are experiencing *downsizing*—reduction in the number of employees. Although downsizing is often necessary, it is too often carried out from a purely economic perspective without consideration of the effects on employees and on the organization itself. The projected savings from layoffs may never materialize for several reasons; for example, the remaining employees are too demotivated to be effective, and too many of the best employees have left. Organizational development can help by considering the human side of organizational change and the best way to carry it out so that the organization remains effective. In this chapter, we explore how organizational development can help and some of the specific techniques involved.

Organizational theories describe how organizations work. Some focus on the structure of organizations, including the various components and how they interrelate. Others are concerned with the interpersonal aspects of organizations, including communication and how people relate to one another. Finally, some focus on the interaction of the interpersonal and technical sides of organizations. In other words, how do people affect the technology of the organization, and how does the technology affect people? All of these approaches are discussed in this chapter as we cover four important organizational theories.

Objectives   **The student who studies this chapter should be able to:**

1. Explain what organizational development is and how it is applied.
2. Describe the organizational development techniques discussed and indicate the effectiveness of each.
3. Discuss each of the organizational theories presented in the chapter.
4. Show the linkages among the four organizational theories discussed.

ORGANIZATIONAL DEVELOPMENT

Organizational development (OD) is a family of techniques designed to help organizations change for the better. They involve the use of behavioral science principles and procedures that help employees improve performance and interact with co-workers more effectively. An OD effort involves an entire organization or a large component of it, and it is intended to result in substantial changes in how the organization operates. Such changes can involve a reorganization in which departments are created and eliminated and functions are moved from area to area and person to person. An OD effort, however, is typically much more than a reorganization. It usually involves changing how people do their work, how they communicate with one another, and how they coordinate their efforts.

An OD effort or program involves employees at all levels of the organization. It is implemented by a person or persons referred to as change agents. The **change agent** is the catalyst for change within the organization. He or she is an expert in working with organizations to improve their functioning. The change agent might be an employee of the organization, as in the case at the end of the chapter. In most instances, however, the change agent is an outside consultant who is hired to implement the OD program. Many consulting firms throughout the world specialize in organizational development.

The change agent's job is to act as a guide and trainer for the organizational development process. He or she might conduct classes in which employees are trained in new ways to communicate or operate within their organizations. He or she might conduct group sessions during which organization members plan changes that will improve the organization. The role of the change agent in these sessions is to serve as the group facilitator or moderator to keep everyone focused on the task at hand and to help mediate disputes among people. In short, the change agent assists the organization members in their OD effort. The change agent usually does not come into the organization with a specific plan for change, only the process by which employees can redesign their organization.

Several specific organizational change techniques are frequently used in OD efforts. Four will be discussed in this chapter: management by objectives (MBO), survey feedback, team building, and T-groups. They have all been used extensively by organizations throughout the world.

Management by Objectives

Management by objectives (MBO) is an organizational change technique that is based on goal setting (see Chapter 8). Each employee's own goals are coordinated with the goals of both supervisors and subordinates. In a typical MBO program, goal setting begins by having those at the top of the organization set broad objectives for the entire organization. The process of setting goals or objectives then filters down level by level, with all employees' goals being related to the goals of their superiors. The goals serve as motivational tools to direct effort, as criteria against which employee performance is appraised, and as the means of coordinating everyone's efforts toward a common set of organizational objectives.

Implementation of an MBO program typically begins with the change agent meeting with the top officials of the organization to set organizationwide goals and objectives. These goals must be as concrete and measurable as possible because everyone else's goals must be linked to them. A goal such as

Improve the functioning of the organization

is a worthy goal, but it is too vague to be of much value in directing effort. A better goal would be

Increase sales by 20%

This goal is specific and measurable, allowing everyone to know precisely what needs to be done and when it has been achieved.

In the next step, the change agent meets with managers and trains them in the goal-setting process. The program will work only when managers understand how to state measurable goals and how to set goals with subordinates and superiors. The third step is a series of meetings involving every subordinate–supervisor pair in the organization, usually beginning at the top and working down the organization level by level. The technique involves active participation by subordinates, who negotiate their goals with their supervisor, with the requirement that subordinates' goals must be consistent with those of the higher levels. Once all goals have been set, employees try to achieve them. After a 6- to 12-month period, each employee's job performance is evaluated against progress toward his or her goals. The entire process is illustrated in Figure 14-1.

Research on MBO has supported its use as an effective means of increasing organizational performance. Rodgers and Hunter (1991) conducted a meta-analysis of the effectiveness of MBO. They found positive effects on employee productivity in 68 of the 70 studies they reviewed. The combined results of 23 of the studies indicated an average increase in productivity of 39% as a result of the program. Rodgers and Hunter (1991) did an additional analysis in which they separated the 23 studies into three groups based on the extent to which top management was committed to the MBO program. As shown in Table 14-1, organizations with the highest levels of management commitment had far better results than those with the lowest levels (57% vs. 6% increase in productivity).

The high success rate found by Rodgers and Hunter (1991) is probably an overestimate of how well MBO has worked across the many organizations in which it has been

FIGURE 14-1
The five steps of implementing a Management by Objectives (MBO) program.

TABLE 14-1
Effect of management commitment on percentage of performance gain after
implementation of management by objectives

LEVEL OF COMMITMENT	PERCENTAGE GAIN IN PRODUCTIVITY
High	56.5
Medium	32.9
Low	6.1

Source: Adapted from "Impact of Management by Objectives on Organizational Productivity," by
R. Rodgers and J. E. Hunter, 1991, *Journal of Applied Psychology, 76,* 322–336.

tried. These studies likely represent some of the better efforts at implementing MBO.
Many organizations have made attempts to implement MBO without full management
commitment or necessary resources. Such half-hearted attempts are likely to have little effect on the organization, with employees setting easy goals and exerting little effort toward
achieving them.

Survey Feedback

Survey feedback is an OD technique that involves conducting a survey of employee attitudes and opinions and then feeding back the results to the entire organization. The idea
is that employees can express their opinions in a nonthreatening way through anonymous
or confidential questionnaires. The survey data can then be used as the starting point for
discussions about needed changes in the organization.

A survey feedback program consists of two major stages. First, the change agent will
design and administer questionnaires to the employees of the organization. Employees are
asked about job attitudes, job satisfaction, perceptions of job conditions, and problems at
work. Standardized scales can be used to assess some of these variables, such as the Job
Descriptive Index (Smith, Kendall, & Hulin, 1969) for job satisfaction (see Chapter 9).
Other items and custom-made scales might be developed specifically for each organization by the change agent after interviews with a sample of employees. The advantage of
using standardized scales is that data from the organization can be compared to similar
information from other organizations. For example, one would know if employee job satisfaction was unusually high or low. The advantage of custom-made scales is that they can
be much more specific and deal with issues of concern to employees only in the specific
organization. Thus, one can find out with a standardized scale how employees feel about
their pay in general. It would take a custom-made scale to find out how they feel about a
particular pay policy.

The second stage of a survey feedback program is providing feedback about the survey to employees. Data from the survey are compiled into a report, and the report is presented to employees, usually at a series of group meetings. Change agents run the
meetings during which employees discuss the results and potential solutions to the problems uncovered by the survey. A successful program will result in the implementation of
solutions to organizational problems.

Studies on the effectiveness of survey feedback have tended to find positive results
from its use. Bowers (1973) reported the results of a large-scale longitudinal study involv-

ing over 14,000 employees from 23 organizations. Positive changes in job satisfaction and employee reports of job conditions were found after survey feedback programs were introduced. In a meta-analysis of OD studies, survey feedback was found to have a modest positive impact on the job satisfaction of employees who participated (Neuman, Edwards, & Raju, 1989). It gives employees an opportunity to air their grievances in a constructive atmosphere. It also can provide for increased participation by employees in policy decisions that affect the entire organization. If done properly, survey feedback can help solve problems and give employees a greater sense of involvement in the organization.

Team Building

Team building refers to many techniques that are designed to enhance the functioning of work teams. As discussed in Chapter 12, team building can focus on interpersonal issues, such as communication, or on tasks, such as smooth coordination of effort. With the task-oriented approach, the change agent helps work teams improve their task performance by learning how to work together more effectively. With the interpersonal approach, the change agent helps work teams improve their communication and interaction. Part of this effort can be directed toward reducing interpersonal conflict within work teams.

Team building can be an essential part of an OD effort because many of the tasks of organizations are conducted by work teams rather than individuals. An organization in which work teams do not work well will have a hard time being effective. Improving team functioning can go a long way toward improving an organization. In Chapter 12 we saw how the U.S. Navy is committed to finding ways to improve team functioning through training. Also noted in Chapter 12 were studies on the effectiveness of team building that had mixed results; some studies found positive effects, and some found no effects (Buller, 1986; Eden, 1985, 1986). Buller (1986) pointed out that the wide variety of team-building interventions across studies makes it difficult to draw firm conclusions about what sorts of techniques are effective. In their meta-analysis, Neuman et al. (1989) found that team building had a positive effect on job satisfaction.

T-Group

The **T-group** or training group is an intervention designed to enhance the communication and interpersonal skills of individual employees through specific group exercise techniques. There are many variations of the T-group. Most are conducted at a site away from work, take place over a three-day to two-week period, and involve several people who do not know one another. The idea is for the group of strangers to experience a series of interpersonal skills exercises with a trainer or facilitator to guide them.

A T-group experience encourages participants to experiment with their interpersonal behavior in a situation in which they receive nonjudgmental feedback. This allows group members to gain insights into their effects on others and how they are perceived by others. The purpose is for organizational members, most often managers, to increase their interpersonal skills in the hope that they will be more effective on the job.

At one time, the T-group was a popular intervention, with many large organizations sending their management staffs to an off-site location for training. It is not as popular at the present time for at least two reasons. First, research on the T-group has found that although individuals can be positively affected by the experience, there can be either no effect or negative effects on the workplace. For example, Bowers (1973) found detrimental changes in reports of job conditions and job satisfaction among employees who participated in T-groups. Second, the T-group experience can be very much like group psychotherapy, with individuals exploring sensitive and potentially threatening aspects of themselves. There have been reports of individuals being hurt and upset by the T-group. Some have raised the issue that it is unethical for an organization to require T-group attendance.

Although T-groups have lost their popularity, organizations are still very much concerned with communication skills. To enhance such skills, organizations can use a variety of other methods. For example (as discussed in Chapter 7), behavior modeling has been found to be effective in training interpersonal skills. This method involves having employees watch people enact appropriate ways to communicate with others on the job. Trainees then practice what they have seen, under the direction of a trainer. This approach can be effective in enhancing interpersonal skills without the potentially harmful effects of the T-group. Thus, organizations have alternatives that they can use to enhance communication skills of their employees.

Effectiveness of OD

The many different approaches to OD make it difficult to define precisely what a legitimate OD program is. Many involve more than one technique, including some combination of the four discussed in this section. An OD program might begin with survey feedback to identify issues. MBO or team building might be implemented next if the survey feedback process suggested that they were appropriate interventions. The wide variety of approaches and the complexity of the programs make it difficult to determine the effectiveness of particular OD techniques.

Another problem is that research on an entire organization is difficult to accomplish. If one implements an OD effort and wishes to assess the results, what will serve as the control group? The ideal OD study would randomly assign a sample of organizations (as opposed to individual subjects) to one of two groups—intervention or control. This sort of design would require the cooperation of many organizations and is obviously not feasible. Most OD studies are conducted in a single organization with comparisons made before and after the OD program. For example, one could compare the performance of employees before and after OD implementation, but one could not be certain what caused any differences that were found. A likely possibility is that improvements were due to a Hawthorne Effect rather than the OD intervention itself.

Perhaps the most reasonable conclusion is that OD programs, if properly applied and supported by top management, can be effective. Meta-analyses have found that many OD techniques are effective (e.g., Guzzo, Jette, & Katzell, 1985; Neuman, Edwards & Raju, 1989). Except for T-groups, there have been few reports of detrimental effects on organizations. The majority of large U.S. corporations seem to believe in the value of OD. In a recent survey of Fortune 500 companies, McMahan and Woodman (1992) found that most had internal OD professionals who were actively working to improve their organizations. Thirty-eight percent of the companies had OD staffs of 6 or more people, and 14% had staffs of 21 or more people. These results are probably an overestimate of the amount of OD activity in large U.S. companies, for the participation rate in the study was only about one-fifth of the eligible companies. Nevertheless, they suggest that OD is an important activity in many large organizations.

ORGANIZATIONAL THEORIES

Organizational theories describe the structure and functioning of organizations and deal with issues such as

1. The distinguishing characteristics of organizations
2. The structure of organizations
3. The interrelationships among people in organizations
4. The interactions among people and technology in organizations

Descriptive theories explain how existing organizations work. A good descriptive theory will provide an accurate picture of how organizations are structured and how they operate. **Prescriptive theories** indicate how organizations should operate. A good prescriptive theory will lead to an effective and efficient organization.

In practice, the distinction between descriptive and prescriptive theories may not be totally clear. Elements of both may appear in a given theory. Prescriptive theories that tell us what to do may in fact be descriptive of certain types of organizations. The first theory we discuss, bureaucracy, describes a particular type of organization, but its developer intended it to be prescriptive.

In this section, we discuss four different theoretical approaches to understanding organizations. *Bureaucracy* is the oldest theory and dates back to the nineteenth century. It is concerned with the structure of a particular type of organization that has been quite popular over the past century. *Theory X/Theory Y* is concerned with the interpersonal aspects of an organization. It is not an overall theory but describes how the attitudes of managers toward subordinates determine the organizational practices that are adopted. *Open system theory* describes the 10 components common to all general systems. *Sociotechnical systems theory* is concerned with the interaction between the people and the technology of an organization.

Bureaucracy

Bureaucracy theory, initially developed by Max Weber in the late 1800s, is a classical theory of the structure of an organization (see Weber, 1947). In the early days of large organizations, little was known about effective techniques to structure and manage an organization. Weber's idea was to create a rational structure and several principles that would allow for the orderly and efficient functioning of an organization. Although we tend to think of a bureaucracy today as an inefficient and unresponsive organization, it represented an improvement over many of the organizational structures that existed at the time. Early organizations were often disorganized and inefficient. Bureaucracy theory provides characteristics and principles that were presumed to be important for an effective organization. We will discuss four of them:

Division of labor

Delegation of authority

Span of control

Line versus staff

These principles can be useful for describing how most organizations operate, even those that are not bureaucratic in nature.

Division of Labor. **Division of labor** refers to the organization's specialized job positions, each of which is responsible for different tasks. For a complex process, such as manufacturing an automobile, the total job is divided into many individual parts. For an entire manufacturing organization, the design, production, sale, and delivery of products are handled by different people in different departments.

The advantage of a division of labor is that each job requires relatively few skills. Therefore, it will not be difficult to find people who have the necessary abilities to do the job; it will take little time to train them; and individuals can become quite proficient because they have few tasks to master. The major disadvantage is that it requires resources to coordinate the activities of many specialized people. In a factory, for example, many managers and supervisors are needed to monitor that all employees do their jobs properly and that the efforts of employees are coordinated. This leads us to the next characteristic, delegation of authority.

Delegation of Authority. Most organizations are hierarchically structured with one person at the top who has ultimate authority and control. Reporting to the top person will be one or more people who have authority and control over others who are below them in the hierarchy. At each level of the hierarchy, except the first, people report to others who are their superior. At the last or bottom level are people who report to someone above them, but no one reports to them. An example of the organizational chart for a hierarchically structured organization is shown in Figure 14-2.

Division of labor means that no one in the organization does the entire work of the organization. Thus, the person at the top is dependent on all those below to produce the organization's goods or services. In order to accomplish this, each person must practice the **delegation of authority** to those below to accomplish a particular job. Thus, the top person might delegate authority for the design of a product to the research and development manager, for the running of a factory to a plant manager, for the selling of the product to a sales manager, and for the distribution of the product to a distribution manager. The people who report to each of these managers will be given authority to do whatever their jobs require. The efforts of different individuals are coordinated through a network of hierarchical supervision or **chain of command**: Each person is responsible for those tasks and functions over which he or she has authority.

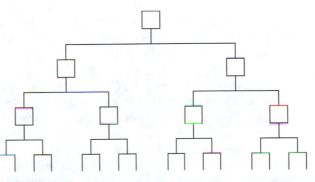

FIGURE 14-2

An organizational chart for a hierarchically structured organization. In these organizations, for example, a bureaucracy, each person reports to a single supervisor.

Span of Control. Span of control refers to the number of subordinates who report to each supervisor. In a given bureaucracy there will be an optimal span of control. Because everyone except the person at the top has a supervisor, too small a span of control would result in needing too many managers. Too large a span of control would be chaotic because one person cannot adequately supervise the work of many people. The number of people someone can adequately supervise depends on two factors. First, the more skilled the subordinates, the less supervisory time they take. A person who is unskilled will need constant help and direction. A person who knows the job well will need only occasional attention. Second, the person's supervisory style helps determine the optimal span of control. A directive style requires considerable time for each subordinate. Each time a decision or problem arises, the supervisor must take time to deal with it. A participative style allows for a larger span of control because subordinates are allowed to deal with many of their own problems and make their own decisions, thereby freeing the time of their supervisors.

Line Versus Staff. Each position in an organization can be classified as either line or staff. A *line position* is involved directly with the organization's major purpose. In the military it would be combat soldiers; in education it would be teachers; in manufacturing it would be assemblers; and in retailing it would be sales staff. Line positions also include all the levels of supervision above these positions. A *staff position* supports the activities of a line position. The administration of salary and fringe benefits, employee selection, and training are all considered to be staff functions performed by people in staff positions.

Theory X/Theory Y

McGregor's (1960) **Theory X/Theory Y** is a human relations theory concerned with the interaction between supervisors and subordinates. The basic idea is that the attitudes and beliefs of supervisors about their subordinates determine the organization's management approach, which in turn affects how subordinates behave. There is a self-fulfilling prophecy in that managers treat subordinates according to how they are expected to behave, and this treatment causes subordinates to behave as expected. For example, a manager who believes that subordinates will not do their jobs properly without close supervision is likely to supervise closely. The closely supervised subordinates will undoubtedly believe that they are not trusted and will probably not work well when the supervisor is absent. Although the manager might believe that the close supervision was the result of subordinate behavior, the opposite is the case.

McGregor (1960) considers Theory X to represent the conventional view of the manager's role and the nature of subordinates. He noted eight propositions that represent widely held beliefs by managers (Table 14-2). They include the idea that managers are responsible for organizing the human and nonhuman (for example, equipment, money, supplies, and tools) elements of the organization and that they should direct and motivate subordinates. The worker is viewed as being indifferent to the organization's needs, lazy, unmotivated, and not very bright. This belief leads managers to adopt one of two strategies. The *hard approach* is to use coercion and threats and to supervise closely, an approach that results in employee resistance, such as counterproductive behavior and restriction of output. The *soft approach* is to be permissive and avoid conflict with subordinates, which leads to an ineffective organization.

TABLE 14-2
McGregor's (1966) Theory X/Theory Y propositions

Theory X
Managers are responsible for organizing elements of the organization.
Managers should direct the activities of subordinates.
Employees are resistant to organizational needs.
The average employee is lazy.
The average employee lacks ambition and dislikes responsibility.
The average employee is concerned for himself or herself and not the organization.
The average employee is resistant to change.
The average employee is gullible and not very bright.

Theory Y
Managers are responsible for organizing elements of the organization.
Employees are not by nature resistant to organization needs. They have become that way because of prior organization experiences.
Managers should make it possible for subordinates to recognize and develop their organizational capabilities.
Managers should create organizational conditions so that subordinates can achieve their own goals through achieving organizational goals.

Source: *The Human Side of Enterprise,* by D. M. McGregor, 1960, New York: McGraw-Hill.

Theory Y is McGregor's preferred management view, which he believes will lead to more satisfied employees and more effective organizations. It has four propositions (see Table 14-2), which cover both the role of managers and the nature of subordinates. According to Theory Y, managers are responsible for organizing rather than directing the various human and nonhuman elements of the organization. Subordinates are capable and not inherently unmotivated or unresponsive to organizational needs. It is the responsibility of managers to arrange conditions so that employees can fulfill their own goals by directing efforts toward organizational goals. This last point is very much like the path-goal leadership theory idea (see Chapter 13) that leaders should provide the means by which subordinates can achieve personal rewards through good job performance. The supervisory approach adopted by the Theory Y manager is likely to be quite different from his or her Theory X counterpart. Rather than relying on directive approaches, the Theory Y manager stresses employee autonomy and development. Emphasis is placed on the setting of goals and objectives for employees, with their supervisors helping by removing constraints and providing guidance.

McGregor believed that movement toward Theory Y would be a slow process because the experiences of most people have been in Theory X situations. Today we can see many examples of the Theory Y approach. For example, the autonomous work team is based on the philosophy that subordinates are capable of managing themselves. As organizations continue to experience pressure to reduce costs by downsizing, it will become necessary to give more responsibility to lower level employees. This will require adoption of a Th ory Y approach.

Theory X and Theory Y are not the only possible approaches for man
William Ouchi (1981) proposed an approach to management that is h

practices. **Theory Z** assumes that long-term employment is the basis of effective organizations. People who can count on spending their entire career in the same organization will have high levels of commitment. They will be willing to put more effort into helping their organizations be successful because they have a personal stake in the long-term success of their employers.

Open System Theory

According to Katz and Kahn's (1978) **open system theory**, an organization can be viewed as a type of open system. The idea comes from the natural sciences, which view plants, animals, bacteria, and viruses as open systems. Although organizations are different from biological organisms, they do share many characteristics (see Figure 14-3).

Katz and Kahn noted 10 characteristics of open systems, which are listed in Table 14-3. Open systems such as organizations import energy, transform the energy into something else, and output some product or products. All organizations import people and materials, produce goods and services, and deliver those goods and services to customers. Even government organizations provide services to citizens, including education, health care, protection, and transportation.

<u>FIGURE 14-3</u>
Organizations can be thought of as open systems that share many of the characteristics of biological organisms.

TABLE 14-3

The 10 organizational characteristics from Katz and Kahn's (1978) open system theory and an organizational example of each

CHARACTERISTIC	EXAMPLE
1. Import energy	Hire people
2. Transform energy	Make products
3. Output products	Sell products
4. Cycles of events	Work shifts
5. Escape entropy	Stay profitable
6. Input information	Do a market survey
7. Homeostasis	Balance the annual budget
8. Specialization	Create specialized job titles
9. Coordination and integration	Supervise employees
10. Equifinality	There are many effective ways to run an organization

Open systems undergo cycles of events, and organizations are no different. Most organize their finances by fiscal years; employees have weekly work schedules; and for many organizations, the day is broken into two or more work shifts. Universities organize instruction by semesters, and semesters are organized into academic years. Many employees are hired according to time-limited contracts, especially in sports organizations such as professional baseball, basketball, football, or soccer.

Open systems must somehow escape entropy—the decay and destruction of the system. With a biological organism, entropy results in death. For an organization, entropy also can result in death, although often "dying" organizations are absorbed by other organizations. With private sector organizations, entropy can be indicated by the economic health of the company. Organizations that are efficient in transforming their inputs into goods and services that can be sold at a reasonable profit will survive. Those that cannot produce goods and services at a profit will have their finances erode until they can no longer pay employees or input energy. When this situation occurs, they will cease to function unless additional energy is available. It might occur if an external entity provides the funds to continue. This is what happened to the Chrysler Corporation in the 1970s when the U.S. government gave it a loan to prevent bankruptcy.

In addition to energy, open systems input information about their environments. Organizations have many people who are information specialists of various types. Organizations have accountants to deal with financial matters and lawyers to deal with legal issues, helping the organization maintain its homeostasis. Just as the thermostat in a house keeps the temperature constant, systems in organizations maintain certain conditions. An organization must maintain an appropriate number of employees, have the proper equipment in working order, have the necessary materials, and balance a budget. All these maintain the organization's homeostasis.

As open systems grow and become more complex, they develop specialized functions. As organizations become larger, they tend to divide work into more and more specialized functions. A small organization might have a single individual perform all accounting, human resource, and legal functions. A large corporation will have entire departments and often divisions for each of these functions. As functions become more specialized, open systems develop structures for coordination and integration. In organizations this function is accomplished through supervision and the chain of command.

The final characteristic of an open system is equifinality—a system can reach a particular state from many different starting points using many different methods. From an organizational perspective, there is no way to structure and operate an organization. Successful organizations can function in a variety of ways. For example, a product can be produced with an autonomous work group or with a traditional assembly line.

Open system theory is descriptive in providing a framework to understand the characteristics of organizations. It does not provide prescriptive insights into how an organization should be run, as does McGregor's Theory X/Theory Y.

Sociotechnical Systems Theory

Sociotechnical systems theory views an organization in terms of the interrelations between people and technology in the context of the organizational environment. *People* include the employees of the organization and their relationships with one another. *Technology* consists of the equipment, materials, tools, and other nonhuman objects in the organization. The *environment* is the physical and social conditions in which the organization must function. The theory deals with how people affect technology and how technology affects people. Sociotechnical systems theory is prescriptive in that it uses research findings to provide principles of good organizational design.

The origins of sociotechnical systems theory can be found in a paper by Trist and Bamforth (1951) in which they describe the effects of technological change in the British coal industry (see Figure 14-4). Prior to the change, coal mining was done by small groups of men who controlled their own work pace. Members of each group worked together in close proximity inside the dangerous environment of the mine. The introduction of machinery resulted in changes in the work group relationships among the men and the loss of worker control over work pace. Individuals now operated large pieces of machinery alone, without the close support of colleagues. This led to increases in absence and health complaints among the miners. This paper made the linkages between the human and technological aspects of organizations very clear.

Since Trist and Bamforth's (1951) paper, sociotechnical systems theory has undergone development and frequent application (Winterton, 1994). Cooper and Foster (1971) noted several principles of the theory. **Joint optimization** is the idea that the social and technological systems should be designed to fit as well as possible. Machines and equipment should be easy for people to use, and people should be organized into tasks and jobs so that machines and equipment can function well. This means not only that human factors should be part of equipment design, but also that available technology be considered in designing the human side of organizations. The introduction of word processing in offices is an example of this approach. To successfully introduce this technology, word processing systems must be designed so that they are easy to learn and use. On the human side, existing employees need training and support because it takes time for people to learn to use computers, which can make people anxious. Many managers of organizations violated sociotechnical systems principles by thinking that all they needed to do was order computers.

Unit control of variances concerns who handles work problems when they arise. In many organizations, each employee is responsible for handling only routine assigned

FIGURE 14-4
Technological changes in coal mining have sometimes disrupted the social system of miners, resulting in employee problems.

tasks. When there is a variance from normal routine—for example, a machine breaks or a customer has a problem—specialists or supervisors are called to handle it. The idea of unit control is that variances should be handled by the employee or employees who encounter them. Thus, the operator of the machine should be allowed to fix it, and the salesclerk should be allowed to help a customer with a problem. In an office, employees who use word processors should be able to solve all but the most difficult problems they encounter. This approach enhances the motivation, self-efficacy, and skills of the employee, and it saves the time of the specialist and supervisor.

Implementation of the sociotechnical systems approach results in self-regulation by the individual employees or groups of employees. Thus, the autonomous work team approach is a major way in which these ideas have been introduced into organizations (Majchrzak & Borys, 1998). The existence of self-regulating or self-managed units implies a different function for management. Rather than directing the actions of employees, managers spend time counseling and supporting the activities of work units and facilitating their interactions.

The ideas of sociotechnical systems theory have been widely applied in organizations and will probably continue to spread for at least two reasons. First, as noted earlier in this chapter, there has been a worldwide trend toward downsizing organizations by trimming the size of management staffs (Kozlowski, Chao, Smith, & Hedlund, 1993). With fewer managers individual employees will have to work more independently. Second, research on sociotechnical systems theory applications has been supportive. Two studies conducted in Britain found that the unit control principle had positive effects on productivity.

Wall, Corbett, Martin, Clegg, and Jackson (1990) hypothesized, based on sociotechnical systems theory, that allowing factory workers to deal with machine problems themselves would reduce the amount of time that machines were "down" for adjustment or repair. They found not only that this form of unit control enhancement decreased downtime, but that it also decreased employee feelings of job pressure and increased job satisfaction. In a similar study in another British factory, Wall, Jackson, and Davids (1992) found that when factory workers assumed responsibility for fixing machine problems, productivity increased because of a reduction of machine downtime (see the Research in Detail box in this chapter).

Meta-analyses of interventions based on sociotechnical systems theory have indicated a high degree of success. Pasmore, Francis, Haldeman, and Shani (1982) analyzed the results of 134 studies and found that the majority had positive effects on criteria of productivity, costs, employee withdrawal, employee attitudes, safety, grievances, and work quality (Table 14-4). Guzzo, Jetter, and Katzell (1985) found positive effects of sociotechnical systems interventions on productivity and turnover.

Comparison of the Theories

Each of the four theories we have discussed is distinct, and each tends to focus on different aspects of organizations. There are some common ideas and connections among them, however. The rigid structure of the bureaucracy lends itself to a rigid Theory X approach. In a bureaucracy each person's job is clearly defined, with the individual having relatively little autonomy or discretion. This tends to be associated with the leadership style defined as Theory X, which includes close supervision and nonparticipative approaches.

Sociotechnical systems theory applications have tended to be consistent with Theory Y ideas. One of the main sociotechnical systems approaches has been the autonomous

TABLE 14-4

Percentage of studies reporting various positive effects of sociotechnical systems theory interventions

EFFECT	PERCENTAGE SUCCESSFUL
Productivity	87
Cost	89
Absence	81
Turnover	65
Attitudes	94
Safety	88
Grievances	89
Quality	97

Source: Adapted from "Sociotechnical Systems: A North American Reflection on Empirical Studies of the Seventies," by W. Pasmore, C. Francis, J. Haldeman, and A. Shani, 1982. *Human Relations, 12,* 1179–1204.

THERE IS PERHAPS no better setting in which to apply the principles of sociotechnical systems theory than an automated factory that mixes people with industrial robots. Such was the case in this study of productivity in a British factory by Wall, Jackson, and Davids (1992). This factory produced drill bits on a robotics assembly line where four humans interacted with six robots. The robots did most of the assembly work, which involved forming metal into drill bits. The workers fed the material to the first robot, unloaded the finished bits from the last robot, and made minor adjustments to the machines.

Relying on principles of sociotechnical systems theory, the researchers recommended to management that the workers' jobs be redesigned to allow them to deal with machine problems, which are common with industrial robots. Management refused the idea because of objections by the engineers who believed that the machine operators could not handle this responsibility. Management had also instituted an incentive system for the operators, however, but because the assembly-line speed was controlled by the robots, the only way to increase productivity was to reduce downtime. The operators took it upon themselves to handle the machine problems, and once they proved they could do so the engineers withdrew their objections. Thus, the "experiment" occurred "accidentally."

Data on downtime were collected for six months before and eight months after the operators expanded their jobs. Downtime was reduced significantly from the period of time before to after the "intervention." It is interesting that the number of short stoppages (less than 15 minutes) increased, but the number of long stoppages (15 minutes to an hour) decreased. Overall, the number of stoppages was the same, but the time lost for stoppages decreased. This suggests that when the operators dealt with the problems themselves, they could do so more quickly and reduce the lost time. The researchers estimated that productivity increases resulted in as much as $2,400 in profit per week.

This study shows that the sociotechnical approach, even when implemented in an unplanned way, can have beneficial effects on productivity. A similar study by some of the same researchers (see Chapter 12) showed that it can have positive effects on people as well (Wall et al., 1990). Organizations could benefit by carefully applying the principles of sociotechnical systems theory. Note that in this study employees were offered an incentive for improving productivity. The combination of increased motivation (the incentive) and accidental job redesign resulted in reduced downtime. Imposing this sort of job change without considering employee motivation and preferences might not have the same effects and could even result in counterproductive behavior if employees resist the change.

Source: Wall, T. D., Jackson, P. R., & Davids, K. (1992). Operator work design and robotics system performance: A serendipitous field study. *Journal of Applied Psychology, 77,* 353–362.

work group (see Chapter 12). The idea is to give employees autonomy and discretion in how they do their jobs. This assumes that management adopts a trusting view of employees. One cannot allow someone discretion without being confident that he or she will do the job properly. Thus, the application of sociotechnical systems theory requires a Theory Y philosophy that employees can be trusted to do the job.

Open system theory is quite different. It describes the functioning of an organization in terms of 10 rather general principles and does not recommend specific practices. One can use the principles to describe the processes of an organization that might be based on the other theories. For example, the ways in which employees are supervised would be covered by the principles of coordination and integration; however, there is little in the theory to tell us how we should coordinate and integrate. Of course, the principle of equifinality tells us that there can be many effective ways to run an organization.

These theories provide a broad perspective on organizations and how they function. Some have led to specific applications such as the autonomous work groups based on sociotechnical systems theory. Others have affected the philosophies of those who manage organizations rather than describing particular techniques. Theory X/Theory Y, for example, is well known to managers and has had some influence on their practices.

FUTURE ISSUES AND CHALLENGES

Perhaps the biggest challenge facing organizations today is dealing effectively with rapid change in both the internal and external environments. Change is produced by both social and technological forces that impinge on organizations. Globalization and rapid advances in computers and related technologies have produced an environment that demands the ability of organizations to adapt and change (Coovert, 1995; Davis, 1995). To avoid chaotic change, techniques discussed in this chapter, such as team development, should be considered. At the same time, it must be kept in mind that change can be extremely stressful for employees (Mack, Nelson, & Quick, 1998). Organizations must take steps to help employees cope with change, which can adversely affect their job performance and well-being.

Global economies require that organizations have the flexibility to deal with people from many different cultural backgrounds, who might have different expectations about acceptable and unacceptable practices. The multicultural nature of a global workforce brings new challenges for finding appropriate and effective ways of dealing with different sorts of people.

Technological change means that organizational practices and structures can quickly become ineffective and obsolete. Technologies for near instant communication, such as e-mail and fax, have already made profound changes in how people work. The almost instant communication now possible makes the pace of organizational life faster, often requiring quick organizational response. For example, such advances now allow people to **telecommute**, that is, commute to work without leaving home by logging into the office computer system with a modem. Chapman, Sheehy, Heywood, Dooley, and Collins (1995) have discussed the advantages of telecommuting to both employees (flexible scheduling and not having to commute to and from the office) and organizations (lower office costs and increased productivity).

Another major challenge is the worldwide trend toward greater efficiency by downsizing. As noted earlier in this chapter, the downsizing of an organization usually means a reduction in the size of its management staff. With fewer supervisors, organizations must find ways for employees to work with greater autonomy. Sociotechnical systems theory has much to say about designing such organizations.

CHAPTER SUMMARY

We took an organizational perspective in this chapter, briefly reviewing two areas—organizational development and organizational theory. Organizational development is concerned with behavioral science techniques designed to improve the functioning of organizations. We discussed four specific techniques that can be used separately or in combination. Management by objectives (MBO) sets interlinked goals throughout an organization. Survey feedback uses the results of a survey of employees as the basis for group discussion and organization improvement. Team building is a family of techniques that can be used with work teams to improve their functioning. T-groups are a series of group exercises designed to enhance the individual's communication and interpersonal skills.

Existing evidence suggests that MBO, survey feedback, and team building can be effective interventions, with positive effects on both employees and organizations. On the other hand, T-groups have not been found to be effective and have been associated with detrimental effects.

Bureaucracy theory is a classical theory that focuses on the structural components of organizations. Theory X/Theory Y is a human relations theory that focuses on how management philosophy affects the behavior of employees. Open system theory describes organizations in terms of 10 characteristics of open systems. Sociotechnical systems theory is concerned with the interrelations between the human and technical sides of organizations. This theory has led to many interventions, and most of those reported in the research literature have been successful.

I/O PSYCHOLOGY IN PRACTICE

THIS CASE IS AN effort to help employees cope with organizational change brought about by a corporate downsizing. Dr. Tom White served as the architect and primary change agent for this organization development project. Dr. White received his Ph.D. in I/O psychology in 1985 from the University of South Florida. Immediately after graduation he moved to Australia, where he has worked as an I/O psychologist ever since. He presently holds the title of organization development manager for Digital Equipment Corporation in Australia. The company is one of the largest manufacturers of computers in the world.

Among Dr. White's responsibilities is facilitating organizational change and development. He is also involved with conflict resolution among employees, leadership development, planning for the future, and team building. His role is mainly that of an internal consultant and facilitator. This means he functions as change agent to help the organization manage frequent change necessitated by rapid technological development in the computer industry.

An important project Dr. White undertook was to help employees cope with a corporate downsizing that was necessary to keep the company profitable in the extremely competitive computer industry. Despite the company's reputation of caring for em-

(Continued next page)

I/O PSYCHOLOGY IN PRACTICE

ployees, heavy losses in recent years required drastic action to cut costs. As many as 30% of employees in some areas had to be let go. This downsizing was a traumatic experience for survivors of the layoffs, many of whom lost close friends at work. The entire company was disrupted, as people found it difficult to work effectively. Dr. White's job was to find a way to help survivors deal with the situation.

The approach chosen was based on techniques to help people cope with death of a family member. A series of two-day sessions was conducted with 100 employees or more each. During the sessions, which were conducted by managers, a series of small-group activities were conducted to help employees grieve their losses while focusing on plans for the future. Two themes were letting go of the past and committing to the future. Dr. White's role was to organize the companywide activity and instruct managers in how to conduct sessions. This is a typical role for a change agent, in that managers have to actually implement change. A psychologist will be a facilitator and resource for those who do the change.

Once the full program was completed, which took one month, an evaluation was conducted to determine its effectiveness. Results showed that employees became more accepting of change and more trusting of management. Employee job performance increased, as did overall productivity of the workforce. Overall, this organizational change effort was beneficial to both the employees and organization.

Discussion Questions

1. Why didn't Dr. White take a more active role in running the sessions?

2. How can a change agent facilitate change if managers have all the power in the organization?

3. What KSAOs are needed for a person to do organizational development?

4. Why is it important to evaluate programs, such as Dr. White's?

REFERENCES

Adams, G. A., King, L. A., & King, D. W. (1996). Relationships of job and family involvement, family social support, and work-family conflict with job and life satisfaction. *Journal of Applied Psychology, 81*, 411–420.

Adams, J. S. (1965). Inequity in social exchange. In L. Berkowitz (Ed.), *Advances in experimental social psychology* (pp. 276–299). New York: Academic Press.

Aguinis, H., Nesler, M. S., Quigley, B. M., Suk-Jae-Lee, & Tedeschi, J. T. (1996). Power bases of faculty supervisors and educational outcomes for graduate students. *Journal of Higher Education, 67*, 267–297.

Akerstedt, T., & Theorell, T. (1976). Exposure to night work: Serum gastrin reactions, psychosomatic complaints and personality variables. *Journal of Psychosomatic Research, 20*, 479–484.

Aldag, R. J., & Fuller, S. R. (1993). Beyond fiasco: A reappraisal of the groupthink phenomenon and a new model of group decision processes. *Psychological Bulletin, 113*, 533–552.

Alderfer, C. P. (1969). An empirical test of a new theory of human needs. *Organizational Behavior and Human Performance, 4*, 142–175.

Alliger, G. M., & Janak, E. A. (1989). Kirkpatrick's levels of training criteria: Thirty years later. *Personnel Psychology, 42*, 331–342.

Alliger, G. M., Tannenbaum, S. I., Bennett, W., Jr., Traver, H., & Shotland, A. (1997). A meta-analysis of the relations among training criteria. *Personnel Psychology, 50*, 341–358.

American Psychological Association. (1992). Ethical principles of psychologists and code of conduct. *American Psychologist, 47*, 1597–1611.

Arvey, R. D., Bouchard, T. J., Segal, N. L., & Abraham, L. M. (1989). Job satisfaction: Environmental and genetic components. *Journal of Applied Psychology, 74*, 187–192.

Ash, R. A., & Levine, E. L. (1980). A framework for evaluating job analysis methods. *Personnel, 57*, 53–59.

Ashton, M. C. (1998). Personality and job performance: The importance of narrow traits. *Journal of Organizational Behavior, 19*, 289–303.

Augustine, M. A., & Coovert, M. D. (1991). Simulations and information order as influences in the development of mental models. *SIGCHI Bulletin, 23*, 33–35.

Bacharach, S. B., Bamberger, P., & Conley, S. (1991). Work-home conflict among nurses and engineers: Mediating the impact of role stress on burnout and satisfaction at work. *Journal of Organizational Behavior, 12*, 39–53.

Baldwin, T. T., & Ford, J. K. (1988). Transfer of training: A review and directions for future research. *Personnel Psychology, 41*, 63–105.

Baldwin, T. T., & Padgett, M. Y. (1993). Management development: A review and commentary. In C. L. Cooper & I. T. Robertson (Eds.), *International review of industrial and organizational psychology 1993* (pp. 35–38). Chichester, UK: John Wiley.

Balzer, W. K., Smith, P. C., Kravitz, D. E., Lovell, S. E., Paul, K. B., Reilly, B. A., & Reilly, C. E. (1990). *User's Manual for the Job Descriptive Index (JDI) and the Job in General (JIG) Scales.* Bowling Green, OH: Bowling Green State University.

Balzer, W. K., & Sulsky, L. M. (1992). Halo and performance appraisal research: A critical examination. *Journal of Applied Psychology, 77*, 975–985.

Bandura, A. (1982). Self-efficacy mechanism in human agency. *American Psychologist, 37*, 122–147.

Banker, R. D., Field, J. M., Schroeder, R. G., & Sinha, K. K. (1996). Impact of work teams on manufacturing performance: A longitudinal field study. *Academy of Management Journal, 39*, 867–890.

Banks, C. G., & Murphy, K. (1985). Toward narrowing the research-practice gap in performance appraisal. *Personnel Psychology, 38*, 335–345.

Banks, M. H., Jackson, P. R., Stafford, E. M., & Warr, P. B. (1983). The Job Components Inventory and the analysis of jobs requiring limited skill. *Personnel Psychology, 36*, 57–66.

Banks, M. H., & Stafford, E. M. (1982). Skills training for clerical work: Action research within the youth opportunities programme. *BACIE Journal, 37*, 57–66.

Barling, J., Fullagar, C., & Bluen S. (1986). Organisational behaviour in South Africa: An historical overview. In J. Barling, C. Fullagar, & S. Bluen (Eds.), *Behaviour in Organisations* (pp. 3–31). Johannesburg: Lexicon.

Barling, J., & MacEwen, K. E. (1988). A multitrait-multimethod analysis of four maternal employment role experiences. *Journal of Organizational Behavior, 9,* 335–344.

Barling, J., Wade, B., & Fullagar, C. (1990). Predicting employee commitment to company and union: Divergent models. *Journal of Occupational Psychology, 63,* 49–61.

Barling, J., Weber, T., & Kelloway, E. K. (1996). Effects of transformational leadership training on attitudinal and financial outcomes: A field experiment. *Journal of Applied Psychology, 81,* 827–832.

Barrett, G. V., Caldwell, M. S., & Alexander, R. A. (1985). The concept of dynamic criteria: A critical reanalysis. *Personnel Psychology, 38,* 41–56.

Barrett, G. V., & Kernan, M. G. (1987). Performance appraisal and terminations: A review of court decisions since *Brito v. Zia* with implications for personnel practices. *Personnel Psychology, 40,* 489–503.

Barrick, M. R., & Mount, M. K. (1991). The Big Five personality dimensions and job performance: A meta-analysis. *Personnel Psychology, 44,* 1–26.

Barton, J., & Folkard, S. (1991). The response of day and night nurses to their work schedules. *Journal of Occupational Psychology, 64,* 207–218.

Bartram, D. (1994). Computer-based assessment. In C. L. Cooper, & I. T. Robertson (Eds.), *International review of industrial and organizational psychology 1994* (pp. 31–69). Chichester, UK: John Wiley.

Bass, B. M., Avolio, B. J., & Atwater, L. (1996). The transformational and transactional leadership of men and women. *Applied Psychology: An International Review, 45,* 5–34.

Bauer, T. N., & Green, S. G. (1996). Development of leader-member exchange: A longitudinal test. *Academy of Management Journal, 39,* 1538–1567.

Becker, B. E., & Huselid, M. A. (1992). Direct estimates of SD_y and the implications for utility analysis. *Journal of Applied Psychology, 77,* 227–233.

Becker, T. E., & Billings, R. S. (1993). Profiles in commitment: An empirical test. *Journal of Organizational Behavior, 14,* 177–190.

Bedeian, A. G., Burke, B. G., & Moffett, R. G. (1988). Outcomes of work-family conflict among married male and female professionals. *Journal of Management, 14,* 475–491.

Begley, T. M., & Czajka, J. M. (1993). Panel analysis of the moderating effects of commitment on job satisfaction, intent to quit, and health following organizational change. *Journal of Applied Psychology, 78,* 552–556.

Bell, P. A. (1981). Physiological, comfort, performance, and social effects of heat stress. *Journal of Social Issues, 37,* 71–94.

Benjamin, L. T., Jr. (1997). Organized industrial psychology before Division 14: The ACP and the AAAP (1930–1945). *Journal of Applied Psychology, 82,* 459–466.

Bernardin, H. J. (1988). Police officer. In S. Gael (Ed.), *Job analysis handbook* (pp. 1242–1254). New York: John Wiley.

Bernardin, H. J., & Beatty, R. W. (1984). *Performance appraisal: Assessing human behavior at work.* Boston: Kent.

Bernardin, H. J., & Pence, E.C . (1980). Rater training: Creating new response sets and decreasing accuracy. *Journal of Applied Psychology, 65,* 60–66.

Bettenhausen, K. L. (1991). Five years of group research: What we've learned and what needs to be addressed. *Journal of Management, 17,* 345–381.

Birdi, K., Warr, P., & Oswald, A. (1995). Age differences in three components of employee well-being. *Applied Psychology: An International Review, 44,* 345–373.

Blanz, F., & Ghiselli, E. E. (1972). The mixed standard scale: A new rating system. *Personnel Psychology, 25,* 185–199.

Blau, G. (1993a). Testing the relationship of locus of control to different performance dimensions. *Journal of Occupational and Organizational Psychology, 66,* 125–138.

Blau, G. (1993b). Further exploring the relationship between job search and voluntary individual turn-over. *Personnel Psychology, 46,* 313–330.

Bluedorn, A. C. (1982). A unified model of turnover from organizations. *Human Relations, 35,* 135–153.

Bluen, S. D. (1994). The psychology of strikes. In C. L. Cooper & I. T. Robertson (Eds.), *International review of industrial and organizational psychology* (pp. 113–145). Chichester, UK: John Wiley.

Bobko, P., Shetzer, L., & Russell, C. (1991). Estimating the standard deviation of professors' worth: The effects of frame and presentation order in utility analysis. *Journal of Occupational Psychology, 64,* 179–188.

Bohle, P., & Tilley, A. J. (1998). Early experience of shiftwork: Influences on attitudes. *Journal of Occupational and Organizational Psychology, 71,* 61–79.

Borman, W. C. (1987). Personal constructs, performance schemata, and "folk theories" of subordinate effectiveness: Explorations in an army officer sample. *Organizational Behavior and Human Decision Processes, 40,* 307–322.

Borman, W. C., Dorsey, D., & Ackerman, L. (1992). Time-spent responses as time allocation strategies: Relations with sales performance in a stockbroker sample. *Personnel Psychology, 45,* 763–777.

Borman, W. C., Peterson, N. G., & Russell, T. L. (1992). Selection, training, and development of personnel. In G. Salvendy (Ed.), *Handbook of industrial engineering* (2nd ed., pp. 882–914). New York: John Wiley.

Boudreau, J. W. (1983). Economic considerations in estimating the utility of human resource productivity improvement programs. *Personnel Psychology, 36,* 551–576.

Bowers, D. G. (1973). OD techniques and their results in 23 organizations: The Michigan ICL study. *Journal of Applied Behavioral Science, 9*, 21–43.

Bragg, J. E., & Andrews, I. R. (1973). Participative decision making: An experimental study in a hospital. *Journal of Applied Behavioral Science, 9*, 727–735.

Brannick, M. T., Michaels, C. E., & Baker, D. (1989). Construct validity of in-basket scores. *Journal of Applied Psychology, 74*, 957–963.

Breaugh, J. A. (1983). The 12-hour work day: Differing employee reactions. *Personnel Psychology, 36*, 277–288.

Broadbent, D. E., & Gath, D. (1981). Symptom levels in assembly-line workers. In G. Salvendy & M. J. Smith (Eds.), *Machine pacing and occupational stress* (pp. 244–252). London: Taylor & Francis.

Brush, D. H., Moch, M. K., & Pooyan, A. (1987). Individual demographic differences and job satisfaction. *Journal of Occupational Behaviour, 8*, 139–155.

Buck, J. R. (1983). Controls and tools. In B. H. Kantowitz & R. D. Sorkin (Eds.), *Human factors* (pp. 195–231). New York: John Wiley.

Budd, J. W., Arvey, R. D., & Lawless, P. (1996). Correlates and consequences of workplace violence. *Journal of Occupational Health Psychology, 1*, 197–210.

Buffum, W. E., & Konick, A. (1982). Employees' job satisfaction, residents' functioning, and treatment progress in psychiatric institutions. *Health & Social Work, 7*, 320–327.

Buller, P. F. (1986). The team building–task performance relation: Some conceptual and methodological refinements. *Group and Organization Studies, 11*, 147–168.

Bunker, K. A., & Cohen, S. L. (1977). The rigors of training evaluation: A discussion and field demonstration. *Personnel Psychology, 30*, 525–541.

Bycio, P., Alvares, K., & Hahn, J. (1987). Situational specificity in assessment center ratings: A confirmatory factor analysis. *Journal of Applied Psychology, 72*, 463–474.

Bycio, P., Hackett, R. D., & Allen, J. S. (1995). Further assessments of Bass's (1985) conceptualization of transactional and transformational leadership. *Journal of Applied Psychology, 80*, 468–478.

Cable, D. M., & Judge, T. A. (1997). Interviewers' perceptions of person–organization fit and organizational selection decisions. *Journal of Applied Psychology, 82*, 546–561.

Caldwell, D. F., & O'Reilly, C. A., III. (1990). Measuring person–job fit with a profile-comparison process. *Journal of Applied Psychology, 75*, 648–657.

Campbell, J. P., Gasser, M. B., & Oswald, F. L. (1996). The substantive nature of job performance variability. In K. R. Murphy (Ed.). *Individual differences and behavior in organizations* (pp. 258–299). San Francisco: Jossey-Bass.

Campbell, J. P., & Pritchard, R. D. (1976). Motivation theory in industrial and organizational psychology. In M. D. Dunnette (Ed.), *Handbook of industrial and organizational psychology* (pp. 63–130). Princeton, NJ: Van Nostrand.

Campion, M. A., & Campion, J. E. (1987). Evaluation of an interviewee skills training program in a natural field experiment. *Personnel Psychology, 40*, 676–691.

Campion, M. A., Palmer, D. K., & Campion, J. E. (1997). A review of structure in the selection interview. *Personnel Psychology, 50*, 655–702.

Campion, M. A., Pursell, E. D., & Brown, B. K. (1988). Structured interviewing: Raising the psychometric properties of the employment interview. *Personnel Psychology, 41*, 27–42.

Carsten, J. M., & Spector, P. E. (1987). Unemployment, job satisfaction, and employee turnover: A meta-analytic test of the Muchinsky model. *Journal of Applied Psychology, 72*, 374–381.

Cascio, W. F. (1987). *Applied psychology in personnel management* (3rd ed.). Englewood Cliffs, NJ: Prentice Hall.

Cascio, W. F., Alexander, R. A., & Barrett, G. V. (1988). Setting cutoff scores: Legal, psychometric, and professional issues and guidelines. *Personnel Psychology, 41*, 1–24.

Chacko, T. I. (1982). Women and equal employment opportunity: Some unintended effects. *Journal of Applied Psychology, 67*, 119–123.

Chan, D. (1996). Criterion and construct validation of an assessment centre. *Journal of Occupational and Organizational Psychology, 69*, 167–181.

Chapman, A. J., Sheehy, N. P., Heywood, S., Dooley, B., & Collins, S. C. (1995). The organizational implications of teleworking. In C. L. Cooper & I. T. Robertson (Eds.), *International review of industrial and organizational psychology 1995* (pp. 1–48). Chichester, UK: John Wiley.

Chen, P. Y., & Spector, P. E. (1992). Relationships of work stressors with aggression, withdrawal, theft and substance use: An exploratory study. *Journal of Occupational and Organizational Psychology, 65*, 177–184.

Clark, A., Oswald, A., & Warr, P. (1996). Is job satisfaction U-shaped in age? *Journal of Occupational and Organizational Psychology, 69*, 57–81.

Clark, T. (1993). Selection methods used by executive search consultancies in four European countries: A survey and critique. *International Journal of Selection and Assessment, 1*, 41–49.

Cleveland, J. N., Barnes-Farrell, J. L., & Ratz, J. M. (1997). Accommodation in the workplace. *Human Resource Management Review, 7*, 77–107.

Coch, L., & French, J.R.P., Jr. (1948). Overcoming resistance to change. *Human Relations, 1*, 512–532.

Cohen, A. (1992). Antecedents of organizational commitment across occupational groups: A meta-analysis. *Journal of Organizational Behavior, 13*, 539–558.

Cohen, A. (1993). Organizational commitment and turnover: A meta-analysis. *Academy of Management Journal, 36*, 1140–1147.

Cohen, S. G., & Ledford, G. E., Jr. (1994). The effectiveness of self-managing teams: A quasi-experiment. *Human Relations, 47*, 13–43.

Cohen, S., & Weinstein, N. (1981). Nonauditory effects of noise on behavior and health. *Journal of Social Issues, 37*, 36–70.

Colarelli, S. M., & Boos, A. L. (1992). Sociometric and ability-based assignment work groups: Some implications for personnel selection. *Journal of Organizational Behavior, 13*, 187–196.

Collins, J. M., & Schmidt, F. L. (1993). Personality, integrity, and white collar crime: A construct validity study. *Personnel Psychology, 46*, 295–311.

Cook, J. D., Hepworth, S. J., Wall, T. D., & Warr, P. B. (1981). *The experience of work*. New York: Academic Press.

Cook, T. D., & Campbell, D. T. (1979). *Quasi-experimentation: Design and analysis issues for field settings*. Chicago: Rand McNally.

Cooper, C. L., & Cartwright, S. (1994). Healthy mind; healthy organization—A proactive approach to occupational stress. *Human Relations, 47*, 455–471.

Cooper, R., & Foster, M. (1971). Sociotechnical systems. *American Psychologist, 26*, 467–474.

Coovert, M. D. (1990). Development and evaluation of five user models of human–computer interaction. In U. E. Gattiker & L. Larwood (Eds.), *End-user training* (pp. 105–139). Berlin: Walter de Gruyter.

Coovert, M. D. (1995). Technological changes in office jobs: What we know and what we can expect. In A. Howard (Ed.), *The changing nature of work* (pp. 175–208). San Francisco: Jossey-Bass.

Cordery, J. L., Mueller, W. S., & Smith, L. M. (1991). Attitudinal and behavioral effects of autonomous group working: A longitudinal field study. *Academy of Management Journal, 34*, 464–476.

Cordes, C. L., & Dougherty, T. W. (1993). A review and an integration of research on job burnout. *Academy of Management Review, 18*, 621–656.

Cornelius, E. T., III, DeNisi, A. S., & Blencoe, A. G. (1984). Expert and naive raters using the PAQ: Does it matter? *Personnel Psychology, 37*, 453–464.

Costa, P. T., Jr., & McCrae, R. R. (1992). *Revised NEO Personality Inventory*. Lutz, FL: Psychological Assessment Resources.

Crampton, S. M., & Wagner, J. A., III. (1994). Percept-percept inflation in microorganizational research: An investigation of prevalence and effect. *Journal of Applied Psychology, 79*, 67–76.

Cropanzano, R., Howes, J. C., Grandey, A. A., & Toth, P. (1997). The relationship of organizational politics and support to work behaviors, attitudes, and stress. *Journal of Organizational Behavior, 18*, 159–180.

Cropanzano, R., James, K., & Konovsky, M. A. (1993). Dispositional affectivity as a predictor of work attitudes and job performance. *Journal of Organizational Behavior, 14*, 595–606.

Dalton, D. R., & Mesch, D. J. (1991). On the extent and reduction of avoidable absenteeism: An assessment of absence policy provisions. *Journal of Applied Psychology, 76*, 810–817.

Dalton, D. R., & Todor, W. D. (1993). Turnover, transfer, absenteeism: An interdependent perspective. *Journal of Management, 19*, 193–219.

Dansereau, F., Jr., Graen, G., & Haga, W. J. (1975). A vertical dyad linkage approach to leadership with formal organizations. *Organizational Behavior and Human Performance, 13*, 46–78.

Daus, C. S., Sanders, D. N., & Campbell, D. P. (1998). Consequences of alternative work schedules. In C. L. Cooper & I. T. Robertson (Eds.), *International review of industrial and organizational psychology 1998* (pp. 185–223). Chichester, UK: John Wiley.

Davis, D. D. (1995). Form, function, and strategy in boundaryless organizations. In A. Howard (Ed.), *The changing nature of work* (pp. 112–138). San Francisco: Jossey-Bass.

Davis, J. H. (1969). *Group performance*. Reading, MA: Addison-Wesley.

Day, D. V., & Sulsky, L. M. (1995). Effects of frame-of-reference training and information configuration on memory organization and rating accuracy. *Journal of Applied Psychology, 80*, 158–167.

Deadrick, D. L., & Madigan, R. M. (1990). Dynamic criteria revisited: A longitudinal study of performance stability and predictive validity. *Personnel Psychology, 43*, 717–744.

DeNisi, A. S., Cafferty, T. P., & Meglino, B. M. (1984). A cognitive view of the performance appraisal process: A model and research propositions. *Organizational Behavior and Human Performance, 33*, 360–396.

Dennis, A. R., & Valacich, J. S. (1993). Computer brainstorms: More heads are better than one. *Journal of Applied Psychology, 78*, 531–537.

Dickinson, T. L., & Glebocki, G. G. (1990). Modification in the format of the mixed standard scale. *Organizational Behavior and Human Decision Processes, 47*, 124–137.

Dickter, D. N., Roznowski, M., & Harrison, D. A. (1996). Temporal tempering: An event history analysis of the process of voluntary turnover. *Journal of Applied Psychology, 81*, 705–716.

Dipboye, R. L. (1990). Laboratory vs. field research in industrial and organizational psychology. In C. L. Cooper & I. T. Robertson (Eds.), *International review of industrial and organizational psychology 1990* (pp. 1–34). Chichester, UK: John Wiley.

Dipboye, R. L., & Gaugler, B. B. (1993). Cognitive and behavioral processes in the selection interview. In N. Schmitt & W. C. Borman (Eds.), *Personnel selection in organizations* (pp. 135–170). San Francisco: Jossey-Bass.

Doerr, K. H., Mitchell, T. R., Klastorin, T. D., & Brown, K. A. (1996). Impact of material flow policies and goals on job outcomes. *Journal of Applied Psychology, 81*, 142–152.

Driskell, J. E., Willis, R., & Copper, C. (1992). Effect of overlearning on retention. *Journal of Applied Psychology, 77*, 615–622.

Dunham, R. B., Grube, J. A., & Castañeda, M. B. (1994). Organizational commitment: The utility of an integrative definition. *Journal of Applied Psychology, 79*, 370–380.

Dunnette, M. D. (1998). Emerging trends and vexing issues in industrial and organizational psychology. *Applied Psychology: An International Review, 47*, 129–153.

Dwyer, D. J., & Ganster, D. C. (1991). The effects of job demands and control on employee attendance and satisfaction. *Journal of Organizational Behavior, 12*, 595–608.

Eagly, A. H., & Johnson, B. T. (1990). Gender and leadership style: A meta-analysis. *Psychological Bulletin, 2*, 233–256.

Earley, P. C. (1989). Social loafing and collectivism: A comparison of the United States and the People's Republic of China. *Administrative Science Quarterly, 34*, 565–581.

Eden, D. (1985). Team development: A true field experiment employing three levels of rigor. *Journal of Applied Psychology, 70*, 94–100.

Eden, D. (1986). Team development: Quasi-experimental confirmation among combat companies. *Group & Organizational Studies, 11*, 133–146.

Eden, D., & Aviram, A. (1993). Self-efficacy training to speed reemployment: Helping people to help themselves. *Journal of Applied Psychology, 78*, 352–360.

Eden, D., & Zuk, Y. (1995). Seasickness as a self-fulfilling prophecy: Raising self-efficacy to boost performance at sea. *Journal of Applied Psychology, 80*, 628–635.

Edwards, J. R. (1991). Person–job fit: A conceptual integration, literature review, and methodological critique. In C. L. Cooper & I. T. Robertson (Eds.), *International review of industrial and organizational psychology, 1991* (pp. 283–357). Chichester, UK: John Wiley.

Erez, M. (1994). Toward a model of cross-cultural industrial and organizational psychology. In H. C. Triandis, M. D. Dunnette, & L. M. Hough (Eds.), *Handbook of industrial and organizational psychology* (pp. 559–607). Palo Alto, CA: Consulting Psychologists Press.

Eyde, L. D. (1983). Evaluating job evaluation: Emerging research issues for comparable worth analysis. *Public Personnel Management Journal, 12*, 425–444.

Facteau, J. D., Dobbins, G. H., Russell, J. E. A., Ladd, R. T., & Kudisch, J. D. (1995). The influence of general perceptions of the training environment on pretraining motivation and perceived training transfer. *Journal of Management, 21*, 1–25.

Farh, J., Podsakoff, P. M., & Organ, D. W. (1990). Accounting for organizational citizenship behaviors: Leader fairness and task scope versus satisfaction. *Journal of Management, 16*, 705–721.

Farr, J. L., Hofmann, D. A., & Ringenbach, K. L. (1993). Goal orientation and action control theory: Implications for industrial and organizational psychology. In C. L. Cooper & I. T. Robertson (Eds.) *International Review of industrial and organizational psychology 1993* (pp. 193–232). Chichester, UK: John Wiley.

Farrell, D., & Stamm, C. L. (1988). Meta-analysis of the correlates of employee absence. *Human Relations, 41*, 211–227.

Federation of Irish Employers. (1991). *Personnel policies and procedures guidelines.* Dublin: Baggot Bridge House.

Feldman, J. M. (1981). Beyond attribution theory: Cognitive processes in performance appraisal. *Journal of Applied Psychology, 66*, 127–148.

Ferris, G. R., Judge, T. A., Rowland, K. M., & Fitzgibbons, D. E. (1994). Subordinate influence and the performance evaluation process: Test of a model. *Organizational and Human Decision Processes, 58*, 101–135.

Fiedler, F. E. (1978). The contingency model and the dynamics of the leadership process. In L. Berkowitz (Ed.), *Advances in Experimental Social Psychology, 11* (pp. 59–112). New York: Academic Press.

Field, R. H. G., & House, R. J. (1990). A test of the Vroom–Yetton model using manager and subordinate reports. *Journal of Applied Psychology, 75*, 362–366.

Fine, S. A., & Wiley, W. W. (1971). *An introduction to functional job analysis, methods for manpower analysis* (Monograph No. 4). Kalamazoo, MI: W. E. Upjohn Inst.

Fitzgerald, L. F., Drasgow, F., Hulin, C. L., Gelfand, M. J., & Magley, V. J. (1997). Antecedents and consequences of sexual harassment in organizations: A test of an integrated model. *Journal of Applied Psychology, 82*, 578–589.

Flanagan, J. C. (1954). The critical incident technique. *Psychological Bulletin, 51*, 327–358.

Fleishman, E. A., & Harris, E. F. (1962). Patterns of leadership behavior related to employee grievances and turnover. *Personnel Psychology, 15*, 43–56.

Fletcher, B. C. (1988). The epidemiology of occupational stress. In C. L. Cooper & R. Payne (Eds.), *Causes, coping and consequences of stress at work* (pp. 3–50). Chichester, UK: John Wiley.

Ford, J. K., & Kraiger, K. (1995). The application of cognitive constructs and principles to the instructional systems model of training: Implications for needs assessment, design, and transfer. In C. L. Cooper & I. T. Robertson (Eds.), *International review of industrial and organizational psychology 1995* (pp. 1–48). Chichester, UK: John Wiley.

Ford, J. K., & Wroten, S. P. (1984). Introducing new methods for conducting training evaluation and for linking training evaluation to program redesign. *Personnel Psychology, 37*, 651–665.

Fowler, F. J., Jr. (1988). *Survey research methods* (Rev. ed.). Newbury Park, CA: Sage.

Fox, J. B., Scott, K. D., & Donohue, J. M. (1993). An investigation into pay valence and performance in a pay-for-performance field setting. *Journal of Organizational Behavior, 14*, 687–693.

Fox, M. L., Dwyer, D. J., & Ganster, D. C. (1993). Effects of stressful job demands and control on physiological and attitudinal outcomes in a hospital setting. *Academy of Management Journal, 36*, 289–318.

Fox, M. L., Hopkins, B. L., & Anger, W. K. (1987). The long-term effects of a token economy on safety performance in open-pit mining. *Journal of Applied Behavior Analysis, 20*, 215–224.

Frankenhaeuser, M., & Johansson, G. (1986). Stress at work: Psychobiological and psychosocial aspects. *International Review of Applied Psychology, 35*, 287–299.

Franklin. J. C. (1993). Industry output and employment. *Monthly Labor Review, 116*, 41–57.

Freeman, S., Walker, M., Borden, R., & Latané, (1975). Diffusion of responsibility and restaurant tipping: Cheaper by the bunch. *Personality and Social Psychology Bulletin, 1,* 584–587.

French, J. R. P., Jr., & Raven, B. (1959). The bases of social power. In D. Cartwright (Ed.), *Studies in social power* (pp. 150–167). Ann Arbor, MI: Institute for Social Research.

Frese, M. (1987). Human-computer interaction in the office. In C. L. Cooper & I. T. Robertson (Eds.), *International review of industrial and organizational psychology 1987* (pp. 117–165). Chichester, UK: John Wiley.

Frese, M., & Zapf, D. (1988). Methodological issues in the study of work stress: Objective vs. subjective measurement of work stress and the question of longitudinal studies. In C. L. Cooper & R. Payne (Eds.), *Causes, coping and consequences of stress at work* (pp. 375–409). Chichester, UK: John Wiley.

Frese, M., & Zapf, D. (1994). Action as the core of work psychology: A German approach. In H. C. Triandis, M. D. Dunnette, & L. M. Hough (Eds.). *Handbook of industrial and organizational psychology* (pp. 271–340). Palo Alto, CA: Consulting Psychologists Press.

Fried, Y., Ben-David, H. A., Tiegs, R. B., Avital, N., & Yeverechyahu, U. (1998). The interactive effect of role conflict and role ambiguity on job performance. *Journal of Occupational and Organizational Psychology, 71,* 19–27.

Fried, Y., & Ferris, G. R. (1987). The validity of the job characteristics model: A review and meta-analysis. *Personnel Psychology, 40,* 287–322.

Fried, Y., & Tiegs, R. B. (1995). Supervisors' role conflict and role ambiguity differential relations with performance ratings of subordinates and the moderating effect of screening ability. *Journal of Applied Psychology, 80,* 282–291.

Frone, M. R., Russell, M., & Cooper, M. L. (1994). Relationship between job and family satisfaction: Causal or noncausal covariation? *Journal of Management, 20,* 565–579.

Furnham, A., & Stringfield, P. (1994). Congruence of self and subordinate ratings of managerial practices as a correlate of supervisor evaluation. *Journal of Occupational and Organizational Psychology, 67,* 57–67.

Gallup Poll (1997, August). Public generally negative toward business, but most workers satisfied with jobs. [Online] Available: http://www.gallup.com/poll/editors/9710busi.html [1998, February 18].

Gallupe, R. B., Bastianutti, L. M., & Cooper, W. H. (1991). Unblocking brainstorms. *Journal of Applied Psychology, 76,* 137–142.

Gallupe, R. B., Cooper, W. H., Grisé, M., & Bastianutti, L. M. (1994). Blocking electronic brainstorms. *Journal of Applied Psychology, 79,* 77–86.

Ganster, D. C., & Schaubroeck, J. (1991). Work stress and employee health. *Journal of Management, 17,* 235–271.

Gardner, W. L., & Avolio, B. J. (1998). The charismatic relationship: A dramaturgical perspective. *Academy of Management Review, 23,* 32–58.

Gaugler, B. B., Rosenthal, D. B., Thornton, G. C., III, & Bentson, C. (1987). Meta-analysis of assessment center. *Journal of Applied Psychology, 72,* 493–511.

Geddes, D. (1994, August). *The relationship between negative feedback and increased organizational aggression.* Paper presented at the 1994 Academy of Management meetings, Dallas.

George, J. M., & Bettenhausen, K. (1990). Under-standing prosocial behavior, sales performance, and turnover: A group-level analysis in a service context. *Journal of Applied Psychology, 75,* 698–709.

Gerhart, B. (1987). How important are dispositional factors as determinants of job satisfaction? Implications for job design and other personnel programs. *Journal of Applied Psychology, 72,* 366–373.

Gerhart, B. (1990). Voluntary turnover and alternative job opportunities. *Journal of Applied Psychology, 5,* 467–476.

Gerstner, C. R., & Day, D. V. (1997). Meta-analytic review of leader–member exchange theory: Correlates and construct issues. *Journal of Applied Psychology, 82,* 827–844.

Giacalone, R. A., & Knouse, S. B. (1990). Justifying wrongful employee behavior: The role of personality in organizational sabotage. *Journal of Business Ethics, 9,* 55–61.

Giacalone, R. A., & Rosenfeld, P. (1987). Reasons for employee sabotage in the workplace. *Journal of Business and Psychology, 1,* 367–378.

Giuliano, V. E. (1982). The mechanization of office work. *Scientific American, 247,* 148–165.

Glick, W. H., Jenkins, G. D., Jr., & Gupta, N. (1986). Method versus substance: How strong are underlying relationships between job characteristics and attitudinal outcomes? *Academy of Management Journal, 29,* 441–464.

Goff, S. J., Mount, M. K., & Jamison R. L. (1990). Employer supported child care, work/family conflict, and absenteeism: A field study. *Personnel Psychology, 43,* 794–809.

Goldstein, I. L. (1993). *Training in organizations: Needs assessment, development, and evaluation* (3rd ed.). Monterey, CA: Brooks/Cole.

Goldstein, I. L., & Gilliam, P. (1990). Training system issues in the year 2000. *American Psychologist, 45,* 134–143.

Gomez-Mejia, L. R., Page, R. C., & Tornow, W. W. (1982). A comparison of the practical utility of traditional, statistical, and hybrid job evaluation approaches. *Academy of Management Journal, 25,* 790–809.

Graen, G., Novak, M. A., & Sommerkamp, P. (1982). The effects of leader–member exchange and job design on productivity and satisfaction: Testing a dual attachment model. *Organizational Behavior and Human Performance, 30,* 109–131.

Green, S. B., & Stutzman, T. (1986). An evaluation of methods to select respondents to structured job-analysis questionnaires. *Personnel Psychology, 39,* 543–565.

Greenberg, J. (1990). Employee theft as a reaction to underpayment inequity: The hidden cost of pay cuts. *Journal of Applied Psychology, 5,* 561–568.

Greenberg, L., & Barling, J. (1996). Employee theft. In C. L. Cooper, & D. M. Rousseau (Eds.), *Trends in organizational behavior,* vol. 3 (pp. 49–64). Chichester, UK: John Wiley.

Greene, C. N. (1989). Cohesion and productivity in work groups. *Small Group Behavior, 20,* 70–86.

Greenhaus, J. H., Parasuraman, S., & Wormley, W. M. (1990). Effects of race on organizational experiences, job performance evaluations, and career outcomes. *Academy of Management Journal, 33,* 64–86.

Griffeth, R. W., & Hom, P. W. (1987). Some multivariate comparisons of multinational managers. *Multivariate Behavioral Research, 22,* 173–191.

Griffin, R. W. (1991). Effects of work redesign on employee perceptions, attitudes, and behaviors: A long-term investigation. *Academy of Management Journal, 34,* 425–435.

Guion, R. M., & Alvares, K. M. (1980). *Selection of police officers* (Report Supplement No. 1: Job Analysis). Bowling Green, OH: Bowling Green State University.

Gupta, N., Jenkins, G. D., Jr., & Beehr, T. A. (1992). The effects of turnover on perceived job quality. *Group & Organization Management, 17,* 431–445.

Gutenberg, R. L., Arvey, R. D., Osburn, H. G., & Jeanneret, P. R. (1983). Moderating effects of decision-making/information-processing job dimensions on test validities. *Journal of Applied Psychology, 68,* 602–608.

Guzzo, R. A., Jette, R. D., & Katzell, R. A. (1985). The effects of psychologically based intervention programs on worker productivity: A meta-analysis. *Personnel Psychology, 38,* 275–291.

Hacker, G. R. (1996). *A theoretical approach to the selection of job analysis respondents.* Unpublished doctoral dissertation, University of South Florida, Tampa.

Hackett, R. D., Bycio, P., & Hausdorf, P. A. (1994). Further assessments of Meyer and Allen's (1991) three-component model of organizational commitment. *Journal of Applied Psychology, 79,* 15–23.

Hackett, R. D., & Guion, R. M. (1985). A reevaluation of the absenteeism—job satisfaction relationship. *Organizational Behavior and Human Decision Processes, 35,* 340–381.

Hackman, J. R., & Oldham, G. R. (1976). Motivation through the design of work: Test of a theory. *Organizational Behavior and Human Performance, 16,* 250–279.

Hackman, J. R., & Oldham, G. R. (1980). *Work redesign.* Reading, MA: Addison-Wesley.

Hackman, J. R., & Porter, L. W. (1968). Expectancy theory predictions of work effectiveness. *Organizational Behavior and Human Performance, 3,* 417–426.

Hall, J. K. (1990). *Locus of control as a moderator of the relationship between perceived role ambiguity and reported work strains.* Unpublished doctoral dissertation, University of South Florida, Tampa.

Harris, M. M. (1989). Reconsidering the employment interview: A review of recent literature and suggestions for future research. *Personnel Psychology, 42,* 691–726.

Harris, M. M., Becker, A. S., & Smith, D. E. (1993). Does the assessment center scoring method affect the cross-situational consistency of ratings? *Journal of Applied Psychology, 78,* 675–678.

Harris, M. M., & Schaubroeck, J. (1988). A meta-analysis of self-supervisor, self-peer, and peer-supervisor ratings. *Personnel Psychology, 41,* 43–62.

Harrison, D. A., & Shaffer, M. A. (1993, August). *Wading through Lake Woebegone: Comparative examinations of self reports and perceived norms of absenteeism.* Paper presented at Academy of Management Convention, Atlanta.

Hedge, J. W., & Kavanagh, M. J. (1988). Improving the accuracy of performance evaluations: Comparison of three methods of performance appraiser training. *Journal of Applied Psychology, 73,* 68–73.

Heilman, M. E., Battle, W. S., Keller, C. E., & Lee, R. A. (1998). Type of affirmative action policy: A determinant of reactions to sex-based preferential selection? *Journal of Applied Psychology, 83,* 190–205.

Heilman, M. E., Block, C. J., & Stathatos, P. (1997). The affirmative action stigma of incompetence: Effects of performance information ambiguity. *Academy of Management Journal, 40,* 603–625.

Heilman, M. E., Block, C. J., Martell, R. F., & Simon, M. C. (1989). Has anything changed? Current characterizations of men, women, and managers. *Journal of Applied Psychology, 74,* 935–942.

Heilman, M. E., & Herlihy, J. M. (1984). Affirmative action, negative reaction? Some moderating conditions. *Organizational Behavior and Human Performance, 33,* 204–213.

Heilman, M. E., Kaplow, S. R., Amato, M. A. G., & Stathatos, P. (1993). When similarity is a liability: Effects of sex-based preferential selection on reactions to like-sex and different-sex others. *Journal of Applied Psychology, 78,* 917–927.

Heilman, M. E., McCullough, W. F., & Gilbert, D. (1996). The other side of affirmative action: Reactions of nonbeneficiaries to sex-based preferential selection. *Journal of Applied Psychology, 81,* 346–357.

Herzberg, F. (1968, January/February). One more time: How do you motivate employees? *Harvard Business Review,* pp. 52–62.

Herzberg, F., Mausner, B., & Snyderman, B. (1959). *The motivation to work.* New York: John Wiley.

Hesketh, B. (1997). Dilemmas in training for transfer and retention. *Applied Psychology: An International Review, 46,* 317–339.

Hesketh, B., & Robertson, I. (1993). Validating personnel selection: A process model for research and practice. *International Journal of Selection and Assessment, 1,* 3–17.

Hofstede, G. (1984). *Culture's consequences: International differences in work-related values.* Abridged Edition. Newbury Park, CA: Sage.

Hogan, J., & Hogan, R. (1989). How to measure employee reliability. *Journal of Applied Psychology, 74,* 273–279.

Hogan, J., & Roberts, B. W. (1996). Issues and non-issues in the fidelity—bandwidth trade-off. *Journal of Organizational Behavior, 17,* 627–637.

Hogan, R., Curphy, G. J., & Hogan, J. (1994). What we know about leadership. *American Psychologist, 49*, 493–504.

Holland, J. L. (1994). *Self-Directed Search Form R.* Lutz, FL: Psychological Assessment Resources.

Hollinger, R. C., Dabney, D. A., Lee, G., Hayes, R., Hunter, J., & Cummings, M. (1996). *1996 national retail security survey final report.* Gainesville, FL: University of Florida.

House, R. J., & Mitchell, T. R. (1974). Path-goal theory of leadership. *Contemporary Business, 3*, 81–98.

Howard, A. (1990). *The multiple facets of industrial-organizational psychology.* Arlington Heights, IL: Society for Industrial and Organizational Psychology.

Hoyos, C. G. (1995). Occupational safety: Progress in understanding the basic aspects of safe and unsafe behaviour. *Applied Psychology: An International Review, 44*, 233–250.

Huffcutt, A. I., & Arthur, W., Jr. (1994). Hunter and Hunter (1984) revisited: Interview validity for entry-level jobs. *Journal of Applied Psychology, 79*, 184–190.

Huffcutt, A. I., Roth, P. L., & McDaniel, M. A. (1996). A meta-analytic investigation of cognitive ability in employment interview evaluations: Moderating characteristics and implications for incremental validity. *Journal of Applied Psychology, 81*, 459–473.

Hugick, L., & Leonard, J. (1991). Job dissatisfaction grows; "moonlighting" on the rise. *The Gallup Poll News Service, 56*, 1–11.

Hui, C. H., Yee, C., & Eastman, K. L. (1995). The relationship between individualism–collectivism and job satisfaction. *Applied Psychology: An International Review, 44*, 276–282.

Hulin, C. L., & Blood, M. R. (1968). Job enlargement, individual differences, and worker responses. *Psychological Bulletin, 69*, 41–55.

Hunter, J. E., & Hunter, R. F. (1984). Validity and utility of alternative predictors of job performance. *Psychological Bulletin, 96*, 72–98.

Hunter, J. E., & Schmidt, F. L. (1990). *Methods of meta-analysis: Correcting error and bias in research findings.* Newbury Park, CA: Sage.

Iaffaldano, M. T., & Muchinsky, P. M. (1985). Job satisfaction and job performance: A meta-analysis. *Psychological Bulletin, 97*, 251–273.

Ilgen, D. R., Barnes-Farrell, J. L., & McKellin, D. B. (1993). Performance appraisal process research in the 1980's: What has it contributed to appraisals in use? *Organizational Behavior and Human Decision Processes, 54*, 321–368.

Ironson, G. H., Smith, P. C., Brannick, M. T., Gibson, W. M., & Paul, K. B. (1989). Constitution of a Job in General scale: A comparison of global, composite, and specific measures. *Journal of Applied Psychology, 74*, 193–200.

Iverson, R. D., & Erwin, P. J. (1997). Predicting occupational injury: The role of affectivity. *Journal of Occupational and Organizational Psychology, 70*, 113–128.

Iverson, R. D., & Roy, P. (1994). A causal model of behavioral commitment: Evidence from a study of Australian blue-collar employees. *Journal of Management, 20*, 15–41.

Jackson, S. E., & Schuler, R. S. (1985). A meta-analysis and conceptual critique of research on role ambiguity and role conflict in work settings. *Organizational Behavior and Human Decision Processes, 36*, 16–78.

Jacobs, R., & Solomon, T. (1977). Strategies for enhancing the prediction of job performance from job satisfaction. *Journal of Applied Psychology, 62*, 417–421.

Jago, A. G., & Ragan, J. W. (1986). The trouble with Leader Match is that it doesn't match Fiedler's contingency model. *Journal of Applied Psychology, 71*, 555–559.

Jamal, M. (1990). Relationship of job stress and type-A behavior to employees' job satisfaction, organizational commitment, psychosomatic health problems, and turnover motivation. *Human Relations, 43*, 727–738.

Janis, I. L. (1972). *Victims of groupthink.* Boston: Houghton Mifflin.

Jaros, S. J., Jermier, J. M., Koehler, J. W., & Sincich, T. (1993). Effects of continuance, affective, and moral commitment on the withdrawal process: An evaluation of eight structural equation models. *Academy of Management Journal, 36*, 951–995.

Jex, S. M., & Beehr, T. A. (1991). Emerging theoretical and methodological issues in the study of work-related stress. *Research in Personnel and Human Resources Management, 9*, 311–365.

Jex, S. M., & Gudanowski, D. M. (1992). Efficacy beliefs and work stress: An exploratory study. *Journal of Organizational Behavior, 13*, 509–517.

Johansson, G. (1981). Psychoneuroendocrine correlates of unpaced and paced performance. In G. Salvendy & M. J. Smith (Eds.), *Machine pacing and occupational stress* (pp. 277–286). London: Taylor & Francis.

Johansson, G. (1989). Stress, autonomy, and the maintenance of skill in supervisory control of automated systems. *Applied Psychology: An International Review, 33*, 45–56.

Joyce, L. W., Thayer, P. W., & Pond, S. B., III. (1994). Managerial functions: An alternative to traditional assessment center dimensions? *Personnel Psychology, 47*, 109–121.

Judge, T. A. (1992). The dispositional perspective in human resources research. *Research in Personnel and Human Resources Management, 10*, 31–72.

Judge, T. A. (1993). Does affective disposition moderate the relationship between job satisfaction and voluntary turnover? *Journal of Applied Psychology, 78*, 395–401.

Judge, T. A., & Watanabe, S. (1993). Another look at the job satisfaction—life satisfaction relationship. *Journal of Applied Psychology, 78*, 939–948.

Kalton, G. (1983). *Introduction to survey sampling* (Sage University Paper series on Quantitative Application in the Social Sciences, 07–035). Newbury Park, CA: Sage.

Kane, J. S., & Bernardin, H. J. (1982). Behavioral observation scales and the evaluation of performance appraisal effectiveness. *Personnel Psychology, 35*, 635–641.

Kanfer, R. (1992). Work motivation: New directions in theory and research. In C. L. Cooper & I. T. Robertson (Eds.), *International review of industrial and organizational psychology 1992* (pp. 1–53). Chichester, UK: John Wiley.

Kantowitz, B. H., & Sorkin, R. D. (1983). *Human factors: Understanding people–system relationships*. New York: John Wiley.

Karasek, R. A., Jr. (1979). Job demands, job decision latitude, and mental strain: Implications for job redesign. *Administrative Science Quarterly, 24*, 285–307.

Karasek, R. A., Jr., Gardell, B., & Lindell, J. (1987). Work and non-work correlates of illness and behaviour in male and female Swedish white collar workers. *Journal of Occupational Behavior, 8*, 187–207.

Karl, K. A., O'Leary-Kelly, A. M., & Martocchio, J. J. (1993). The impact of feedback and self-efficacy on performance in training. *Journal of Organizational Behavior, 14*, 379–394.

Katz, D., & Kahn, R. L. (1978). *The social psychology of organizations* (2nd ed.). New York: John Wiley.

Katzell, R. A., & Austin, J. T. (1992). From then to now: The development of industrial-organizational psychology in the United States. *Journal of Applied Psychology, 77*, 803–835.

Keenan, A., & Newton, T. J. (1985). Stressful events, stressors and psychological strains in young professional engineers. *Journal of Occupational Behavior, 6*, 151–156.

Keenan, T. (1995). Graduate recruitment in Britain: a survey of selection methods used by organizations. *Journal of Organizational Behavior, 16*, 303–317.

Keller, R. T. (1986). Predictors of the performance of project groups in R & D organizations. *Academy of Management Journal, 29*, 715–726.

Keller, R. T. (1989). A test of the path-goal theory of leadership with need for clarity as a moderator in research and development organizations. *Journal of Applied Psychology, 74*, 208–212.

Keller, R. T. (1997). Job involvement and organizational commitment as longitudinal predictors of job performance: A study of scientists and engineers. *Journal of Applied Psychology, 82*, 539–545.

King, W. C., Jr., & Miles, E. W. (1995). A quasi-experimental assessment of the effect of computerizing noncognitive paper-and-pencil measurements: A test of measurement equivalence. *Journal of Applied Psychology, 80*, 643–651.

Kirkpatrick, D. L. (1977). Evaluating training programs: Evidence versus proof. *Training and Development Journal, 31*, 9–12.

Kirkpatrick, S. A., & Locke, E. A. (1996). Direct and indirect effects of three core charismatic leadership components on performance and attitudes. *Journal of Applied Psychology, 81*, 36–51.

Kleiman, L. S., & Faley, R. H. (1988). Voluntary affirmative action and preferential treatment: Legal and research implications. *Personnel Psychology, 41*, 481–496.

Klein, H. J., & Kim, J. S. (1998). A field study of the influence of situational constraints, leader–member exchange, and goal commitment on performance. *Academy of Management Journal, 41*, 88–95.

Kogan, N., & Wallach, M. A. (1964). *Risk taking: A study in cognition and personality*. New York: Holt, Rinehart and Winston.

Koh, W. L., Steers, R. M., & Terborg, J. R. (1995). The effects of transformational leadership on teacher attitudes and student performance in Singapore. *Journal of Organizational Behavior, 16*, 319–333.

Kohler, S. S., & Mathieu, J. E. (1993). Individual characteristics, work perceptions, and affective reactions influences on differentiated absence criteria. *Journal of Organizational Behavior, 14*, 515–530.

Koller, M., Kundi, M., & Cervinka, R. (1978). Field studies of shift work at an Austrian oil refinery: I. Health and psychosocial wellbeing of workers who drop out of shiftwork. *Ergonomics, 21*, 835–847.

Koppes, L. L. (1997). American female pioneers of industrial and organizational psychology during the early years. *Journal of Applied Psychology, 82*, 500–515.

Korsgaard, M. A., & Roberson, L. (1995). Procedural justice in performance evaluation: The role of instrumental and non-instrumental voice in performance appraisal discussions. *Journal of Management, 21*, 657–669.

Koslowsky, M., Sagie, A., Krausz, M., & Singer, A. D. (1997). Correlates of employee lateness: Some theoretical considerations. *Journal of Applied Psychology, 82*, 79–88.

Kossek, E. E., & Ozeki, C. (1998). Work-family conflict, policies, and the job-life satisfaction relationship: A review and directions for organizational behavior-human resources research. *Journal of Applied Psychology, 83*, 139–149.

Kozlowski, S. W. J., Chao, G. T., Smith, E. M., & Hedlund, J. (1993). Organizational downsizing: Strategies, interventions, and research implications. In C. L. Cooper & I. T. Robertson (Eds.), *International review of industrial and organizational psychology, 1993* (pp. 263–332). Chichester, UK: John Wiley.

Krausz, M., & Freibach, N. (1983). Effects of flexible working time for employed women upon satisfaction, strains, and absenteeism. *Journal of Occupational Psychology, 56*, 155–159.

Kravitz, D. A., Harrison, D. A., Turner, M. E., Levine, E. L., Chaves, W., Brannick, M. T., Denning, D. L., Russell, C. J., & Conard, M. A. (1997). *Affirmative action: A review of psychological and behavior research*. Bowling Green, OH: Society for Industrial & Organizational Psychology.

Kravitz, D. A., & Martin, B. (1986). Ringelmann rediscovered: The original article. *Journal of Personality and Social Psychology, 50*, 936–941.

Kristof, A. L. (1996). Person–organization fit: An integrative review of its conceptualizations, measurement, and implications. *Personnel Psychology, 49*, 1–49.

Lamm, H., & Myers, D. G. (1978). Group-induced polarization of attitudes and behavior. In L. Berkowitz (Ed.), *Advances in Ex-*

perimental and Social Psychology, *11*, pp. 145–195. New York: Academic Press.

Lance, C. E., LaPointe, J. A., & Stewart, A. M. (1994). A test of the context dependency of three causal models of halo rater error. *Journal of Applied Psychology*, *79*, 332–340.

Lance, C. E., Lautenschlager, G. J., Sloan, C. E., & Varca, P. E. (1989). A comparison between bottom-up, top-down, and bidirectional models of relationships between global and life facet satisfaction. *Journal of Personality*, *57*, 601–624.

Landy, F. J. (1997). Early influences on the development of industrial and organizational psychology. *Journal of Applied Psychology*, *82*, 467–477.

Landy, F. J., Farr, J. L., & Jacobs, R. R. (1982). Utility concepts in performance measurement. *Organizational Behavior and Human Performance*, *30*, 15–40.

Langan-Fox, J. (1998). Women's careers and occupational stress. In C. L. Cooper & I. T. Robertson (Eds.), *International review of industrial and organizational psychology 1998* (pp. 273–304). Chichester, UK: John Wiley.

Latané, B., Williams, K., & Harkins, S. (1979). Many hands make light the work: The causes and consequences of social loafing. *Journal of Personality and Social Psychology*, *37*, 822–832.

Latham, G. P. (1986). Job performance and appraisal. In C. L. Cooper & I. T. Robertson (Eds.), *International review of industrial and organizational psychology 1986* (pp. 117–155). Chichester, UK: John Wiley.

Latham, G. P., & Saari, L. M. (1979). Application of social-learning theory to training supervisors through behavioral modeling. *Journal of Applied Psychology*, *64*, 239–246.

Latham, G. P., Skarlicki, D., Irvine, D., & Siegel, J. P. (1993). The increasing importance of performance appraisals to employee effectiveness in organizational settings in North America. In C. L. Cooper & I. T. Robertson (Eds.), *International review of industrial and organizational psychology 1993* (pp. 87–132). Chichester, UK: John Wiley.

Latham, G. P., & Wexley, K. N. (1977). Behavioral observation scales for performance appraisal purposes. *Personnel Psychology*, *30*, 255–268.

Lautenschlager, G. J., & Flaherty, V. L. (1990). Computer administration of questions: More desirable or more social desirability? *Journal of Applied Psychology*, *75*, 310–314.

Leck, J. D., Saunders, D. M., & Charbonneau, M. (1996). Affirmative action programs: an organizational justice perspective. *Journal of Organizational Behavior*, *17*, 79–89.

Lee, R. T., & Ashforth, B. E. (1996). A meta-analytic examination of the correlates of the three dimensions of job burnout. *Journal of Applied Psychology*, *81*, 123–133.

Levine, E. L. (1983). *Everything you always wanted to know about job analysis*. Tampa, FL: Mariner.

Levine, E. L., Ash, R. A., Hall, H., & Sistrunk, F. (1983). Evaluation of job analysis methods by experienced job analysts. *Academy of Management Journal*, *26*, 339–348.

Levine, E. L., & Baker, D. P. (1987). Job analysis of deputy sheriff in the Pinellas County Sheriff's Office. Unpublished paper, University of South Florida, Tampa.

Locke, E. A. (1980). Latham versus Komaki: A tale of two paradigms. *Journal of Applied Psychology*, *65*, 16–23.

Locke, E. A., & Henne, D. (1986). Work motivation theories. In C. L. Cooper & I. T. Robertson (Eds.), *International review of industrial and organizational psychology 1986* (pp. 1–35). Chichester, UK: John Wiley.

Locke, E. A., & Latham G. P. (1990). *A theory of goal setting & task performance*. Englewood Cliffs, NJ: Prentice Hall.

Loher, B. T., Noe, R. A., Moeller, N. L., & Fitzgerald, M. P. (1985). A meta-analysis of the relation of job characteristics to job satisfaction. *Journal of Applied Psychology*, *70*, 280–289.

Lord, R. G., Binning, J. F., Rush, M. C., & Thomas, J. C. (1978). The effect of performance cues and leader behavior on questionnaire ratings of leadership behavior. *Organizational Behavior and Human Performance*, *21*, 27–39.

Lord, R. G., & Maher, K. J. (1989). Cognitive processes in industrial and organizational psychology. In C. L. Cooper & I. T. Robertson (Eds.), *International review of industrial and organizational psychology 1989* (pp. 49–91). Chichester, UK: John Wiley.

Lord, R. G., de Vader, C. L., & Alliger, G. M. (1986). A meta-analysis of the relation between personality traits and leadership perceptions: An application of validity generalization procedures. *Journal of Applied Psychology*, *71*, 402–410.

Lowin, A., & Craig, J. R. (1968). The influence of level of performance on managerial style: An experimental object-lesson in the ambiguity of correlational data. *Organizational Behavior and Human Performance*, *3*, 440–458.

Ludwig, T. D., & Geller, E. S. (1997). Assigned versus participative goal setting and response generalization: Managing injury control among professional pizza deliverers. *Journal of Applied Psychology*, *82*, 253–261.

Lyness, K. S., & Thompson, D. E. (1997). Above the glass ceiling? A comparison of matched samples of female and male executives. *Journal of Applied Psychology*, *82*, 359–375.

Mack, D. A., Nelson, D. L., & Quick, J. C. (1998). *Applied Psychology: An International Review*, *47*, 219–232.

MacKenzie, S. B., Podsakoff, P. M., & Fetter, R. (1991). Organizational citizenship behavior and objective productivity as determinants of managerial evaluations of salespersons' performance. *Organizational Behavior and Human Decision Processes*, *50*, 123–150.

Maertz, C. P., Jr., & Campion, M. A. (1998). 25 years of voluntary turnover research: A review and critique. In C. L. Cooper & I. T. Robertson (Eds.), *International review of industrial and organizational psychology 1998* (pp. 49–81). Chichester, UK: John Wiley.

Majchrzak, A., & Borys, B. (1998). Computer-aided technology and work: Moving the field forward. In C. L. Cooper & I. T. Robertson (Eds.), *International review of industrial and organiza-*

tional psychology 1998 (pp. 305–354). Chichester, UK: John Wiley.

Marchese, M. C., & Muchinsky, P. M. (1993). The validity of the employment interview: A meta-analysis. *International Journal of Selection and Assessment, 1,* 18–26.

Marion-Landais, C. A. (1993). *A cross-cultural study of leader–member exchange quality and job satisfaction as correlates of intradyadic work-value congruence.* Unpublished master's thesis, University of South Florida, Tampa.

Marks, M. L., Mirvis, P. H., Hackett, E. J., & Grady, J. F., Jr. (1986). Employee participation in a quality circle program: Impact on quality of work life, productivity, and absenteeism. *Journal of Applied Psychology, 71,* 61–69.

Martin, C. L., & Nagao, D. H. (1989). Some effects of computerized interviewing on job applicant responses. *Journal of Applied Psychology, 74,* 72–80.

Martocchio, J. J. (1994). The effects of absence culture on individual absence. *Human Relations, 47,* 243–262.

Maslach, C., & Jackson, S. (1981). *The Maslach Burnout Inventory.* Palo Alto, CA: Consulting Psychologists.

Maslow, A. H. (1943). A theory of human motivation. *Psychological Review, 50,* 370–396.

Mathieu, J. E., & Kohler, S. S. (1990). A cross-level examination of group absence influences on individual absence. *Journal of Applied Psychology, 75,* 217–220.

Mathieu, J. E., Martineau, J. W., & Tannenbaum, S. I. (1993). Individual and situational influences on the development of self-efficacy: Implications for training effectiveness. *Personnel Psychology, 46,* 125–147.

Mathieu, J. E., & Zajac, D. M. (1990). A review and meta-analysis of the antecedents, correlates, and consequences of organizational commitment. *Psychological Bulletin, 108,* 171–194.

McBride, J. R. (1998). Innovations in computer-based ability testing: Promise, problems, and perils. In M. D. Hakel (Ed.). *Beyond multiple choice: Evaluating alternatives to traditional testing for selection* (pp. 23–39). Mahway, NJ: Lawrence Erlbaum Associates.

McCormick, E. J., Jeanneret, P. R., & Mecham, R. C. (1972). A study of job characteristics and job dimensions as based on the position analysis questionnaire (PAQ). *Journal of Applied Psychology, 56,* 347–368.

McCulloch, S. (1993). Recent trends in international assessment. *International Journal of Selection and Assessment, 1,* 59–61.

McEvoy, G. M., & Beatty, R. W. (1989). Assessment centers and subordinate appraisals of managers: A seven-year examination of predictive validity. *Personnel Psychology, 42,* 37–52.

McEvoy, G. M., & Cascio, W. F. (1989). Cumulative evidence of the relationship between employee age and job performance. *Journal of Applied Psychology, 74,* 11–17.

McGregor, D. M. (1960). *The human side of enterprise.* New York: McGraw-Hill.

McIntire, S. A., & Levine, E. L. (1991). Combining personality variables and goals to predict performance. *Journal of Vocational Behavior, 38,* 288–301.

McMahan, G. C., & Woodman, R. W. (1992). The current practice of organization development within the firm. *Group and Organization Management, 17,* 117–134.

McNeely, B. L., & Meglino, B. M. (1994). The role of dispositional and situational antecedents in prosocial organizational behavior: An examination of the intended beneficiaries of prosocial behavior. *Journal of Applied Psychology, 79,* 836–844.

Meglino, B. M., DeNisi, A. S., & Ravlin, E. C. (1993). Effects of previous job exposure and subsequent job status on the functioning of a realistic job preview. *Personnel Psychology, 46,* 803–822.

Melamed, S., Ben-Avi, I., Luz, J., & Green, M. S. (1995). Objective and subjective work monotony: Effects on job satisfaction, psychological distress, and absenteeism in blue-collar workers. *Journal of Applied Psychology, 80,* 29–42.

Meyer, J. P., & Allen, N. J. (1997). *Commitment in the workplace: Theory, research, and application.* Thousand Oaks, CA: Sage.

Meyer, J. P., & Allen, N. J., & Smith, C. A. (1993). Commitment to organizations and occupations: Extension and test of a three-component conceptualization. *Journal of Applied Psychology, 78,* 538–551.

Meyer, J. P., Bobocel, D. R., Allen, N. J. (1991). Development of organizational commitment during the first year of employment: A longitudinal study of pre- and post-entry influences. *Journal of Management, 17,* 717–733.

Mitchell, K. K., Alliger, G. M., & Morfopoulos, R. (1997). Toward an ADA-appropriate job analysis. *Human Resource Management Review, 7,* 5–26.

Mitra, A., Jenkins, G. D., Jr., & Gupta, N. (1992). A meta-analytic review of the relationship between absence and turnover. *Journal of Applied Psychology, 77,* 879–889.

Mobley, W. H., Griffeth, R. W., Hand, H. H., & Meglino, B. M. (1979). Review and conceptual analysis of the employee turnover process. *Psychological Bulletin, 86,* 493–522.

Moorhead, G., Ference, R., & Neck, C. P. (1991). Group decision fiascoes continue: Space shuttle Challenger and a revised groupthink framework. *Human Relations, 44,* 539–550.

Morgeson, F. P., & Campion, M. A. (1997). Social and cognitive sources of potential inaccuracy in job analysis. *Journal of Applied Psychology, 82,* 627–655.

Morrison, A. M., & Von Glinow, M. A. (1990). Women and minorities in management. *American Psychologist, 45,* 200–208.

Morrow, C. C., Jarrett, M. Q., & Rupinski, M. T. (1997). An investigation of the effect and economic utility of corporate-wide training. *Personnel Psychology, 50,* 91–119.

Mowday, R. T., Steers, R. M., & Porter, L. W. (1979). The measurement of organizational commitment. *Journal of Vocational Behavior, 14,* 224–247.

Moyle, P. (1995). The role of negative affectivity in the stress process: tests of alternative models. *Journal of Organizational Behavior, 16*, 647–668.

Mullarkey, S., Jackson, P. R., Wall, T. D., Wilson, J. R., & Grey-Taylor, S. M. (1997). The impact of technology characteristics and job control on worker mental health. *Journal of Organizational Behavior, 18*, 471–489.

Münsterberg, H. (1913). *Psychology and industrial efficiency.* Boston: Houghton Mifflin.

Murphy, K. R. (1988). Psychological measurement: Abilities and skills. In C. L. Cooper & I. T. Robertson (Eds.), *International review of industrial and organizational psychology 1988* (pp. 213–244). Chichester, UK: John Wiley.

Murphy, K. R., Gannett, B. A., Herr, B. M., & Chen, J. A. (1986). Effects of subsequent performance on evaluations of previous performance. *Journal of Applied Psychology, 71*, 427–431.

Murphy, K. R., & Jako, R. A. (1989). Under what conditions are observed intercorrelations greater or smaller than true intercorrelations? *Journal of Applied Psychology, 74*, 827–830.

Murphy, K. R., Jako, R. A., & Anhalt, R. L. (1993). Nature and consequences of halo error: A critical analysis. *Journal of Applied Psychology, 78*, 218–225.

Murphy, L., Gershon, R. M., & DeJoy, D. (1996). Stress and occupational exposure to HIV/AIDS. In C. L. Cooper (Ed.), *Handbook of stress, medicine, and health* (pp. 177–190). Boca Raton, FL: CRC Press.

Nathan, B. R., & Lord, R. G. (1983). Cognitive categorization and dimensional schemata: A process approach to the study of halo in performance ratings. *Journal of Applied Psychology, 68*, 102–114.

Nathan, B. R., & Tippins, N. (1990). The consequences of halo "error" in performance ratings: A field study of the moderating effect of halo on test validation results. *Journal of Applied Psychology, 75*, 290–296.

National Safety Council. (1992a). *Blood pathogens.* Itasca, IL: Author.

National Safety Council (1992b). *Sound sense.* Itasca, IL: Author.

National Safety Council (1992c). *Accident facts, 1992 edition.* Itasca, IL: Author.

National Safety Council (1996). *Accident facts.* [Online] Available: http://www.nsc.org/lrs/statinfo/afp48.htm [1998, February 18].

Netemeyer, R. G., Boles, J. S., & McMurrian, R. (1996). Development and validation of work–family conflict and family–work conflict scales. *Journal of Applied Psychology, 81*, 400–410.

Neuman, G. A., Edwards, J. E., & Raju, N. S. (1989). Organizational development interventions: A meta analysis of their effects on satisfaction and other attitudes. *Personnel Psychology, 42*, 461–483.

Neuman, J. H., & Baron, R. A. (1997). Aggression in the workplace. In R. A. Giacalone & J. Greenberg (Eds.), *Antisocial behavior in organizations* (pp. 37–67). Newbury Park, CA: Sage.

Newton, T., & Keenan, T. (1991). Further analyses of the dispositional argument in organizational behavior. *Journal of Applied Psychology, 76*, 781–787.

Nicholson, N., & Johns, G. (1985). The absence culture and the psychological contract—who's in control of absence? *Academy of Management Review, 10*, 397–407.

Noe, R. A. (1986). Trainees' attributes and attitudes: Neglected influences on training effectiveness. *Academy of Management Review, 11*, 736–749.

Noe, R. A., & Schmitt, N. (1986). The influence of trainee attitudes on training effectiveness: Test of a model. *Personnel Psychology, 39*, 497–523.

O'Brien, G. E. (1983). Locus of control in work and retirement. In H. M. Lefcourt (Ed.), *Research in locus of control* (Vol. 3, pp. 7–71). New York: Academic Press.

O'Connor, E. J., Peters, L. H., Rudolf, C. J., & Pooyan, A. (1982). Situational constraints and employee affective reactions: A partial field replication. *Group & Organization Studies, 7*, 418–428.

O'Driscoll, M. P., & Beehr, T. A. (1994). Supervisor behaviors, role stressors and uncertainty as predictors of personal outcomes for subordinates. *Journal of Organizational Behavior, 15*, 141–155.

Occupational Safety and Health Administration (1997, December 11). *Ergonomics* [Online] Available: http://www.osha-slc.gov/SLTC/Ergonomics [1998, February, 18].

Oldham, G. R., Cummings, A., Mischel, L. J., Schmidtke, J. M., & Zhou, J. (1995). Listen while you work? Quasi-experimental relations between personal-stereo headset use and employee work responses. *Journal of Applied Psychology, 80*, 547–564.

Ones, D. S., & Viswesvaran, C. (1996). Bandwidth—fidelity dilemma in personality measurement for personnel selection. *Journal of Organizational Behavior, 17*, 609–626.

Ones, D. S., & Viswesvaran, C. (1998). Gender, age, and race differences on overt integrity tests: Results across four large-scale job applicant data sets. *Journal of Applied Psychology, 83*, 35–42.

Ones, D. S., & Viswesvaran, C., & Schmidt, F. L. (1993). Comprehensive meta-analysis of integrity test validities: Findings and implications for personnel selection and theories of job performance. *Journal of Applied Psychology, 78*, 679–703.

Organ, D. W., & Konovsky, M. (1989). Cognitive versus affective determinants of organizational citizenship behavior. *Journal of Applied Psychology, 74*, 157–164.

Osborn, A. F. (1957). *Applied imagination* (Rev. ed.). New York: Scribner.

Osgood, C. E., Tannenbaum, P. H., & Suci, G. J. (1957). *The measurement of meaning.* Urbana: University of Illinois Press.

Ouchi, W. G. (1981). *Theory Z.* New York: Avon.

Parker, C. P., Baltes, B. B., & Christiansen, N. D. (1997). Support for affirmative action, justice perceptions, and work attitudes: A study of gender and racial-ethnic group differences. *Journal of Applied Psychology, 82*, 376–389.

Pasmore, W., Francis, C., Haldeman, J., & Shani, A. (1982). Sociotechnical systems: A North American reflection on empirical studies of the seventies. *Human Relations, 12*, 1179–1204.

Pearce, J. A., II, & Ravlin, E. C. (1987). The design and activation of self-regulating work groups. *Human Relations, 40*, 751–782.

Pearlman, I., Schmidt, F. L., & Hunter, J. E. (1980). Validity generalization results for tests used to predict job proficiency and training success in clerical occupations. *Journal of Applied Psychology*, 65, 373–406.

Pearn, M. A. (1989). Fairness in employment selection: A comparison of UK and USA experience. In M. Smith & I. T. Robertson (Eds.), *Advances in selection and assessment* (pp. 155–163). Chichester, UK: John Wiley.

Pearson, C.A.L., & Chong, J. (1997). Contributions of job content and social information on organizational commitment and job satisfaction: An exploration in a Malaysian nursing context. *Journal of Occupational and Organizational Psychology*, 70, 357–374.

Pedalino, E., & Gamboa, V. U. (1974). Behavior modification and absenteeism: Intervention in one industrial setting. *Journal of Applied Psychology*, 59, 694–698.

Perlow, R., & Latham, L. L. (1993). Relationship of client abuse with locus of control and gender: A longitudinal study. *Journal of Applied Psychology*, 78, 831–834.

Pervin, L. A. (1993). *Personality: Theory and research* (6th ed.). New York: John Wiley.

Peters, L. H., Hartke, D. D., & Pohlman, J. T. (1985). Fiedler's contingency theory of leadership: An application of the meta-analysis procedures of Schmidt and Hunter. *Psychological Bulletin*, 97, 274–285.

Peters, L. H., & O'Connor, E. J. (1980). Situational constraints and work outcomes: The influences of a frequently overlooked construct. *Academy of Management Review*, 5, 391–397.

Peters, L. H., O'Connor, E. J., & Rudolf, C. J. (1980). The behavioral and affective consequences of performance-relevant situational variables. *Organizational Behavior and Human Performance*, 25, 79–96.

Petty, M. M., McGee, G. W., & Cavender, J. W. (1984). A meta-analysis of the relationships between individual job satisfaction and individual performance. *Academy of Management Review*, 9, 712–721.

Phillips, J. S., & Lord, R. G. (1982). Schematic information processing and perceptions of leadership in problem-solving groups. *Journal of Applied Psychology*, 67, 486–492.

Pierce, J. L., & Dunham, R. B. (1992). The 12-hour work day: A 48-hour, eight-day week. *Academy of Management Journal*, 35, 1086–1098.

Pierce, J. L., & Newstrom, J. W. (1982). Employee responses to flexible work schedules: An inter-organization, inter-system comparison. *Journal of Management*, 8, 9–25.

Podsakoff, P. M., Ahearne, M., & MacKenzie, S. B. (1997). Organizational citizenship behavior and the quantity and quality of work group performance. *Journal of Applied Psychology*, 82, 262–270.

Podsakoff, P. M., MacKenzie, S. B., Ahearne, M., & Bommer, W. H. (1995). Searching for a needle in a haystack: Trying to identify the illusive moderators of leadership behaviors. *Journal of Management*, 21, 422–470.

Potosky, D., & Bobko, P. (1997). Computer versus paper-and-pencil administration mode and response distortion in noncognitive selection tests. *Journal of Applied Psychology*, 82, 293–299.

Powell, G. N., & Butterfield, D. A. (1994). Investigating the "glass ceiling" phenomenon: An empirical study of actual promotions to top management. *Academy of Management Journal*, 37, 68–86.

Powell, G. N., & Butterfield, D. A. (1997). Effect of race on promotions to top management in a federal department. *Academy of Management Journal*, 40, 112–128.

Premack, S. L., & Wanous, J. P. (1985). A meta-analysis of realistic job preview experiments. *Journal of Applied Psychology*, 70, 706–719.

Prewett-Livingston, A. J., Feild, H. S., Veres, J. G., III, & Lewis, P. M. (1996). Effects of race on interview ratings in a situational panel interview. *Journal of Applied Psychology*, 81, 178–186.

Pulakos, E. D., Schmitt, N., & Ostroff, C. (1986). A warning about the use of a standard deviation across dimensions within ratees to measure halo. *Journal of Applied Psychology*, 71, 29–32.

Raggatt, P. T. (1991). Work stress among long-distance coach drivers: A survey and correlational study. *Journal of Organizational Behavior*, 12, 565–579.

Rain, J. S., Lane, I. M., & Steiner, D. D. (1991). A current look at the job satisfaction/life satisfaction relationship: Review and future considerations. *Human Relations*, 44, 287–305.

Raju, N. S., Burke, M. J., & Normand, J. (1990). A new approach for utility analysis. *Journal of Applied Psychology*, 75, 3–12.

Ralston, D. A. (1989). The benefits of flextime: Real or imagined? *Journal of Organizational Behavior*, 10, 369–373.

Randle, C. W. (1956). How to identify promotable executives. *Harvard Business Review*, 34, 122–134.

Ree, M. J., & Carretta, T. R. (1998). General cognitive ability and occupational performance. In C. L. Cooper & I. T. Robertson (Eds.), *International review of industrial and organizational psychology 1998* (pp. 159–184). Chichester, UK: John Wiley.

Reilly, R. R., Henry, S., & Smither, J. W. (1990). An examination of the effects of using behavior checklists on the construct validity of assessment center dimensions. *Personnel Psychology*, 43, 71–84.

Reilly, R. R., & Israelski, E. W. (1988). Development and validation of minicourses in the telecommunication industry. *Journal of Applied Psychology*, 73, 721–726.

Rice, R. W., Frone, M. R., & McFarlin, D. B. (1992). Work-nonwork conflict and the perceived quality of life. *Journal of Organizational Behavior*, 13, 155–168.

Rice, R. W., Phillips, S. M., & McFarlin, D. B. (1990). Multiple discrepancies and pay satisfaction. *Journal of Applied Psychology*, 75, 386–393.

Robbins, T. L., & DeNisi, A. S. (1994). A closer look at interpersonal affect as a distinct influence on cognitive processing in performance evaluations. *Journal of Applied Psychology*, 79, 341–353.

Robertson, I. T., & Downs, S. (1989). Work-sample tests of trainability: A meta-analysis. *Journal of Applied Psychology, 74,* 402–410.

Robertson, I. T., Gratton, L., & Sharpley, D. (1987). The psychometric properties and design of managerial assessment centres: Dimensions into exercises won't go. *Journal of Occupational Psychology, 60,* 187–195.

Robertson, I. T., & Kandola, R. S. (1982). Work sample tests: Validity, adverse impact and applicant reaction. *Journal of Occupational Psychology, 55,* 171–183.

Robinson, D. D., Wahlstrom, O. W., & Mecham, R. C. (1974). Comparison of job evaluation methods: A "policy-capturing" approach using the position analysis questionnaire. *Journal of Applied Psychology, 59,* 633–637.

Rodgers, R., & Hunter, J. E. (1991). Impact of management by objectives on organizational productivity. *Journal of Applied Psychology, 76,* 322–336.

Roethlisberger, F. J. (1941). *Management and morale.* Cambridge, MA: Harvard University Press.

Roethlisberger, F. J., & Dickson, W. J. (1939). *Management and the worker.* Cambridge, MA: Harvard University Press.

Ronen, S., & Primps, S. B. (1981). The compressed work week as organizational change: Behavioral and attitudinal outcomes. *Academy of Management Review, 6,* 61–74.

Rosenthal, R. (1991). *Meta-analytic procedures for social research* (Rev. ed.). Newbury Park, CA: Sage.

Roth, P. E., & Campion, J. E. (1992). An analysis of the predictive power of the panel interview and pre-employment tests. *Journal of Occupational and Organizational Psychology, 65,* 51–60.

Rothstein, H. R., Schmidt, F. L., Erwin, F. W., Owens, W. A., & Sparks, C. P. (1990). Biographical data in employment selection: Can validities be made generalizable? *Journal of Applied Psychology, 75,* 175–184.

Roznowski, M. (1989). Examination of the measurement properties of the Job Descriptive Index with experimental items. *Journal of Applied Psychology, 74,* 805–814.

Russell, C. J., Colella, A., & Bobko, P. (1993). Expanding the context of utility: The strategic impact of personnel selection. *Personnel Psychology, 46,* 781–801.

Russell, C. J., & Domm, D. R. (1995). Two field tests of an explanation of assessment centre validity. *Journal of Occupational and Organizational Psychology, 68,* 25–47.

Rytina, N. F. (1981). Occupational segregation and earnings differences by sex. *Monthly Labor Review, 104,* 49–53.

Saari, L. M., Johnson, T. R., McLaughlin, S. D., & Zimmerle, D. M. (1988). A survey of management training and education in U.S. companies. *Personnel Psychology, 41,* 731–743.

Sackett, P. R., Burris, L. R., & Callahan, C. (1989). Integrity testing for personnel selection: An update. *Personnel Psychology, 42,* 491–529.

Sagie, A., & Koslowsky, M. (1994). Organizational attitudes and behaviors as a function of participation in strategic and tactical change decisions: An application of path-goal theory. *Journal of Organizational Behavior, 15,* 37–47.

Salgado, J. F. (1997). The five factor model of personality and job performance in the European community. *Journal of Applied Psychology, 82,* 30–43.

Sanchez, J. I., & Levine, E. L. (1994). The impact of raters' cognition on judgment accuracy: An extension to the job analysis domain. *Journal of Business and Psychology, 9,* 47–57.

Sanchez, J. L., & Fraser, S. L. (1992). On the choice of scales for task analysis. *Journal of Applied Psychology, 77,* 545–553.

Sarafino, E. P. (1990). *Health psychology: Biopsychosocial interactions.* New York: John Wiley.

Savery, L. K., & Wooden, M. (1994). The relative influence of life events and hassles on work-related injuries: Some Australian evidence. *Human Relations, 47,* 283–305.

Scandura, T. A., & Lankau, M. J. (1997). Relationships of gender, family responsibility and flexible work hours to organizational commitment and job satisfaction. *Journal of Organizational Behavior, 18,* 377–391.

Schaubroeck, J., Ganster, D. C., & Fox, M. C. (1992). Dispositional affect and work-related stress. *Journal of Applied Psychology, 77,* 322–335.

Schaubroeck, J., & Kuehn, K. (1992). Research design in industrial and organizational psychology. In C. L. Cooper & I. T. Robertson (Eds.), *International review of industrial and organizational psychology 1992* (pp. 99–121). Chichester, UK: John Wiley.

Schein, V. E., Mueller, R., Lituchy, T., & Liu, J. (1996). Think manager—think male: a global phenomenon? *Journal of Organizational Behavior, 17,* 33–41.

Schmidt, F. L., & Hunter, J. E. (1977). Development of a general solution to the problem of validity generalization. *Journal of Applied Psychology, 62,* 529–540.

Schmidt, F. L., Hunter, J. E., McKenzie, R. C., & Muldrow, T. W. (1979). Impact of valid selection procedures on work-force productivity. *Journal of Applied Psychology, 64,* 609–626.

Schmidt, F. L., Mack, M. J., & Hunter, J. E. (1984). Selection utility in the occupation of U.S. park ranger for three modes of test use. *Journal of Applied Psychology, 69,* 490–497.

Schmit, M. J., Ryan, A. M., Stierwalt, S. L., & Powell, A. B. (1995). Frame-of-reference effects on personality scale scores and criterion-related validity. *Journal of Applied Psychology, 80,* 607–620.

Schmitt, N., Gilliland, S. W., Landis, R. S., & Devine, D. (1993). Computer-based testing applied to selection of secretarial applicants. *Personnel Psychology, 46,* 149–165.

Schmitt, N., Gooding, R. Z., Noe, R. A., & Kirch, M. (1984). Meta-analyses of validity studies published between 1964 & 1982 and the investigation of study characteristics. *Personnel Psychology, 37,* 407–422.

Schnake, M. (1991). Organizational citizenship: A review, proposed model, and research agenda. *Human Relations, 44,* 735–759.

Schneider, B., & Dachler, H. P. (1978). A note on the stability of the Job Descriptive Index. *Journal of Applied Psychology, 63,* 650–653.

Schneider, K. T., Swan, S., & Fitzgerald, L. F. (1997). Job-related and psychological effects of sexual harassment in the workplace: Empirical evidence from two organizations. *Journal of Applied Psychology, 82,* 401–415.

Schneider, R. J., Hough, L. M., & Dunnette, M. D. (1996). Broadsided by broad traits: how to sink science in five dimensions or less. *Journal of Organizational Behavior, 17,* 639–655.

Schriesheim, C. A., Powers, K. J., Scandura, T. A., Gardiner, C. C., & Lankau, M. J. (1993). Improving construct measurement in management research: Comments and quantitative approach for assessing the theoretical content adequacy of paper-and-pencil survey-type instruments. *Journal of Management, 19,* 385–417.

Schriesheim, J. F. (1980). The social context of leader–subordinate relations: An investigation of the effects of group cohesiveness. *Journal of Applied Psychology, 65,* 183–194.

Schwab, D. P., & Grams, R. (1985). Sex-related errors in job evaluation: A "real-world" test. *Journal of Applied Psychology, 70,* 533–539.

Scott, W. D. (1908). *The theory of advertising.* Boston: Small, Maynard.

Shackleton, V., & Newell, S. (1991). Management selection: A comparative survey of methods used in top British and French companies. *Journal of Occupational Psychology, 64,* 23–36.

Shechtman, Z. (1992). A group assessment procedure as a predictor of on-the-job performance of teachers. *Journal of Applied Psychology, 77,* 383–387.

Sheehy, N. P., & Chapman, A. J. (1987). Industrial accidents. In C. L. Cooper & I. T. Robertson (Eds.), *International review of industrial and organizational psychology 1987* (pp. 201–228). Chichester, UK: John Wiley.

Shirom, A. (1989). Burnout in work organizations. In C. L. Cooper & I. T. Robertson (Eds.), *International review of industrial and organizational psychology 1989* (pp. 25–48). Chichester, UK: John Wiley.

Shore, L. M., Barksdale, K., & Shore, T. H. (1993, April). *Managerial perceptions of employee commitment to the organization.* Paper presented at the Society for Industrial and Organizational Psychology conference, San Francisco.

Simon, S. J., & Werner, J. M. (1996). Computer training through behavior modeling, self-paced, and instructional approaches: A field experiment. *Journal of Applied Psychology, 81,* 648–659.

Sinclair, R. C. (1988). Mood, categorization breadth, and performance appraisal: The effects of order of information acquisition and affective state on halo, accuracy, information retrieval, and evaluations. *Organizational Behavior and Human Decision Processes, 42,* 22–46.

Skarlicki, D. P., & Folger, R. (1997). Retaliation in the workplace: The roles of distributive, procedural, and interactional justice. *Journal of Applied Psychology, 82,* 434–443.

Slaying was store's 176th call to police. (1993, July 7). *Tampa Tribune.*

Smith, C. A., Organ, D. W., & Near, P. J. (1983). Organizational citizenship behavior: Its nature and antecedents. *Journal of Applied Psychology, 68,* 653–663.

Smith, J. E., & Hakel, M. D. (1979). Convergence among data sources, response bias, and reliability and validity of a structured job analysis questionnaire. *Personnel Psychology, 32,* 677–692.

Smith, M., & George, D. (1992). Selection methods. In C. L. Cooper & I. T. Robertson (Eds.), *International review of industrial and organizational psychology 1992* (pp. 55–97). Chichester, UK: John Wiley.

Smith, M. J., Hurrell, J. J., Jr., & Murphy, R. K., Jr. (1981). Stress and health effects in paced and unpaced work. In G. Salvendy & M. J. Smith (Eds.), *Machine pacing and occupational stress* (pp. 261–267). London: Taylor & Francis.

Smith, P. B., & Misumi, J. (1989). Japanese management—A sun rising in the West? In C. L. Cooper & I. T. Robertson (Eds.), *International review of industrial and organizational psychology, 1989* (pp. 330–369). Chichester, UK: John Wiley.

Smith, P. C., & Kendall, L. M. (1963). Retranslation of expectations: An approach to the construction of unambiguous anchors for rating scales. *Journal of Applied Psychology, 47,* 149–155.

Smith, P. C., Kendall, L. M., & Hulin, C. L. (1969). *Measurement of satisfaction in work and retirement.* Chicago: Rand McNally.

Snyder, R. A., Verderber, K., Langmeyer, L., & Myers, M. (1992). A reconsideration of self- and organization-referent attitudes as "causes" of the glass ceiling effect. *Group and Organization Management, 17,* 260–278.

Society for Industrial and Organizational Psychology. (1985). *Guidelines for education and training at the doctoral level in industrial/organizational psychology.* College Park: University of Maryland.

Society for Industrial and Organizational Psychology. (1992). *Graduate training programs in industrial/organizational psychology and related fields.* Arlington Heights, IL: Author.

Solomonson, A. L., & Lance, C. E. (1997). Examination of the relationship between true halo and halo error in performance ratings. *Journal of Applied Psychology, 82,* 665–674.

Sparks, K., Cooper, C., Fried, Y., & Shirom, A. (1997). The effects of hours of work on health: A meta-analytic review. *Journal of Occupational and Organizational Psychology, 70,* 391–408.

Spector, P. E. (1982). Behavior in organizations as a function of employees' locus of control. *Psychological Bulletin, 91,* 482–497.

Spector, P. E. (1985). Measurement of human service staff satisfaction: Development of the Job Satisfaction Survey. *American Journal of Community Psychology, 13,* 693–713.

Spector, P. E. (1986). Perceived control by employees: A meta-analysis of studies concerning autonomy and participation at work. *Human Relations, 11,* 1005–1016.

Spector, P. E. (1992). A consideration of the validity and meaning of self-report measures of job conditions. In C. L. Cooper & I. T. Robertson (Eds.), *International review of industrial and organizational psychology 1992* (pp. 123–151). Chichester, UK: John Wiley.

Spector, P. E., Brannick, M. T., & Coovert, M. D. (1989). Job analysis. In C. L. Cooper & I. T. Robertson (Eds.), *International review of industrial and organizational psychology 1989* (pp. 281–328). Chichester, UK: John Wiley.

Spector, P. E., Dwyer, D. J., & Jex, S. M. (1988). Relation of job stressors to affective, health, and performance outcomes: A comparison of multiple data sources. *Journal of Applied Psychology, 73,* 11–19.

Spector, P. E., & Jex, S. M. (1991). Relations of job characteristics from multiple data sources with employee affect, absence, turnover intentions, and health. *Journal of Applied Psychology, 76,* 46–53.

Spector, P. E., & Wimalasiri, J. (1986). A cross-cultural comparison of job satisfaction dimensions in the United States and Singapore. *Applied Psychology: An International Review, 35,* 147–158.

Spychalski, A. C., Quiñones, M. A., Gaugler, B. B., & Pohley, K. (1997). A survey of assessment center practices in organizations in the United States. *Personnel Psychology, 50,* 71–90.

Stajkovic, A. D., & Luthans, F. (1997). A meta-analysis of the effects of organizational behavior modification on task performance, 1975–95. *Academy of Management Journal, 40,* 1122–1149.

Staw, B. M., Bell, N. E., & Clausen, J. A. (1986). The dispositional approach to job attitudes: A lifetime longitudinal test. *Administrative Science Quarterly, 31,* 56–77.

Staw, B. M., & Ross, J. (1985). Stability in the midst of change: A dispositional approach to job attitudes. *Journal of Applied Psychology, 70,* 469–480.

Steel, R. P., & Ovalle, N. K., II. (1984). A review and meta-analysis of research on the relationship between behavioral intentions and employee turnover. *Journal of Applied Psychology, 69,* 673–686.

Steiner, D. D., & Gilliland, S. W. (1996). Fairness reactions to personnel selection techniques in France and the United States. *Journal of Applied Psychology, 81,* 134–141.

Stogdill, R. M. (1963). *Manual for the Leader Behavior Description Questionnaire—Form XII.* Columbus: Ohio State University.

Stokes, G. S., & Reddy, S. (1992). Use of background data in organizational decisions. In C. L. Cooper & I. T. Robertson (Eds.), *International review of industrial and organizational psychology 1992* (pp. 285–321). Chichester, UK: John Wiley.

Storms, P. L., & Spector, P. E. (1987). Relationships of organizational frustration with reported behavioural reactions: The moderating effect of locus of control. *Journal of Occupational Psychology, 60,* 227–234.

Strauss, A., & Corbin, J. (1990). *Basics of qualitative research.* Newbury Park, CA: Sage.

Stroh, L. K., Brett, J. M., & Reilly, A. H. (1992). All the right stuff: A comparison of female and male managers' career progression. *Journal of Applied Psychology, 77,* 252–260.

Strube, M. J., & Garcia, J. E. (1981). A meta-analytic investigation of Fiedler's contingency model of leadership effectiveness. *Psychology Bulletin, 90,* 307–321.

Sundstrom, E., De Meuse, K. P., & Futrell, D. (1990). Work teams applications and effectiveness. *American Psychologist, 45,* 120–133.

Sweeney, P. D., & McFarlin, D. B. (1997). Process and outcome: gender differences in the assessment of justice. *Journal of Organizational Behavior, 18,* 83–98.

Taylor, F. W. (1911). *Scientific management.* New York: Harper & Row.

Taylor, M. S., & Schmidt, D. W. (1983). A process-oriented investigation of recruitment source effectiveness. *Personnel Psychology, 36,* 343–354.

Taylor, M. S., Tracy, K. B., Renard, M. K., Harrison, J. K., & Carroll, S. J. (1995). Due process in performance appraisal: A quasi-experiment in procedural justice. *Administrative Science Quarterly, 40,* 495–523.

Terpstra, D. E., & Cook, S. E. (1985). Complainant characteristics and reported behaviors and consequences associated with formal sexual harassment charges. *Personnel Psychology, 38,* 559–574.

Tett, R. P., & Meyer, J. P. (1993). Job satisfaction, organizational commitment, turnover intention, and turnover: Path analysis based on meta-analytic findings. *Personnel Psychology, 46,* 259–293.

Tett, R. P., Jackson, D. N., & Rothstein, M. (1991). Personality measures as predictors of job performance: A meta-analytic review. *Personnel Psychology, 44,* 703–742.

Tharenou, P. (1993). A test of reciprocal causality for absenteeism. *Journal of Organizational Behavior, 14,* 269–290.

Thomas, L. T., & Ganster, D. C. (1995). Impact of family-supportive work variables on work-family conflict and strain: A control perspective. *Journal of Applied Psychology, 80,* 6–15.

Thorndike, E. L. (1913). *Educated psychology: The psychology of learning* (Vol. 2). New York: Teachers College Press.

Three die in postal shootings in Michigan, California. (1993, May 7). *The Atlanta Journal/The Atlanta Constitution.*

Totterdell, P., Spelten, E., Smith, L., Barton, J., & Folkard, S. (1995). Recovery from work shifts: How long does it take? *Journal of Applied Psychology, 80,* 43–57.

Tracy, J. B., Tannenbaum, S. I., & Kavanagh, M. J. (1995). Applying trained skills on the job: The importance of the work environment. *Journal of Applied Psychology, 80,* 239–252.

Treiman, D. J. (1979). *Job evaluation: An analytical review* (Interim Report to the Equal Employment Commission). Washington, DC: National Academy of Sciences.

Trevor, C. O., Gerhart, B., & Boudreau, J. W. (1997). Voluntary turnover and job performance: Curvilinearity and the moderating influences of salary growth and promotions. *Journal of Applied Psychology, 82,* 44–61.

Trice, A. D., & Tillapaugh, P. (1991). Children's estimates of their parents' job satisfaction. *Psychological Reports, 69,* 63–66.

Triplett, N. (1897). The dynamogenic factors in pacemaking competition. *American Journal of Psychology, 8,* 507–533.

Trist, E. L., & Bamforth, K. W. (1951). Some social and psychological consequences of the longwall method of coal-getting. *Human Relations, 4,* 3–38.

Tuch, S. A., & Martin, J. K. (1991). Race in the workplace: Black/white differences in the sources of job satisfaction. *The Sociological Quarterly, 32,* 103–116.

Tziner, A., & Vardi, Y. (1983). Ability as a moderator between cohesiveness and tank crews performance. *Journal of Occupational Behaviour, 4,* 137–143.

Uniform guidelines on employee selection procedures. (1978). *Federal Register, 43,* Section 60-3, 38296, August 25.

U.S. Bureau of Labor Statistics. (1995). *Incidence rates for nonfatal occupational injuries and illnesses involving days away from work per 10,000 full-time workers for selected characteristics and industry division, 1995.* [Online] Available: http://www.bls.gov/news.release/osh2.t06.htm [1998, February 18].

U.S. Bureau of Labor Statistics. (1996). *National census of fatal occupational injuries, 1996.* [Online] Available: http://stats.bls.gov/news.release/cfoi.new.htm [1998, February 18].

U.S. Bureau of Labor Statistics. (1998). *Workers on flexible and shift schedules in 1997 summary.* [Online] Available: http://www.bls.gov/news/release/flex.new.htm [1998, April 8].

U.S. Department of Labor. (1977). *Dictionary of occupational titles* (4th ed.). Washington DC: U.S. Government Printing Office.

U.S. Department of Labor. (1991). *Dictionary of occupational titles* (5th ed.). Washington DC: U.S. Government Printing Office.

U.S. Department of Labor. (1998). *Occupational Information Network, ONET.* [Online] Available: http://www.doleta.gov/programs/onet [1998, June 23].

Valacich, J. S., Dennis, A. R., & Nunamaker. J. E., Jr. (1992). Group and anonymity effects on computer-mediated idea generation. *Small Group Research, 23,* 49–73.

Van De Water, T. J. (1997). Psychology's entrepreneurs and the marketing of industrial psychology. *Journal of Applied Psychology, 82,* 486–499.

Van Eerde, W., & Thierry, H. (1996). Vrooms's expectancy models and work-related criteria: A meta-analysis. *Journal of Applied Psychology, 81,* 575–586.

Van Fleet, D. D., & Griffin, R. W. (1989). Quality circles: A review and suggested future directions. In C. L. Cooper & I. T. Robertson (Eds.), *International review of industrial and organizational psychology 1989* (pp. 213–233). Chichester, UK: John Wiley.

Vinchur, A. J., Schippmann, J. S., Smalley, M. D., & Rothe, H. F. (1991). Productivity consistency of foundry chippers and grinders: A 6-year study. *Journal of Applied Psychology, 76,* 134–136.

Violanti, J. M., Vena, J. E., & Marshall, J. R. (1986). Disease risk and mortality among police officers: New evidence and contributing factors. *Journal of Police Science and Administration, 14,* 17–23.

Vroom, V. (1964). *Work and motivation.* New York: John Wiley.

Vroom, V. H., & Jago, A. G. (1988). *The new leadership: Managing participation in organizations.* Englewood Cliffs, NJ: Prentice Hall.

Vroom, V. H., & Yetton, P. W. (1973). *Leadership and decision-making.* Pittsburgh: University of Pittsburgh Press.

Wagner, J. A., III. (1994). Participation's effects on performance and satisfaction: A reconsideration of research evidence. *Academy of Management Review, 19,* 312–330.

Wagner, J. A., III. (1995). Studies of individualism-collectivism: Effects on cooperation in groups. *Academy of Management Journal, 38,* 152–172.

Wall, T. D., Corbett, J. M., Martin, R., Clegg, C. W., & Jackson, P. R. (1990). Advanced manufacturing technology, work design, and performance: A change study. *Journal of Applied Psychology, 6,* 691–697.

Wall, T. D., & Davids, K. (1992). Shopfloor work organization and advanced manufacturing technology. In C. L. Cooper & I. T. Robertson (Eds.), *International review of industrial and organizational psychology 1992* (pp. 363–398). Chichester, UK: John Wiley.

Wall, T. D., Jackson, P. R., & Davids, K. (1992). Operator work design and robotics system performance: A serendipitous field study. *Journal of Applied Psychology, 77,* 353–362.

Wall, T. D., Jackson, P. R., Mullarkey, S., & Parker, S. K. (1996). The demands-control model of job strain: A more specific test. *Journal of Occupational and Organizational Psychology, 69,* 153–166.

Wall, T. D., Kemp, N. J., Jackson, P. R., & Clegg, C. W. (1986). Outcomes of autonomous workgroups: A long-term field experiment. *Academy of Management Journal, 29,* 280–304.

Wall, T. D., & Martin, R. (1987). Job and work design. In C. L. Cooper & I. T. Robertson (Eds.), *International review of industrial and organizational psychology 1987* (pp. 61–92). Chichester, UK: John Wiley.

Wallack, J. T. (1989). AIDS anxiety among health care professionals. *Hospital and Community Psychiatry, 40,* 507–510.

Wanous, J. P. (1989). Installing a realistic job pre-view: Ten tough choices. *Personnel Psychology, 42,* 117–133.

Wanous, J. P., & Zwany, A. (1977). A cross-sectional test of need hierarchy theory. *Organizational Behavior and Human Performance, 18,* 78–97.

Warr, P., & Payne, R. (1983). Affective outcomes of paid employment in a random sample of British workers. *Journal of Occupational Behavior, 4,* 91–104.

Watson, D., Pennebaker, J. W., & Folger, R. (1986). Beyond negative affectivity: Measuring stress and satisfaction in the workplace. *Journal of Organizational Behavior Management, 8,* 141–157.

Wayne, S. J., Shore, L. M., & Liden, R. C. (1997). Perceived organizational support and leader-member exchange: A social exchange perspective. *Academy of Management Journal, 40,* 82–111.

Weaver, C. N. (1978). Job satisfaction as a component of happiness among males and females. *Personnel Psychology, 31,* 831–840.

Weber, M. (1947). *The theory of social and economic organization* (A. M. Henderson & T. Parsons, Trans. and Eds.). New York: Oxford University Press.

Weiss, D. J., Dawis, R., Lofquist, L. H., & England, G. W. (1966). *Instrumentation for the theory of work adjustment* (Minnesota Studies in Vocational Rehabilitation: XXI). University of Minnesota, Minneapolis.

Werner, J. M. (1994). Dimensions that make a difference: Examining the impact of in-role and extrarole behaviors on supervisory ratings. *Journal of Applied Psychology, 79,* 98–107.

Werner, J. M., & Bolino, M. C. (1997). Explaining U.S. courts of appeals decisions involving performance appraisal: Accuracy, fairness, and validation. *Personnel Psychology, 50,* 1–24.

West, M. A., Borrill, C. S., & Unsworth, K. L. (1998). Team effectiveness in organizations. In C. L. Cooper & I. T. Robertson (Eds.), *International review of industrial and organizational psychology 1998* (pp. 1–48). Chichester, UK: John Wiley.

Westman, M. (1992). Moderating effect of decision latitude on stress-strain relationship: Does organizational level matter? *Journal of Organizational Behavior, 13,* 713–722.

Westman, M., & Eden, D. (1997). Effects of a respite from work on burnout: Vacation relief and fade-out. *Journal of Applied Psychology, 82,* 516–527.

Wiesner, W. H., & Cronshaw, S. F. (1988). A meta-analytic investigation of the impact of interview format and degree of structure on the validity of the employment interview. *Journal of Occupational Psychology, 61,* 275–290.

Wilhelm, C. C., Herd, A. M., & Steiner, D. D. (1993). Attributional conflict between managers and sub-ordinates: An investigation of leader-member exchange effects. *Journal of Organizational Behavior, 14,* 531–544.

Williams, K., Harkins, S., & Latané, B. (1981). Identifiability as a deterrent to social loafing: Two cheering experiments. *Journal of Personality and Social Psychology, 40,* 303–311.

Williams, L. J., & Hazer, J. T. (1986). Antecedents and consequences of satisfaction and commitment in turnover models: A reanalysis using latent variable structural equation methods. *Journal of Applied Psychology, 71,* 219–231.

Wilson, M. A., Harvey, R. J., & Macy, B. A. (1990). Repeating items to estimate the test–retest reliability of task inventory ratings. *Journal of Applied Psychology, 75,* 158–163.

Winterton, J. (1994). Social and technological characteristics of coal-face work: A temporal and special analysis. *Human Relations, 47,* 89–118.

Witt, L. A., & Nye, L. G. (1992). Gender and the relationship between perceived fairness of pay or promotion and job satisfaction. *Journal of Applied Psychology, 77,* 910–917.

Wofford, J. C., & Liska, L. Z. (1993). Path-goal theories of leadership: A meta-analysis. *Journal of Management, 19,* 857–876.

Wong, C., Hui, C., & Law, K. S. (1998). A longitudinal study of the job perception–job satisfaction relationship: A test of the three alternative specifications. *Journal of Occupational and Organizational Psychology, 71,* 127–146.

Woolley, R. M., & Hakstian, A. R. (1993). A comparative study of integrity tests: The criterion-related validity of personality-based and overt measures of integrity. *International Journal of Selection and Assessment, 1,* 27–40.

Wright, P. M., Lichtenfels, P. A., & Pursell, E. D. (1989). The structured interview: Additional studies and a meta-analysis. *Journal of Occupational Psychology, 62,* 191–199.

Yearta, S. K., Maitlis, S., & Briner, R. B. (1995). An exploratory study of goal setting in theory and practice: A motivational technique that works? *Journal of Occupational and Organizational Psychology, 68,* 237–252.

Yukl, G. A. (1989). *Leadership in organizations.* Englewood Cliffs, NJ: Prentice Hall.

Yukl, G. A., & Latham, G. P. (1975). Consequences of reinforcement schedules and incentive magnitudes for employee performance: Problems encountered in an industrial setting. *Journal of Applied Psychology, 60,* 294–298.

Zajonc, R. B. (1965). Social facilitation. *Science, 149,* 269–274.

Zickar, M., & Taylor, R. (1995). Income of SIOP members in 1994, [Online] Available: http://www.siop.org/TIPDec95/Zickar.html [1998, April 1].

GLOSSARY

Ability: The capability of developing a skill or learning a task; a person's aptitude for learning.

Ability test: A test designed to assess a person's abilities or aptitudes.

Achievement test: A psychological test designed to assess a person's level of knowledge or skill; also called a knowledge and skill test.

Action theory: A motivation theory that links a person's goals to their behavior.

Actual criterion: The way in which the theoretical criterion is assessed; the operationalization of a construct.

Additive task: A task in which a group's performance is the sum of individual members' performances. For example, total sales for a group of salespeople in a store are the sum of each person's individual sales.

Adverse impact: Potential unfairness in the treatment of minority group or protected class members. In hiring it occurs if the protected class's selection ratio is less than four-fifths of the nonprotected class's selection ratio.

Affirmative action: A program designed to increase the number of minority or protected class members in an organization.

Analysis of variance (ANOVA): A statistical test used to compare group means.

Application form: A form completed by a job applicant; asks for background information.

Apprenticeship: An on-the-job training method. The trainee learns by assisting an experienced employee; most often used to teach a skilled trade such as carpentry or plumbing.

Arithmetic mean: The sum of scores divided by the number of scores.

Assessment center: A series of assessment exercises including simulations of work tasks that are used to assess a person's potential for a job. They are most frequently used to determine an employee's suitability for promotion into management positions.

Audiovisual instruction: A training method that uses pictures and sound to present material.

Autoinstruction: Any self-taught method of training.

Automaticity: A skill or task that is so well learned that a person can do it automatically with little conscious monitoring or thought. Professional athletes achieve this level of task performance.

Autonomy: The extent to which an employee is able to decide how to do his or her job.

Baserate: How often something occurs. In selection it is the proportion of people hired who will be successful on the job.

Behavior criteria: Methods of evaluating training by assessing changes in trainee behavior on the job.

Behavior Observation Scale (BOS): A behavior-based job performance instrument. Raters are given a list of behaviors and are asked to indicate how often the ratee performs each one.

Behaviorally Anchored Rating Scale (BARS): A behavior-based job performance instrument. Raters are given several behaviors shown on a scale and are asked to indicate which one is most characteristic of the ratee's performance.

Big Five: The five dimensions considered to represent the major factors of human personality.

Biographical inventory: A selection tool in which the job applicant provides extensive background information.

353

Brainstorming: A group method whereby individuals meet to generate solutions to a problem.

Bureaucracy: A highly structured organizational form having the characteristics outlined in Max Weber's bureaucracy theory.

Burnout: An aversive emotional state that is thought to be the result of job stress. It is characterized by a lack of enthusiasm for the job and a lost sense of the importance of the job.

Cadre: A term from leader–member exchange (LMX) theory that refers to individuals who are favored by their supervisors.

Career ladder: A system in an organization that defines a progression of promotion opportunities, such as ranks in the military.

Carpal tunnel syndrome: A repetitive strain injury of the wrist brought on by continually performing the same motions.

Categorical measurement: A measurement technique in which numbers represent arbitrary categories of a variable rather than positions along an underlying continuum.

Central tendency error: The tendency for a rater to give everyone mid-range ratings across all dimensions of performance.

Chain of command: In bureaucracy theory the idea that directives flow down the organization from supervisor to subordinate.

Change agent: The person or persons who implement the changes in organizational development plans.

Charismatic leader: A leader who has an unusual amount of influence on followers and can change their attitudes and beliefs.

Classical measurement theory: States that a measure is composed of a true score component and an error component.

Coercive power: Power based on the use of punishments.

Cognitive ability tests: Tests that assess cognitive or mental abilities, such as mathematical or verbal reasoning. The most commonly used cognitive ability tests are intelligence tests.

Cohesiveness: The attraction that group members have toward the group; the importance of the group to group members.

Collectivism: A culture value referring to the focus a person has on others rather than the self. It is the opposite of individualism.

Combination Job Analysis Method (C-JAM): A job analysis technique that involves several methods, including interviews and questionnaires.

Comparable worth: The idea that jobs having equivalent value to an organization should be paid the same; refers to differences in pay levels between jobs held predominantly by men and jobs held predominantly by women.

Compensable factors: In job evaluation the variables that are used as the basis of the analysis.

Concurrent validation study: A validation strategy in which the predictor and criterion are assessed at the same time.

Conference: A training method in which trainees meet to discuss the material.

Confounding: A state that occurs when two or more variables are tangled up such that conclusions about either one alone cannot be made.

Consideration: A supervisory style characterized by concern with the well-being of subordinates. One of the dimensions of the Leader Behavior Description Questionnaire that was developed during the Ohio State Leadership Studies.

Construct validity: The ability to confidently interpret the meaning of an instrument and the ability to conclude that we understand what it is that an instrument actually measures.

Content validity: A characteristic of a test that adequately covers the entire domain intended. For a final examination, content validity would mean that all of the curriculum has been included as opposed to only a small part.

Continuous measurement: A measurement technique in which numbers represent an underlying continuum of a variable from low to high.

Control: Any of a number of research procedures that eliminate the possibility that unwanted variables caused the results.

Control group: A comparison group in an experiment; often a group that did not receive the treatment of interest.

Correlation: The association between two variables.

Correlation coefficient: A statistic that indicates the strength of association between two variables.

Criterion: A standard of comparison. For performance appraisal, it is the definition of good performance.

Criterion contamination: The extent to which an actual criterion assesses something other than the theoretical criterion.

Criterion deficiency: The extent to which a theoretical criterion is not assessed by the actual criterion.

Criterion-related validity: The instrument in question is related to a criterion that it is theoretically expected to relate to.

Criterion relevance: The extent to which the actual criterion assesses the theoretical criterion.

Critical incident: An example of either good or poor job performance; often used to conduct job analysis.

Cross-sectional design: A design for a study in which all data are collected at the same time.

Cross-validate: To replicate the results of one sample with those of another sample.

Cutoff score: A score that serves as the threshold for selection. Individuals who reach the cutoff are hired, whereas those who are below the cutoff are not.

Decibel (dB): A measure of sound intensity.

Delegation of authority: From bureaucracy theory, the principle that each manager should assign the responsibility for portions of work to subordinates.

Demand/control model: A model of job stress that suggests how control can reduce the negative effects of job stressors.

Dependent variable: In an experiment the variable that changes as a result of manipulating the independent variable.

Descriptive statistics: Statistics that summarize a distribution of scores, such as means and standard deviations.

Descriptive theory: An organizational theory that explains how organizations operate.

Dictionary of Occupational Titles (DOT): A book that contains descriptions of over 20,000 jobs in the United States.

Division of labor: Principle from bureaucracy theory that suggests how work should be divided into a series of tasks that are assigned to different individuals.

Dynamic criterion: The idea that job performance changes over time.

Engineering psychology: The branch of psychology concerned with the interaction of people and technology, also called ergonomics or human factors.

Equity theory: A theory that bases work motivation on the balance between perceived contributions (inputs) and rewards (outcomes).

Ergonomics: The branch of psychology concerned with the interaction of people and technology, also called engineering psychology or human factors.

Error: According to classical test theory, the part of an observed score that does not represent the construct of interest.

Error variance: Variability among subjects in the same experimental condition.

Essential function: The idea that certain job tasks are necessary for an employee to perform.

Existence, Relatedness, Growth (ERG) theory: A theory that bases motivation on three categories of need.

Expectancy: The belief that effort will lead to good job performance.

Expectancy theory: A theory that bases work motivation on a person's expectancy that behavior will lead to desired rewards.

Experiment: A research design in which subjects are randomly assigned to conditions or treatments created by the researcher.

Expert power: Influence based on the perceived expertise of the individual.

Face validity: What a measure appears to assess.

Facet: A dimension of job satisfaction, such as pay or supervision.

Factorial analysis of variance (ANOVA): A statistical technique for analyzing data from experiments with more than one independent variable.

Factorial design: An experimental design for a study that has two or more independent variables.

Feedback: Information given to a person about his or her performance.

Fiedler's contingency theory: A theory that considers leader effectiveness to be a joint outcome of the leader and the leadership situation.

Field experiment: An experiment conducted in the setting in which the behavior in question naturally occurs.

Field setting: A research setting in which behavior naturally occurs.

Flextime: A work schedule that allows employees to choose some of their work hours.

Force: The term in expectancy theory that represents the level of motivation to engage in a behavior.

Formal role: An established role in an organization, such as supervisor.

Four-fifths rule: The threshold for adverse impact.

Frame of reference training: A form of training for raters who conduct performance appraisal in which they are given a common and consistent frame of reference on which to base judgments.

Frustration-regression: A principle of ERG theory that says people will revert to a lower level need when fulfillment of a higher level need is blocked.

Functional Job Analysis (FJA): Method of job analysis that produces scores on common dimensions; used to compile the Dictionary of Occupational Titles.

Galatea effect: A type of self-fulfilling prophecy in which a belief in being able to do something well results in better performance by an individual. It is similar to self-efficacy.

General principles: A general overview of the area being trained that should be given to trainees.

Generalizability: The extent to which findings in a study can be extended to other settings.

Glass ceiling: The phenomenon that minorities and women can progress only to a certain level in organizations.

Goal-setting theory: A motivation theory that considers motivation to be enhanced by the setting of goals.

Graphic rating form: A performance appraisal technique in which employees are rated on dimensions of performance, such as work quality or work quantity.

Group cohesiveness: *See* Cohesiveness.

Group polarization: The tendency of a group to take more extreme positions than the mean of individuals' positions.

Group test: A psychological test administered to groups of individuals at the same time.

Groupthink: Poor decision making that results from certain group processes.

Growth need strength (GNS): A personality variable from job characteristics theory that concerns the level of a person's need for things that can be gotten from complex work, such as recognition and sense of accomplishment.

Halo error: The tendency for a rater to give an individual the same rating across different dimensions of performance.

Hawthorne Effect: Study results that are produced by the subjects' knowledge that they are research participants.

Hired hands: In leader–member exchange (LMX) theory, the individuals who are not favored by the supervisor.

Human factors: The branch of psychology concerned with the interaction of people and technology, also called engineering psychology or ergonomics.

Hygiene factors: In two-factor theory the job factors that fall outside the nature of the work itself, such as pay and other rewards.

Hypothesis: A researcher's guess about the outcome of a study.

Identical elements: In training the correspondence between responses made in training and responses necessary on the job.

In-basket exercise: A simulation exercise used in an assessment center; asks the assessee to show what he or she would do with a series of items that might be found in a manager's in-basket.

In-group: *See* Cadre.

Incentive system: A compensation system in which employees are paid for their level of productivity.

Independent variable: The variable in an experiment that is manipulated by the researcher.

Individual test: A psychological test administered to only one person at a time.

Individualism: A culture value referring to the focus a person has on the self as opposed to others. It is the opposite of collectivism.

Industrial/organizational (I/O) psychology: Applied branch of psychology that is concerned with understanding people in organizations.

Inferential statistics: Branch of statistics that is concerned with generalizing results from the data at hand to all possible cases. It relies on statistical tests that are based on probability.

Informal role: A role that develops in a work group that was not intended by the organization.

Informed consent form: Explains a study to a potential subject before he or she agrees to participate.

Initiating structure: A leadership style characterized by concern with task accomplishment; one of the dimensions of the Leader Behavior Description Questionnaire from the Ohio State Leadership Studies.

Inputs: In equity theory the contributions made by an employee.

Instrumentality: In expectancy theory the belief that performance will lead to rewards.

Integrity test: A paper-and-pencil test designed to predict employee counterproductive behavior.

Internal consistency reliability: The agreement among multiple items in a test or multiple ratings by different raters.

Inter-rater reliability: The association between the ratings of two (or more) raters who rate the same subject on the same variable.

Interview: A face-to-face meeting between two or more people for the purpose of sharing information; used for data collection and employee selection.

Job analysis: A method for describing jobs and characteristics necessary for jobs.

Job characteristics model: A model that relates employee motivation and satisfaction to job characteristics.

Job Components Inventory (JCI): A method of job analysis that matches job requirements to characteristics of people.

Job Descriptive Index (JDI): A five-facet measure of job satisfaction.

Job evaluation: A mathematical procedure for determining the relative value of a job to an organization.

Job in General (JIG) scale: A measure of overall job satisfaction.

Job-oriented job analysis: Any job analysis method that focuses on the content of jobs.

Job satisfaction: A person's attitudes and feelings about his or her job and facets of the job.

Job strain: A physical or psychological reaction to a stressful job condition.

Job stressor: A stressful job condition.

Joint optimization: The concept from sociotechnical systems theory that the social system and technical system of an organization must be designed to complement one another.

Knowledge: What it is necessary to know for a job.

Knowledge and skill test: A psychological test designed to assess a person's knowledge or skills; also called an achievement test.

KSAOs: The knowledge, skills, abilities, and other personal characteristics necessary for good job performance.

Laboratory setting: Research setting in which the behavior of interest does not naturally occur.

Leader Behavior Description Questionnaire (LBDQ): Scale to assess leadership style, including consideration and initiating structure.

Leader Match: A procedure based on Fiedler's contingency theory that trains leaders to modify situations to match their personal characteristics.

Leader-member exchange (LMX) theory: A theory that views leadership from the perspective of individual leader-subordinate pairs.

Leaderless group exercise: An assessment center exercise in which assessees are placed in a group without a leader to observe their interpersonal behavior.

Learning criteria: Measures that indicate how much trainees have learned from training.

Least Preferred Coworker (LPC) scale: A measure used to assess a personality characteristic of a leader. The LPC is an important component of Fiedler's contingency theory.

Lecture: A training method in which trainees listen to a presentation.

Legitimate power: Influence based on followers' beliefs that a person has the right to ask for compliance, usually based on rank or title.

Leniency error: The tendency for a rater to give everyone high ratings across dimensions of performance.

Life satisfaction: A person's attitudes about his or her overall life.

Locus of control: A personality variable that refers to people's tendencies to attribute rewards to themselves (internals) or to other people or things (externals).

Longitudinal design: A design for a study in which data are collected at different times.

Management by objectives (MBO). An organizational change technique that involves setting interrelated goals throughout an organization.

Masculinity: A culture value reflecting an emphasis on achievement as opposed to the well-being of others.

Massed training: Training that is done all at one time; opposite of spaced training.

Mean: A measure of the center of a distribution; the sum of observations divided by the number of observations.

Measurement: The process of assigning numbers to characteristics of people or things.

Median: A measure of the center of a distribution; the middle score in a rank-ordered group of observations.

Mental model: A person's conception or cognitive representation of something, such as how a computer works.

Merit pay: Pay based on level of job performance.

Meta-analysis: A mathematical summary of the results of several samples or studies of the same phenomenon.

Minnesota Satisfaction Questionnaire (MSQ): A 20-facet job satisfaction scale.

Mixed Standard Scale (MSS): A behavior-based performance appraisal method.

Modeling: A training method in which the trainee first observes someone executing a behavior and then practices it.

Moderator variable: A variable that affects the relation between two other variables.

Motivation: The underlying force that explains why people engage in a behavior.

Motivation Potential Score (MPS): From job characteristics theory, the overall complexity or scope of a job.

Motivator factors: In two-factor theory the job factors that are inherent in the job itself.

Motor task: A task that involves body movements, such as placing pegs in holes or walking.

Multiple hurdle: A selection method whereby applicants must achieve a certain score on each predictor to be hired.

Multiple regression: A statistical procedure for combining several predictors to forecast a criterion.

Need hierarchy theory: A theory that considers motivation to be based on a hierarchy of five basic human needs.

Negative affectivity (NA): A personality variable that refers to a tendency to experience negative emotions across many different situations.

Nominal group: Several noninteracting people who serve as a comparison to an interacting group in group research.

Norm: A standard of behavior in a group of people.

Objective test: A test that has fixed response choices that the test taker picks for each item.

Observational design: A research design in which people are observed on the job.

Obtrusive method: A data collection method in which subjects are aware that they are being studied.

Occupational Information Network, O*NET: The U.S. Department of Labor's extensive database on jobs and worker requirements for jobs.

On-the-job-training: A training method in which the trainee learns the job while doing it.

Open-ended test: A test that requires the test taker to write out his or her answer, such as an essay examination.

Open system theory: A theory that describes organizations as having all the features of an open system.

Organizational citizenship behavior (OCB): Behavior that is not required of employees but benefits the organization.

Organizational commitment: The attachment that a person has for his or her job.

Organizational constraints: Conditions in an organization that prevent employees from performing well.

Organizational development (OD): One of a family of methods used to improve the functioning of organizations.

Other: In equity theory the person used for comparison of inputs and outcomes.

Other personal characteristics: Characteristics of people relevant to jobs other than knowledge, skill, or ability.

Outcome: In equity theory the rewards a person gets from a job.

Out-group: *See* Hired hands.

Overlearning: Training that continues after a trainee first reaches a criterion of learning the skill.

Paper-and-pencil test: A written test that requires either indicating the correct answer from several choices or writing an answer to an open-ended question.

Part training: Training of individual subtasks one at a time; opposite of whole training.

Path-goal theory: A leadership theory that emphasizes how leaders can enhance subordinate motivation by clarifying the paths between behavior and rewards.

Pearson product-moment correlation: The most frequently used measure of association between two continuous variables.

Performance appraisal: The formal procedures that an organization uses to assess job performance of employees.

Performance-level criteria: Measures that indicate how well training transfers to the job.

Performance test: A test that requires the test taker to perform tasks involving manipulation of objects.

Person-oriented job analysis: Any job analysis method that focuses on characteristics necessary for a job.

Personality test: A test designed to assess people's patterns of behavior or feelings.

Personality trait: The tendency of a person to engage in certain types of behavior or respond to situations in particular ways.

Piece-rate system: A system that pays employees for each unit of productivity.

Position Analysis Questionnaire (PAQ): A job analysis method that describes jobs and necessary job characteristics along common dimensions.

Power: The ability to influence other people.

Power distance: A culture value of tolerance for large power and status differences among levels in an organization.

Power test: A test without a time limit.

Predictive validity design: A design in which predictor information is used to forecast a criterion that is assessed at a later time.

Predictor: A variable that is used to forecast a criterion.

Prescriptive theory: An organizational theory that explains how an organization should function.

Pretest–posttest design: A research design in which the same criterion variable is assessed before and after the treatment occurs.

Procedural justice: The fairness of a process by which rewards are allocated.

Process loss: Time spent by group members that is not devoted to task accomplishment.

Programmed instruction: A training method in which trainees work at their own pace.

Protected class: Groups of people who are given special legal protection because of past discrimination against them.

Psychological test: A sample of behavior assessed under standardized conditions to measure characteristics of people.

Psychomotor ability test: A psychological test designed to assess physical abilities, such as eye–hand coordination.

Qualitative method: Research that minimizes the use of quantitative and statistical methods.

Quality circle: A group of employees who meet to discuss ways to improve their work.

Quasi-experimental design: A research design that has some but not all the features of an experiment. For example, there might not be random assignment of subjects to conditions.

Questionnaire: A paper-and-pencil instrument used to collect information; can be completed by respondents themselves.

Random assignment: Placing subjects into treatment conditions in an experiment so that each subject has an equal chance of being in each condition.

Random selection: Choosing subjects for a study so that every possible subject has an equal chance of participating.

Rater error training (RET): A training program designed to familiarize individuals who rate performance with rating errors and techniques to avoid them.

Reactions criteria: Measures of trainee reactions to training.

Realistic job preview (RJP): Information given to job applicants to let them know what the job and organization are like.

Reasonable accommodation: A principle from the Americans With Disabilities Act that requires organizations to provide reasonable assistance or modifications to the job or workplace so that disabled people can perform the job.

Referent power: Influence based on the subordinate's liking for the supervisor.

Regression equation: A mathematical equation that allows the prediction of one variable from another.

Reinforcement theory: A motivation theory that considers behavior to be a function of rewards.

Reliability: The consistency of a measure; how well scores on the same subject are replicable across repeated measurements of the same variable.

Repetitive strain injury: An injury brought on by making the same motion continuously, such as typing on a computer keyboard.

Research design: The structure of a research study.

Response rate: The percentage or proportion of contacted people who participate in a survey.

Results criteria: Measures of training impact on the organization, such as profits.

Reward power: Influence based on giving rewards.

Role: A person's position in a group or team.

Role ambiguity: Employee uncertainty about what is expected of him or her on the job.

Role conflict: Incompatible demands placed on an employee.

Role play: A training technique that involves having the trainee pretend to perform a task.

Salary survey: A survey of employers to determine salary levels for certain jobs.

Sample: The subjects chosen for a study.

Schemata: A cognitive category or frame of reference.

Scientific Management: The application of scientific principles to managing people's job performance; developed by Frederick Winslow Taylor.

Scope: The complexity of a job.

Selection ratio: The proportion of job applicants who are hired for a job.

Self-efficacy: The belief that a person has in his or her ability to perform a task well.

Self-efficacy theory: A motivation theory based on the idea that people perform well when they believe they are capable of doing the job.

Severity error: In performance appraisal the assignment of low ratings to all ratees.

Sexual harassment: Behavior of a sexual nature that adversely affects a person's ability to do his or her job.

Simulation: A training method that allows people to practice a skill in an artificial and controlled situation.

Skill: How well a person is able to do a task.

Skill variety: A dimension of the job characteristics model that involves the number of skills required to do a job.

Social facilitation: The improvement in performance that sometimes occurs when in the presence of other people. Research has shown that simple or well-learned tasks are facilitated by the presence of others, while performance on complex or new tasks is inhibited.

Social loafing: A group phenomenon whereby the larger the group, the less effort made by each member on a task.

Sociotechnical systems theory: A theory that states that organizations should consider both the human and technological demands of tasks in designing work environments.

Spaced training: Training in which sessions are spread out over time; opposite of massed training.

Span of control: A principle of bureaucracy theory that is concerned with the number of people that a supervisor can oversee.

Speed test: A test with a time limit.

Standard deviation: A measure of dispersion for a distribution of scores; the square root of the variance.

Statistical significance: A rule of thumb for evaluating the results of a statistical test.

Statistical test: A quantitative procedure based on probability that allows for the interpretation of study outcomes.

Stress: Physiological and psychological responses to demands that are perceived to be challenging or threatening.

Structured interview: An interview in which the questions are standardized across interviewees.

Subject matter expert: A person who is knowledgeable about a topic.

Survey design: A design in which subjects are asked to answer questions, usually with an interview or questionnaire.

Survey feedback: An organizational change technique in which employees are surveyed and the survey information is fed back to all levels of the organization.

T-group: An organizational change technique that has employees attend training sessions over a period of days to learn interpersonal skills.

T-test: A statistical test used to compare two means.

Tailored testing: A testing procedure that adjusts the level of item difficulty to the test taker's ability.

Task identity: A dimension from the job characteristics model that identifies the extent to which a person does an entire job.

Task inventory: A job analysis technique that produces a detailed list of the tasks for a job.

Task significance: A dimension from the job characteristics model that represents the extent to which a particular job impacts other people.

Team building: A procedure that is used to improve the functioning of work teams.

Telecommute: Work at home while communicating with work-related people via modem and the telephone.

Test–retest reliability: The consistency of a measure when it is repeated over time.

Theoretical criterion: The conceptual definition of what constitutes good job performance.

Theory X/Theory Y: A theory that proposes that how a manager views subordinate characteristics affects his or her approach to supervision.

Theory Z: The Japanese style of management for large organizations that assumes employees will spend their entire careers with one organization.

360 degree feedback: A performance appraisal technique that provides feedback from several perspectives, including peers, subordinates, supervisors, and self.

Time and motion study: An analysis of task performance involving the observation and timing of subject motions. The purpose is to determine ways to eliminate or modify motions to make performance more efficient.

Training-level criteria: Measures of how well a trainee does in training.

Transfer of training: The application of what was learned in training to the job itself.

Transformational leader: *See* Charismatic leader.

True halo: The extent to which a person's performance across different dimensions is at the same level.

Turnover: An employee quitting his or her job.

Two-factor theory: A theory that considers job satisfaction and dissatisfaction to be separate factors rather than opposite ends of the same continuum.

Type A/B personality: A personality variable; a person can be hard driving and impatient (Type A) or easygoing and relaxed (Type B).

Uncertainty avoidance: A culture value reflecting tolerance for ambiguity and uncertainty, which is reflected in the tendency to be rule oriented.

Uniform Guidelines on Employee Selection: A document produced by the U.S. government that describes appropriate and legally defensible selection procedures.

Unit control of variances: A principle of sociotechnical systems theory that recommends allowing employees who encounter problems to solve them.

Universal precautions: Suggested safety procedures for health care workers to reduce chances of accidental exposure to infectious diseases such as AIDS/HIV or Hepatitis B.

Unobtrusive method: A method of research in which subjects do not know that they are being studied.

Utility analysis: The analysis of the financial benefits to an organization of taking a course of action, such as implementing a particular selection system.

Valence: In expectancy theory the value or worth a person gives to an outcome.

Validity: The interpretation given to the meaning of a measure.

Validity generalization: A principle that states if a predictor is a valid indicator of a criterion in one setting, it will be valid in another similar setting.

Variable: A characteristic of a person or thing that varies.

Variance: The degree to which scores differ among individuals in a distribution of scores.

Vocational interest test: A test that matches the interests of test takers to people in various professions.

Vroom-Yetton model: A model that indicates the best approach to making decisions that involve subordinates.

Whole training: Training that focuses on an entire task at one time rather than parts of the task; opposite of part training.

Work–family conflict: A form of role conflict in which family demands and work demands conflict.

Work group: Two or more individuals who interact and share common task goals.

Work sample: A test that includes tasks from a job.

Work team: A work group in which members have interdependent tasks and individual task-related roles.

NAME INDEX

SUBJECT INDEX

PHOTO CREDITS